Camping
Oregon

Help Us Keep This Guide Up to Date

Every effort has been made by the author and editors to make this guide as accurate and useful as possible. However, many things can change after a guide is published—trails are rerouted, regulations change, techniques evolve, facilities come under new management, etc.

We would love to hear from you concerning your experiences with this guide and how you feel it could be improved and kept up to date. While we may not be able to respond to all comments and suggestions, we'll take them to heart and we'll also make certain to share them with the author. Please send your comments and suggestions to the following address:

The Globe Pequot Press
Reader Response/Editorial Department
P.O. Box 480
Guilford, CT 06437

Or you may e-mail us at:

editorial@GlobePequot.com

Thanks for your input, and happy trails!

Camping
Oregon

Second Edition

Rhonda and George Ostertag

FALCON GUIDE®

GUILFORD, CONNECTICUT
HELENA, MONTANA
AN IMPRINT OF THE GLOBE PEQUOT PRESS

Acknowledgments

We would like to thank the staffs of the local chambers of commerce, the visitor centers, the city and county parks departments, the state parks and forest departments, the state and federal fish and wildlife offices, Crater Lake National Park, and the district offices of the USDA Forest Service and Bureau of Land Management for the help they provided us in compiling this book. We also would like to thank the people we met along the way who shared their enthusiasm for camping in Oregon.

Introduction

Oregon is one of the most naturally diverse states in the Union, with elevations ranging from sea level to 11,000 feet. Along the Pacific Coast, you may encounter quiet coves, uninterrupted sandy strands, and the exciting collision of wave and headland. As you move east toward the Cascades, you pass through temperate rain forests, chiseled coastal mountains, and the fertile Willamette Valley—destination of early settlers following the Oregon Trail. The Cascade Range will captivate you with its chain of conical volcanic peaks, extensive fir forests, and high-mountain lakes, including its crown jewel, Crater Lake.

In the shadow of the Cascades, shaping the central part of Oregon, are plateaus, lava fields, desert plains, and, to the south, a sweeping expanse of playas, lakes, and wildlife lands. Farther to the east, the signature peaks and meadows of the Blue Mountains set the stage. The state's northeastern corner features a stirring juxtaposition: the glacial high country of the Wallowa Mountains and the arid steppes of Hells Canyon National Recreation Area. Secreted in the southeastern corner are colorful canyons, rocky rims, and lonesome sagebrush flats.

This amazingly varied terrain combines with distinctive climatic differences to produce habitats for a menagerie of wildlife. A number of public and private wildlife lands harbor native and migrant species. Antelope congregate in Hart Mountain National Antelope Refuge, Kiger wild horses gallop at Steens Mountain, great gray owls nest in the Blue Mountains, elk gather at the winter feeding stations in Union and Baker counties, and gray whales migrate along the Oregon coast each spring and fall. Each of these events suggest a potential vacation theme.

Other seasonal changes and natural events may serve as impetus for a camping trip: the blaze of fall foliage, the bloom of rhododendrons, the harvest season, the ripening of the huckleberries, or the Perseid meteor showers, to name a few. At the annual Mosquito Festival in Paisley ("if you can't beat 'em, celebrate 'em") there is even a tongue-in-cheek crowning of Oregon's very own "Miss-Quito." (By the way, the birding in the area is fabulous.)

Oregon's many spectacular rivers, which served as highways for the Native Americans, early explorers, and arriving settlers, now guide contemporary explorers through the best the state has to offer. Among the contiguous United States, Oregon leads the way in protecting its waterways. As a result, the recreational opportunities are superb. You can indulge in summer swimming; salmon, steelhead, sturgeon, and trout fishing; white-water rafting, canoeing, and kayaking; drift boating; mailboat rides; and sternwheeler tours. There is also an impressive collection of waterfalls and hot springs. You will be surprised by what Oregon can do with a raindrop!

While Oregon's natural bounty is unparalleled, the state also caters to more refined tastes, with fine museums, concerts, wineries, art galleries, aquariums, zoos, and shops. The Ashland Shakespeare Festival has an excellent national reputation, and festivals, Saturday markets, community theaters, and art fairs add to the allure of town-and-country outings. If you are ready to "let 'er rip,"

Campsite raider.

the Pendleton Rodeo is an ideal venue, or you may choose to try your luck at one of a growing number of Indian-owned casinos.

Best of all, Oregon has fine public campgrounds from which to explore its exciting attractions. This book includes not only detailed campground information, but information about a myriad of nearby activities, ranging from urban excursions to outdoor adventures to driving tours.

How to Use This Book

This book focuses on public campgrounds and parks that are readily accessible by car, motor home, and recreational vehicle. While the list is not exhaustive, it is comprehensive. Some public campgrounds were excluded because they were unreasonably isolated, were in disrepair, or had rough access roads, too few sites, or no facilities. Group campgrounds and strictly walk-in facilities were also omitted.

Choosing a Campground

To help you locate and select a campground, we have basically organized the book using the seven travel regions established by Oregon's Department of Tourism: Coast, the Portland area, the Willamette Valley (and Western Cascades Slope), Mount Hood and the Columbia River Gorge, Southern Oregon, Central Oregon, and Eastern Oregon (see map). Within these regions, we have assembled the campgrounds based on their proximity to key towns or landmarks. In each of these subsections, campgrounds are listed alphabetically.

Each campground description includes key information on location, season, the number of sites, maximum RV length, availability of facilities and services, fee per night, the management agency, contact information, how to get there, and what you can expect to see and do once you are at the campground. The numbers assigned to the campgrounds coincide with those on the regional maps. By consulting the appropriate regional map and scanning the descriptions, you should be able to select a campground that both appeals to your interest and is most convenient for your travel plans.

Helpful Information

The specific categories in the campground sections are Location, Season, Sites, Maximum length, Facilities, Fee per night, Management, Contact, and Finding the campground. The following explains some of the information provided within several of these categories, along with a few tips.

Season: Many campgrounds remain open during fair weather, closing when frost, ice, and snow threaten plumbing and safety, or when rain makes the ground and roads unsuitable for camping. We have listed the typical operating seasons for the camps, but visitors should still check with the managing agency if their trip occurs at the edges of the operating season.

For some of the USDA Forest Service and Bureau of Land Management campgrounds, the more remote and primitive offerings can remain open year-round but go without service after the summer visitor season (June through August). Snow, though, can prevent access. When frequenting these camps after the peak camping season, bring your own toilet tissue, water, and other comforts, and pack out all garbage—never leave unburned garbage in a fire ring or grill.

In some parks, winter camping may be restricted to self-contained RVs only or have limited sites, reduced services, or dry camping only. For general information on the state parks, including their operating seasons, call the Oregon Department of Parks and Recreation information number (800–551–6949).

Keep in mind that even the listed operating times are subject to change. Weather, budget cuts, ongoing events, a change-over in the concessionaire, and vandalism can all influence opening and closing policies. The price of a phone call is small relative to the cost of a misspent trip.

Within camp descriptions, the mentioned nearby attractions may also have seasonal schedules. If the success of your trip depends on seeing a particular museum or attraction, you may wish to call ahead.

Sites: The sites are labeled as hookup, basic, RV, tent, or walk-in tent. Throughout this book, RV refers to the broad class of recreational vehicles on the road: trailers, campers, motor homes, tent trailers, and vans. Basic sites are those suitable for either tent or RV camping but without hookups.

Under this heading we have also indicated if any cabins, tepees, or yurts are available for rent. Yurts are domed canvas structures with wooden floors, heating, electricity, lock-secured doors, and bunks. Yurt users bring their own bedding or sleeping bags and have access to the camp restroom/shower facilities.

Fee per night: The price codes used throughout the book are based on the prices in 2004. A range is used because prices can fluctuate year-to-year. The purpose of the symbols is to assist in cost comparisons and provide a relative idea of out-of-pocket cost.

$ = Less than $10
$$ = $10 to $19
$$$ = $20 or more

The price refers to single campsites only. Expect cabins, yurts, tepees, and double sites to cost more. Many camps have add-on fees for additional vehicles, pets, or large parties, which could increase your costs.

In some cases a Northwest Forest Pass may be required in lieu of the campground fee. These can be purchased from the USDA Forest Service, the USDA Nature of the Northwest (an information center for nature and outdoor recreation in Oregon and Washington; contact www.naturenw.org), or select outdoor stores.

Reservations: Making reservations is a good idea, especially during peak summer travel months, holidays, fish runs, or when your travel plans hinge on getting a campsite and there are no alternative camping options in the area. The state park system has a contract with a fee reservation service to handle the booking of state park campsites (800–452–5687).

Although most USDA Forest Service campgrounds are offered on a first come, first served basis, the agency does have a reservation line for a few of its larger, more popular campgrounds; this, too, is a fee service. Contact the National Recreation Reservation Service (877–444–6777 or www.reserveusa

.com). In Oregon, many Forest Service campgrounds are run by concession-aires, who set their own pricing and rules for reservation.

Water: We have tried to list each of the campgrounds that have developed drinking water systems. Because these systems can pass water quality tests one week and fail the next, however, you should always carry an emergency supply of safe drinking water and be prepared to treat campground water by boiling. This becomes especially true the farther you travel from safe urban water sources.

Pets: Unless it is specified otherwise in the campground descriptions, pets restrained on leashes are generally allowed.

The quick reference charts with each area give information about the campground services available. Following is a key to abbreviations used in these charts:

Hookups:	W = Water, E = Electric, S = Sewer, C = Cable, P = Phone, I = Internet
Total Sites:	T = Tents only
Max. RV length:	given in feet
Toilets:	F = Flush, NF = No flush
Recreation:	H = Hiking, S = Swimming, F = Fishing, B = Boating, L = Boat launch, O = Off-highway driving, R = Horseback riding, C = Cycling

Getting to the Campground

The best way to reach your intended campsite is to use the campground directions in conjunction with a detailed state map or the appropriate Forest Service or Bureau of Land Management (BLM) map. Maps in the book are meant only as general locator tools.

Outdoor and Camping Refresher Course

Responsible use of the outdoors and campground and trail facilities is the best way to protect and preserve the privilege of a quality outdoor experience. It is also the best way to control campground costs.

Preparation

The drive: Traveling to campgrounds and parks along major highways poses little problem. The roads are well maintained, a town or passing vehicle is never far off, and the reception of your cellular phone seems just fine.

But backcountry roads are quite a different story. For this type of travel, it is mandatory that you keep your tires and engine in good repair. Top the gas tank at the last point of civilization and carry emergency vehicle gear: jack, spare tire and belts, tire pump, jumper cables, and, if the weather is foul, tire chains.

Basic survival gear: This includes water, food, blankets, matches, a first-aid kit, and a flashlight. You may also want to add a shovel and bucket to the list. A downed tree, road washout, or rock slide need not spoil a trip if you carry supplies for an unintended stop and maps for plotting an alternative destination or route. Before any long journey from home, it is advisable to phone the appropriate agency about facility openings and road conditions.

Notification safeguard: Because being stranded or injured in the wild poses a greater problem than similar situations at home or in town, it is critical before any outdoor adventure to notify a responsible party of your intended destination and time of return. Contacting that individual upon return completes the safety procedure. This also works in reverse: If an emergency occurs on the homefront, someone will be able to alert you or help authorities locate you.

Camping

Zero-impact camping should be the goal of everyone, even at developed campgrounds. Do not rearrange the site, pound nails, remove ground cover, or dig drainage channels, and if you build a campfire, keep it small and inside the provided container. If grills or fire rings are not provided, do not build a campfire. Heed all regulations on campfires, smoking, and wood gathering.

Setting up: Exercise courtesy with your site selection and keep it neat. Avoid blocking roads and spilling out of your assigned space into your neighbor's site.

Storing food: Food should be stored in closed containers when not in use. At night, be sure all foods and coolers are stowed away in the vehicle. In some areas, you will also want to cover the coolers, as bears have learned that coolers hold food and have ripped open car doors just to reach them.

Garbage: Dispose of litter properly and often. If no facility is provided, pack it out. Use sturdy garbage bags to collect the garbage at your site, storing the bags where they are handy for use but not an eyesore to fellow campers. At night, you should stash the garbage bags in a vehicle to avoid raids by raccoons or bears. Never put garbage down toilets, leave it in the outhouse, or abandon it in the fire pit. If you did not burn your flammable garbage during your stay, pack it out.

Sanitation: In campgrounds, dispose of waste water in the provided sites. Bathing or washing dishes should be done well away from natural waters such as lakes or streams and away from the campground supplies of drinking water.

Smoking: Where fires present extreme danger or where habitats are particularly sensitive, smoking may be prohibited; heed regulations. Where and when smoking is allowed, stop to have your smoke; never smoke while hiking. Use an ashtray at camp. In the wild, clear an area to the mineral soil, smoke the cigarette, and then crush it out in the dirt. Pack out cigarette butts.

Pets: In campgrounds that allow pets, keep your animal(s) at your site, restrained, and quiet. If your pet is not comfortable around strangers, it does not belong in a public campground. On trails, pets must be leashed at all times to protect habitat and wildlife.

Courtesy: Keep your noise down and your site neat, ration your use of showers, and clean up after yourself and your youngsters in the restrooms. There is no maid service here!

Stay limits: Public campgrounds typically have stay limits ranging from a few days up to two weeks, although a few facilities will accommodate campers on a monthly basis. Be sure to limit your stay accordingly.

Gearing Up for the Outdoors

Clothing: Layering is the way to go. Wool is the fabric for cold, wet, or changeable weather conditions. It retains heat even when wet. Cotton is the fabric of warm summer days. In Oregon, a clothing necessity is a good suit of rain gear—jacket and pants (or chaps).

Footgear: Sneakers are appropriate for town walks or nature trails, but for longer hikes, boots provide both comfort and protection.

Equipment: The quantity and variety of equipment you carry will depend on where you are going and how long you will be away from the vehicle or campsite. Day packs with padded straps or fanny packs offer convenient storage and portability while keeping hands free. Water, snacks, a sweater, money, keys, tissues, sunglasses, a camera, and binoculars are fine for short hops. The greater the adventure, the greater the quantity of required gear, including safety and first-aid materials.

Atlases, maps, and brochures: Maps are important tools. They provide an orientation to the area, suggest alternative routes, present new areas to explore, and aid in the planning and preparation. Be sure to have the correct maps for your trip. The farther your travels take you from the beaten path, the more important specific area maps become. County, Forest Service, Bureau of Land Management, and topographic maps can all show greater detail than the standard state road map.

Fees and permits: Trail park passes, wilderness permits, and day-use permits may be required to travel the trails in the area where you are camped. While some may be picked up or purchased at the site, others must be secured in advance at the ranger station.

Activities

Beachcombing: Learn the rules for tide pooling and collecting, and check on any wildlife closures; these are generally posted at each beach. Before taking a long stroll on the beach, find out the times and heights of high and low tides to avoid becoming stranded. Make sure there will be adequate time to complete your hike or reach safety before the incoming tide. Irregular "sneaker" waves occur along the Oregon coast and can arrive suddenly, sweeping you off your feet. Drift logs do not provide a safe haven from incoming waves because the logs can shift in the surf, unseating and striking would-be riders.

Fishing: A current fishing license from the state of Oregon is a must, and for a few places along the Deschutes River, you will also need to purchase an Indian fishing license from the Confederated Tribes of Warm Springs. It is essential that you possess and study a copy of the current year's *Oregon Sport Fishing Regulations.* The booklet specifically outlines what state waters are open to angling, the season, what types of bait are allowed, catch limits, and size restrictions. Copies may be picked up where fishing licenses are sold and at bait and tackle, sporting goods, and outdoor stores. A state map will help you sort out your options and ensure compliance with the rules, which can vary depending on your location along a river or stream.

Since the initiation of the Salmon Recovery Program in 1997, and with the evolving federal and state listings of threatened and endangered fish species, regulations are changing continuously, so do not trust memory or hearsay. What was acceptable in the past may no longer be permissible. Use only barbless hooks in catch-and-release waters, and always wet your hands before handling fish. Minimize your contact with fish being returned to the wild.

Swimming: Swimming areas mentioned in this book are typically unguarded, so swim at your own risk. Visitors should never swim alone. Also, always supervise children; survey the area for hazards beforehand; and use common sense with regard to water levels, flow, and water temperature. Chilly temperatures and undercurrents can disable even the strongest swimmer. Horseplay, drinking, and diving are inappropriate and dangerous.

Hiking with children: When hiking with young children, choose simple destinations and do not insist on reaching any particular destination. Allow for their differences in attention span, interests, and energy level. Encourage children's natural curiosity, but come prepared for sun, mosquitoes, wasps, and poison oak. Do not become so focused on what you want to share with your children that you dismiss their discoveries. Get down on your hands and knees, peer into that puddle, admire that ugly rock. For safety's sake, discuss what to do should you become separated (hug a tree); even small ones should carry some essential items: a sweater, water bottle, and food.

Hiking shared-use trails: Unless otherwise posted, mountain bikers are expected to yield the right of way to hikers and horseback riders, while hikers, in turn, should yield to equestrians. Because horses can spook and put riders at risk, yielding means stopping, with all party members stepping to the same side of the trail. Avoid any sudden movements, but feel free to speak in normal tones. Voices reassure the horse that you are indeed human and not some alien creature; backpacks, tripods, and walking sticks can confuse or alarm horses.

Hiking with pets: Owners should strictly adhere to posted rules for pets. Controlling your animal on a leash is not just a courtesy reserved for times when other campers and hikers are present; it is an ongoing responsibility to protect wildlife and ground cover. Know that dogs represent a threat to horses and may create problems with bears. Clean up after your pet, keeping trails free of debris.

Safety

While this book attempts to alert users to safe methods and warn of potential dangers, it can only accomplish so much. Nature is unpredictable, and humans are fallible. Good judgment and common sense remain your best allies. When you travel the backcountry, you assume the risks, but you also reap the rewards.

Water: To avoid dehydration, carry ample drinking water with you. When taking water from an outdoor source, be sure to treat the water by using an approved filter or by boiling it for ten minutes. Even if you plan to use trailside sources, you should carry an emergency supply in case those sources have dried up or become fouled. Even on short nature walks and city outings, water is a good companion. If you are thirsty, you cannot enjoy the offering.

Getting lost: Before venturing on any hike, leave word with someone about the planned destination and time of return. Then keep to your plan and notify the informed party upon your return. Do not go alone. If you become lost, sit down and try to think calmly. You are in no immediate danger, as long as you have packed properly and followed the notification procedure. If hiking with a group, stay together and do not wander off on your own. If you do become separated, try signaling to the others by shouting or whistling in sets of three, which is universally recognized as a distress call. If it is getting late, use the remaining light to prepare for night and conserve your energy.

Hypothermia: Hypothermia is a dramatic cooling of the body. Cold, wet, and windy weather conditions demand respect. Eating properly, avoiding fatigue, and being alert to the symptoms (sluggishness, clumsiness, and incoherence) remain the best protection. Should someone display symptoms, stop and get that person dry and warm. Hot fluids can help restore body heat.

Heat exhaustion: Overwhelming your body's own cooling system during warm weather is also a danger. Wear a hat, drink plenty of water, eat properly, and take rests as needed.

Poison oak and ivy: To avoid the irritating oils of these plants, learn what the plants look like and in what environments they grow. There are creams and lotions that can be applied both before and after contact with the plant to reduce the risk of rash. Avoidance, though, is the best tactic.

Stings and bites: The best protection against stings and bites is knowledge. It is important to become aware of any personal allergies or sensitivities that you may have and to learn about the habits and habitats of snakes, bees, ticks, and other potential threats. If you are experiencing any unexplained symptoms or poor health, seek medical advice and volunteer the information that you have been hiking or camping, which can help with the diagnosis. In the case of a tick bite, after removal of the tick, watch for signs of redness and swelling, which could be an early indication of Lyme disease. Consult a physician when bites or wounds show any sign of infection.

Bears: Bears have a supersensitive sense of smell and tend to be curious, so avoid any strong smells that could intrigue them. In particular, be careful of how and where you store food, and never store food in your tent. (See earlier section on storing food for proper protocol.) If you are tent camping, avoid sleeping in clothes that may have picked up cooking odors. Also, be wary of sweet-smelling creams, cosmetics, or lotions that may be enticing to a bear. While hiking, make ample noise, and try never to come between a sow and her cubs. If you should see a bear, do not try to get closer for a better look.

Outdoor Awareness

There is risk associated with any trip into the backcountry. Changes occur all the time, in nature and in the maintenance of roads, campgrounds, and trails. Just because a campground or trip is represented within these pages does not mean it will be safe when you get there. Common sense and good judgment, paired with careful preparation and a realistic assessment of your skills and abilities, are the best means for ensuring a safe, fun, fulfilling outing.

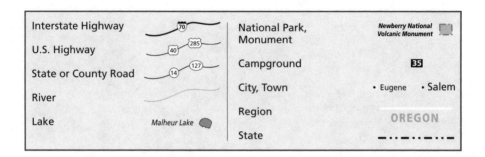

Interstate Highway	National Park, Monument
U.S. Highway	
State or County Road	Campground
River	City, Town
Lake	Region
	State

Malheur Lake

Newberry National Volcanic Monument

35

• Eugene   • Salem

OREGON

Coast

Next to thick carpets of trees and, of course, rain, Oregon is probably best known for its coastline. In the shadow of the Coast Range and Siskiyou Mountains, rumpled dunes, sandy strands, natural spits, rugged headlands, sea lion rookeries, sea stacks, and verdant coastal valleys combine to create one incredible welcome mat. The explorers who first visited the coast—James Cook, Robert Gray, Lewis and Clark, and Don Bruno de Heceta—live on in the place names. Gold rushes and Indian encounters pepper the coastal tale of Oregon, while lighthouses and shipwrecks supply the romance. To preserve this 350-mile-long treasure, the state has elected to keep its beaches public; nearly one hundred state parks and waysides help to do just that, providing residents and visitors with unmatched coastal access.

The coastal mountains and the rivers that drain them extend the bounty, with elk herds, waterfalls, hidden lakes, record-size trees, pockets of old growth, natural meadows, and Oregon's lone redwood forest. Historically, the rivers hosted sizable salmon and steelhead runs, but modern-day pressures leave the fishing in question. Today's anglers must keep current with sport-fishing regulations and restrictions.

Nonetheless, outdoor activities abound. Hiking, kite flying, beachcombing and tide pooling, whale watching, birding, surf and freshwater fishing, crabbing and clamming, dune play, all-terrain-vehicle driving, and horseback riding will get you started. Shopping, museums, and aquariums allow you to dodge the raindrops when necessary. Festivals crowd the beach calendar, with kites, sandcastles, storms, azaleas, rhododendrons, and cranberries, all providing reasons to celebrate.

Coastal recreation is year-round. In winter, storm fronts laden with rain pass over the coast interspersed with bold breaks of sunshine. In summer, soaring temperatures in the Willamette Valley create an inversion that cloaks the coast in morning fog and summons sea-cooled afternoon winds. (Do not pack those jackets at the bottom of your suitcase.) Spring and fall promise clear skies, mild temperatures, and less wind. In the coastal mountains, you will find a vibrant temperate rain forest in winter and sun-drenched peaks and shady canyons in summer.

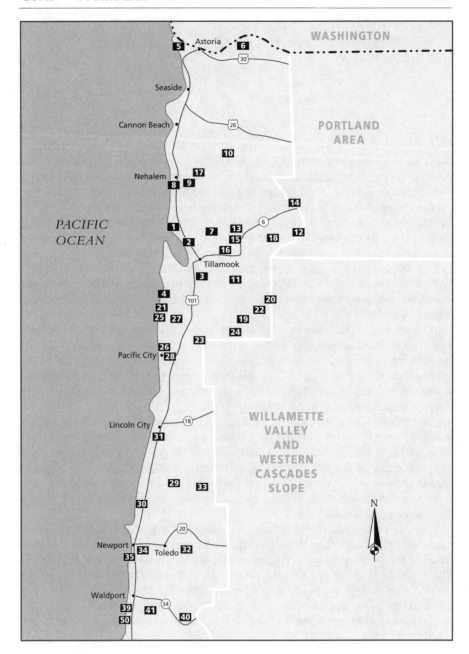

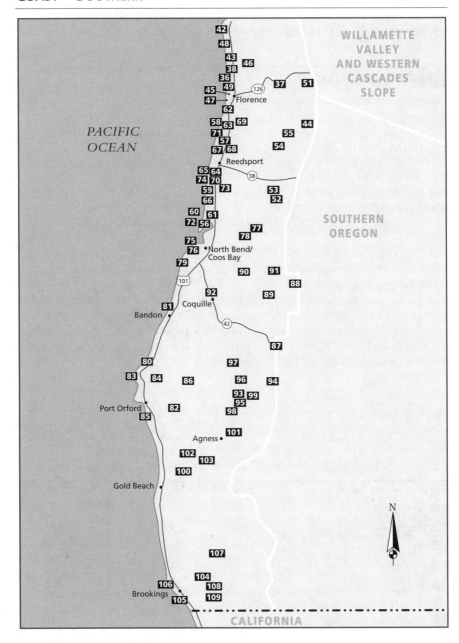

PACIFIC OCEAN

WILLAMETTE VALLEY AND WESTERN CASCADES SLOPE

SOUTHERN OREGON

Florence

Reedsport

North Bend/ Coos Bay

Coquille

Bandon

Port Orford

Agness

Gold Beach

Brookings

CALIFORNIA

N

Astoria–Tillamook Area

1 Barview Jetty County Park

Location: In Barview, about 12 miles north of Tillamook
Season: Year-round
Sites: 59 hookup sites, 186 basic sites; water, electric, and sewer hookups
Maximum length: 40 feet
Facilities: Tables, flush toilets, drinking water, showers, dump station, telephone
Fee per night: $$–$$$
Management: Tillamook County
Contact: (503) 322–3522, reservations accepted; www.co.tillamook.or.us/gov/parks
Finding the campground: From U.S. Highway 101 in Barview, 1.5 miles north of Garibaldi, turn west on Cedar Street and follow it 0.2 mile to its end at the campground and beach.
About the campground: Occupying a large coastal flat, this campground is framed by a tall dune bank to the east and a wild beach strewn with drift logs to the west. Sites are roomy and private in a natural setting of low, twisted shore pine and salal. Fishing from North Jetty is popular. Youngsters will like romping, sliding, and exploring the dune.

Astoria–Tillamook Area

	Hookup sites	Total sites	Maximum RV length	Hookups	Toilets	Showers	Drinking water	Dump station	Recreation	Fee	Can reserve
1 Barview Jetty County Park	59	245	40	WES	F	•	•	•	HSF	$$–$$$	•
2 Bay City Park	4	11	small	WS	F	•				$$	
3 Blimp Base RV Park		64	50		F	•				$	
4 Cape Lookout State Park	39	228	60	WES	F	•	•	•	HSF	$$–$$$	•
5 Fort Stevens State Park	477	534	50	WES	F	•	•	•	HSFBRC	$$–$$$	•
6 Gnat Creek		6	small		NF				HF	$	
7 Kilchis River County Park		34	40		F	•		•	SFBL	$$	•
8 Nehalem Bay State Park	267	302	60	WE	F	•	•	•	HSFRC	$$	•
9 Roy Creek		4	30		NF				FBL	$	
10 Spruce Run		37	30		NF	•			FB	$–$$	
11 Trask County Park		60	40		NF	•		•	HSFBL	$$	•

Whalehead Rocks, one of many coastal attractions.

2 Bay City Park

Location: In Bay City, about 5 miles north of Tillamook
Season: May–October
Sites: 4 hookup sites, 7 tent sites; water and sewer hookups
Maximum length: Small RV units
Facilities: Tables, grills, flush toilets, drinking water, playground, sports courts
Fee per night: $$
Management: Bay City
Contact: (503) 377-2288
Finding the campground: In Bay City, turn east off U.S. Highway 101 onto Hayes Oyster Drive, then take the first left on Fourth Street. Follow it to the park at the corner of Fourth and Trade Streets.
About the campground: This campground occupies a city park in a quiet residential area removed from the highway. Alders shade its grassy sites. A bridge spans the small creek threading the park and links the camp to the play areas. The coastal-maritime diversions are just a skip away.

3   Blimp Base RV Park

Location: South end of Tillamook
Season: February–December
Sites: 52 basic sites, 12 tent sites; no hookups
Maximum length: 50 feet
Facilities: Tables, flush toilets, drinking water
Fee per night: $
Management: Port of Tillamook Bay
Contact: (503) 842–7152; www.potb.org/rv-park.htm
Finding the campground: From the junction of U.S. Highway 101 and Oregon 6 in Tillamook, go 2.8 miles south on US 101 and turn east on Blimp Boulevard. Drive 0.2 mile to the campground.
About the campground: Located near Tillamook County Airport and the Air Museum, this large campground sits on an open grassy plain with views of the coastal foothills. Sites have ample room for setting out chairs or raising tents. Shade sources can make a stay more pleasant. The attractions of Tillamook and the Tillamook–Three Capes coast await. In winter, prolonged, heavy rains can flood some sites.

4   Cape Lookout State Park

Location: About 12 miles southwest of Tillamook
Season: Year-round
Sites: 39 hookup sites, 176 basic sites, 13 yurts; water, electric, and sewer hookups
Maximum length: 60 feet
Facilities: Tables, grills, flush toilets, drinking water, showers, dump station, telephone
Fee per night: $$–$$$
Management: Oregon State Parks and Recreation Department
Contact: (503) 842–4981; (800) 452–5687 for reservations; www.oregonstate parks.org
Finding the campground: From U.S. Highway 101 in Tillamook, head west and southwest on Netarts Highway–Three Capes Scenic Route for 12 miles. The park entrance is west off the scenic loop.
About the campground: This large coastal campground, with closely spaced beachside or forest sites, provides campers with convenient access to an ocean spit with 5 miles of uninterrupted beach, dunes, and bay shoreline. Harbor seals haul out on the spit's tip. A forested headland and cedar swamp add to the park discovery. Three Capes Scenic Route provides easy outward exploration to Cape Meares State Park, to the north, with its lighthouse and octopus spruce, and Cape Kiwanda State Park, to the south, with its hang gliders and dory fleet. Along this coast, scenic offshore rocks delight photographers and provide seabird nesting.

5 Fort Stevens State Park

Location: About 5 miles west of Astoria, near Hammond
Season: Year-round
Sites: 477 full and partial hookup sites, 42 basic sites, 15 yurts; water, electric, and sewer hookups
Maximum length: 50 feet
Facilities: Tables, grills, flush toilets, drinking water, showers, dump station, playground, nearby boat docks and launch
Fee per night: $$–$$$
Management: Oregon State Parks and Recreation Department
Contact: (503) 861–1671; (800) 452–5687 for reservations; www.oregonstate parks.org
Finding the campground: From the junction of U.S. Highways 30 and 101 in Astoria, go 2.7 miles south on US 101, turn right on East Harbor Drive, and travel 4.4 miles to Hammond. From there, go south 1 mile on Lake Drive.
About the campground: This large campground could be considered a miniature town. Sites are closely spaced, but you are not likely to spend much time in camp because you can bicycle, explore the historic military bunkers, fish Coffenbury Lake, hike the trails, or walk the beach along the ocean or at the Columbia River mouth, all without ever leaving the state park. From mid-December to mid-May, you will want to take along your binoculars because bald eagles congregate near the river mouth to feed on the migrating shore-birds weakened from their journey south. Astoria area attractions include the Column, the Columbia River Maritime Museum, and Fort Clatsop National Memorial, where Lewis and Clark wintered on the Oregon coast before their return east.

6 Gnat Creek

Location: About 17 miles east of Astoria
Season: Year-round
Sites: 6 tent sites; no hookups
Maximum length: Small units only
Facilities: Tables, fire pits, vault toilet; no drinking water
Fee per night: $
Management: Clatsop State Forest
Contact: (503) 325–5451; www.odf.state.or.us
Finding the campground: The campground is north off U.S. Highway 30 at milepost 78, about 17 miles east of Astoria and 1 mile west of the Gnat Creek Fish Hatchery.
About the campground: Along Gnat Creek near Gnat Creek Fish Hatchery, this rustic forest campground appeals to anglers and hikers. A foot trail links the camp to the hatchery, where additional trails enter Nicolai Watershed and lead to a waterfall. Area anglers find 2.5 miles of fishing access; consult cur-rent fishing regulations. The hatchery rears both summer and winter steel-head. Hatchery visitors will find a show pond with large rainbow trout and sturgeon, as well as picnicking spots.

7 Kilchis River County Park

Location: About 7 miles northeast of Tillamook
Season: May–late September
Sites: 34 basic sites; no hookups
Maximum length: 40 feet
Facilities: Tables, fire rings, flush toilets, drinking water, dump station, telephone, playground, horseshoe pits, primitive boat launch
Fee per night: $$
Management: Tillamook County
Contact: (503) 842–6694, reservations accepted; www.co.tillamook.or.us/gov/parks
Finding the campground: From U.S. Highway 101, 1.5 miles north of Tillamook, turn east on Alderbrook Road. At the fork in 1 mile, bear right on Kilchis River Road and proceed 4 miles to the park.
About the campground: This family campground sits along the Kilchis River. The paved loop road through camp rings a playing field; sites are grassy with framing alders and statuesque Sitka spruce. The Kilchis is a beautiful coastal river coursing through a scenic, forested canyon. Drift boating, fishing, relaxing, and bird watching help guests while away the day.

8 Nehalem Bay State Park

Location: Near Manzanita, about 24 miles north of Tillamook
Season: Year-round
Sites: 267 hookup sites, 17 horse campsites, 18 yurts; water and electric hookups
Maximum length: 60 feet
Facilities: Tables, grills, flush toilets, drinking water, showers, dump station, corrals at horse sites
Fee per night: $$
Management: Oregon State Parks and Recreation Department
Contact: (503) 368–5154; (800) 452–5687 for reservations; www.oregonstateparks.org
Finding the campground: It is 1.5 miles west off U.S. Highway 101, 21 miles south of the US 101–US 26 junction, 3 miles south of Manzanita.
About the campground: Sheltered by a coastal dune, this bayside campground offers convenient access to the old-growth Sitka spruce forests at Oswald West State Park and Cape Falcon and to the summit views of Neahkahnie Mountain, all to the north. Within Nehalem Bay State Park, visitors can stroll a 2-mile-long spit and 6 miles of coastal beach. Binoculars bring birds, whales, and harbor seals into focus. Boating and fishing similarly top lists of things to do. Tent campers, however, may prefer the walk-in sites in the deep old-growth woods of Oswald West State Park.

Cannon Beach sand castle contest near Nehalem Bay State Park.

9 Roy Creek

Location: About 5 miles east of Nehalem
Season: Year-round
Sites: 4 basic sites; no hookups
Maximum length: 30 feet
Facilities: Tables, fire rings, vault toilet, primitive boat launch; no drinking water
Fee per night: $
Management: Tillamook County
Contact: (503) 322–3477; www.co.tillamook.or.us/gov/parks
Finding the campground: From U.S. Highway 101, 8.5 miles north of Rockaway Beach and 1.5 miles south of Nehalem, turn east on Oregon 53 toward Mohler and Portland. Go 1.4 miles and turn right toward Nehalem River and Foley Creek, and in another 0.9 mile turn left on Foss Road. Follow it 0.2 mile to the campground on the right.
About the campground: This primitive campground is tucked between the Nehalem River and the road in a setting of alders and cottonwoods. Sites have partial shade and easy river access. The primitive boat launch sits where the river deepens and slows.

10 Spruce Run

Location: About 32 miles southeast of Seaside
Season: Year-round
Sites: 32 basic sites, 5 walk-in tent sites; no hookups
Maximum length: 30 feet
Facilities: Tables, fire rings, vault toilets, drinking water (maintained in summer)
Fee per night: $-$$
Management: Clatsop State Forest
Contact: (503) 325-5451; www.odf.state.or.us
Finding the campground: From U.S. Highway 26, east of Elsie and west of Jewell Junction, turn south at a sign on Lower Nehalem River Road and proceed 7 miles to camp.
About the campground: In the Nehalem River Valley, this 128-acre rustic camp claims a tree-shaded and grassy flat parted by Spruce Run Creek. The lower river is open to canoeing for a short season, and river sightseeing is always inviting. Visitors may wish to make an excursion to Jewell Meadows Wildlife Area for elk viewing. Wild turkey can sometimes be seen at the wildlife area as well.

11 Trask County Park

Location: About 14 miles east of Tillamook
Season: May–late September
Sites: 60 basic sites; no hookups
Maximum length: 40 feet
Facilities: Tables, grills, vault toilets, drinking water, dump station, telephone, horseshoe pits; boat launch 4 miles downstream at Peninsula Day Use
Fee per night: $$
Management: Tillamook County
Contact: (503) 842-4559, reservations accepted; www.co.tillamook.or.us/gov /parks
Finding the campground: From U.S. Highway 101 in Tillamook, go east on Oregon 6 for 2.5 miles and turn right (south) on Trask River Road. Drive 1.8 miles and bear left to remain on Trask River Road. Proceed another 10 miles to the park.
About the campground: Situated along the Trask River and its North Fork is this rustic campground and day use. The campground is woodsy, with earthen roads and parking; some sites are more level than others. The day-use area claims a grassy flat above the river. When adequately high, the Trask River is popular with rafters. Its fast channels are interspersed with quiet flows. A foot trail allows exploration along the river at Peninsula boat launch.

Tillamook State Forest

12 Browns Off-Highway-Vehicle Campground

Location: About 21 miles northwest of Forest Grove
Season: March–November
Sites: 29 basic sites; no hookups
Maximum length: 40 feet
Facilities: Tables, grills, vault toilets, drinking water, OHV loading ramps and staging area
Fee per night: $$
Management: Tillamook State Forest
Contact: (503) 357-2191; www.odf.state.or.us/AREAS/northwest/tillamook/tsf /camping.asp
Finding the campground: At the summit on Oregon 6, 19 miles west of Forest Grove and 31.3 miles east of Tillamook, turn south at the sign for Browns Camp and quickly bear right, following a single-lane dirt road riddled with potholes. Go 0.8 mile and again bear right, proceeding 0.4 mile. There bear left, coming to a T junction in another 0.2 mile. Head left for 0.3 mile, then bear right, proceeding 0.4 mile more to the campground on Scoggins Creek Road.
About the campground: Edged by alders and conifers, this campground for the off-highway-vehicle (OHV) enthusiast lays out like a three-leaf clover, with each camping loop nudging the central revegetated area. Boulders shape the graveled sites and avenues, while Scoggins Creek threads past camp. Trails and roads open to OHVs are the primary draw, so you can expect a noisy neighborhood. Elsewhere in historic Tillamook State Forest, visitors can enjoy the quieter pursuits of horseback riding, hiking, fishing, and sightseeing.

Tillamook State Forest

	Hookup sites	Total sites	Maximum RV length	Hookups	Toilets	Showers	Drinking water	Dump station	Recreation	Fee	Can reserve
12 Browns OHV Campground		29	40		NF		•		HO	$$	
13 Diamond Mill		20	40		NF				O		
14 Gales Creek		23	25		NF		•		HFR	$–$$	
15 Jones Creek		38	40		NF		•		HSF	$–$$	
16 Jordan Creek OHV Staging Area		6	40		NF				O	$	
17 Nehalem Falls		18	30		NF		•		SFB	$–$$	
18 Stagecoach Horse Camp		11	25		NF				HR	$	

13 Diamond Mill

Location: About 24 miles east of Tillamook
Season: March–November
Sites: 20 basic sites; no hookups
Maximum length: 40 feet
Facilities: Tables, pit toilets; no drinking water
Fee per night: None
Management: Tillamook State Forest
Contact: (503) 842–2545; www.odf.state.or.us/AREAS/northwest/tillamook/tsf/camping.asp
Finding the campground: From Oregon 6, 23 miles east of Tillamook and 29 miles west of Forest Grove, head north on the gravel North Fork Road for 0.3 mile. There bear right and proceed 1.3 miles to the campground.
About the campground: Tables mark off the campsites that border a central, gravel off-highway-vehicle (OHV) staging area. A fir-and-alder forest shapes the perimeter. Although noisy, the camp attracts a like-minded group interested in the sport of OHV riding.

14 Gales Creek

Location: About 17 miles northwest of Forest Grove
Season: May–October
Sites: 19 basic sites, 4 walk-in tent sites; no hookups
Maximum length: 25 feet
Facilities: Tables, grills, vault toilets, drinking water
Fee per night: $–$$
Management: Tillamook State Forest
Contact: (503) 357–2191; www.odf.state.or.us/AREAS/northwest/tillamook/tsf/camping.asp
Finding the campground: The campground is 0.7 mile north off Oregon 6, 17 miles west of Forest Grove and 33.6 miles east of Tillamook.
About the campground: In historic Tillamook State Forest, this campground offers family campsites in a second-growth forest of alders and firs along Gales Creek. The series of fires that burned the forest in the 1930s are considered one of the worst disasters to strike the Pacific Northwest; the reforestation is one of the region's great success stories. From camp, hikers may access the historic Gales Creek Trail, which in turn leads to University Falls Loop. Additional trails in the state forest serve hikers, equestrians, and off-highway-vehicle users. Fishing, sightseeing, and relaxing also engage campers. Tent campers, however, might prefer the offering at Elk Creek Campground, 7 miles farther west on Oregon 6. It has 15 forested walk-ins tucked along Elk Creek and a bend of the Wilson River and similar services. Elk Mountain Trail leaves from camp, and the Wilson River Trail offers a tie from the Elk Mountain Trail to Kings Mountain Trail.

15 Jones Creek

Location: About 22 miles east of Tillamook
Season: Memorial Day–October
Sites: 29 basic sites, 9 walk-in tent sites; no hookups
Maximum length: 40 feet
Facilities: Tables, grills, vault toilets, drinking water, horseshoe pit
Fee per night: $-$$
Management: Tillamook State Forest
Contact: (503) 842–2545; www.odf.state.or.us/AREAS/northwest/tillamook/tsf /camping.asp
Finding the campground: From U.S. Highway 101 at Tillamook, go east on Oregon 6 for 21.5 miles and turn left, crossing the river bridge, to reach the campground in 0.3 mile.
About the campground: In historic Tillamook State Forest, this campground offers beautiful sites in a mature, even-aged Douglas fir forest riddled with alders. The campsites are aesthetically pleasing and spacious with long, gravel parking pads. A few sites sit close to the Wilson River. The park offers convenient access to the varied recreation of the forest: off-highway-vehicle driving, horseback riding, hiking, fishing, and sightseeing, with swimming and kayaking also possible. River Trail offers a short walk to a picturesque rock ledge.

16 Jordan Creek Off-Highway-Vehicle (OHV) Staging Area

Location: About 20 miles east of Tillamook
Season: March–November
Sites: 6 basic sites; no hookups
Maximum length: 40 feet
Facilities: Tables, fire rings, vault toilets; no drinking water
Fee per night: $
Management: Tillamook State Forest
Contact: (503) 842–2545; www.odf.state.or.us/AREAS/northwest/tillamook/tsf /camping.asp
Finding the campground: From the junction of U.S. Highway 101 and Oregon 6 in Tillamook, go east on OR 6 for 17.4 miles and turn right on gravel Jordan Creek Road at the sign for the off-highway-vehicle staging area. Go 2.2 mile to the staging area and take a right. The campground is 0.1 mile ahead.
About the campground: This campground serving off-highway-vehicle (OHV) enthusiasts sits beside Jordan Creek and consists of a large central gravel parking area with the site tables and grills dispersed in forest along its perimeter. Alders overhang the picturesque creek. State forest roads and designated trails provide OHV users ample discovery.

17 Nehalem Falls

Location: About 11 miles northeast of Nehalem
Season: Memorial Day–Labor Day
Sites: 14 basic sites, 4 walk-in tent sites; no hookups
Maximum length: 30 feet
Facilities: Tables, grills, vault toilets, drinking water
Fee per night: $–$$
Management: Tillamook State Forest
Contact: (503) 842–2545; www.odf.state.or.us/AREAS/northwest/tillamook/tsf/camping.asp
Finding the campground: From U.S. Highway 101, 8.5 miles north of Rockaway Beach and 1.5 miles south of Nehalem, turn east on Oregon 53 toward Mohler and Portland. Go 1.4 miles and turn right toward Nehalem River and Foley Creek, and in another 0.9 mile turn left on Foss Road. Follow it 7 miles to the campground entrance on the left.
About the campground: Within earshot of the Nehalem River, this pleasant family campground sits among alders, bigleaf maples, and mixed conifers. The walk-in sites are tucked away in an old-growth stand. A few old stumps pierce the undergrowth of thimbleberry and fern. The river shows dark, deep pools alternating with riffles. A path leads to the river falls contained in an outcrop gorge. A fish ladder bypasses the falls.

18 Stagecoach Horse Camp

Location: About 24 miles west of Forest Grove
Season: May–mid-September
Sites: 11 basic sites; no hookups
Maximum length: 25 feet
Facilities: Tables, grills, vault toilets, shelter, corrals, water only for horses; no drinking water
Fee per night: $
Management: Tillamook State Forest
Contact: (503) 357–2191; www.odf.state.or.us/AREAS/northwest/tillamook/tsf/camping.asp
Finding the campground: At the summit on Oregon 6, 19 miles west of Forest Grove and 31.3 miles east of Tillamook, turn south at the sign for Browns Camp and quickly bear right, following a single-lane gravel road riddled by potholes. Continue to bear right at the junctions at 0.8 mile, 1.2 miles, 2.7 miles, and 4.4 miles, staying on the primary gravel road. Then at 4.7 miles, turn left on Rutherford Road for a steep, 0.3-mile descent into camp. A state forest map is helpful.
About the campground: Equestrians will appreciate this relaxing camp snuggled in a second-growth fir forest, with a lush understory. An information board in camp shows the location of trailheads. The Tillamook State Forest historic trails (all signed) are open to hikers and equestrians only. For the most part, these trails keep the animals safely away from off-highway vehicles. Still, when riding the trails, remain attentive at intersections.

Pacific City–Nestucca River Area

19 Alder Glen Recreation Site

Location: About 16 miles northeast of Beaver, 28 miles northeast of Pacific City
Season: April–November
Sites: 11 basic sites; no hookups
Maximum length: 40 feet
Facilities: Tables, grills, vault toilets, drinking water, fishing dock
Fee per night: $
Management: Salem District Bureau of Land Management
Contact: (503) 375-5646; www.or.blm.gov/salem
Finding the campground: From U.S. Highway 101 at Beaver, turn east onto Nestucca River Road, a BLM Back Country Byway, and go 16.4 miles to the campground.
About the campground: In a moss-draped alder and maple setting, this welcoming Nestucca River campground sits across the river from a lacy, pyramid-shaped falls. Sites have paved parking spaces, and a paved path leads to a small fishing dock. The relaxing sound of the water erases campers' cares.

20 Dovre Recreation Site

Location: About 25 miles northeast of Beaver, 37 miles northeast of Pacific City
Season: April–November
Sites: 10 basic sites; no hookups
Maximum length: 30 feet
Facilities: Tables, grills, vault toilets, drinking water, covered picnic shelter
Fee per night: $

Pacific City–Nestucca River Area	Hookup sites	Total sites	Maximum RV length	Hookups	Toilets	Showers	Drinking water	Dump station	Recreation	Fee	Can reserve
19 Alder Glen Recreation Site		11	40		NF		•		F	$	
20 Dovre Recreation Site		10	30		NF		•		F	$	
21 East Dunes and West Winds		140	40		F,NF		•		HSFO	$$	
22 Fan Creek Recreation Site		11	24		NF		•		F	$	
23 Hebo Lake		15	18		NF		•		HFB	$	
24 Rocky Bend		6	30		NF				F		
25 Sandbeach		101	30		F		•	•	HFO	$$	•
26 Webb County Park		30	30		F		•	•	HSF	$$	
27 Whalen Island County Park		26	25		F		•	•	F	$$	
28 Woods County Park	5	8	40	WES	F		•		FBL	$$	

Management: Salem District Bureau of Land Management
Contact: (503) 375–5646; www.or.blm.gov/salem
Finding the campground: From U.S. Highway 101 at Beaver, turn east on Nestucca River Road and go 25 miles to the campground.
About the campground: At this Nestucca River campground, the sites terrace the riverside slope of tall hemlocks and Douglas firs. Mossy rocks and cascading ferns dress the opposite shore, and a large side creek adds to the river's song. If quiet is your goal, you will find it at this campground. Most sites have paved parking pads, but a few have graveled road-shoulder parking. The lower reaches of camp provide direct access to the river, which alternately shows riffles and glassy pools.

21 East Dunes and West Winds

Location: About 12 miles north of Pacific City
Season: Year-round
Sites: 100 basic sites at East Dunes, 40 basic sites at West Winds; no hookups
Maximum length: 40 feet
Facilities: Flush and pit toilets, drinking water, playground
Fee per night: $$
Management: Siuslaw National Forest
Contact: (503) 392–3161; www.fs.fed.us/r6/siuslaw/recreation
Finding the campground: From the junction of U.S. Highway 101 and Oregon 6 in Tillamook, go south on US 101 for 10.7 miles. Turn west on Sand Lake Road, and proceed 4.3 miles. Turn left to remain on Sand Lake Road and continue another 0.9 mile. Turn right on Galloway, go 2.3 miles, and keep right at the junction. The campgrounds are just ahead, with West Winds at road's end.
About the campgrounds: This pair of campgrounds caters to off-highway-vehicle (OHV) enthusiasts. Large, open, paved parking areas serve the RVers and truck campers pulling OHV trailers. Sites sit side-by-side. At the edge of the parking lot, a few determined individuals manage to pitch tents where the pavement meets the dunes. The roar of engines can be heard 24 hours a day, so come prepared.

22 Fan Creek Recreation Site

Location: About 22 miles northeast of Beaver, 34 miles northeast of Pacific City
Season: April–November
Sites: 11 basic sites; no hookups
Maximum length: 24 feet
Facilities: Tables, grills, vault toilets, drinking water
Fee per night: $
Management: Salem District Bureau of Land Management
Contact: (503) 375–5646; www.or.blm.gov/salem
Finding the campground: From U.S. Highway 101 at Beaver, turn east on Nestucca River Road and go 22.4 miles for the campground. From McMinnville, it is 30 miles northwest of town via Meadow Lake and Nestucca Access roads.

About the campground: In a mixed forest of hemlocks, firs, and alders, this campground occupies the shores of Nestucca River and Fan Creek. Thorny salmonberry abounds in the understory, helping to assure site privacy. All sites have paved parking, with some more level than others. Tent campers may opt instead for the 5 walk-in sites under a canopy of bigleaf maples at Elk Bend, 3.5 miles west. This no-fee camp has river access and similar amenities.

23 Hebo Lake

Location: About 5 miles east of Hebo, 15 miles northeast of Pacific City
Season: Mid-April–mid-November
Sites: 15 basic sites; no hookups
Maximum length: 18 feet
Facilities: Tables, grills, vault toilets, drinking water, rustic picnic shelter, barrier-free fishing docks
Fee per night: $
Management: Siuslaw National Forest
Contact: (503) 392–3161; www.fs.fed.us/r6/siuslaw/recreation
Finding the campground: From Oregon 22 at Hebo, turn east onto Forest Road 14 just north of the Hebo Ranger District office and proceed 4.5 miles to the campground on the right.
About the campground: Centerpiece to the camp is Hebo Lake, a coastal mountain lake stocked with pan-sized trout and said to have some big catfish. Rafts or small rowboats may ply the water, but three is definitely a crowd. A rich coastal woods enfolds the lake and camp, and a barrier-free trail travels two-thirds of the way around Hebo Lake. Lily pads, alder reflections, and newts add to the lake's charm. From camp, the 7-mile Pioneer–Indian Trail leads hikers over Mount Hebo and past vegetated North Lake to end at the larger, more isolated South Lake, which also offers fishing. En route to camp, you will pass the Hebo Plantation Trail; this 0.5-mile interpretive walk relates the mountain's history of fire and reforestation.

24 Rocky Bend

Location: About 14 miles northeast of Beaver, 26 miles northeast of Pacific City
Season: Year-round
Sites: 6 basic sites; no hookups
Maximum length: 30 feet
Facilities: Tables, grills, pit toilets; no drinking water
Fee per night: None
Management: Salem District Bureau of Land Management/Siuslaw National Forest
Contact: (503) 392–3161; www.fs.fed.us/r6/siuslaw/recreation
Finding the campground: From U.S. Highway 101 at Beaver, turn east onto Nestucca River Road and go 13.8 miles to the campground.
About the campground: Jointly operated by the Bureau of Land Management and Hebo Ranger District, this tiny, primitive camp occupies an alder-clad shore along the Nestucca River. Sites have gravel parking.

25 Sandbeach

Location: About 12 miles north of Pacific City
Season: Year-round
Sites: 101 basic sites; no hookups
Maximum length: 30 feet
Facilities: Tables, grills, flush toilets, drinking water, dump station
Fee per night: $$
Management: Siuslaw National Forest
Contact: (503) 392–3161; (877) 444–6777 for reservations; www.fs.fed.us/r6 /siuslaw/recreation
Finding the campground: From the junction of U.S. Highway 101 and Oregon 6 in Tillamook, go south on US 101 for 10.7 miles and turn west on Sand Lake Road. Proceed 4.3 miles and turn left to remain on Sand Lake Road, following it another 0.9 mile. Turn right on Galloway and continue 2.3 miles to take a left at the junction for Sandbeach Campground.
About the campground: Although off-highway vehicles (OHVs) are prohibited from driving through camp, the engine roars still carry over the dunes 24 hours a day. Camp guests with OHVs reach the dunes via a designated bypass. For more quiet pursuits, the beach is closed to OHV driving between the campground and Fisherman's Parking; this stretch of beach is just 0.1 mile away via Sand Lake Estuary. Sand Lake is a big, shallow tidal lake that reduces to a sand flat at low tide. The lake holds flounder and perch, which, at low tide, dig into the wet sand or collect in lingering pools, making easy pickings for eagles and other birds. Because the campground sits in a weather gap between coastal capes, it is often basked in sun when the rest of the coast is cloaked in fog. Sites have fairly good privacy in the dune–shore pine setting.

26 Webb County Park

Location: In Pacific City
Season: Year-round
Sites: 30 basic sites; no hookups
Maximum length: 30 feet
Facilities: Tables, grills, flush toilets, drinking water, dump station
Fee per night: $$
Management: Tillamook County
Contact: (503) 965–5001; www.co.tillamook.or.us/gov/parks
Finding the campground: From Cape Kiwanda Drive 1.1 miles northwest of Pacific City center, turn right on Webb Park Road (opposite the parking for Cape Kiwanda State Natural Area) and follow it into the park.
About the campground: Inland from Haystack Rock, this pleasant campground claims a private, out-of-the-way, shore pine–shaded spot. The campground sits within easy walking distance of a state beach where dories (flat-bottomed fishing boats) are launched into the surf and where hang gliders soar from the Cape Kiwanda headland. Other area activities include driving Three Capes Scenic Route, hiking the spit at Robert W. (Bob) Straub State Park, and fishing the Nestucca River or tiny Hebo Lake (see campground 23).

27 Whalen Island County Park

Location: About 7 miles north of Pacific City
Season: Year-round
Sites: 26 basic sites; no hookups
Maximum length: 25 feet
Facilities: Tables, fire rings, flush toilets, drinking water, dump station
Fee per night: $$
Management: Tillamook County
Contact: (503) 965–5001; www.co.tillamook.or.us/gov/parks
Finding the campground: From the junction of U.S. Highway 101 and Oregon 6 in Tillamook, go south on US 101 for 10.7 miles, turn west on Sand Lake Road, and proceed another 4.3 miles. Turn left to remain on Sand Lake Road for another 3.3 miles. Turn right and cross a Sand Lake levee road to enter camp in 0.2 mile.
About the campground: Most of the sites of this campground stretch across a treeless, grassy flat overlooking the Sand Lake estuary; a few occupy a rise at wood's edge. Bald eagles, shorebirds, and frogs contribute amusement to a stay. Fishing, crabbing, and exploring the Three Capes Scenic Route or area dunes engage campers. This camp offers a quiet alternative to the area's popular off-highway-vehicle campgrounds.

28 Woods County Park

Location: Less than a mile east of Pacific City
Season: Year-round
Sites: 5 hookup sites, 3 tent sites; water, electric, and sewer hookups
Maximum length: 40 feet
Facilities: Tables at tent sites and a shelter with tables and fireplace, flush toilets, drinking water. There is a public boat launch and fishing access 0.4 mile west of camp.
Fee per night: $$
Management: Tillamook County
Contact: (503) 965–5001; www.co.tillamook.or.us/gov/parks
Finding the campground: From the center of Pacific City, go 0.8 mile east on Brooten Road to find the campground on the corner at Woods Bridge.
About the campground: In a rural-residential setting, this small campground occupies a corner green at Woods Bridge above the Nestucca River. The camp's small, sandy river access often holds the tracks of the previous night's wildlife, and the river shows a tidal influence. Meadowlarks serenade campers from the open field across from the park. Sites occupy an open lawn, but trees grow toward shore. RVers should avoid camping here when conditions are wet, as the soft grassy sites turn to mud under the weight of the vehicle.

Lincoln City–Newport Area

29 A. W. "Jack" Morgan County Park

Location: About 20 miles southeast of Lincoln City
Season: Mid-March–mid-November
Sites: 9 basic sites; no hookups
Maximum length: 35 feet
Facilities: Tables, grills, nonflush toilets, drinking water, drift/car-top boat launch (across road from camp)
Fee per night: $
Management: Lincoln County
Contact: (541) 265-5747; www.co.lincoln.or.us/lcparks
Finding the campground: From U.S. Highway 101 south of Lincoln City, turn east on Oregon 229 to reach the campground in 17 miles. The campground is 6 miles northwest of Siletz.
About the campground: Across the highway from the Siletz River, this campground occupies a grassy spot beneath towering western hemlocks and spruces. Some site are more open than others. The camp has gravel roads and parking. The coastal river draws campers away for fishing or drift boating.

30 Beverly Beach State Park

Location: About 7 miles north of Newport
Season: Year-round
Sites: 128 full or partial hookup sites, 128 basic sites, 21 yurts; water and electric hookups, with sewer and cable hookups available at some sites
Maximum length: 65 feet
Facilities: Tables, grills, flush toilets, drinking water, showers, dump station, telephone, playground, visitor center

Lincoln City–Newport Area

	Hookup sites	Total sites	Maximum RV length	Hookups	Toilets	Showers	Drinking water	Dump station	Recreation	Fee	Can reserve
29 A. W. "Jack" Morgan County Park		9	35		NF		•		FBL	$	
30 Beverly Beach State Park	128	277	65	WESC	F	•	•	•	HSF	$$–$$$	•
31 Devils Lake State Recreation Area	32	97	62	WESC	F	•	•		SFBL	$$–$$$	•
32 Elk City Park		12	40		F		•		FBL	$$	
33 Moonshine County Park		38	40		F		•		FBL	$$	
34 Newport Marina RV Park	114	114	60	WESC	F	•	•	•	FBL	$$$	•
35 South Beach State Park	228	261	60	WE	F	•	•	•	HSF	$$–$$$	•

Fee per night: $$-$$$
Management: Oregon State Parks and Recreation Department
Contact: (541) 265-9278; (800) 452-5687 for reservations; www.oregonstate
parks.org
Finding the campground: From Newport, go about 7 miles north on U.S.
Highway 101. The campground is on the east side of the highway.
About the campground: Threaded by Spencer Creek, this campground oc-
cupies a coastal forest setting of Sitka spruce, wax myrtle, and rhododendron.
It features beach access and a short nature trail and lies within easy reach of
Yaquina Head Outstanding Natural Area, with its visitor center, historic light-
house, and wildlife watching. Visitors can spy nesting seabirds on Colony
Rock, migrating gray whales, and harbor seals. Newport adds its city, port, and
beach enticements.

31 Devils Lake State Recreation Area

Location: In Lincoln City
Season: Year-round
Sites: 32 full or partial hookup sites, 55 basic sites, 10 yurts; water and elec-
tric hookups, with sewer and cable hookups available at some sites
Maximum length: 62 feet
Facilities: Tables, grills, flush toilets, drinking water, showers, telephone,
launch, dock, moorage slips
Fee per night: $$-$$$
Management: Oregon State Parks and Recreation Department
Contact: (541) 994-2002; (800) 452-5687 for reservations; www.oregonstate
parks.org
Finding the campground: From U.S. Highway 101 in Lincoln City, head east
on Sixth Street for 0.1 mile to enter the campground.
About the campground: Attractive shore pines shade and seclude these
campsites, which are not far from the shore of Devils Lake. The individual
sites are level, with paved parking pads. Lake access is available at the dock
here and at the park's day use off First Street. Besides fishing and boating at
the lake, you can spend your time prowling the coastal beaches, visiting the
shops and eateries of Lincoln City, joining in the spring or fall kite festival, or
taking a chance at Chinook Winds Indian Casino.

32 Elk City Park

Location: About 10 miles southeast of Toledo, 20 miles southeast of Newport
Season: April–October
Sites: 12 basic sites; no hookups
Maximum length: 40 feet
Facilities: Tables, grills, flush toilets, drinking water, concrete boat ramp and
dock
Fee per night: $$
Management: Lincoln County
Contact: (541) 265-5747; www.co.lincoln.or.us/lcparks

Finding the campground: From the junction of Main Street and Butler Bridge Road in Toledo, follow Butler Bridge Road for 0.8 mile as it rounds south past the Georgia-Pacific Paper Mill and crosses the Yaquina River. Bear left at the fork onto Elk City Road. Follow it 8.7 miles upstream to the park at the intersection of Elk City and Harlan Roads.

About the campground: At the confluence of Big Elk Creek and the Yaquina River, this campground occupies a large meadow flat with a handful of shade trees. It mainly attracts anglers and boaters, with ample boater parking in addition to the campsites. Vultures commonly soar overhead. In 1866, the first stage line between the Willamette Valley and the coast stopped here; coast-bound travelers would then have to continue by boat on the Yaquina River.

33 Moonshine County Park

Location: About 12 miles northeast of Siletz
Season: April–October; in winter, dry camping only
Sites: 24 RV sites, 14 tent sites; no hookups
Maximum length: 40 feet
Facilities: Tables, grills, flush toilets, drinking water, drift/car-top boat launch, horseshoe pits
Fee per night: $$
Management: Lincoln County
Contact: (541) 265-5747; www.co.lincoln.or.us/lcparks
Finding the campground: From Oregon 229 at Siletz, 23 miles southeast of Lincoln City and 7 miles north of Toledo, go east on East Logsden Road, which becomes Upper Siletz Road. Drive 7.5 miles to Logsden, turn left (north) at a sign for the park, and continue another 4 miles to the camp.

About the campground: This park serves up Siletz River hospitality in an attractive river valley location. Campsites occupy a large, open lawn above the river, with dispersed pine, spruce, and cedar trees distributing bits of shade. Paved pads are available at the RV sites, while tent sites dot the lawn. Across from camp, a tributary waterfall spills into the coastal river that supports salmon and steelhead.

34 Newport Marina RV Park

Location: In Newport
Season: Year-round
Sites: 114 hookup sites; water, electric, sewer, and cable hookups
Maximum length: 40 feet at marina sites, 60 feet at the south RV area
Facilities: Flush toilets, drinking water, showers, laundry, dump station, telephone, camp store, cafe, pier, charters, dock, boat rental, fish-cleaning station
Fee per night: $$$
Management: Port of Newport
Contact: (541) 867-3321, reservations accepted
Finding the campground: From the south end of Yaquina Bay Bridge in Newport, take Southeast Pacific Way, following the signs for the Oregon Coast

Aquarium, to reach the marina in 0.6 mile. The park sits east of the bridge.

About the campground: RVers may choose between the two camp areas: the paved lot of the marina for waterfront camping or the inland coastal flat of the south RV area, which has grass and a few shore pines. The marina offers everything that nautical and fishing enthusiasts might want, and its sites are within a hat's throw of a microbrewery, the Oregon Coast Aquarium, and the Mark O. Hatfield Marine Science Center. Seasonal attractions include jigging for herring, crabbing on the pier, clamming in the bay, and watching the larceny of the sea lions or the diving of loons. Newport and the coastal beaches may lure you away from camp.

35 South Beach State Park

Location: About 1.5 miles south of Newport
Season: Year-round
Sites: 228 hookup sites, 6 basic sites, 27 yurts; water and electric hookups
Maximum length: 60 feet
Facilities: Tables, grills, flush toilets, drinking water, showers, dump station, telephone, playground, volleyball and basketball courts
Fee per night: $$–$$$
Management: Oregon State Parks and Recreation Department
Contact: (541) 867-4715; (800) 452-5687 for reservations; www.oregonstate parks.org
Finding the campground: From the Yaquina Bay Bridge in Newport, drive 1.5 miles south on U.S. Highway 101 and turn west to enter the park.
About the campground: This jumbo campground occupies a broad coastal plain behind the swale and low dunes of a prized beach. Shore pines isolate and lend shade to the campsites, which are nicely spaced for privacy and comfort. The paths to the beach range between 0.25 and 0.5 mile in length. Hiking north along the beach, you can reach a jetty, where you can fish or watch the sea lions and harbor seals in the bay. The state park is within easy drive of the tourist shops and Old Town attractions of Newport, coastal offerings, Oregon Coast Aquarium, and Mark O. Hatfield Marine Science Center.

Waldport–Florence Area

36 Alder Dune

Location: About 6 miles north of Florence
Season: Mid-May–September
Sites: 38 basic sites; no hookups
Maximum length: 30 feet
Facilities: Tables, grills, flush toilets, drinking water
Fee per night: $$
Management: Siuslaw National Forest
Contact: (541) 902–6940; www.fs.fed.us/r6/siuslaw/recreation
Finding the campground: From the junction of U.S. Highway 101 and Oregon 126 in Florence, go 6.4 miles north on US 101. The campground is on the west side of the highway.
About the campground: This campground, with paved sites and roads, occupies a coastal forest of alders and conifers along Alder and Dune Lakes.

Waldport–Florence Area

	Hookup sites	Total sites	Maximum RV length	Hookups	Toilets	Showers	Drinking water	Dump station	Recreation	Fee	Can reserve
36 Alder Dune		38	30		F		•		HSF	$$	
37 Archie Knowles		9	18		F		•			$$	
38 Baker Beach Recreation Site		5	25		NF				HSFR	$$	
39 Beachside State Recreation Area	33	80	30	WE	F	•	•		HSF	$$–$$$	•
40 Blackberry		32	40		F		•		FBL	$$	•
41 Canal Creek		12	22		NF		•		F	$$	•
42 Cape Perpetua		38	32		F		•	•	HF	$$	•
43 Carl G. Washburne Memorial State Park	58	67	45	WES	F	•	•	•	HSF	$$–$$$	
44 Clay Creek Recreation Site		21	32		NF		•		HSFBL	$	
45 Harbor Vista	32	38	40	WE	F,NF	•	•	•		$$$	•
46 Horse Creek Trailhead		10	60		NF				HR	donation	
47 Port of Siuslaw RV Park and Marina	85	85	40	WESC	F	•	•	•	FBL	$$	•
48 Rock Creek		16	T		F		•		HF	$$	
49 Sutton Creek Recreation Area	23	90	30	E	F		•		HFBL	$$	
50 Tillicum Beach		62	40		F		•		HSF	$$	•
51 Whittaker Creek Recreation Site		31	32		NF		•		HFBL	$	

Dune Lake is green and picturesque, with an irregular shoreline. Alder Lake has a marshy side arm and grassy spits, but its main body is larger and deeper than Dune Lake. Fishing, swimming, and canoeing are possible. Hiking trails pass through dunes and coastal forest and link the camp to Sutton Creek Recreation Area to the south. East off US 101, 1.6 miles south of camp, is the nature trail touring Darlingtonia Wayside. The trail visits a bog of rare cobra lilies (or pitcher plants), carnivores of the plant kingdom. They flower in May and June. Sutton Lake, slightly farther to the south, has a ramp for boating.

37 Archie Knowles

Location: About 3 miles east of Mapleton, 18 miles east of Florence
Season: Mid-May–Labor Day
Sites: 9 basic sites; no hookups
Maximum length: 18 feet
Facilities: Tables, grills, flush toilets, drinking water
Fee per night: $$
Management: Siuslaw National Forest
Contact: (541) 902–6940; www.fs.fed.us/r6/siuslaw/recreation
Finding the campground: It is south off Oregon 126, 3 miles east of Mapleton and 42 miles west of Eugene.
About the campground: Sites have gravel pads and are well spaced across the grassy flat above Knowles Creek. Big alders, hemlocks, and firs lend shade. Because this charming campground is just off OR 126, vehicle noise can be intrusive. Primarily, this is a campground for kicking back, opening a newspaper, and reading it from cover to cover. From camp, you may go 9 miles east for Siuslaw River recreation or venture west to the coastal attractions around Florence.

38 Baker Beach Recreation Site

Location: About 8 miles north of Florence
Season: Year-round
Sites: 5 basic sites; no hookups
Maximum length: 25 feet
Facilities: Tables, grills, vault toilets; no drinking water
Fee per night: $$
Management: Siuslaw National Forest
Contact: (541) 902–6940; www.fs.fed.us/r6/siuslaw/recreation
Finding the campground: From the junction of U.S. Highway 101 and Oregon 126 in Florence, go 7.6 miles north on US 101 and turn west on Baker Beach Road. The recreation site is 0.4 mile ahead.
About the campground: Within sound of the surf, this campground, popular with equestrians, consists of a large gravel parking lot with sites fanning off into the edging shore pines and vegetated dunes. A trail crosses the dunes to the beach. To protect the threatened snowy plover, the beach is closed behind the high tide from March 15 through September 15.

39 Beachside State Recreation Area

Location: About 3 miles south of Waldport
Season: Mid-March–October
Sites: 33 hookup sites, 45 basic sites, 2 yurts; water and electric hookups
Maximum length: 30 feet
Facilities: Tables, grills, flush toilets, drinking water, showers, telephone
Fee per night: $$–$$$
Management: Oregon State Parks and Recreation Department
Contact: (541) 563–3220; (800) 452–5687 for reservations; www.oregonstate parks.org
Finding the campground: From the junction of Oregon 34 and U.S. Highway 101 in Waldport, go 3.4 miles south on US 101. The park is on the west side of the highway.
About the campground: This beach campground features private, well-shaded sites in a coastal pine–Sitka spruce forest. The understory salal and wax myrtle contribute to site privacy. The camp affords easy access to miles of broad, sandy beach and beautiful ocean. Traffic noise from US 101 carries to the sites closest to the highway. The hookup sites typically have longer parking spurs. Besides beachcombing, beach strolling, sunning, and surf play, campers can try their hands at clamming and crabbing in Alsea Bay or fishing for steelhead or salmon on the Alsea River, both north of the park. For trout fishing, there is the Yachats River, to the south.

40 Blackberry

Location: About 17 miles east of Waldport
Season: Year-round
Sites: 32 basic sites; no hookups
Maximum length: 40 feet
Facilities: Tables, grills, flush toilets, drinking water, telephone, drift/car-top boat launch
Fee per night: $$
Management: Siuslaw National Forest
Contact: (541) 563–3211; (877) 444–6777 for reservations; www.fs.fed.us/r6 /siuslaw/recreation
Finding the campground: It is south off Oregon 34, 17.1 miles east of Waldport.
About the campground: Overnighters will enjoy this beautiful riverside campground with paved parking pads, lots of open grass, and towering hemlocks, Sitka spruces, and Douglas firs. Bigleaf maples shade the Alsea River. Some sites directly overlook the river, but all lie within easy access of it. Fishing and relaxing are the primary draws to this campground, and the coast is only minutes away.

41 Canal Creek

Location: About 11 miles southeast of Waldport
Season: Mid-May–September
Sites: 12 basic sites; no hookups
Maximum length: 22 feet
Facilities: Tables, grills, vault toilets, drinking water
Fee per night: $$
Management: Siuslaw National Forest
Contact: (541) 563–3211; (877) 444–6777 for reservations; www.fs.fed.us/r6/siuslaw/recreation
Finding the campground: From U.S. Highway 101 in Waldport, go 6.7 miles east on Oregon 34 and turn south on Canal Creek Road. Proceed another 3.8 miles to the campground. The road is narrow, paved, and winding, with turnouts for passing.
About the campground: This scenic, out-of-the-way campground in alders and firs along Canal Creek suggests a quiet getaway. The creek is open to catch-and-release fishing only, but thickets of prickly salmonberry may keep you away from the creek altogether. In camp, the salmonberry thickets shape ideal privacy borders between sites. Elsewhere, attractive mosses coat the tree trunks and posts.

42 Cape Perpetua

Location: About 3 miles south of Yachats, 11 miles south of Waldport
Season: Memorial Day–September
Sites: 38 basic sites; no hookups
Maximum length: 32 feet
Facilities: Tables, grills, flush toilets, drinking water, dump station, telephone at interpretive center
Fee per night: $$
Management: Siuslaw National Forest
Contact: (541) 563–3211; (877) 444–6777 for reservations; www.fs.fed.us/r6/siuslaw/recreation
Finding the campground: It is east off U.S. Highway 101, 3.3 miles south of Yachats.
About the campground: This serene campground along Cape Creek charms guests with its grassy sites and framing wooded hillside. Footbridges span the creek and link the campground to a nature trail, which leads to a 500-year-old Sitka spruce and the area's interpretive center. An underpass allows safe passage beneath US 101 to a trail system along the ragged seashore, which is punctuated by blow holes, high-splashing waves, chasms, and tide pools. A scenic drive or foot trail leads to the top of the headland for whale watching; longer trails explore ridge and creek canyon. Captain James Cook named this headland Cape Perpetua, in 1778.

43 Carl G. Washburne Memorial State Park

Location: About 14 miles north of Florence
Season: Year-round
Sites: 58 hookup sites, 7 walk-in tent sites, 2 yurts; water, electric, and sewer hookups
Maximum length: 45 feet
Facilities: Tables, grills, flush toilets, drinking water, showers, telephone, dump station across U.S. Highway 101
Fee per night: $$–$$$
Management: Oregon State Parks and Recreation Department
Contact: (541) 547–3416; www.oregonstateparks.org
Finding the campground: From US 101, 11.4 miles south of Yachats and 13.9 miles north of Florence, turn east for the park campground. The park's beach and day-use area are on the west side of the highway.
About the campground: Snuggled in a coastal forest with a lush understory that includes rhododendron blooms in early summer, this spacious campground offers a pleasing retreat at which to relax. China and Blowout Creeks thread through the park. Elk and tide pools are possible nature discoveries. A trail from camp passes under US 101 for safe, convenient access to the beach, while another trail links the park to Heceta Head Lighthouse. You can also drive the 2.1 miles south to this photogenic lighthouse. Sea Lion Caves, a popular private attraction featuring a Steller's sea lion rookery, is 3.2 miles south of the park.

44 Clay Creek Recreation Site

Location: About 28 miles southeast of Mapleton
Season: May–October
Sites: 21 basic sites; no hookups
Maximum length: 32 feet
Facilities: Tables, grills, vault toilets, drinking water, playground, ballfield, horseshoe pits, car-top boat launch
Fee per night: $
Management: Eugene District Bureau of Land Management
Contact: (541) 683–6600; www.edo.or.blm.gov
Finding the campground: From Oregon 126, 12 miles east of Mapleton and 33 miles west of Eugene, turn south on Siuslaw River Road, go 9.7 miles, and bear left on Siuslaw River Access Road. Proceed another 6 miles and turn right to reach the entrance to the recreation site.
About the campground: Spacious sites with paved parking pads, mossy vine-maple tangles, and tall straight firs make up this camp area along Clay Creek and the Siuslaw River. The river flows broad, cloudy, and green and calls to anglers; check current fishing regulations. A small swimming area invites you to cool off. The 1-mile Clay Creek Trail ascends a ridge above camp to visit a remnant old-growth stand. From camp, cross the concrete bridge on Clay Creek Road and ford or rock hop across Clay Creek to begin the hike.

45 Harbor Vista

Location: In Florence
Season: Year-round
Sites: 32 hookup sites, 6 tent sites; water and electric hookups
Maximum length: 40 feet
Facilities: Tables, grills, flush and chemical toilets, drinking water, showers, dump station, telephone, playground, vista shelter
Fee per night: $$$
Management: Lane County
Contact: (541) 997–5987, reservations accepted; www.co.lane.or.us/parks
Finding the campground: In Florence, turn west off U.S. Highway 101 onto Heceta Beach Road, go 1.8 miles, and turn left on Rhododendron Drive. Proceed another 1.2 miles and turn right on Jetty Road North to find the campground on the left in 0.1 mile. Alternatively, turn west off US 101 on Thirty-fifth Street, go 0.9 mile, and turn right on Rhododendron Drive. Proceed another 1.3 miles, and turn left on Jetty Road North to reach the campground in 0.1 mile.
About the campground: This campground offers a quiet, clean, comfortable base from which to explore the area. Sites rest in a coastal vegetation of shore pine, salal, rhododendron, and wax myrtle; some sites are more open than others. From the vista shelter, you can see North Jetty and the Siuslaw River mouth. Outward explorations lead to ocean beaches, dunes, coastal lakes, and Old Town Florence.

46 Horse Creek Trailhead

Location: About 14 miles northeast of Florence
Season: Year-round
Sites: 10 basic sites; no hookups
Maximum length: 60 feet
Facilities: Tables, grills, vault toilets, corrals, hitching posts, horse loading ramp; no drinking water
Fee per night: Donation
Management: Siuslaw National Forest
Contact: (541) 902–6940; www.fs.fed.us/r6/siuslaw/recreation
Finding the campground: From U.S. Highway 101, 10.3 miles north of Florence and 0.5 mile south of Sea Lion Caves, turn east onto Horse Creek Road (Forest Road 5800), which begins paved but becomes single-lane gravel with turnouts. Follow it 3.2 miles to campground.
About the campground: In a dense forest of tall Sitka spruce, this pleasant, isolated campground serves a burgeoning hiker/horse trail system that already encompasses 14 miles of trail through the coastal mountains. The camp is functional, clean, and comfortable, and the sites are well spaced for campers with horses.

47 Port of Siuslaw RV Park and Marina

Location: On the bay in Florence
Season: Year-round
Sites: 85 full and partial hookup sites; water, electric, sewer, and cable hookups
Maximum length: 40 feet
Facilities: Tables, flush toilets, drinking water, showers, laundry, dump station, telephone, boat launch, sport marina
Fee per night: $$
Management: Port of Siuslaw
Contact: (541) 997-3040, reservations accepted
Finding the campground: In Florence, take the Old Town Loop off U.S. Highway 101 to First Street. The campground is at the corner of First and Harbor Streets, less than a quarter mile off US 101.
About the campground: At the Port of Siuslaw, in the heart of Old Town Florence, campers have a choice between pleasant, shore pine–shaded lawn sites or the open, graveled sites directly overlooking the bay. This is an ideal base for outward explorations or simply planting yourself in camp. Easy walks lead to the marina and marine offerings and to the shops and eateries of Florence. The beach and dunes are just a short drive away. Boating, sport fishing, crabbing from the dock, or clamming in the mudflats are popular pursuits.

48 Rock Creek

Location: About 16 miles north of Florence
Season: Memorial Day–September
Sites: 16 basic sites; no hookups
Maximum length: Tent units only
Facilities: Tables, grills, flush toilets, drinking water
Fee per night: $$
Management: Siuslaw National Forest
Contact: (541) 563-3211; www.fs.fed.us/r6/siuslaw/recreation
Finding the campground: From U.S. Highway 101, 9.7 miles south of Yachats and 15.6 miles north of Florence, turn east to enter campground.
About the campground: Gateway to Rock Creek Wilderness, this small campground sits where Rock Creek yawns to the ocean and the valley floor broadens into scenic meadows. Rock Creek is a beautiful, sparkling coastal water emerging from a forested canyon. A fisherman's path heads upstream from camp, providing the only access to the wilderness, but check current fishing regulations before fishing the creek. The path passes through old homestead meadows that are now frequented by elk. It is an easy jaunt from the campground to Cape Perpetua, Old Town Florence, and the northern reaches of Oregon Dunes National Recreation Area.

Sutton Creek Recreation Area.

49 Sutton Creek Recreation Area

Location: About 5 miles north of Florence
Season: May–September
Sites: 23 hookup sites, 67 basic sites; electric hookups only
Maximum length: 30 feet
Facilities: Tables, grills, flush toilets, drinking water, playground, boat launch (at Sutton Lake to the north)
Fee per night: $$
Management: Siuslaw National Forest
Contact: (541) 902–6940; www.fs.fed.us/r6/siuslaw/recreation
Finding the campground: From the junction of U.S. Highway 101 and Oregon 126 in Florence, go 4.5 miles north on US 101 and turn west to enter Sutton Creek Recreation Area. The campground is reached off the recreation area entrance road.
About the campground: This charming coastal campground is nestled in cedars, shore pines, hemlocks, and spruces along Sutton Creek. It extends a comfortable stay, with good site privacy and ample space. Parking spurs are paved. Area trails visit dune, ocean, estuary, and lake attractions. In camp, a

short nature trail reveals a bog of carnivorous *Darlingtonia* (or pitcher plant); Darlingtonia Wayside, 0.1 mile north on US 101, offers another chance to view this rare plant. Sutton Lake draws boaters and anglers. Florence and the Oregon Dunes National Recreation Area are but a short drive south. Sea Lion Caves are 9 miles north on US 101.

50 Tillicum Beach

Location: About 5 miles south of Waldport
Season: Year-round
Sites: 62 basic sites; no hookups
Maximum length: 40 feet
Facilities: Tables, grills, flush toilets, drinking water
Fee per night: $$
Management: Siuslaw National Forest
Contact: (541) 563–3211; (877) 444–6777 for reservations; www.fs.fed.us/r6 /siuslaw/recreation
Finding the campground: From the junction of Oregon 34 and U.S. Highway 101 in Waldport, go 4.5 miles south on US 101 and turn west to enter the campground.
About the campground: On a low bluff above the beach, a dense growth of low shore pines, salal, evergreen huckleberry, and wax myrtle enfolds this campground. Sites closer to shore are more exposed and receive more sun. Silvered snags and wind-sculpted spruce add to sunset photography. Beach pursuits and visits to Cape Perpetua or Waldport further engage campers.

51 Whittaker Creek Recreation Site

Location: About 14 miles southeast of Mapleton
Season: May–October, with a few sites kept open year-round
Sites: 31 basic sites; no hookups
Maximum length: 32 feet
Facilities: Tables, grills, vault or pit toilets, drinking water, horseshoe pits, drift/car-top boat launch
Fee per night: $
Management: Eugene District Bureau of Land Management
Contact: (541) 683–6600; www.edo.or.blm.gov
Finding the campground: From Oregon 126, 12 miles east of Mapleton and 33 miles west of Eugene, turn south on Siuslaw River Road, go 1.5 miles, and turn right on Whittaker Creek Road. Go another 0.2 mile to find the entrance to the recreation site on the right.
About the campground: This campground is bisected by Whittaker Creek, which houses an experimental fish trap and is closed to fishing. Sites occupy either alder woodland or fir forest. Close by, the Siuslaw River suggests launching a drift boat or fishing, but check current fishing regulations first. This large coastal river flows broad, cloudy, and green. The interpretive Old Growth Ridge National Recreation Trail begins in camp and climbs 1.4 miles to a river overlook and an old-growth grove. Look for the trailhead across from campsites 23 and 24.

Reedsport Area

52 East Shore Recreation Site

Location: About 21 miles southeast of Reedsport
Season: Memorial Day weekend–October
Sites: 6 basic sites; no hookups
Maximum length: 40 feet
Facilities: Tables, grills, vault toilets, boat dock; no drinking water
Fee per night: $$
Management: Coos Bay District Bureau of Land Management
Contact: (541) 756-0100; www.or.blm.gov/coosbay
Finding the campground: From Oregon 38, 22.5 miles west of Elkton and 13 miles east of Reedsport, head south on winding Loon Lake Road to reach the recreation site in 7.5 miles.
About the campground: This small campground occupies a forested slope above Loon Lake; there is a separate day-use area across the road on the lakeshore. Fishing, boating, Jet Skiing, and swimming are popular pursuits. A boat launch is located at Loon Lake Recreation Site (see below).

53 Loon Lake Recreation Site

Location: About 20 miles southeast of Reedsport
Season: Memorial Day weekend–September
Sites: 52 basic sites, 8 tent sites; no hookups
Maximum length: 40 feet
Facilities: Tables, flush toilets, drinking water, showers, dump station, telephone, playground, boat launch, fish-cleaning station
Fee per night: $$
Management: Coos Bay District Bureau of Land Management
Contact: (541) 756-0100; www.or.blm.gov/coosbay

Reedsport Area

	Hookup sites	Total sites	Maximum RV length	Hookups	Toilets	Showers	Drinking water	Dump station	Recreation	Fee	Can reserve
52 East Shore Recreation Site		6	40		NF				SFB	$$	
53 Loon Lake Recreation Site		60	40		F	•	•	•	SFBL	$$	
54 Smith River Falls Recreation Site		9	small		NF				SF		
55 Vincent Creek Recreation Site		6	small		NF						

Finding the campground: From Oregon 38, 22.5 miles west of Elkton and 13 miles east of Reedsport, head south 6.6. miles on winding Loon Lake Road to reach the recreation site.

About the campground: Situated in a stately Douglas fir forest interspersed with bigleaf maples and coastal shrubs is this fully accommodating campground on Loon Lake. Although the terrain has a mild slope, campsite parking is level and paved. Guests have access to boating, fishing, swimming, and waterskiing on lovely Loon Lake. During the first week in August, the popular annual fishing derby is fun for the whole family.

54 Smith River Falls Recreation Site

Location: About 26 miles northeast of Reedsport
Season: Year-round
Sites: 9 basic sites; no hookups
Maximum length: Small units only
Facilities: Tables, grills, vault toilets; no drinking water
Fee per night: None
Management: Coos Bay District Bureau of Land Management
Contact: (541) 756–0100; www.or.blm.gov/coosbay
Finding the campground: From U.S. Highway 101, 0.3 mile north of the Umpqua River bridge on the northern outskirts of Reedsport, turn east on Smith River Road (County Road 48) and go 25.3 miles to reach the recreation site on the right.

About the campground: Located 0.2 mile upstream from Smith River Falls, this small, rustic campground occupies the terraces of a river slope. Alders grow toward the river; conifers shade the campsites. A few glorious old-growth trees tower above camp. Because of the short, uneven gravel or earthen parking pads and the sometimes awkward approach to sites, this campground is better suited for tents or pickup campers. At Smith River Falls, rounded rock ledges part and fold the river, creating tiers of cascading water. Near the falls, flat-topped rocks appeal to sunbathers; elsewhere, potholes lend interest to the river rock. A fish enhancement project is located near the falls.

55 Vincent Creek Recreation Site

Location: About 29 miles northeast of Reedsport
Season: Year-round
Sites: 6 basic sites; no hookups
Maximum length: Small units only
Facilities: Tables, grills, vault or pit toilets; no drinking water
Fee per night: None
Management: Coos Bay District Bureau of Land Management
Contact: (541) 756–0100; www.or.blm.gov/coosbay
Finding the campground: From U.S. Highway 101, 0.3 mile north of the Umpqua River bridge at the northern outskirts of Reedsport, turn east on

Smith River Road (County Road 48) and go 28.7 miles to reach the recreation site on the right. The entry road travels past a guard station on its way into camp.

About the campground: This small, primitive, no-frills campground sits near the confluence of Vincent Creek and the Smith River. Alders and firs shade the river bench. The sites lack established parking pads, and you should be aware that rain-soaked ground can cause trouble for heavier vehicles.

Oregon Dunes National Recreation Area

56 Bluebill

Location: About 4 miles north of North Bend/Coos Bay
Season: Mid-May–September
Sites: 18 basic sites; no hookups
Maximum length: 30 feet
Facilities: Tables, grills, flush toilets, drinking water
Fee per night: $$
Management: Siuslaw National Forest
Contact: (541) 271–3611; www.fs.fed.us/r6/siuslaw/recreation

Oregon Dunes National Recreation Area

	Hookup sites	Total sites	Maximum RV length	Hookups	Toilets	Showers	Drinking water	Dump station	Recreation	Fee	Can reserve
56 Bluebill		18	30		F		•		HF	$$	
57 Carter Lake		23	35		F		•		HFBL	$$	•
58 Driftwood II		59	40		F	•	•		FO	$$	•
59 Eel Creek		51	30		F		•		H	$$	•
60 Horsfall		70	50		F	•	•		O	$$	•
61 Horsfall Beach		41	50		F		•		HSFOR	$$	
62 Jessie M. Honeyman Memorial State Park	166	367	60	WES	F	•	•	•	HSFBLO	$$–$$$	•
63 Lagoon		38	35		F		•		HF	$$	
64 Salmon Harbor Marina RV Park		300	40		F	•	•	•	FBL	$	•
65 Salmon Harbor Marina RV Resort	138	163	40	WESCP	F	•	•	•	FBLC	$$$	•
66 Spinreel		36	40		F		•		O	$$	
67 Tahkenitch		31	30		F				HFBL	$$	•
68 Tahkenitch Landing		27	30		NF				FBL	$$	•
69 Tyee		16	22		NF		•		FBL	$$	•
70 Umpqua Lighthouse State Park	20	54	45	WES	F	•	•		HSF	$$–$$$	•
71 Waxmyrtle		55	35		F		•		HFO	$$	
72 Wild Mare Horse Camp		12	50		NF		•		HR	$$	•
73 William M. Tugman State Park	100	113	50	WE	F	•	•	•	FBL	$$	•
74 Windy Cove	64	93	30	WESC	F	•	•		FBL	$$	•

Finding the campground: From U.S. Highway 101, 0.6 mile north of the Coos Bay Bridge, turn west toward Horsfall Dune and Beach. Go 1 mile, and turn right on Horsfall Beach Road to reach the campground in another 1.7 miles.

About the campground: This family campground near Bluebill Lake and seasonal ponds and lagoons has paved parking and at least partial shade afforded by the shore pines and myrtles. Pussy willows and Indian plum grow in the wetlands. Bluebill Lake Trail offers an easy walk to and around the lake. Nearby off-highway-vehicle areas offer more boisterous pursuits.

57 Carter Lake

Location: About 8 miles south of Florence
Season: Mid-May–September
Sites: 23 basic sites; no hookups
Maximum length: 35 feet
Facilities: Tables, grills, flush toilets, drinking water, boat launch (0.4 mile south of campground)
Fee per night: $$
Management: Siuslaw National Forest
Contact: (541) 271–3611; (877) 444–6777 for reservations; www.fs.fed.us/r6/siuslaw/recreation
Finding the campground: From the Siuslaw River Bridge in Florence, drive 7.4 miles south on U.S. Highway 101 and turn west to reach the campground and Taylor Dunes Trailhead.

About the campground: Located next to an undisturbed dune field and mile-long Carter Lake, this campground particularly appeals to naturalists. A tall coastal forest intermingled with rhododendrons enfolds camp, but some highway noise carries across the lake. A 0.5-mile wheelchair-accessible trail travels through the dunes to Taylor Lake, while cedar posts guide hikers along a 1.5-mile route west across the open dunes to the beach. With off-highway vehicles prohibited on the dunes, hikers can discover nature's tracks and wind patterns in the sand. The mirror-black water of Carter Lake welcomes the use of small rowboats and rafts and calls to anglers.

58 Driftwood II

Location: About 8 miles south of Florence
Season: Year-round
Sites: 59 basic sites; no hookups
Maximum length: 40 feet
Facilities: Flush toilets, drinking water, showers, sand access point for OHVs
Fee per night: $$
Management: Siuslaw National Forest
Contact: (541) 271–3611; (877) 444–6777 for reservations; www.fs.fed.us/r6/siuslaw/recreation
Finding the campground: From the Siuslaw River Bridge in Florence, drive 6.8 miles south on U.S. Highway 101 and turn west into Siltcoos Recreation

Area to reach the campground in 1.2 miles.

About the campground: Used almost exclusively by off-highway-vehicle enthusiasts, this campground is more practical than scenic. It consists of a large paved parking area for vehicle camping; only a few areas among the edging shore pines are suitable for tents. Islands of shore pines also divide the blocks of paved sites, lending modest shade and a sense of landscaping. One side of the OHV camp abuts the dunes—the primary draw for camp guests. Hiking, lake and ocean fishing, and beachcombing may also appeal to visitors.

59 Eel Creek

Location: About 10 miles south of Reedsport
Season: Mid-May–September
Sites: 51 basic sites; no hookups
Maximum length: 30 feet
Facilities: Tables, grills, flush toilets, drinking water
Fee per night: $$
Management: Siuslaw National Forest
Contact: (541) 271–3611; (877) 444–6777 for reservations; www.fs.fed.us/r6 /siuslaw/recreation
Finding the campground: It is west off U.S. Highway 101 about 10 miles south of Reedsport.
About the campground: This family campground sits in a reclaimed-dune forest and rich coastal thicket at the back side of a picturesque dune field. Sites have paved parking and basic amenities; tree frogs and hummingbirds provide seasonal entertainment. Adjacent to camp and closed to motorized vehicles, Umpqua Scenic Dunes invite carefree wandering and nature study, with cedar posts to guide you across the dunes and through the deflation plain to the beach. Some dunes stretch 400 feet high. Eel Lake at William M. Tugman State Park, 1 mile to the north, offers fishing and boating (10 miles per hour maximum). To the south, Tenmile Lake offers bass fishing, speed boating, and waterskiing.

60 Horsfall

Location: About 3 miles north of North Bend/Coos Bay
Season: Year-round
Sites: 70 basic sites; no hookups
Maximum length: 50 feet
Facilities: Some tables and fire rings, flush toilets, drinking water, showers, telephone
Fee per night: $$
Management: Siuslaw National Forest
Contact: (541) 271–3611; (877) 444–6777 for reservations; www.fs.fed.us/r6 /siuslaw/recreation
Finding the campground: From U.S. Highway 101, 0.6 mile north of the Coos Bay Bridge, turn west toward Horsfall Dune and Beach. Go 1 mile, and turn right on Horsfall Beach Road to reach the campground in another 0.5 mile.

About the campground: This campground features clusters of single paved sites rimmed by shore pines and coastal scrub and separated by meridians of natural vegetation. The camp provides a pleasant base for off-highway-vehicle enthusiasts, when they take a break from roving the dunes. There is direct dune access from camp.

61 Horsfall Beach

Location: About 5 miles north of North Bend/Coos Bay
Season: Year-round
Sites: 41 basic sites; no hookups
Maximum length: 50 feet
Facilities: Flush toilets, drinking water, telephone
Fee per night: $$
Management: Siuslaw National Forest
Contact: (541) 271–3611; www.fs.fed.us/r6/siuslaw/recreation
Finding the campground: From U.S. Highway 101, 0.6 mile north of the Coos Bay Bridge, turn west toward Horsfall Dune and Beach. Go 1 mile, and turn right on Horsfall Beach Road to reach the campground at road's end in 2.3 miles.
About the campground: Primarily for off-highway-vehicle enthusiasts, this campground consists of a large, open paved area, with numbered sites. A foredune separates the campground from the beach, but paths cross over it, allowing for wave play or surf fishing on the ocean shore. Horse trails extend south.

62 Jessie M. Honeyman Memorial State Park

Location: About 3 miles south of Florence
Season: Year-round
Sites: 166 full and partial hookup sites, 191 basic sites, 10 yurts; water, electric, and sewer hookups
Maximum length: 60 feet
Facilities: Tables, grills, flush toilets, drinking water, showers, dump station, telephone, boat launches, boat rentals, swimming beaches, playground, food concession
Fee per night: $$–$$$
Management: Oregon State Parks and Recreation Department
Contact: (541) 997–3641; (800) 452–5687 for reservations; www.oregonstate parks.org
Finding the campground: It is west off U.S. Highway 101, 2.5 miles south of the Siuslaw River Bridge at the south end of Florence.
About the campground: This bustling campground receives some noise from the off-highway vehicles on the neighboring dunes, but mostly it offers a pleasant stay for active families. Sites are spacious and private. Hookup sites occupy a shore pine plain, while sites without hookups rest in the lovely tall forest of hemlocks, spruces, and towering rhododendrons. Campers have direct access to two freshwater, coastal lakes: Cleawox (closest to camp) and

Woahink (the larger of the two, across US 101). Nonmotorized boating alone is allowed on Cleawox Lake; Woahink Lake serves larger, motorized boats. Both welcome swimming. Dune play and OHV driving likewise engage campers. OHVs have direct dune access from loop L at the southern end of camp. Area dunes can be up to 500 feet high.

63 Lagoon

Location: About 8 miles south of Florence
Season: Mid-May–September
Sites: 38 basic sites; no hookups
Maximum length: 35 feet
Facilities: Tables, grills, flush toilets, drinking water, telephone
Fee per night: $$
Management: Siuslaw National Forest
Contact: (541) 271–3611; www.fs.fed.us/r6/siuslaw/recreation
Finding the campground: From the Siuslaw River Bridge in Florence, drive 6.8 miles south on U.S. Highway 101 and turn west into Siltcoos Recreation Area. The campground is on the right in 0.8 mile.
About the campground: Adjacent to a scenic black lagoon, this family campground occupies a semi-open coastal shore pine forest. Of the Siltcoos Recreation Area camps, this one sits the farthest from the off-highway-vehicle activity. Operation of OHVs in camp is prohibited. The natural offerings that engage guests include hiking the trails along the lagoon and the Siltcoos River or into Siltcoos Lake (the lake trailhead is across US 101 from the recreation area turnoff). Nature lovers may also seek out the section of beach near the river mouth that is off-limits to OHVs.

64 Salmon Harbor Marina RV Park

Location: About 4 miles south of Reedsport, in Winchester Bay
Season: Year-round
Sites: 300 RV sites, 0 tent sites; no hookups
Maximum length: 40 feet
Facilities: Small gazebo, flush toilets, drinking water, showers, dump station, telephone, playground (at adjacent county park at far end of camp area), 2 boat launches, 850 slips, fish-cleaning station, boat wash, designated fishing and crabbing docks
Fee per night: $
Management: Salmon Harbor
Contact: (541) 271–3407, reservations accepted
Finding the campground: In Winchester Bay, 4 miles south of Reedsport, turn west off U.S. Highway 101 onto Salmon Harbor Drive and go 0.2 mile to the marina complex.
About the campground: Located a mile upstream from where the Umpqua River meets the ocean is this 5-acre open, paved camping area, which suits the nautical, the through-traveler, and those seeking a base from which to explore the coast. Gulls, seabirds, diving birds, and Canada geese share the bay loca-

tion. The docks and boat moorings add atmosphere; sidewalks welcome morning and evening strolls along the marina. You may view recreational and working boats, along with a sternwheeler. Area attractions include fishing charters, a commercial cannery, the dunes, Umpqua River Lighthouse, a vessel tour of the *Hero* at Reedsport, and Dean Creek Elk Viewing Site (east of Reedsport on Oregon 38).

65 Salmon Harbor Marina RV Resort

Location: About 4 miles south of Reedsport, in Winchester Bay
Season: Year-round
Sites: 138 hookup sites, 25 tent sites; water, electric, sewer, cable, and phone hookups
Maximum length: 40 feet
Facilities: Flush toilets, drinking water, showers, dump station (at marina complex), laundry, playground, telephone; convenient access to 2 boat launches, 850 slips, fish-cleaning station, and designated fishing and crabbing docks (at marina complex)
Fee per night: $$$
Management: Salmon Harbor
Contact: (541) 271–0287, reservations accepted; www.marinarvresort.com
Finding the campground: In Winchester Bay, 4 miles south of Reedsport, turn west off U.S. Highway 101 onto Salmon Harbor Drive and go 0.25 mile to reach the resort on the right.
About the campground: Upstream from where the Umpqua River meets the ocean is this new, landscaped RV resort, surrounded on three sides by water. Lawn, shrubs, and native shore pines dress the grounds, and a mile-long paved pedestrian/bicycle trail encircles the resort. Campers enjoy a wide range of amenities and have convenient access to the marina and to the attractions of Reedsport and Winchester Bay.

66 Spinreel

Location: About 14 miles south of Reedsport
Season: Year-round
Sites: 36 basic sites; no hookups
Maximum length: 40 feet
Facilities: Tables, grills, flush toilets, drinking water
Fee per night: $$
Management: Siuslaw National Forest
Contact: (541) 271–3611; www.fs.fed.us/r6/siuslaw/recreation
Finding the campground: From the junction of U.S. Highway 101 and Oregon 38 in Reedsport, go 13.4 miles south on US 101 and turn west onto Wildwood Drive. The campground is on the left in 0.3 mile.
About the campground: This campground provides off-highway-vehicle access to the dunes and is located near a dune-vehicle rental for the curious who might wish to try the sport. Wide, paved sites suitable for OHVs serve campers; a backdrop of natural coastal shrubs and trees adds to the camp's ambience.

67 Tahkenitch

Location: About 12 miles south of Florence
Season: Mid-May–September
Sites: 31 basic sites; no hookups
Maximum length: 30 feet
Facilities: Tables, grills, flush toilets, drinking water (sometimes smells of sulfur and tastes bad), boat launch (on Tahkenitch Lake at Tahkenitch Landing 0.2 mile north). Recommend you bring drinking water.
Fee per night: $$
Management: Siuslaw National Forest
Contact: (541) 271–3611; (877) 444–6777 for reservations; www.fs.fed.us/r6 /siuslaw/recreation
Finding the campground: From the Siuslaw River Bridge in Florence, drive 12 miles south on U.S. Highway 101 and turn west to enter the campground.
About the campground: This coastal campground sits at the base of a forested dune. Its proximity to US 101 does mean some vehicle noise, but the traffic generally quiets by nightfall. From camp, you may explore a natural dune area where off-highway vehicles are prohibited; it is ideal for enjoying a carefree romp, nature study, and photography. From camp, the Tahkenitch Dunes Trail travels 2.75 miles through coastal woods, over dunes, and along the beach, finding Threemile Lake along the way. Anglers may try their luck at Threemile Lake, Tahkenitch Lake, or in the ocean surf.

68 Tahkenitch Landing

Location: About 12 miles south of Florence
Season: Year-round
Sites: 27 basic sites; no hookups
Maximum length: 30 feet
Facilities: Tables, grills, vault toilets, barrier-free dock, boat launch; no drinking water
Fee per night: $$
Management: Siuslaw National Forest
Contact: (541) 271–3611; (877) 444–6777 for reservations; www.fs.fed.us/r6 /siuslaw/recreation
Finding the campground: From the Siuslaw River Bridge in Florence, drive 11.8 miles south on U.S. Highway 101 and turn east to enter the campground.
About the campground: This attractive campground offers prized sites overlooking Tahkenitch Lake, a large, coastal lake with mostly undeveloped shores. A forest frames the lake basin. At the day use, just below camp, you will find a rustic dock and boat ramp. The western arm of the lake is capped with lily pads. Osprey soar over the lake and dive for fish, while geese plod along shore in search of handouts. On the west side of US 101, the Tahkenitch Dunes Trail travels 2.75 miles through woods, over dunes, and along the beach, encountering Threemile Lake along the way. (See Tahkenitch campground above.)

69 Tyee

Location: About 6 miles south of Florence
Season: Late April–October
Sites: 16 basic sites; no hookups
Maximum length: 22 feet
Facilities: Tables, grills, vault toilets, drinking water, boat launch
Fee per night: $$
Management: Siuslaw National Forest
Contact: (541) 271-3611; (877) 444-6777 for reservations; www.fs.fed.us/r6 /siuslaw/recreation
Finding the campground: From the Siuslaw River Bridge in Florence, drive 5.5 miles south on U.S. Highway 101 and turn east on Pacific Avenue. The campground is reached soon after taking the turn.
About the campground: Along the Siltcoos River sits this mostly wooded campground, although some sites nudge an open lawn that overlooks the glassy river. An attractive rockwork border can be found toward the river. Boating and fishing are the chief activities, with large, adjacent Siltcoos Lake hosting much of the fun. Vying for visitors' time are dune recreation and the area hiking trails at Siltcoos Recreation Area (to the south). The trails lead to Siltcoos Lake and along a lagoon and beach.

70 Umpqua Lighthouse State Park

Location: About 6 miles south of Reedsport
Season: Year-round
Sites: 20 hookup sites, 24 basic sites, 8 yurts, 2 cabins; water, electric, and sewer hookups
Maximum length: 45 feet
Facilities: Tables, grills, flush toilets, drinking water, showers, telephone
Fee per night: $$–$$$
Management: Oregon State Parks and Recreation Department
Contact: (541) 271-4118; (800) 452-5687 for reservations; www.oregonstate parks.org
Finding the campground: From the junction of U.S. Highway 101 and Oregon 38 in Reedsport, go south on US 101 for 5 miles and turn west on Umpqua Lighthouse Road. Go 0.2 mile and turn right to enter the campground in another 0.3 mile.
About the campground: This campground sits adjacent to the Umpqua River Lighthouse, built in 1894. Sites occupy a wooded slope above Lake Marie, a scenic coastal lake rimmed by forest and possessing dark, still reflections. Shrub divides, paved parking, and groomed personal spaces make the sites appealing. Trails and fishing at Lake Marie keep campers engaged at the park. Oregon Dunes, Reedsport, and Deans Creek Elk Viewing Site make worthwhile outings.

71 Waxmyrtle

Location: About 8 miles south of Florence
Season: May–September
Sites: 55 basic sites; no hookups
Maximum length: 35 feet
Facilities: Tables, grills, flush toilets, drinking water
Fee per night: $$
Management: Siuslaw National Forest
Contact: (541) 271–3611; www.fs.fed.us/r6/siuslaw/recreation
Finding the campground: From the Siuslaw River Bridge in Florence, drive 6.8 miles south on U.S. Highway 101 and turn west into Siltcoos Recreation Area. The campground is on the left in 0.9 mile, opposite a black lagoon.
About the campground: Along the Siltcoos River, this family campground features wooded sites in a setting of tall shore pines; privacy borders are shaped by the black huckleberries and wax myrtles. Although the driving of off-highway vehicles is prohibited in camp, OHV enthusiasts do have an access to their "field of dreams," via a path that skirts camp. Hiking trails along the river and lagoon, a section of beach near the river mouth that is closed to OHVs, and a trail to Siltcoos Lake appeal to the foot-powered crowd.

72 Wild Mare Horse Camp

Location: About 4 miles north of North Bend/Coos Bay
Season: Year-round
Sites: 12 basic sites; no hookups
Maximum length: 50 feet
Facilities: Tables, grills, vault toilets, drinking water, rustic horse corrals
Fee per night: $$
Management: Siuslaw National Forest
Contact: (541) 271–3611; (877) 444–6777 for reservations; www.fs.fed.us/r6/siuslaw/recreation
Finding the campground: From U.S. Highway 101, 0.6 mile north of the Coos Bay Bridge, turn west toward Horsfall Dune and Beach. Go 1 mile, turn right on Horsfall Beach Road, and proceed 1.8 miles to the campground.
About the campground: Closed to off-highway vehicles, this campground exclusively serves equestrians. It accesses a network of fine horse trails through the dunes and scrub habitat and has well-spaced, substantial sites for comfort and ease of parking. Shore pines and coastal scrub surround and divide the sites. The North Bend/Coos Bay area suggests outings for services, coastal recreation, and perhaps an evening at the casino.

73 William M. Tugman State Park

Location: About 9 miles south of Reedsport
Season: Year-round
Sites: 100 hookup sites, 13 yurts; water and electric hookups
Maximum length: 50 feet

Facilities: Tables, grills, flush toilets, drinking water, showers, dump station, fishing docks for the disabled, boat launch
Fee per night: $$
Management: Oregon State Parks and Recreation Department
Contact: (541) 759-3604; (800) 452-5687 for reservations; www.oregonstate parks.org
Finding the campground: It is east off U.S. Highway 101, about 9 miles south of Reedsport.
About the campground: This landscaped campground and adjoining day use provide convenient boating and fishing access to Eel Lake, a scenic, big coastal lake. Visitors can also enjoy nearby Tenmile Lake, which allows faster boat speeds and is noted for its bass fishing. Other destinations include Umpqua Scenic Dunes, a natural dune area open for quiet exploration, and the coastal and inland attractions of the Reedsport area.

74 Windy Cove

Location: About 4 miles south of Reedsport, in Winchester Bay
Season: Year-round
Sites: 64 hookup sites, 29 tent sites; water, electric, sewer, and cable hookups
Maximum length: 30 feet
Facilities: Tables, flush toilets, drinking water, showers, telephone, boat docks and launch (across road from park at Salmon Harbor Marina)
Fee per night: $$
Management: Douglas County
Contact: (541) 957-7001, reservations accepted; www.co.douglas.or.us/parks
Finding the campground: In Winchester Bay, 4 miles south of Reedsport, turn west off U.S. Highway 101 onto Salmon Harbor Drive and go 0.2 mile to enter this park on the left. It sits opposite Salmon Harbor Marina.
About the campground: At the foot of a forested hill, this 10-acre park encompasses a pair of landscaped camp areas; tent and RV sites are kept separate. From camp, guests can easily access Salmon Harbor's fishing, boating, and sightseeing; explore Oregon Dunes National Recreation Area via foot or dune vehicle; visit Umpqua River Lighthouse; tour the *Hero* at Reedsport; or put a spotting scope on a bull elk at Dean Creek Elk Viewing Site (east of Reedsport along Oregon 38).

North Bend–Coos Bay Area

75 Bastendorff Beach County Park

Location: About 10 miles west of North Bend/Coos Bay, outside Charleston
Season: Year-round
Sites: 56 hookup sites, 35 tent sites; water and electric hookups
Maximum length: 50 feet
Facilities: Tables, grills, flush toilets, drinking water, showers, dump station, telephone, playground, horseshoe pits, basketball court, fish-cleaning sink
Fee per night: $$
Management: Coos County
Contact: (541) 888–5353, reservations accepted; www.co.coos.or.us/ccpark
Finding the campground: From Charleston, 8 miles west of North Bend/Coos Bay, drive 1.6 miles west on Cape Arago Highway and turn right at the sign for the county park. Proceed about 0.2 mile more to reach the campground.
About the campground: This quiet county park encompasses 91 acres, with a long sandy beach and a rich coastal woods. Natural thickets shape privacy borders between campsites. Despite the paved parking, some campsites are more level than others. The Cape Arago Coast is famous for its cliffs, coves, and offshore rocks topped by seals and barking sea lions. South Slough National Estuarine Reserve, with its visitor center and hiking and canoe trails, offers an alternative outing.

76 Charleston Marina RV Park

Location: About 8 miles west of North Bend/Coos Bay, in Charleston
Season: Year-round
Sites: 96 hookup sites, 8 tent sites, 2 yurts; water, electric, sewer, and cable hookups
Maximum length: 35 feet
Facilities: Tables, flush toilets, drinking water, showers, dump station, laundry, telephone, playground, boat launch, crab cooking area

North Bend–Coos Bay Area

	Hookup sites	Total sites	Maximum RV length	Hookups	Toilets	Showers	Drinking water	Dump station	Recreation	Fee	Can reserve
75 Bastendorff Beach County Park	56	91	50	WE	F	•	•	•	HSF	$$	•
76 Charleston Marina RV Park	96	106	35	WESC	F	•	•	•	FBL	$$–$$$	
77 Nesika County Park		20	small		NF				F	$$	
78 Rooke–Higgins County Park		26	small		NF				FBL	$$	
79 Sunset Bay State Park	65	139	45	WES	F	•	•		HSF	$$–$$$	•

Fee per night: $$–$$$
Management: Port of Coos Bay
Contact: (541) 888-2548; www.charlestonmarina.com/rvpark
Finding the campground: From Cape Arago Highway in Charleston, take Boat Basin Drive north for 0.2 mile and turn right on Kingfisher Drive to reach the marina RV park.
About the campground: This port campground consists of numbered, paved sites paired with gravel meridians and tables and a separate, grassy tent area. Raucous gulls contribute to the seaside ambience. Campers enjoy direct access to the bay and marina, where they can go boating, book a sportfishing charter, or try crabbing. Restaurants lie within walking distance, and the Cape Arago Coast lays out a scenic drive.

77 Nesika County Park

Location: About 18 miles northeast of North Bend/Coos Bay
Season: April–September.
Sites: 20 basic sites; no hookups
Maximum length: Best suited for smaller units
Facilities: Tables, fire rings, vault toilets; no drinking water
Fee per night: $$
Management: Coos County
Contact: (541) 396-3121, ext. 355
Finding the campground: From the Coos River Junction at the south end of Coos Bay, turn east off U.S. Highway 101 onto Sixth Avenue, following the signs for Allegany. You will zigzag through the outskirts of town and soon come out on Coos River Road. Remain on it all the way to Allegany (13.5 miles from US 101). From there, follow the signs for Golden and Silver Falls State Park, continuing 4.2 miles east on East Fork Millicoma Road. You'll find the campground on the right 0.2 mile past the county park's day use. The route is winding and narrow.
About the campground: This attractive, rustic, linear campground occupies a low terrace along the East Fork Millicoma River and offers relatively spacious, private sites nestled in a forest of Douglas firs and myrtles. Thimbleberry and salmonberry abound in the understory. Most sites have gravel parking; a few are grassy. A stairway descends to the shallow Millicoma River, which courses over bedrock and is punctuated by low cascades. A 0.2-mile foot trail links the camp and day-use areas. Golden and Silver Falls State Park is reached 6 miles east of here off Glenn Creek Road. Its short trails offer perspectives on a pair of 200-foot waterfalls.

78 Rooke–Higgins County Park

Location: About 9 miles east of Coos Bay
Season: Year-round
Sites: 26 basic sites; no hookups
Maximum length: Best suited for smaller units

Facilities: Tables, fire rings, vault toilets, boat launch (0.2 mile east); no drinking water
Fee per night: $$
Management: Coos County
Contact: (541) 396–3121, ext. 355
Finding the campground: From the Coos River Junction at the south end of Coos Bay, turn east off U.S. Highway 101 onto Sixth Avenue, following the signs for Allegany. You will zigzag through the outskirts of town and soon come out on Coos River Road. Remain on it all the way to the park campground, 9.3 miles from US 101.
About the campground: Across the road from the tidewater-influenced Millicoma River, this campground spreads across a wooded flat at the foot of a forested slope. It offers a quiet, rustic camping experience. Fishing and drift boating or canoeing the sleepy Millicoma are common diversions. If you continue driving upstream past Allegany, you can visit Golden and Silver Falls State Park, with its pair of cool, shady waterfall glens.

79 Sunset Bay State Park

Location: About 12 miles southwest of North Bend/Coos Bay
Season: Year-round
Sites: 65 full and partial hookup sites, 66 basic sites, 8 yurts; water, electric, and sewer hookups
Maximum length: 45 feet
Facilities: Tables, grills, flush toilets, drinking water, showers, telephone, playground
Fee per night: $$–$$$
Management: Oregon State Parks and Recreation Department
Contact: (541) 888–3778; (800) 452–5687 for reservations; www.oregonstate parks.org
Finding the campground: From U.S. Highway 101 in North Bend/Coos Bay, go 12 miles southwest on Cape Arago Highway, following the signs to Charleston and the state park. The campground is on the left.
About the campground: This campground sits across the road from Sunset Bay, a scenic, quiet ocean cove that reflects the setting sun. The landscaped sites are closely spaced. Surf fishing and swimming are popular, and a segment of the Oregon Coast Trail follows the shoreline through the park, visiting eroded cliffs, the sculptured gardens at Shore Acres, and an overlook of an offshore reef where sea lions—and, in recent years, elephant seals—haul out. Shore Acres State Park and Simpson Reef Viewpoint may also be accessed by Cape Arago Highway. Other possibilities for outings are South Slough National Estuarine Reserve and the Mill Casino.

Bandon–Port Orford Area

80 Boice–Cope County Park

Location: About 17 miles south of Bandon
Season: Year-round
Sites: 23 RV sites, 11 tent sites; no hookups
Maximum length: 40 feet
Facilities: Tables, grills, flush toilets, drinking water, showers, dump station, telephone, boat launch
Fee per night: $$
Management: Curry County
Contact: (541) 247–3306
Finding the campground: From downtown Bandon, go 14.2 miles south on U.S. Highway 101 and turn west on Floras Lake Loop Road. Proceed 1.1 miles and turn right on Curry County 136, following the signs for a boat ramp. In another 1.3 miles, bear left, go 0.1 mile, and turn right on Boice-Cope Road. The campground is 0.3 mile ahead on the left; the boat ramp is just beyond the camp at road's end.
About the campground: Rimmed by Sitka spruces and shore pines, this crisp, clean campground occupies a groomed lawn above Floras Lake. The dunes and seashore are but a short walk beyond the picturesque lake, which attracts sailboarders, anglers, and migrating birds. A footbridge at the outlet leads to the dunes and the long, wild beach. Hikers must heed the protective closures for the snowy plover. Information about when and which areas are closed is posted at the bridge.

Bandon–Port Orford Area

	Hookup sites	Total sites	Maximum RV length	Hookups	Toilets	Showers	Drinking water	Dump station	Recreation	Fee	Can reserve
80 Boice–Cope County Park		34	40		F	•	•	•	HFBL	$$	
81 Bullards Beach State Park	185	206	55	WES	F	•	•	•	HSFBLR	$$–$$$	•
82 Butler Bar		7	small		NF		•		F		
83 Cape Blanco State Park	53	63	65	WE	F	•	•	•	HSFR	$$	•
84 Edson Creek Recreation Site		25	40		NF				F	$	
85 Humbug Mountain State Park	33	99	55	WE	F	•	•	•	HSFC	$$	
86 Sixes River Recreation Site		19	small		NF				F	$	

81 Bullards Beach State Park

Location: 2 miles north of Bandon
Season: Year-round
Sites: 185 full and partial hookup sites, 8 horse sites, 13 yurts; water, electric, and sewer hookups
Maximum length: 55 feet
Facilities: Tables, grills, flush toilets, drinking water, showers, dump station, telephone, playground, boat ramp, corrals at horse camp
Fee per night: $$–$$$
Management: Oregon State Parks and Recreation Department
Contact: (541) 347-2209; (800) 452-5687 for reservations; www.oregonstate parks.org
Finding the campground: It is west off U.S. Highway 101, 2 miles north of Bandon.
About the campground: At the Coquille River mouth, in a protected area of shore pines and coastal thicket behind a beach foredune, sits this large coastal campground with paved sites. Campers have access to hiking and horse trails, a long stretch of wild beach, jetty fishing, and the photogenic Coquille River

Coquille River Lighthouse.

Lighthouse, built in 1896. The adjoining Bandon Marsh Wildlife Refuge brings a bounty of birds to your doorstep. The shops and waterfront of Old Town Bandon invite investigation.

82 Butler Bar

Location: About 22 miles east of Port Orford
Season: Year-round
Sites: 7 basic sites; no hookups
Maximum length: Best suited for smaller units
Facilities: Tables and fire rings, vault toilet, drinking water in summer
Fee per night: None
Management: Siskiyou National Forest
Contact: (541) 439–6200; www.fs.fed.us/r6/rogue-siskiyou
Finding the campground: From U.S. Highway 101, about 3 miles north of Port Orford, turn east on Elk River Road, which later becomes Forest Road 5325. Follow the river upstream for 19 miles, turn left onto FR 5201, and proceed 0.1 mile to the campground.
About the campground: This scenic, rustic campground sits on a forested bench above the Elk Wild and Scenic River. Grassy Knob Wilderness is its neighbor across the river. The Elk River is an enchantress, flowing blue-green. Because gorge walls often contain the river, the campground's easy river access is all the more prized.

83 Cape Blanco State Park

Location: About 9 miles north of Port Orford
Season: Year-round
Sites: 53 hookup sites, 6 horse sites, 4 cabins; water and electric hookups
Maximum length: 65 feet
Facilities: Tables, grills, flush toilets, drinking water, showers, dump station, telephone, corrals at horse camp
Fee per night: $$
Management: Oregon State Parks and Recreation Department
Contact: (541) 332–6774; (800) 452–5687 for reservations; www.oregonstate parks.org
Finding the campground: From Port Orford, go 4 miles north on U.S. Highway 101, turn west on Cape Blanco Road, and follow it 5 miles to the park.
About the campground: Inland from the bluff, in a protective stand of trees, you will find this comfortable family campground. The horse camp occupies a coastal grassland below. At this exciting, wild strip of Oregon Coast, you can photograph the 1870 Cape Blanco Lighthouse, which braves wind and storm from atop the bluff, or tour the 1898 Hughes House, which sits above the floodplain of the Sixes River. Beachcombers scour the black sands and gravels for prized, naturally polished agates, many of them golden in hue. Anglers fish for salmon on the Sixes River, and the Elk River is just a short drive away. The Oregon Coast Trail and the wild beach invite hiking. Equestrians enjoy 7 miles of horse trail and 150 acres of open riding range.

84 Edson Creek Recreation Site

Location: About 9 miles northeast of Port Orford
Season: Year-round, but sometimes closes in December and January; call in winter
Sites: 25 basic sites; no hookups
Maximum length: 40 feet
Facilities: Tables, grills, vault toilets; no drinking water
Fee per night: $
Management: Coos Bay District Bureau of Land Management
Contact: (541) 756–0100; www.or.blm.gov/coosbay
Finding the campground: From U.S. Highway 101, 5 miles north of Port Orford, turn east on Sixes River Road and go 4.1 miles to reach campground on the left.
About the campground: This campground claims a grassy bench with myrtles and alders along Edson Creek, just above its confluence with the Sixes River. Campers can choose between sunny or shady locations. RVers should avoid the area during rainy weather, because the parking areas are grassy, not paved. River fishing and coastal attractions lie within convenient reach.

85 Humbug Mountain State Park

Location: 6 miles south of Port Orford
Season: Year-round
Sites: 33 hookup sites, 66 basic sites; water and electric hookups
Maximum length: 55 feet
Facilities: Tables, grills, flush toilets, drinking water, showers, dump station, telephone
Fee per night: $$
Management: Oregon State Parks and Recreation Department
Contact: (541) 332–6774; www.oregonstateparks.org
Finding the campground: It is east off U.S. Highway 101 (near milepost 307), 6 miles south of Port Orford.
About the campground: This campground occupies a scenic lawn and shore pine flat in the shadow of Humbug Mountain. Brush Creek serenades campers. Underpasses allow campers to safely access both the beach and the 3-mile trail to the top of the mountain. At the foot of the camp's eastern ridge, an abandoned section of Old Highway 101 welcomes exercise walks and jogs. You can also search for agates on shore, fish the nearby Elk and Sixes Rivers, or visit he harbor at Port Orford.

86 Sixes River Recreation Site

Location: About 16 miles northeast of Port Orford
Season: Year-round
Sites: 19 basic sites; no hookups
Maximum length: Small units only
Facilities: Tables, grills, vault toilets; no drinking water

Fee per night: $

Management: Coos Bay District Bureau of Land Management

Contact: (541) 756–0100; www.or.blm.gov/coosbay

Finding the campground: From U.S. Highway 101, 5 miles north of Port Orford, turn east on Sixes River Road and go 10.7 miles to reach this campground. The road narrows, becoming dirt for final 0.5 mile. Be careful on the descent into camp.

About the campground: This restful, terraced campground occupies a slope above the beautiful Sixes River. Myrtles, alders, and maples frame and shade the sites, with a few fir lending punctuation. Recreational gold panning (study posted restrictions) and fishing are the river pursuits.

Coquille–Myrtle Point Area

87 Bear Creek Recreation Site

Location: About 30 miles southeast of Myrtle Point
Season: Year-round; currently, a 24-hour stay limit
Sites: 8 basic sites; no hookups
Maximum length: 25 feet
Facilities: Tables, grills, vault toilets; no drinking water
Fee per night: None
Management: Coos Bay District Bureau of Land Management
Contact: (541) 756–0100; www.or.blm.gov/coosbay/recreation
Finding the campground: From U.S. Highway 101 south of Coos Bay, head east on Oregon 42 toward Coquille. The campground is 0.3 mile north off OR 42, 48 miles east of US 101, and 23 miles west of Winston.
About the campground: This attractive campground in the myrtle trees offers a pleasant overnight stop on the banks of Bear Creek. The water level in the creek fluctuates with the season, and by summer it is quite small. Boulders and outcrops accent the creek, while a large moon bridge spans the creek to access a short trail to a swimming hole. Some road noise creeps in from OR 42.

88 Burnt Mountain Recreation Site

Location: About 39 miles northeast of Myrtle Point
Season: Year-round; winter access is dependent on snow
Sites: 6 basic sites; no hookups
Maximum length: Small units
Facilities: Tables, grills, pit toilets; no drinking water
Fee per night: None
Management: Coos Bay District Bureau of Land Management
Contact: (541) 756–0100; www.or.blm.gov/coosbay
Finding the campground: From Oregon 42, at the west end of Myrtle Point,

Coquille–Myrtle Point Area

	Hookup sites	Total sites	Maximum RV length	Hookups	Toilets	Showers	Drinking water	Dump station	Recreation	Fee	Can reserve
87 Bear Creek Recreation Site		8	25		NF				SF		
88 Burnt Mountain Recreation Site		6	small		NF						
89 Frona County Park		17	small		NF					$$	
90 Laverne County Park	46	76	40	WE	F,NF	•	•	•	SF	$–$$	•
91 Park Creek Recreation Site		16	small		NF						
92 Sturdivant City Park		9	25		F,NF		•		FBL	$$	

turn north at the sign for Sitkum, Dora, and Gravelford and follow Myrtle Point–Sitkum Road for 25.7 miles to Sitkum. There, turn north (left) on Brummit Creek Road, which starts as dirt but becomes paved, and follow it 6.4 miles to a T-junction. Turn right on paved Burnt Mountain Access Road, and in 0.7 mile again turn right to remain on this access road. You are now following the Growing Forest Driving Tour. Go 5.5 miles and proceed straight on BLM 27-11-12.0 (still Burnt Mountain Access Road) to reach the campground in another 0.6 mile.

About the campground: This small campground lies just 8.5 miles west of the key attraction on the BLM's Growing Forest Driving Tour. It is stop 5, the trailhead for the Doerner Fir Trail. This trail weaves 0.6 mile through an enchanting old-growth grove to the champion coastal Douglas fir. The Doerner Fir shoots 329 feet skyward, boasts a diameter of 11.5 feet, and is estimated to be between 700 and 900 years old. The trees in the campground are much younger but still tall second-growth firs. Salal, rhododendron, and Oregon grape lend to the campground understory.

89 Frona County Park

Location: About 17 miles northeast of Myrtle Point
Season: Year-round
Sites: 17 basic sites; no hookups
Maximum length: Best suited for smaller units
Facilities: Tables, fire rings, pit toilet; no drinking water
Fee per night: $$
Management: Coos County
Contact: (541) 396–3121, ext. 355
Finding the campground: From Myrtle Point, turn north off Oregon 42 onto Eighth Street, which becomes Myrtle Point–Sitkum Road, heading toward Dora. Go 17.1 miles to reach the campground on the left.
About the campground: This rustic campground is graced by tall Douglas fir and attractive myrtle trees and has a grass and wildflower floor. It offers campers an off-the-beaten track retreat for relaxing and forgetting the workaday world.

90 Laverne County Park

Location: About 14 miles northeast of Coquille
Season: Year-round
Sites: 46 hookup sites, 30 basic sites; water and electric hookups
Maximum length: 40 feet
Facilities: Tables, grills, flush and vault toilets, drinking water, showers, dump station, telephone, playground
Fee per night: $–$$
Management: Coos County
Contact: (541) 396–2344, reservations accepted; www.co.coos.or.us/ccpark
Finding the campground: From Oregon 42 (Main Street) in Coquille, turn north on North Central Boulevard and go 0.7 mile. Turn right and continue 13 miles on Coquille-Fairview Road to reach the camp on the right.

About the campground: This family campground occupies a 350-acre wooded flat above the North Fork Coquille River. Tall Douglas firs, myrtles, and mossy stumps contribute to the coolness and relaxation of camp; the remoteness helps ensure quiet. Fishing and swimming are popular pursuits.

91 Park Creek Recreation Site

Location: About 23 miles northeast of Coquille
Season: Year-round
Sites: 16 basic sites; no hookups
Maximum length: Small units only
Facilities: Tables, grills/barbecues, vault toilets; no drinking water
Fee per night: None
Management: Coos Bay District Bureau of Land Management
Contact: (541) 756-0100; www.or.blm.gov/coosbay
Finding the campground: From Coquille, take Coquille-Fairview Road northeast 9 miles to Fairview. Turn south onto Fairview–Middle Creek Road, heading toward Dora. Go 3.8 miles and turn left on Middle Creek Road, now proceeding toward Burnt Mountain Access Road and Park Creek. Continue 7.8 miles and bear right at the fork to remain on Middle Creek Road. Go 2.4 miles more, turn right, and follow the paved single-lane entry road 0.2 mile into camp.
About the campground: The reward for the long, out-of-the-way drive is an attractive, remote forest campground. Cloaked in scenic, big, mossy maples and myrtles, the campground sits at the confluence of Park and Middle Creeks. If you do not require a lot of diversions to be happy and content, this is the camp for you. Bring a soft pillow and a good book.

92 Sturdivant City Park

Location: In Coquille
Season: Year-round
Sites: 9 basic sites; no hookups
Maximum length: 25 feet
Facilities: Tables, fire rings, flush and chemical toilets, drinking water, telephone, playground, ballfield, horseshoe pits, boat launch and dock
Fee per night: $$
Management: City of Coquille
Contact: (541) 396-5131
Finding the campground: In Coquille, turn south off Oregon 42 onto OR 42S, the Coquille-Bandon Highway. Cross the railroad tracks to enter the park on the right in 0.1 mile.
About the campground: Campsites dot a grassy bench at one edge of this recreational park on the Coquille River. Besides tables and fire rings, a few young planted trees contribute to sites. The river flows broad and slow. In Coquille, you might want to check out the old-fashioned melodrama playing at the Sawdust Theater on summer Saturday nights.

Powers Area

93 Daphne Grove

Location: 14 miles south of Powers
Season: Year-round
Sites: 14 basic sites; no hookups
Maximum length: 35 feet
Facilities: Tables, fire rings, vault toilets, drinking water (June–October), covered day-use shelter
Fee per night: $ when water provided, otherwise free
Management: Siskiyou National Forest
Contact: (541) 439–6200; www.fs.fed.us/r6/rogue-siskiyou
Finding the campground: From Powers, go south toward Agness on Powers Road South/Forest Road 33. The campground is on the right in 14 miles.
About the campground: This campground occupies a semi-open flat above the South Fork Coquille River. Live oak, maple, myrtle, tan oak, and conifer trees shape the setting. The campground has paved roads and parking. Although this stretch of the South Fork is closed to angling, the river still supplies a soothing hush and a place to cool your ankles.

94 Eden Valley

Location: About 30 miles southeast of Powers
Season: Year-round
Sites: 11 basic sites; no hookups
Maximum length: 30 feet
Facilities: Tables, grills, vault toilets; no drinking water
Fee per night: None
Management: Siskiyou National Forest
Contact: (541) 439–6200; www.fs.fed.us/r6/rogue-siskiyou

Powers Area

	Hookup sites	Total sites	Maximum RV length	Hookups	Toilets	Showers	Drinking water	Dump station	Recreation	Fee	Can reserve
93 Daphne Grove		14	35		NF		•		S	$	
94 Eden Valley		11	30		NF				C		
95 Island		5	T		NF					$	
96 Myrtle Grove		5	T		NF				S		
97 Powers County Park	40	71	40	WE	F	•	•	•	F	$–$$	
98 Rock Creek		7	small		NF		•		HF	$	
99 Squaw Lake		6	small		NF		•		F		

Finding the campground: From Powers, go south toward Agness on Powers Road South/Forest Road 33. After going 16.1 miles, turn left (east) onto FR 3348 and continue for another 13.6 miles to the campground. It is on the right off FR 280.

About the campground: East of Foggy Creek, this recreation area spans both sides of FR 3348. The camp has gravel roads and parking, The scenic, full Douglas fir forest contributes to a relaxing stay. If you are looking for some exercise, this campground sits along the Glendale to Powers Bicycle Recreation Area route.

95 Island

Location: About 16 miles south of Powers
Season: Year-round
Sites: 5 basic sites; no hookups
Maximum length: Suitable for tents only
Facilities: Tables, fire rings or grills, vault toilets; no drinking water
Fee per night: $
Management: Siskiyou National Forest
Contact: (541) 439–6200; www.fs.fed.us/r6/rogue-siskiyou
Finding the campground: From Powers, go south toward Agness on Powers Road South/Forest Road 33. After going 15.3 miles, turn right onto FR 3300.490 to enter the campground.

About the campground: This small developed campground extends a pleasant stay along the South Fork Coquille River. The camp has gravel roads and parking and an attractive woods setting. Rhododendrons complement the bountiful understory. Sites are partially shaded most of the day. Check regulations before fishing.

96 Myrtle Grove

Location: About 8 miles south of Powers
Season: Year-round
Sites: 5 tent sites; no hookups
Maximum length: Suitable for tents only
Facilities: Tables, fire rings, vault toilets; no drinking water
Fee per night: None
Management: Siskiyou National Forest
Contact: (541) 439–6200; www.fs.fed.us/r6/rogue-siskiyou
Finding the campground: From Powers, head south toward Agness on Powers Road South/Forest Road 33. Go 8.4 miles to enter the campground on the right.

About the campground: Myrtles, maples, and a few firs shade this small, attractive campground along the South Fork Coquille River. Big boulders add to the character of the river. With the river closed to fishing, swimming and relaxing are the favored pastimes. Elk Creek Falls (its trailhead is 3 miles north of camp on FR 33) is worth the hike to see.

97 Powers County Park

Location: About 19 miles southeast of Myrtle Point, at the north end of Powers
Season: Year-round
Sites: 40 hookup sites, 30 tent sites, 1 cabin; water and electric hookups
Maximum length: 40 feet
Facilities: Tables, grills, flush toilets, drinking water, showers, dump station, telephone, playground, fish-cleaning station, horseshoe pits, sports courts and fields
Fee per night: $–$$
Management: Coos County
Contact: (541) 439–2791; www.co.coos.or.us/ccpark
Finding the campground: From the Powers Junction on Oregon 42, 2.5 miles east of Myrtle Point, go 16.7 miles south to arrive at this park on northern outskirts of Powers.
About the campground: Restful, spotlessly clean, and landscaped in native vegetation, this campground serves family campers well. Wake up to bird-songs, and study the stars at night. A 30-acre pond at the park is stocked with trout and occasionally with surplus steelhead. There is ample room to roam, or you can just settle back and relax at your site.

98 Rock Creek

Location: About 18 miles south of Powers
Season: Year-round
Sites: 7 basic sites; no hookups
Maximum length: Best for small units
Facilities: Tables, grills, vault toilets, drinking water
Fee per night: $
Management: Siskiyou National Forest
Contact: (541) 439–6200; www.fs.fed.us/r6/rogue-siskiyou
Finding the campground: From Powers, go 16.5 miles south on Powers Road South/Forest Road 33 and turn southwest on FR 3347. Drive 1 mile more to reach the camp.
About the campground: This small campground along Rock Creek engages with its stand of old-growth firs intermingled with myrtles and tan oaks. Rock Creek rushes clear over rounded stones, collecting in a few deeper pools. Upstream from camp is the trailhead for the 1.2-mile trail to Azalea Lake. This 2-acre lake is stocked with trout and decorated in July by azalea blooms. By backtracking north on FR 33 to its junction with FR 3348 and following 3348 east for 1.6 miles, you will find the Coquille River Falls trailhead. The exciting falls is reached via a short, steep trail.

99 Squaw Lake

Location: About 21 miles southeast of Powers
Season: Year-round
Sites: 6 basic sites; no hookups
Maximum length: Small units only
Facilities: Tables, grills, vault toilets, drinking water (June–October)
Fee per night: None
Management: Siskiyou National Forest
Contact: (541) 439–6200; www.fs.fed.us/r6/rogue-siskiyou
Finding the campground: From Powers, go south toward Agness on Powers Road South/Forest Road 33. In 16.1 miles, turn left (east) on FR 3348 and proceed 4 miles to FR 080. Turn right and continue 0.8 mile to enter this campground on the left.
About the campground: The well-spaced campsites occupy the basin of Squaw Lake, which is fringed by a remnant stand of old-growth trees. Alders and willows edge the lakeshore. Campers can choose between full or partial shade. But without developed parking pads, the sites are better suited for tent camping. You can try your luck at reeling in a lake trout for the evening meal.

Gold Beach–Agness Area

100 Huntley Park

Location: About 7 miles east of Gold Beach
Season: Year-round
Sites: 63 basic sites; no hookups
Maximum length: 40 feet
Facilities: Tables, fire rings, vault and flush toilets, drinking water, showers, horseshoe pits
Fee per night: $
Management: Port of Gold Beach
Contact: (541) 247-9377
Finding the campground: From U.S. Highway 101 at Gold Beach, on the south side of Patterson (Rogue River) Bridge, head east on Jerry's Flat Road (County Road 595). Go 6.9 miles to enter the campground on the left.
About the campground: This Rogue River campground and adjoining picnic area enjoy a rich setting of myrtles and firs. Access to the Rogue is via the big gravel river bar. Sites closest to the water are more open. Quail coveys are common in camp, and deer are no strangers. The Rogue River recreation, including salmon fishing and taking a jetboat tour, and sightseeing in the Gold Beach area will keep you entertained.

101 Illahe

Location: 5 miles north of Agness
Season: Year-round
Sites: 14 basic sites; no hookups
Maximum length: 22 feet, but the road is better suited for smaller units
Facilities: Tables, fire rings, vault and flush toilets, drinking water May–October, boat launch (1 mile farther north at Foster Bar)
Fee per night: $
Management: Siskiyou National Forest
Contact: (541) 247-3600; www.fs.fed.us/r6/rogue-siskiyou
Finding the campground: From the town of Agness, go 5 miles north on County 375.

Gold Beach–Agness Area

	Hookup sites	Total sites	Maximum RV length	Hookups	Toilets	Showers	Drinking water	Dump station	Recreation	Fee	Can reserve
100 Huntley Park		63	40		F,NF	•	•		F	$	
101 Illahe		14	22		F,NF		•		HFBL	$	
102 Lobster Creek		6	20		F				FBL	$	
103 Quosatana		43	30		F		•	•	SFBL	$	

About the campground: This Rogue River campground has nicely spaced sites in second-growth forest and a river access trail. You can fish right from camp, or put in with a raft or boat upstream at Foster Bar. From the Foster Bar Trailhead (near the boating access), hikers can strike out on the 40-mile Rogue River National Recreation Trail, which follows the wild and scenic river upstream.

102 Lobster Creek

Location: About 9 miles northeast of Gold Beach
Season: Year-round
Sites: 6 basic sites, with open camping on the gravel river bar; no hookups
Maximum length: 20 feet (for basic sites)
Facilities: Tables, grills, flush toilets, telephone, boat launch; no drinking water. Gravel bar camping: No facilities at all.
Fee per night: $
Management: Siskiyou National Forest
Contact: (541) 247–3600; www.fs.fed.us/r6/rogue-siskiyou
Finding the campground: On the south side of Patterson Bridge, at Gold Beach, turn east off U.S. Highway 101 onto Jerry's Flat Road, which becomes Forest Road 33. Travel 9.3 miles to the campground on the left.
About the campground: Tucked away in a lush myrtle woodland is this small campground primarily for tent campers. A few sites are suitable for RVs, but most RVers choose to set up along the gravel bar for direct access to the lower Rogue River. Fishing and boating are key draws, but there are trails in the area to explore as well.

103 Quosatana

Location: About 14 miles northeast of Gold Beach
Season: Year-round
Sites: 43 basic sites; no hookups
Maximum length: 30 feet
Facilities: Tables, grills, flush toilets, drinking water, dump station, telephone, boat launch
Fee per night: $
Management: Siskiyou National Forest
Contact: (541) 247–3600; www.fs.fed.us/r6/rogue-siskiyou
Finding the campground: On the south side of Patterson Bridge, at Gold Beach, turn east off U.S. Highway 101 onto Jerry's Flat Road, which later becomes Forest Road 33. Go 13.9 miles to the campground.
About the campground: This beautiful, sprawling campground claims a prized flat on the lower Rogue River. Campers can select from sites at the meadow's edge or within the tranquil myrtle grove. Seasonally, the mature myrtles scent the air with their eucalyptus-like aroma. Photographers are attracted by the mossy multiple trunks. River access for fishing, boating, and swimming and an open, mowed field for sports engage guests, as does the camp quiet. Deer and wild turkeys are campground interlopers.

Brookings Area

104 Alfred A. Loeb State Park

Location: Northeast of Brookings
Season: Year-round
Sites: 48 hookup sites, 3 cabins; water and electric hookups
Maximum length: 50 feet
Facilities: Tables, grills, flush toilets, drinking water, showers, telephone, boat ramp
Fee per night: $$
Management: Oregon State Parks and Recreation Department
Contact: (541) 469-2021; www.oregonstateparks.org
Finding the campground: From the junction of U.S. Highway 101 and North Bank Chetco River Road in Brookings, go 8 miles northeast on North Bank Chetco River Road to reach the park on the right.
About the campground: Along the north bank of the pristine Chetco River, this quiet campground occupies a scenic grove of old-growth myrtles inter-mixed with evergreens. The park's Riverside Trail journeys upstream along the steep riverbank to link up with the Forest Service's Redwood Nature Trail, which tours the nation's northernmost redwood grove. A crosswalk links the two trails for a 2.5-mile round-trip hike. The big attraction, though, is fishing the Chetco River, and for sheer relaxation, how can you miss with such an inviting camp setting?

105 Beachfront RV Park

Location: In Brookings
Season: Year-round
Sites: 81 full hookup sites, 9 partial hookup sites, 19 basic sites, 28 tent sites; water, electric, and sewer hookups
Maximum length: 40 feet

Brookings Area

	Hookup sites	Total sites	Maximum RV length	Hookups	Toilets	Showers	Drinking water	Dump station	Recreation	Fee	Can reserve
104 Alfred A. Loeb State Park	48	51	50	WE	F	•	•		HSFBL	$$	
105 Beachfront RV Park	90	137	40	WES	F	•	•	•	FBL	$$–$$$	•
106 Harris Beach State Park	86	155	50	WESCP	F	•	•	•	HSF	$$–$$$	•
107 Little Redwood		12	25		NF		•		SFBL	$$	
108 Ludlum		7	20		NF		•		SF	$$	
109 Winchuck		15	40		NF		•		HSF	$$	

Facilities: Tables, barbecues in tent area, flush toilets, drinking water, showers, laundry, dump station, telephone, restaurant, public boat launch
Fee per night: $$–$$$
Management: Port of Brookings
Contact: (541) 469-5867; (800) 441-0856 for reservations; www.port-brookings-harbor.org/rv_park
Finding the campground: From U.S. Highway 101 in Brookings, turn west on Lower Harbor Road, go 0.1 mile, and bear left at the junction. Proceed 0.8 mile and turn right on Boat Basin Road to enter the park in another 0.1 mile.
About the campground: This RV park offers camping on an open, shadeless gravel flat overlooking the ocean. To the back of the campground is the harbor. The park is clean, orderly, and convenient. Ocean views, the sound of the surf, and the briny breeze together set the stage for your stay. Only at the tent area will you find a lawn and a few low shore pines. Beachcombing and jetty fishing for perch and fall salmon are among the popular pastimes. Along the harbor, you will find fresh-fish counters, seafood eateries, and fishing charters.

106 Harris Beach State Park

Location: In Brookings
Season: Year-round
Sites: 86 full and partial hookup sites, 63 basic sites, 6 yurts; water, electric, sewer, cable, and phone hookups
Maximum length: 50 feet
Facilities: Tables, grills, flush toilets, drinking water, showers, dump station, telephone, playground
Fee per night: $$–$$$
Management: Oregon State Parks and Recreation Department
Contact: (541) 469-2021; (800) 452-5687 for reservations; www.oregonstate parks.org
Finding the campground: It is west off U.S. Highway 101 at the north end of Brookings.
About the campground: Occupying a prized coastal location, this developed campground sits back from the ocean in dense vegetation. A wildlife refuge on Goat Island, weathered cliffs, sea stacks, and a sandy beach are among its attractions. The Viewpoint Trail from camp leads to an overlook of a natural bridge. Sea- and shorebirds can animate the scene. To the north, Samuel H. Boardman State Park offers hiking, picnicking, quiet beaches, and ocean vistas. Fishing the Chetco River or visiting the shops and eateries of Brookings can help fill out an itinerary.

107 Little Redwood

Location: About 13 miles northeast of Brookings
Season: Mid-May–September
Sites: 12 basic sites; no hookups
Maximum length: 25 feet

Southern Oregon coastline.

Facilities: Tables, grills, vault toilets, drinking water, drift/car-top boat launch (0.1 mile upstream at Redwood Bar)
Fee per night: $$
Management: Siskiyou National Forest
Contact: (541) 412–6000; www.fs.fed.us/r6/rogue-siskiyou
Finding the campground: From U.S. Highway 101 in Brookings, turn east on North Bank Chetco River Road and continue 12.6 miles to this campground. It is on the left 4 miles after you cross the bridge to the south side of the river.
About the campground: Along the Chetco River stretches this attractive, linear forested campground, with nicely spaced sites, paved roads, and parking. Big Douglas firs, tan oaks, vine maples, and huckleberry bushes shape a restful backdrop, and the river is an easy walk away. For additional, but more primitive, camping or for boat access, you will find Redwood Bar 0.1 mile upstream. It is an open, no-frills gravel bar for recreational use; a camp fee is charged.

108 Ludlum

Location: About 14 miles southeast of Brookings
Season: Mid-May–September
Sites: 7 basic sites; no hookups
Maximum length: 20 feet
Facilities: Tables, grills, vault toilets, drinking water, Ludlum House (available for overnight rental, reservation required)
Fee per night: $$ (house rental is more)
Management: Siskiyou National Forest
Contact: (541) 412–6000; www.fs.fed.us/r6/rogue-siskiyou
Finding the campground: From the Chetco River Bridge in Brookings, travel south on U.S. Highway 101 for 4.1 miles and turn east on Winchuck River Road (County Road 896), which becomes Forest Road 1107. Go 8 miles and turn left on FR 1108, following it another 2 miles to Ludlum Recreation Area. Turn right to enter the campground; the rental house is reached by following the campground road.
About the campground: This quiet, remote forest campground adjacent to Wheeler Creek and the Winchuck River is within a half hour's drive of the ocean beaches and northern California redwoods. When not relaxing along the waters, swimming, or fishing, campground guests can explore area trails, such as the Chimney Camp Trail along Wheeler Creek.

109 Winchuck

Location: About 12 miles southeast of Brookings
Season: Mid-May–mid-October
Sites: 15 basic sites; no hookups
Maximum length: 40 feet
Facilities: Tables, grills, vault toilets, drinking water, wheelchair-accessible river access
Fee per night: $$
Management: Siskiyou National Forest
Contact: (541) 412–6000; www.fs.fed.us/r6/rogue-siskiyou
Finding the campground: From the Chetco River Bridge in Brookings, go south on U.S. Highway 101 for 4.1 miles and turn east on Winchuck River Road (County Road 896), which becomes Forest Road 1107. Go 8 miles, bear right, and proceed 0.1 mile to this campground that straddles the road.
About the campground: The halves of this relaxing forest campground are wrapped in a bend of the sparkling green Winchuck River, another prized coastal waterway of incredible clarity. Crosswalks link the camp areas, and short trails explore along the river. Myrtles, tan oaks, alders, and mossy boulders and outcrops add to the river's soothing spell. Fishing and an upstream gravel-bar beach and swimming hole keep campers entertained.

Portland Area

At the confluence of the Willamette and Columbia Rivers, Portland, the "City of Roses," succeeds in blending culture, progress, industry, and nature into a very livable metropolis. It is noted for its bridges and great beauty. The downtown district is vibrant and highly walkable, or visitors can hop on the Max-line or a Metro bus to get about town. City enticements include fine museums, theaters and concert halls, gardens, and the Portland Saturday Market, where artisans sell their creations. The acclaimed Oregon Zoo and Oregon Museum of Science and Industry (OMSI) have long been favorite destinations, and Forest Park is an unrivaled wilderness island within a city of this size. The trails that explore it are first-rate. Elsewhere, wetlands and estuarine lakes attract wildlife and naturalists.

Portland waterfront.

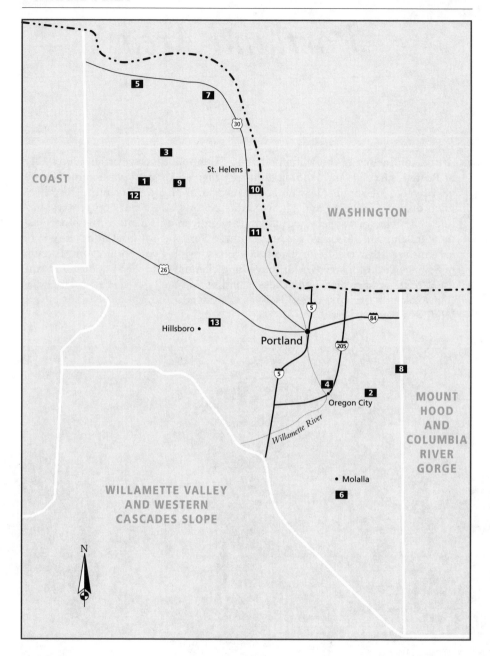

Special events include the Rose Festival, with its Grand Floral Parade, Dragon Boat Races, and the arrival of the Festival Fleet; The Bite, an annual waterfront event at which local eateries serve up their specialties; the Brewer's Festival; and the sailing of the Christmas Ships. Restaurants cater to an array of ethnic tastes, street concerts enliven Pioneer Courthouse Square, and the Trail Blazers bring basketball fans to their feet at the Rose Garden. The waterfront invites sunset gazing and romancing.

Outside the metropolitan center, you will find the pace slows. Images of farms and vineyards, the fir-clad Coast Range foothills, and the shores of the Columbia River provide a counterbalance to the hum of the city. U-Pick farms and roadside stands parade out a colorful assortment of fruits and vegetables. Hot-air balloons may draw eyes skyward, and abandoned railroad grades may suggest a hike or bicycle ride through the countryside.

The Portland area shares in the mild year-round climate of the Willamette Valley. Winds funneling out of the Columbia Gorge can invigorate senses. Summers are warm and inviting; spring and fall feature a mix of showers and sunshine; and winter brings rain interspersed with crisp, clear, cool days. You can also expect snow and ice for a day or two each winter—the perfect time to purchase a latte and curl up with a good book. With more book stores per capita than any other U.S. city, Portland is known as the "reading capital of the nation," and, like Seattle, Portland pioneered in the specialty-coffee fad.

Portland Area

1 Anderson Park

Location: In Vernonia, about 35 miles northwest of Portland
Season: Year-round
Sites: 19 hookup sites, 37 no-hookup sites; water, electric, and sewer hookups
Maximum length: 40 feet
Facilities: Flush toilets, drinking water, showers, dump station, playground
Fee per night: $-$$
Management: City of Vernonia
Contact: (503) 429-5291; (503) 429-2531 for reservations; www.vernonia-or
.gov/vernonia_parks
Finding the campground: From Oregon 47 in Vernonia, turn southeast on
Jefferson Avenue at the sign for Anderson Park and proceed 0.2 mile to the
park.
About the campground: This peaceful park and campground spreads along
the north shore of the upper Nehalem River near the Rock Creek confluence.
A scattering of big conifers lends shade to the camp's open lawn. Campers
have direct access to river fishing, with bass caught at nearby Vernonia Lake.
The northern terminus to the 21-mile Banks–Vernonia Rails-to-Trails Linear
State Park is in Anderson Park. The first 7 miles of the grade are paved for
family bike rides, hikes, or exercise walks. The park is at its busiest during Ver-

Portland Area

		Hookup sites	Total sites	Maximum RV length	Hookups	Toilets	Showers	Drinking water	Dump station	Recreation	Fee	Can reserve
1	Anderson Park	19	56	40	WES	F	•	•	•	HFC	$-$$	•
2	Barton County Park	84	98	40	WE	F	•	•	•	SFBL	$$	•
3	Big Eddy	15	34	40	WE	F		•	•	FBL	$$	•
4	Clackamette Park	38	38	40	WE	F		•	•	FBL	$$	
5	Clatskanie City Park	4	4	40	WES	F	•	•		SFBL	$-$$	
6	Feyrer Memorial County Park	20	20	40	WE	F	•	•	•	FBL	$$	•
7	Hudson/Parcher County Park	25	33	40	WES	F	•	•	•		$$	•
8	Oxbow Regional Park		67	35		F	•	•		HSFBL	$$	
9	Scaponia County Park		10	small		NF	•				$	
10	Scappoose Bay Marine Park		open	40		F		•		HFBL	$$	
11	Scappoose RV Park	7	10	40	WES	F	•	•	•		$$	•
12	Vernonia Airport Park		22	40		NF		•		F	$	
13	Washington County FairPlex RV Park	14	14	30	WE			•	•		$$	

nonia Days, the first weekend in August. Events celebrate the tradition of logging, and there is a small-town parade.

2 Barton County Park

Location: About 10 miles east of Oregon City, near Barton
Season: May–September
Sites: 84 hookup sites, 14 basic sites; water and electric hookups
Maximum length: 40 feet
Facilities: Tables, grills, flush toilets, drinking water, showers, dump station, telephone, playground, horseshoe pits, sports fields, boat ramp (drift boat or raft)
Fee per night: $$
Management: Clackamas County
Contact: (503) 353–4414, reservations accepted; www.co.clackamas.or.us/dtd/parks
Finding the campground: From Oregon 224 at Barton, 9 miles northwest of Estacada and 9.5 miles southeast of Interstate 205 at exit 12 (north of Oregon City), head southwest on Bakers Ferry Road; it is signed for the park. Go 0.2 mile and bear left to enter the park.
About the campground: At this park on the Clackamas River, the campsites are either secluded in trees or lined up at the edge of the woods ringing a central lawn above the river. Big cottonwood, ash, and cedar trees contribute shade. The park is a popular river take-out point for rafters starting their float trip at Milo McIver State Park (located west of Estacada, off OR 224). Fishing and swimming are also popular, and there is a large riverside day use.

3 Big Eddy

Location: About 8 miles north of Vernonia
Season: Year-round
Sites: 15 hookup sites, 19 tent sites; water and electric hookups
Maximum length: 40 feet
Facilities: Tables, grills, flush toilets, drinking water, dump station, telephone, playground, horseshoe pits, primitive boat launch
Fee per night: $$
Management: Columbia County
Contact: (503) 556–9050, reservations accepted; www.co.columbia.or.us/Colparks
Finding the campground: The park is west off Oregon 47, 7.8 miles north of Vernonia.
About the campground: This large, mostly shaded family campground sits where an eddy occurs along a snaking bend of the Nehalem River. Sites have gravel parking spurs. Ample lawn and tall firs and cedars contribute to the camp atmosphere, and alders and bigleaf maples grow riverside. The river is open to drift boats and canoes, and fishing is popular. Vernonia may beckon a visit, with its Banks–Vernonia Rail Trail, the Vernonia Days celebration in August, and the Columbia County Historical Museum.

Portland parks offer many opportunities to study nature.

4 | Clackamette Park

Location: In Oregon City
Season: Year-round
Sites: 38 hookup sites; water and electric hookups
Maximum length: 40 feet
Facilities: Tables, flush toilets, drinking water, dump station, horseshoe pits, swings, skateboard area, boat launch
Fee per night: $$
Management: Oregon City
Contact: (503) 657–8299; www.orcity.org/parks-and-recreation
Finding the campground: From Interstate 205, take exit 9 at Oregon City, head north on McLoughlin Boulevard about 0.1 mile, and turn west into this park on the river.
About the campground: On the Willamette River at the Clackamas River confluence, this park is popular with boaters and anglers. Salmon, shad, and sturgeon provide the action. The camp itself is mostly a gravel flat with a few big cottonwoods along the river. Oregon City is home to the End of the Oregon Trail Interpretive Center.

5 | Clatskanie City Park

Location: In Clatskanie, about 60 miles northwest of Portland
Season: Year-round
Sites: 4 hookup sites, open areas for both dry camping and tent camping; water, electric, and sewer hookups
Maximum length: 40 feet
Facilities: Flush toilets, drinking water, showers (at city pool during summer months), playground, horseshoe pits, volleyball, tennis and basketball courts, ballfields, swimming pool, boat launch, picnic shelters
Fee per night: $–$$
Management: City of Clatskanie
Contact: (503) 728–2038
Finding the campground: From U.S. Highway 30, 1 block east of the traffic signal at Nehalem Street, turn north on Conyers Street, go 1 block, and turn right on Park Street to enter this city park/campground.
About the campground: This city park welcomes overnighters, with its 4 graveled hookup sites, dry camping in the parking area, and tent camping anywhere on the grounds except at the picnic area. The park is an attractive, groomed recreational facility, bordered by the tide-influenced Clatskanie River on two sides. If you are traveling through town on US 30, keep this camp in mind.

6   Feyrer Memorial County Park

Location: About 2 miles southeast of Molalla and 40 miles south of Portland
Season: May–September
Sites: 20 hookup sites; water and electric hookups
Maximum length: 40 feet
Facilities: Tables, grills, flush toilets, drinking water, showers, dump station, telephone, playground, horseshoe pits, sports fields, boat ramp for raft or drift boats
Fee per night: $$
Management: Clackamas County
Contact: (503) 353–4414, reservations accepted; www.co.clackamas.or.us/dtd /parks
Finding the campground: From Oregon 211 at the east side of Molalla, turn south on South Mathias Road and go 0.3 mile. Bear left (east) on Feyrer Park Road and drive 1.5 miles to reach the park's campground on the left. The boat ramp is on the right.
About the campground: This park on the Molalla River offers both camping and day use. The campsites have paved parking and sit back from the day-use area at the edge of a mature, mixed forest, with an effusive understory. Family recreation, fishing, and wading entertain campers. The Molalla River flows shallow over a rocky bed, with cobble bars and a forested far shore.

7   Hudson/Parcher County Park

Location: About 4 miles west of Rainier
Season: Year-round
Sites: 15 full hookup sites, 10 partial hookup sites, 8 basic sites; water, electric, and sewer hookups
Maximum length: 40 feet
Facilities: Tables, fire pits, flush toilets, drinking water, showers, dump station, telephone, playground, ballfield
Fee per night: $$
Management: Columbia County
Contact: (503) 556–9050, reservations recommended; www.co.columbia.or.us /Colparks
Finding the campground: From Rainier, go west on U.S. Highway 30 for 3.1 miles and turn left (south) on Larson Road to reach park in another 0.8 mile.
About the campground: This relaxing family park on a grassy flat enjoys shade from the mature conifer and deciduous trees. Preacher Creek, which threads through the park and supports native trout, is closed to fishing. The campground supplies a convenient stopover for US 30 travelers passing between Portland and the coast. It also lies within easy reach of the Columbia River, where you can indulge in boating, windsurfing, and fishing.

8 Oxbow Regional Park

Location: About 8 miles east of Gresham
Season: Year-round unless river is high; gates locked at sunset
Sites: 67 basic sites; no hookups
Maximum length: 35 feet
Facilities: Tables, flush toilets, drinking water, showers, telephone, playground, horseshoe pits, boat ramp. No pets allowed.
Fee per night: $$
Management: Metro Regional Parks and Greenspaces
Contact: (503) 797–1850; www.metro-region.org
Finding the campground: From Interstate 205 in Portland, go east on Division Street and Oxbow Parkway, following signs 13 miles to the park.
About the campground: This park, cupped in a horseshoe bend of the Sandy Wild and Scenic River, encompasses 1,000 wooded acres to explore. You can fish, swim, canoe, raft, or go drift boating in the Sandy River. The campsites rest mainly in second-growth forest within an easy walk of the river. Areas of old growth also remain in the park, contributing to the diversity of birds and other wildlife. Footpaths travel Alder Ridge, the bend of the river, and the river flat. A popular 10-mile float trip begins at this park and ends at Lewis and Clark State Park, which is south off Interstate 84 east of Troutdale. Fall visitors sometimes are treated to the natural spectacle of spawning chinook salmon.

9 Scaponia County Park

Location: About 10 miles northeast of Vernonia
Season: May–December
Sites: 10 basic sites; no hookups
Maximum length: Best for tents and small units
Facilities: Tables, grills, pit toilets, drinking water
Fee per night: $
Management: Columbia County
Contact: (503) 397–2353; www.co.columbia.or.us/Colparks
Finding the campground: From Vernonia, travel 5 miles north on Oregon 47 and turn east on Scappoose-Vernonia Road to reach the park on the right in another 5.2 miles. It is 15 miles west of Scappoose.
About the campground: This small, rustic wayside campground rests in a second-growth forest along the slow-moving, creek-sized East Fork Nehalem River. Although the quiet is occasionally broken by the sound of traffic, the park welcomes relaxation. It has informal parking and shady lawn sites. In fall, hunters use the camp as a base.

10 Scappoose Bay Marine Park

Location: About 2 miles southwest of St. Helens
Season: Year-round
Sites: Self-contained RV camping; no hookups
Maximum length: 40 feet
Facilities: Flush toilets, drinking water, pump-out station, telephone, three-lane boat launch, marina, moorage, store, picnic shelter, kayak rental
Fee per night: $$
Management: Port of St. Helens
Contact: (503) 397–2888
Finding the campground: From U.S. Highway 30, 5 miles northwest of Scappoose and 1.5 miles southeast of St. Helens city center, turn east onto Millard Road, go 0.3 mile, and turn right on Old Portland Road. Follow it 0.4 mile to this park on the left.
About the campground: This 23-acre facility on the Columbia River features a well-kept marina and allows self-contained, dry camping in the parking area. Some large oaks dot the grassy perimeter of the "camp." Primarily, this is a boater's access on Scappoose Bay, which feeds into Multnomah Channel on the Columbia River. Nature trails allow you to stretch your legs.

11 Scappoose RV Park

Location: About 2 miles north of Scappoose
Season: Year-round
Sites: 7 RV hookup sites, 3 tent sites; water, electric, and sewer hookups
Maximum length: 40 feet
Facilities: Tables, grills, flush toilets, drinking water, showers, dump station, playground
Fee per night: $$
Management: Columbia County
Contact: (503) 556–9050, reservations accepted; www.co.columbia.or.us /Colparks
Finding the campground: From Scappoose, go 1.5 miles northwest on U.S. Highway 30 and turn east on West Lane Road at the sign for the park. Continue 0.6 mile and turn left on North Honeyman Road. Go 0.1 mile and enter the park on the right.
About the campground: This small, well-kept park is located near the rural airport and surrounded by open fields. Despite some noise from a nearby gravel operation, the sites are pleasant, with lawn and full shade from the park's mature firs and bigleaf maples. Scappoose celebrates Airport Appreciation Day in June and the Sauerkraut Festival in October.

12 Vernonia Airport Park

Location: About 4 miles southwest of Vernonia
Season: Year-round
Sites: 22 basic sites, no hookups
Maximum length: 40 feet
Facilities: Tables, grills, vault toilets, drinking water, playground
Fee per night: $
Management: City of Vernonia
Contact: (503) 429–5291; www.vernonia-or.gov/vernonia_parks
Finding the campground: From Oregon 47, 12.7 miles north of U.S. Highway 26 and 2 miles south of Vernonia, turn west onto Timber Road at the park sign. Go 1.1 miles, turn right onto Airport Road, and continue following the signs 0.4 mile into the park.
About the campground: Near the small rural airport, this campground occupies a mixed conifer and maple and alder setting along the Nehalem River. Sites have gravel parking. Fishing and wading are possible pastimes, along with hiking or cycling the Banks–Vernonia Linear State Park rail trail, which has marked trailheads off OR 47 and in Vernonia.

13 Washington County FairPlex RV Park

Location: In Hillsboro
Season: Closed to the public in July, otherwise open as space allows
Sites: 14 RV hookup sites (self-contained only), no tent sites; water and electric hookups
Maximum length: 30 feet
Facilities: Drinking water, showers, telephone (at fairgrounds)
Fee per night: $$
Management: Washington County
Contact (503) 648–1416 (call ahead; sometimes closes for seasonal events); www.faircomplex.com
Finding the campground: From Cornell Road, turn south at the FairPlex entrance across from the Portland Hillsboro Airport.
About the campground: This small overnight facility, which primarily serves fairground participants and through-travelers, is an extension of the main fairground's parking lot. The side-by-side sites are numbered, and all require backing in toward a mesh fence. But the camp does overlook an area of lawn and conifers.

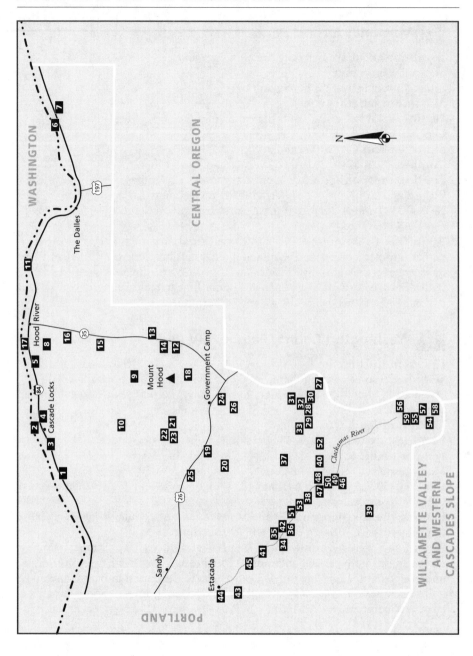

Mount Hood and the Columbia River Gorge

Two striking geographic features are the centerpieces of this region. The first is Mount Hood, the tallest, most famous, and most climbed peak in the Oregon Cascades. At a height of 11,235 feet, it reigns above a prized wilderness, sweeping forests, high mountain lakes, and wild and scenic waterways. The second feature is the Columbia River Gorge, the picturesque divide between Oregon and Washington recognized as a national scenic area. The Oregon side of the gorge has more than a dozen major waterfalls streaking its 3,000-foot cliffs. The stiff winds that funnel through the gorge challenge sailboarders to ride the choppy Columbia River.

Uniting the dynamic duo is the Mount Hood–Columbia Gorge Scenic Loop. This sightseeing drive begins along the river and follows Interstate 84 and the Historic Columbia River Highway east from Troutdale to the city of Hood River. From there, the tour continues south on Oregon 35 and west on U.S. Highway 26 to Gresham. In Gresham, the tour heads north on 242nd Avenue to return to I–84 and Troutdale.

Historically, the Columbia River attracted Indian fishing camps, carried Lewis and Clark and the Corps of Discovery west to the Pacific Ocean, and tested the mettle of the Oregon Trail pioneers in the years before Barlow Road provided an overland route around Mount Hood to the Willamette Valley. Mount Hood has long been an explorer's landmark, adventurer's challenge, and artist's inspiration.

Spectacular scenery and outstanding outdoor recreation are common to both areas, but overall, the Columbia River Gorge is probably better suited for car touring, with the many waterfalls, apple and cherry orchards, museums, the Bonneville Dam fish hatchery and fish-counting station, the sternwheeler tour, and historic train rides. But the outdoor enthusiast is not overlooked. The gorge serves up hiking, salmon and sturgeon fishing, windsurfing, and boating. Mount Hood caters to an active crowd, with mountain climbing, downhill and cross-country skiing, snowboarding, snowmobiling, fishing, hiking, golfing, and huckleberry picking. Mount Hood is also one of the few areas in the country to offer summer downhill skiing.

Both areas have historic lodges, wonderful campgrounds, and superb vistas. While both are popular playgrounds for the Portland metropolitan area, they still hold places for quiet reflection and unspoiled wilds.

At Mount Hood and the Columbia River Gorge, you can enjoy all four seasons. At the higher elevations, you will find comfortable summer temperatures and winter snow. Generally, the lower elevations remain mild most of the year, with the drier, eastern part of the gorge heating up in summer. In summer, the gorge funnels ocean-cooled west winds; in winter, icy east winds sweep through the gorge. While subfreezing temperatures can make for treacherous gorge travel, they transform the waterfalls into frozen art. Rain, though, is the more common winter signature, both in the gorge and at the lower mountain elevations.

Mount Hood.

Cascade Locks–Multnomah Falls Area

1 Ainsworth State Park

Location: About 9 miles west of Cascade Locks
Season: Mid-April–October
Sites: 45 hookup sites; water, electric, and sewer hookups
Maximum length: 60 feet
Facilities: Tables, grills, flush toilets, drinking water, showers, dump station
Fee per night: $$
Management: Oregon State Parks and Recreation Department
Contact: (503) 695-2301; www.oregonstateparks.org
Finding the campground: Take exit 35 off Interstate 84, 35 miles east of Portland and 9 miles west of Cascade Locks. On the south side of the freeway, follow the historic highway west for 0.6 mile to the park entrance on the left.
About the campground: The developed campsites rest in close proximity to one another, separated by small divides of nonnative landscaping, but they serve as a convenient base for exploring the area. The Columbia River Gorge has a wealth of vistas, natural attractions, trails, and history. Driving west on the historic Columbia River Highway opens the doorway to discovery. By following the Gorge Trail, which skirts camp, you may visit Oneonta Gorge and Ponytail, Horsetail, and Triple Falls. Autumn visitors to Multnomah Falls can spy spawning salmon in Multnomah Creek below the falls. At 620 feet, Multnomah Falls is the fourth tallest falls in the nation; its historic lodge—with visitor center, gift shop, and restaurant—is a popular stop.

2 Cascade Locks Marine Park

Location: In Cascade Locks
Season: Year-round
Sites: 16 hookup sites; water and electric hookups
Maximum length: 40 feet

Cascade Locks–Multnomah Falls Area

	Hookup sites	Total sites	Maximum RV length	Hookups	Toilets	Showers	Drinking water	Dump station	Recreation	Fee	Can reserve
1 Ainsworth State Park	45	45	60	WES	F	•	•	•	H	$$	
2 Cascade Locks Marine Park	16	16	40	WE	F	•	•	•	FBL	$$–$$$	
3 Eagle Creek		20	20		F		•		H	$$	
4 Herman Creek Horse Camp		7	24		NF		•		HR	$$	
5 Wyeth		14	32		F		•		H	$$	

Facilities: Tables, flush toilets, drinking water, showers, dump station, telephone, playground, gift shop, boat ramp, fish-cleaning station, small marina
Fee per night: $$–$$$
Management: Port of Cascade Locks
Contact: (541) 374–8619
Finding the campground: From Interstate 84 eastbound, take exit 44 for Cascade Locks, head 0.5 mile east on Wanapa Street, and turn north at the sign for the marine park. The exit from I–84 westbound is also labeled exit 44. From here, though, follow Wanapa Street west through town to the signed turnoff for the marine park. An underpass with a 12-foot height and 20-foot width clearance leads into the park.
About the campground: This convenient overnight spot in the Columbia River Gorge is found within the marine park, just above the boat launch area. It has developed parking pads and groomed lawn. Its central location is ideal if you want to explore the gorge. Within the marine park, you can fish for salmon or sturgeon, tour the Cascade Locks Historical Museum, or book a trip on the Columbia River sternwheeler.

3 Eagle Creek

Location: About 3 miles west of Cascade Locks
Season: Mid-May–September
Sites: 20 basic sites; no hookups
Maximum length: 20 feet
Facilities: Tables, grills, flush toilets, drinking water
Fee per night: $$
Management: Columbia River Gorge National Scenic Area
Contact: (541) 308–1700; www.fs.fed.us/r6/columbia/forest/recreation
Finding the campground: From Interstate 84 eastbound, take exit 41 to the campground. If you are traveling westbound from Cascade Locks, follow I–84 west to the Bonneville Dam exit and get onto I–84 heading east. Take exit 41 and proceed to the campground.
About the campground: Tucked away on a wooded hillside above Eagle Creek is this small, family campground—the first USDA Forest Service campground in the nation. The popular Eagle Creek Trail explores upstream from the camp, stringing past picturesque waterfalls to enter the Mark O. Hatfield Wilderness Area. Other trails trace the southern wall of the gorge or top hills for vistas. In fall, salmon migrate up the gravelly bed of Eagle Creek, sometimes drawing a following of bald eagles (hence the creek's name). Next door to the campground is the Cascade Salmon Fish Hatchery, but it is not set up for visitors. Bonneville Dam, to the west, though, has a visitor center with fish-viewing windows as well as a fish hatchery that can spark the imaginations of anglers.

Columbia River Gorge.

4 Herman Creek Horse Camp

Location: About 2 miles east of Cascade Locks
Season: Mid-May–October
Sites: 7 basic sites; no hookups
Maximum length: 24 feet
Facilities: Tables, grills, vault toilets, drinking water, hitching rails
Fee per night: $$
Management: Columbia River Gorge National Scenic Area
Contact: (541) 308–1700; www.fs.fed.us/r6/columbia/forest/recreation
Finding the campground: At the east end of Cascade Locks, take Forest Lane east for 1.7 miles, quickly crossing to the south side of Interstate 84. Past the Herman Creek Work Center, turn right for the campground and trailhead.
About the campground: Located east of Herman Creek in a low-elevation forest is this small, basic camp facility, which can accommodate stock. The trail up Herman Creek into the Mark O. Hatfield Wilderness begins on the west side of camp and ascends to Wahtum Lake, the Pacific Crest National Scenic Trail (PCT), and a host of other trail connections. Individuals with horses can transport them across the Bridge of the Gods into Washington to follow the PCT north; parking is at the north end of the bridge. The camp also serves fishing enthusiasts.

5 Wyeth

Location: About 8 miles east of Cascade Locks
Season: Mid-May–October
Sites: 14 basic sites; no hookups
Maximum length: 32 feet
Facilities: Tables, grills, flush toilets, drinking water
Fee per night: $$
Management: Columbia River Gorge National Scenic Area
Contact: (541) 308–1700; www.fs.fed.us/r6/columbia/forest/recreation
Finding the campground: From Interstate 84, 7 miles east of Cascade Locks, take exit 51 and follow the county road east along the south side of the freeway to the campground in 0.5 mile.
About the campground: This mostly forested campground along Gorton Creek has paved roads and site parking, with ample spacing between the sites. Small firs and bigleaf maples offer shade. By here, the Columbia River Gorge is beginning to transition out of thick woods on its west end to the grassland steppes on its east end. You can access the Gorge and Wyeth Trails from camp. Small cascades and falls contribute to the character of Gorton Creek.

The Dalles–Hood River Area

6 | Celilo Park

Location: About 15 miles east of The Dalles
Season: Year-round
Sites: Open camping; no hookups
Maximum length: 40 feet
Facilities: Flush toilets, drinking water, playground, boat launch
Fee per night: None
Management: U.S. Army Corps of Engineers
Contact: (541) 296–1181 or (541) 298–7650; www.nwp.usace.army.mil
Finding the campground: From Interstate 84, 12 miles east of The Dalles, take exit 97 to reach this park on the north side of the freeway.
About the campground: Formerly a day use, this Columbia River park now doubles as a campground, with RVs setting up in the parking area and tents pitched on the lawns. Boating, fishing, and windsurfing are the river recreations. The cross-river views are of the grassy hills and cliffs of Washington. Mature shade trees offer escape from the sun.

The Dalles–Hood River Area

	Hookup sites	Total sites	Maximum RV length	Hookups	Toilets	Showers	Drinking water	Dump station	Recreation	Fee	Can reserve
6 Celilo Park		open	40		F			•	SFBL		
7 Deschutes River State Recreation Area	33	59	50	WE	F			•	HFBLRC	$$	•
8 Kingsley County Park		20	small		NF			•	FBL	$	
9 Kinnikinnick		20	16		NF				HFBL	$$	
10 Lost Lake		142	32		NF	•	•	•	HFBLR	$$–$$$	•
11 Memaloose State Park	43	110	60	WES	F	•	•	•		$$	•
12 Nottingham		23	32		NF				HF	$$	
13 Routson County Park		10	T		F			•	HF	$	
14 Sherwood		14	16		NF				HF	$$	
15 Toll Bridge County Park	65	88	40	WES	F	•	•	•	F	$$	•
16 Tucker County Park	13	79	30	WE	F	•	•		HF	$$	
17 Viento State Park	57	75	30	WE	F	•	•		H	$$	

7 Deschutes River State Recreation Area

Location: About 18 miles east of The Dalles
Season: Year-round
Sites: 33 hookup sites, 25 basic sites, 1 covered wagon; water and electric hookups
Maximum length: 50 feet
Facilities: Tables, grills, flush toilets, drinking water, telephone, boat launch (on opposite shore of river), Oregon Trail exhibit
Fee per night: $$
Management: Oregon State Parks and Recreation Department
Contact: (541) 739-2322; (800) 452-5687 for reservations; www.oregonstate parks.org
Finding the campground: From Interstate 84, 12 miles east of The Dalles, take exit 97 and go east along the south side of the freeway for 3 miles to enter the park on the right.
About the campground: The campground's highly appealing tree-shaded lawn faces out on the Deschutes Wild and Scenic River, just upstream from its confluence with Columbia River. The camp is an oasis in an arid canyon of sagebrush and basalt. There is direct river access from camp, as well as foot trails that travel both shores. A bike trail likewise explores the canyon. The Deschutes offers world-class fishing, attracting fly-fishers from around the world, and the river is equally popular with boaters and floaters. A public launch is located across the river at Heritage Landing, a day use. Come with binoculars because the river corridor attracts its share of birds.

8 Kingsley County Park

Location: About 12 miles southwest of Hood River, on Upper Green Point Reservoir
Season: April–October
Sites: Up to 20 sites; no hookups
Maximum length: Small units
Facilities: A few tables, fire rings, vault toilets, drinking water (but suggest you bring some drinking water in case pump fails), boat launch and dock near dam
Fee per night: $
Management: Hood River County
Contact: (541) 387-6889
Finding the campground: From U.S. Highway 30 in Hood River, head south on Thirteenth Street for 0.4 mile. Merge onto Twelfth Street, which later becomes Tucker Road; go another 3.4 miles, taking several right turns to remain on Tucker Road. Turn right onto Portland Drive and go 2 miles to enter the community of Oak Grove and bear right on Binns Hill Road. Follow it 0.3 mile to Kingsley Road, turn left, and continue 5.9 miles to reach the park. All but the last 0.8 mile is paved.

About the campground: This park offers open, primitive camping along the east bank of Upper Green Point Reservoir. Sites are dispersed through the select-cut fir forest. Parking is what you can make of it, but the sites are generally well shaded. This moderate-sized reservoir welcomes boating (5 miles per hour) and fishing. Mount Defiance, topped by a radio tower, is seen across the reservoir.

9 Kinnikinnick

Location: About 24 miles southwest of Hood River, on Laurance Lake
Season: Mid-May–October
Sites: 3 basic sites, 17 tent sites; no hookups
Maximum length: 16 feet
Facilities: Tables, grills, vault toilets, small boat ramp (nonmotorized boating); no drinking water
Fee per night: $$
Management: Mount Hood National Forest
Contact: (541) 352–6002; www.fs.fed.us/r6/mthood/recreation
Finding the campground: From Hood River, go south on Oregon 35 for 14 miles and bear right (west) on Cooper Spur Road at Mount Hood Corner. Proceed 4.6 miles and turn right on Evans Creek Road/Forest Road 2840, signed for Laurance Lake. Continue another 5 miles to the lake and campground.
About the campground: This camp occupies a dry, conifer-forested shore on Laurance Lake, a reservoir on the Clear Branch of the Middle Fork Hood River, at the northern foot of Mount Hood. But Mount Hood can only be seen while rowing or fishing the lake or hiking the area trails. A cliff shapes one side of the lake basin, the dam area is open, and elsewhere brush dominates shore. Rocky locations provide habitat for pikas, big-eared rodents with high-pitched squeaks. A side trip heads south from camp along Cooper Spur Road and up through the Cloud Cap–Tilly Jane Historic Area, an old mining district, to Cloud Cap. Here, you can hike the Timberline Trail rounding Mount Hood, take in glorious views, discover the historic 1889 Cloud Cap Inn, or watch the Clark's nutcrackers.

10 Lost Lake

Location: About 33 miles southwest of Hood River, on Lost Lake
Season: May–mid-October
Sites: 120 basic sites, 3 group sites, 6 horse sites, 7 cabins, 6 rooms; no hookups
Maximum length: 32 feet
Facilities: Tables, grills, vault toilets, drinking water, showers, dump station, boat rental, boat ramp (nonmotorized boating), fish-cleaning stations, barrier-free trails, corrals
Fee per night: $$–$$$
Management: Mount Hood National Forest. Operated by Lost Lake Resort Inc.

Mount Hood from Lost Lake.

Contact: (541) 352–6002; (541) 386–6366 (resort and reservations); www.fs .fed.us/r6/mthood/recreation and for resort: www.lostlakeresort.org

Finding the campground: From Oregon 35, about 14 miles south of the town of Hood River and 0.5 mile north of the community of Mount Hood, turn west on Woodworth Road and follow it 2.1 miles to Dee Highway. Turn right, head 4 miles north to the old mill town of Dee, and cross the river bridge. Keep left to follow Lost Lake Road/Forest Road 13 the remaining 13.4 miles to the recreation area.

About the campground: Although it takes a bit of navigating to get here, Lost Lake and its outdoor playground more than satisfy. The 240-acre triangular lake offers quiet boating, fine fishing, and one of the best clear-day views of Mount Hood to be had anywhere. Old-growth forest and bountiful rhododendrons shape glorious realms to explore by trail or savor at camp. Set back from shore, the wooded camp is highly attractive and well ordered, with paved roads and parking. The concessionaire has designated sites by party size and number of vehicles. Some sites occupy a split level, with the tables and grills on a different terrace than the parking. Trails explore the lakeshore, old-growth grove, Lost Lake Butte, and the Old Skyline route. The Old-Growth Trail and the eastern part of the Lakeshore Trail are barrier-free, with long stretches of boardwalk.

11 Memaloose State Park

Location: 11 miles west of The Dalles
Season: Mid-March–October
Sites: 43 hookup sites; 67 basic sites; water, electric, and sewer hookups
Maximum length: 60 feet
Facilities: Tables, grills, flush toilets, drinking water, showers, dump station, telephone
Fee per night: $$
Management: Oregon State Parks and Recreation Department
Contact: (541) 478-3008; (800) 452-5687 for reservations; www.oregonstate parks.org
Finding the campground: The campground is north off Interstate 84, 11 miles west of The Dalles. Westbound access only.
About the campground: This park takes the name of a Columbia River island that was used by Indians as a sacred burial ground and was flooded with the damming of the river. The landscaped camp rests above the river and below the freeway; planted shade trees bring added comfort to a stay. With no river access at the park, visitors must seek their entertainment away from camp. The Columbia Gorge welcomes fishing, hiking, boating, windsurfing, and sightseeing. Historic The Dalles and the Columbia Gorge Discovery Center (at the outskirts of town) warrant a look.

12 Nottingham

Location: About 27 miles south of Hood River
Season: Late May–mid-October
Sites: 23 basic sites; no hookups
Maximum length: 32 feet
Facilities: Tables, grills, vault toilets; no drinking water
Fee per night: $$
Management: Mount Hood National Forest
Contact: (541) 352-6002; www.fs.fed.us/r6/mthood/recreation
Finding the campground: It is west off Oregon 35, 26.3 miles south of Hood River; 12.3 miles north of the junction of U.S. Highway 26 and Oregon 35.
About the campground: This family campground rests in a open conifer forest along the East Fork Hood River, which originates on Mount Hood. Special fishing regulations apply to the river. Area trails explore along the river and climb to Badger Creek Wilderness. Mount Hood sightseeing is popular, with Cloud Cap and Timberline within reasonable distances of the camp. Pioneer Woman's Grave and a segment of the Oregon Trail can be found near the junction of US 26 and OR 35.

13 Routson County Park

Location: About 21 miles south of Hood River
Season: April–October
Sites: 10 tent sites; no hookups
Maximum length: Suitable for tents only
Facilities: Some tables and grills, flush toilets, drinking water
Fee per night: $
Management: Hood River County
Contact: (541) 387–6889
Finding the campground: It is east off Oregon 35, 20.7 miles south of Hood River. A narrow, gravel road overhung by trees leads into camp.
About the campground: Despite the running-water facilities, the sites themselves are more primitive and somewhat random. They occupy a stand of tall fir set back slightly from the racing, glacier-born East Fork Hood River; special fishing regulations apply. An impressive cliff claims the opposite shore. Although small RV units could park on the earthen flat, the entrance road's blind access, overhanging limbs, and tight turnaround at camp make this park better suited for tent campers.

14 Sherwood

Location: About 25 miles south of Hood River
Season: Late May–mid-October
Sites: 14 basic sites; no hookups
Maximum length: 16 feet
Facilities: Tables, grills, vault toilets; no drinking water
Fee per night: $$
Management: Mount Hood National Forest
Contact: (541) 352–6002; www.fs.fed.us/r6/mthood/recreation
Finding the campground: It is west off Oregon 35, 24.6 miles south of Hood River.
About the campground: This campground on the East Fork Hood River offers a pleasant forest stay, with access to fishing and hiking, but its proximity to OR 35 brings with it some traffic sounds. Special fishing regulations apply to protect salmon and steelhead. Trails travel along the river and upstream along Cold Spring Creek, which flows into the river north of camp. Tamanawas Falls—an elegant waterfall with lacy streamers tumbling 100 feet over a basalt cliff—puts an exclamation mark on the journey up Cold Spring Creek.

15 Toll Bridge County Park

Location: About 15 miles south of Hood River
Season: April–October
Sites: 20 full hookup sites, 45 partial hookup sites, 23 tent sites; water, electric, and sewer hookups

Maximum length: 40 feet
Facilities: Tables, grills, flush toilets, drinking water, showers, dump station, telephone
Fee per night: $$
Management: Hood River County
Contact: (541) 352-5522 for information and reservations
Finding the campground: From Hood River, go 15 miles south on Oregon 35, turn right (west) on Toll Bridge Road, and continue 0.3 mile to this campground on the right.
About the campground: This campground and its large, adjacent day-use area sit along the East Fork Hood River, which originates on Mount Hood. The full-hookup sites occupy a parklike grounds, with lawn shaded by pines and firs. Elsewhere, the campsites are tucked into a semi-open, mixed woods, with tree species common to both eastern and western Oregon. Fishing and sightseeing in the orchard country of Hood River County may provide amusement. In Parkdale, you may wish to visit the Hutson Museum, with its Native American, pioneer, and gemstone collections.

16 Tucker County Park

Location: About 5 miles south of Hood River
Season: April–October
Sites: 13 hookup sites, 66 basic sites; water and electric hookups
Maximum length: 30 feet
Facilities: Tables, grills, flush toilets, drinking water, showers, telephone, playground, horseshoe pits
Fee per night: $$
Management: Hood River County
Contact: (541) 387-6889
Finding the campground: From U.S. Highway 30 in Hood River, go 0.4 mile south on Thirteenth Street. Merge onto Twelfth Street, which later becomes Tucker Road; travel 4.3 miles, taking several right turns to remain on Tucker Road. Bear right toward Dee on Hood River Highway and go 0.4 mile to enter the park on the right.
About the campground: You will find this family campground in an open, mostly natural forest setting of ponderosa pines and oaks above the Hood River. Noisy and turbulent, the river courses past camp; a short nature trail provides access and views. Wood ducks may sometimes be seen along the waterway. The camp lies within convenient reach of the Columbia River Gorge to the north. Lost Lake can be reached by traveling south and west via Hood River Highway and Forest Road 13.

17 Viento State Park

Location: 8 miles west of Hood River
Season: Mid-April–late October
Sites: 57 hookup sites, 18 basic sites; water and electric hookups

Maximum length: 30 feet
Facilities: Tables, grills, flush toilets, drinking water, showers, telephone
Fee per night: $$
Management: Oregon State Parks and Recreation Department
Contact: (541) 374–8811; www.oregonstateparks.org
Finding the campground: The park is reached off Interstate 84, 8 miles west of Hood River. The primary campground is on the north side of the freeway, while tent camping is on the south side.
About the campground: Just off the interstate, this tidy campground among the maples and oaks is convenient for both through travelers and visitors to the Columbia River Gorge National Scenic Area. The separate tent area occupies a natural woodland. The Columbia River is a 0.2-mile walk from camp. Possible excursions include visits to the attractions of Bonneville Dam, Cascade Locks, and the Washington shore; a waterfall-sightseeing trip along the Old Scenic Highway; and windsurfing at Koberg Beach in Hood River. For hiking, head to Starvation Creek State Park (2 miles west), where trails climb to Mount Defiance and the heights of the gorge. A number of first-rate trails also begin off the Old Scenic Highway, and the old road between the campground and Starvation Creek Falls makes a good walking path.

Zigzag–Government Camp Area

18 Alpine

Location: About 4 miles north of Government Camp
Season: July–Labor Day
Sites: 6 tent sites; no hookups
Maximum length: Suitable for tents only
Facilities: Tables, grills, nonflush toilets, drinking water
Fee per night: $$
Management: Mount Hood National Forest
Contact: (503) 622–3191; www.fs.fed.us/r6/mthood/recreation
Finding the campground: From U.S. Highway 26 east of Government Camp, turn north on Timberline Road and go 4.2 miles to reach this campground.
About the campground: This lofty camp puts you in an alpine meadow setting just below timberline on majestic Mount Hood. Mount Hood offers year-round skiing and snowboarding and is one of the most climbed peaks in the country. The superb Timberline Trail encircles the mountain, and you can visit historic Timberline Lodge, which is noted for its fine stone masonry and woodwork. This small camp is well suited for tents, although some small RV units do venture to this spot. Because the camp appeals to snowboarders, it tends to have a livelier atmosphere than other Mount Hood area campgrounds.

Zigzag–Government Camp Area	Hookup sites	Total sites	Maximum RV length	Hookups	Toilets	Showers	Drinking water	Dump station	Recreation	Fee	Can reserve
18 Alpine		6	T		NF		•		H	$$	
19 Camp Creek		25	22		NF		•		HFR	$$	•
20 Green Canyon		15	22		NF				HSF	$$	
21 Lost Creek		16	22		NF		•		HF	$$	•
22 McNeil		34	22		NF				H	$$	
23 Riley Horse Camp		14	16		NF		•		HR	$$	•
24 Still Creek		27	16		NF		•		H	$$	•
25 Tollgate		15	16		NF		•		HFR	$$	•
26 Trillium Lake		57	40		NF		•		HSFBL	$$	•

19 Camp Creek

Location: About 5 miles east of Zigzag
Season: Mid-May–Labor Day
Sites: 25 basic sites; no hookups
Maximum length: 22 feet
Facilities: Tables, grills, vault toilets, drinking water
Fee per night: $$
Management: Mount Hood National Forest
Contact: (503) 622–3191; (877) 444–6777 for reservations; www.fs.fed.us/r6 /mthood/recreation
Finding the campground: It is south off U.S. Highway 26, 19.2 miles east of Sandy and 2.6 miles east of Rhododendron.
About the campground: In a deep, old-growth forest alongside sparkling Camp Creek sits this inviting campground, which makes an ideal base for exploring the Mount Hood area. The camp oozes charm with its many big trees and rich greenery. A small tributary through camp supports bountiful skunk cabbage, pungent in spring. The sites have defined, surfaced parking and are well spaced for comfort. Creek fishing, hiking, and sightseeing may pull you away from camp. The Pioneer Bridle Trail parallels US 26 at the north side of the campground, following the route of the Oregon Trail. Little Zigzag Falls and Flag Mountain Trails are also not far from camp; a visit to the Mount Hood Visitor Information Center in Zigzag (south off US 26 west of camp) will help you with trip planning.

20 Green Canyon

Location: About 5 miles south of Zigzag
Season: Mid-May–Labor Day
Sites: 15 basic sites; no hookups
Maximum length: 22 feet
Facilities: Tables, grills, vault toilets. Bring drinking water.
Fee per night: $$
Management: Mount Hood National Forest
Contact: (503) 622–3191; www.fs.fed.us/r6/mthood/recreation
Finding the campground: From U.S. Highway 26 at Zigzag, go south on Salmon River Road/Forest Road 2618 for 4.5 miles to enter this camp on the right.
About the campground: On an old-growth-forested flat along the Salmon Wild and Scenic River, you will find this quiet campground, where you can either retreat from the flurry of activity around Mount Hood or join right in. The Mount Hood area welcomes fishing, hiking, berry picking, sightseeing, history tracking, and summer skiing; a stop at the Mount Hood Visitor Center in Zigzag can help you plot your itinerary. Near camp, trails parallel the Salmon River in both directions; the upstream hike enters Salmon–Huckleberry Wilderness. The more challenging Green Canyon Way Trail begins across the road from camp and strikes straight uphill into the wilderness. The Salmon River offers catch-and-release fishing only.

21 Lost Creek

Location: About 7 miles northeast of Zigzag
Season: Mid-May–Labor Day
Sites: 10 wheelchair-accessible basic sites, 6 pack-in/roll-in wheelchair sites; no hookups
Maximum length: 22 feet
Facilities: Tables, grills, vault toilets, drinking water. Entire campground is wheelchair accessible.
Fee per night: $$
Management: Mount Hood National Forest
Contact: (503) 622–3191; (877) 444–6777 for reservations; www.fs.fed.us/r6 /mthood/recreation
Finding the campground: From U.S. Highway 26 at Zigzag, turn north on East Lolo Pass Road (Forest Road 18) and go 4.2 miles. Turn right on FR 1825 and follow it for another 2.7 miles to enter the campground on the right.
About the campground: In a picturesque mountain hemlock forest sits this accessible campground with its level and paved sites. Lost Creek lends a soothing backdrop, and rhododendrons seasonally color the scene. A fine interpretive trail begins at camp and explores the immediate area. Fishing also provides entertainment.

A sign along Lost Creek's interpretive trail.

22 McNeil

Location: About 5 miles northeast of Zigzag
Season: Late May–Labor Day
Sites: 34 basic sites; no hookups
Maximum length: 22 feet
Facilities: Tables, grills, vault toilets; no drinking water
Fee per night: $$
Management: Mount Hood National Forest
Contact: (503) 622–3191; www.fs.fed.us/r6/mthood/recreation
Finding the campground: From U.S. Highway 26 at Zigzag, turn north on East Lolo Pass Road (Forest Road 18) and go 4.2 miles. Turn right on FR 1825 and go 0.8 mile to enter this camp on the left.
About the campground: This camp above the Sandy River sits in an open lodgepole pine forest on Old Maid Flat—a lahar (volcanic flow of mud and debris) from Mount Hood's active days. Sites are for the most part sunny and dry. The camp has a difficult river access but is within reach of the Mount Hood Wilderness trails and lies just off the 70-mile Mount Hood Loop Drive. The auto tour loop travels East Lolo Pass Road (paved and gravel) to the north side of the mountain, passes through Dee and Parkdale, then follows Oregon 35 south and US 26 west to complete the cinch around Mount Hood.

McNeil campground.

23 Riley Horse Camp

Location: About 5 miles northeast of Zigzag
Season: Late May–Labor Day
Sites: 14 basic sites; no hookups
Maximum length: 16 feet
Facilities: Tables, grills, vault toilets, drinking water, tie stalls
Fee per night: $$
Management: Mount Hood National Forest
Contact: (503) 622–3191; (877) 444–6777 for reservations; www.fs.fed.us/r6 /mthood/recreation
Finding the campground: From U.S. Highway 26 at Zigzag, turn north on East Lolo Pass Road (Forest Road 18) and go 4.1 miles. Turn right on FR 1825, go 1.1 miles, and turn right on FR 1825.382 to reach camp.
About the campground: This quiet camp rests in a mixed conifer forest at the western foot of Mount Hood, just outside Mount Hood Wilderness Area. Equestrians find easy access to trails that enter the wilderness and link up with the Pacific Crest Trail. Lost Creek flows past the camp, and the sites are mostly shaded.

24 Still Creek

Location: About 1 mile southeast of Government Camp.
Season: Late May–Labor Day
Sites: 27 basic sites; no hookups
Maximum length: 16 feet
Facilities: Tables, grills, vault toilets, drinking water
Fee per night: $$
Management: Mount Hood National Forest
Contact: (503) 622–3191; (877) 444–6777 for reservations; www.fs.fed.us/r6 /mthood/recreation
Finding the campground: From Government Camp, go 0.5 mile east on U.S. Highway 26 and turn south onto Forest Road 2650. Go 0.3 mile to enter camp.
About the campground: This peaceful camp along Still Creek offers comfortable, well-spaced sites in a rich forest of hemlock and fir, with a huckleberry and mixed shrub understory. At the south end of camp is the Old Barlow Road, which you can follow west on foot across Still Creek; a cedar post at its start indicates you are on the actual Oregon Trail. By driving 0.4 mile east on Old Barlow Road, you will find Summit Meadows and a pioneer grave. Fishing and quiet boating are possible at Trillium Lake, only 2 miles east; a day-use fee is charged. Because the Still Creek–Trillium Lake area is popular for cross-country skiing, you may wish to check it out for your winter recreation.

25 Tollgate

Location: 3 miles east of Zigzag
Season: Late May–Labor Day
Sites: 15 basic sites; no hookups
Maximum length: 16 feet
Facilities: Tables, grills, vault toilets, drinking water, rustic picnic shelter
Fee per night: $$
Management: Mount Hood National Forest
Contact: (503) 622–3191; (877) 444–6777 for reservations; www.fs.fed.us/r6
/mthood/recreation
Finding the campground: It is south off U.S. Highway 26, 17 miles east of
Sandy and 0.4 miles east of Rhododendron.
About the campground: Despite its proximity to US 26, this cozy campground occupies a lovely forested flat of mature firs and cedars above the
Zigzag River. The campsites have defined, surfaced parking, but a few are a
bit awkward to get into with longer vehicles because of the angle of approach
and the many trees. A rustic picnic shelter and remnant mossy fireplaces add
to the camp's charm. East of the campground, you will find the historic tollgate on Old Barlow Road, which was part of the Oregon Trail. This interpretive site can be reached via the Pioneer Bridle Trail, at the north end of camp,
or via US 26. Special fishing rules apply to the river. A visit to the Mount Hood
Visitor Center, south off US 26 in Zigzag, can help you plan your activities.

26 Trillium Lake

Location: About 3 miles southeast of Government Camp, on Trillium Lake
Season: Memorial Day weekend–mid-October, depending on snow
Sites: 57 basic sites; no hookups
Maximum length: 40 feet
Facilities: Tables, grills, vault toilets, drinking water, telephone, boat launch,
fishing pier
Fee per night: $$
Management: Mount Hood National Forest
Contact: (503) 622–3191; (877) 444–6777 for reservations; www.fs.fed.us/r6
/mthood/recreation
Finding the campground: From Government Camp, go 1.7 miles east on
U.S. Highway 26, turn south on Forest Road 2656, and proceed 1.4 miles to
enter the campground on the right.
About the campground: This campground occupies a rich, diverse forest
along the east shore of Trillium Lake, which rests in the shadow of Mount
Hood. Lodgepole pine, cedar, fir, mountain hemlock, rhododendron, and beargrass weave an enchanting backdrop. Campers enjoy superb views and photographic opportunities. The quiet mountain lake welcomes family recreation
with nonmotorized boating, fishing, and hiking on a lakeside trail. The lake's
small dam provides a direct volcano view.

Timothy Lake Area

27 Clackamas Lake

Location: About 20 miles south of Government Camp
Season: June–Labor Day
Sites: 46 basic sites (horses allowed in sites 1–19); no hookups
Maximum length: 32 feet
Facilities: Tables, grills, vault toilets, drinking water, hitching posts, pioneer cabin monument
Fee per night: $$
Management: Mount Hood National Forest
Contact: (503) 622-3191; (877) 444-6777 for reservations; www.fs.fed.us/r6/mthood/recreation
Finding the campground: From Government Camp, go 11.5 miles southeast on U.S. Highway 26 and turn right on paved Forest Road 42 (Skyline Road). Follow it another 8.6 miles and turn left, going 0.1 mile to enter campground on the left.
About the campground: This campground occupies a mixed forest at the upper edge of Clackamas Meadow, site of the historic Miller Cabin. A boardwalk from camp leads to tiny Clackamas Lake, which feeds into the scenic Oak Grove Fork of the Clackamas River. Springs percolate up through the sandy bottom of this shallow lake. Outings from camp may include visits to Timothy Lake and the Clackamas Historic Ranger Station. The nearby Miller Trail leads to the Pacific Crest Trail.

Timothy Lake Area

	Hookup sites	Total sites	Maximum RV length	Hookups	Toilets	Showers	Drinking water	Dump station	Recreation	Fee	Can reserve
27 Clackamas Lake		46	32		NF		•		HFR	$$	•
28 Gone Creek		50	32		NF		•		HFBL	$$	•
29 Hoodview		43	32		NF		•		HFBL	$$	•
30 Joe Graham Horse Camp		14	40		NF		•		HFR	$$	•
31 Little Crater Lake		16	22		NF		•		H	$$	•
32 Oak Fork		47	32		NF		•		HFBL	$$	•
33 Pine Point		25	32		NF		•		HFBL	$$	•

28 Gone Creek

Location: About 21 miles south of Government Camp, on Timothy Lake
Season: Mid-May–Labor Day
Sites: 50 basic sites; no hookups
Maximum length: 32 feet
Facilities: Tables, grills, vault toilets, drinking water, boat launch
Fee per night: $$
Management: Mount Hood National Forest
Contact: (503) 622-3191; (877) 444-6777 for reservations; www.fs.fed.us/r6/mthood/recreation
Finding the campground: From Government Camp, go 11.5 miles southeast on U.S. Highway 26 and turn right onto paved Forest Road 42 (Skyline Road). Follow it for 8.3 miles and turn right on FR 57. Proceed 1.6 miles to this campground on right.
About the campground: This campground on the south shore of manmade Timothy Lake sits in mixed age conifer forest with several older firs and hemlocks towering above camp. Most sites receive partial shade. Mount Hood is visible across the reservoir. Camp stays generally include boating (10 miles per hour maximum), fishing, or hiking the Timothy Lake Trail.

29 Hoodview

Location: About 22 miles south of Government Camp, on Timothy Lake
Season: Mid-May–Labor Day
Sites: 43 basic sites; no hookups
Maximum length: 32 feet
Facilities: Tables, grills, vault toilets, drinking water, boat launch
Fee per night: $$
Management: Mount Hood National Forest
Contact: (503) 622-3191; (877) 444-6777 for reservations; www.fs.fed.us/r6/mthood/recreation
Finding the campground: From Government Camp, go 11.5 miles southeast on U.S. Highway 26 and turn right onto paved Forest Road 42 (Skyline Road). Follow it for 8.3 miles, turn right on FR 57, and proceed 2.6 miles to this campground on right.
About the campground: On the south shore of manmade Timothy Lake, this campground boasts some big firs and mountain hemlocks in its mixed age forest that offers good shade. In early summer, rhododendron pompoms decorate camp. Premium-priced sites overlook the lake, with Mount Hood seen from shore. Boating (10 miles per hour maximum), fishing, and the 13-mile Timothy Lake Trail, which circles the lake, keep campers occupied.

30 Joe Graham Horse Camp

Location: About 19 miles south of Government Camp
Season: Mid-May–September
Sites: 14 basic sites; no hookups
Maximum length: 40 feet
Facilities: Tables, grills, vault toilets, drinking water, corrals
Fee per night: $$
Management: Mount Hood National Forest
Contact: (503) 622–3191; (877) 444–6777 for reservations; www.fs.fed.us/r6 /mthood/recreation
Finding the campground: From Government Camp, go 11.5 miles southeast on U.S. Highway 26 and turn right onto paved Forest Road 42 (Skyline Road). Follow it 7.2 miles and turn left on FR 021 for the horse camp.
About the campground: Adjacent to the Oak Grove Fork Clackamas River and picturesque Clackamas Meadow, this campground for the exclusive use of equestrians rests in an old-growth forest of fir and hemlock. The camp has large pole corrals and spacious sites to accommodate horse trailers and camp vehicles. It offers a peaceful, attractive stay and has access to area horse and hiking trails and fishing.

31 Little Crater Lake

Location: About 18 miles south of Government Camp, on Little Crater Lake
Season: Late May–Labor Day
Sites: 16 basic sites; no hookups
Maximum length: 22 feet
Facilities: Tables, grills, vault toilets, drinking water, paved trail to Little Crater Lake
Fee per night: $$
Management: Mount Hood National Forest
Contact: (503) 622–3191; (877) 444–6777 for reservations; www.fs.fed.us/r6 /mthood/recreation
Finding the campground: From Government Camp, go 11.5 miles southeast on U.S. Highway 26 and turn right on paved Forest Road 42 (Skyline Road). Follow it 4.1 miles and turn right on paved FR 58, heading toward High Rock. Go 2.3 miles and turn left to enter this camp.
About the campground: Little Crater Lake, the star attraction of camp, is an artesian-fed lake of dazzling color. Though only an acre in size, the lake has a depth of 45 feet. The water is 34° Fahrenheit, and its clarity reveals silvery logs on the lake bottom. The lake's rustic viewing platform is just a pleasant meadow walk from camp; meadow wildlife sightings are common. Lupine, gentian, and false hellebore sprinkle color in the meadow. An earthen trail beyond the lake links up with the Pacific Crest Trail in a half mile, for longer adventures. The campground itself is tucked in the forest and has gravel parking spurs.

32 Oak Fork

Location: About 21 miles south of Government Camp, on Timothy Lake
Season: Late May–mid-October
Sites: 47 basic sites; no hookups
Maximum length: 32 feet
Facilities: Tables, grills, vault toilets, drinking water, boat launch, dock
Fee per night: $$
Management: Mount Hood National Forest
Contact: (503) 622-3191; (877) 444-6777 for reservations; www.fs.fed.us/r6 /mthood/recreation
Finding the campground: From Government Camp, go 11.5 miles southeast on U.S. Highway 26 and turn right on paved Forest Road 42 (Skyline Road). Follow it for 8.3 miles, turn right on FR 57, and proceed 1.4 miles to this campground on right.
About the campground: On the southeast shore of Timothy Lake, these campsites sit slightly back from the reservoir's edge in a rich atmosphere of full shade. The camp offers sites with lake views, gravel parking (some pull-through), and a recreational lineup that includes boating (10 miles per hour maximum), fishing, and hiking the Timothy Lake Trail or Miller Trail, which also visits the lake area.

33 Pine Point

Location: About 23 miles south of Government Camp, on Timothy Lake
Season: Late May–Labor Day
Sites: 25 basic sites; no hookups
Maximum length: 32 feet
Facilities: Tables, grills, vault toilets, drinking water, boat launch
Fee per night: $$
Management: Mount Hood National Forest
Contact: (503) 622-3191; (877) 444-6777 for reservations; www.fs.fed.us/r6 /mthood/recreation
Finding the campground: From Government Camp, go 11.5 miles southeast on U.S. Highway 26 and turn right onto paved Forest Road 42 (Skyline Road). Follow it for 8.3 miles, turn right on FR 57, and proceed 3.2 miles to this campground on the right.
About the campground: This campground occupies a second-growth forest on the southwest shore of Timothy Lake, a manmade lake with gravelly sand beaches. Timber cutting has left a patchwork on the enfolding hills and younger forest rims the lake. Located near the dam, this campground offers semi-open sites, with gravel parking pads (some pull-through). Several sites have lake views. Boating is kept to 10 miles per hour maximum to preserve the quiet. Fishing or hiking along the Timothy Lake Trail also engages campers.

Old-growth forest.

Estacada–Clackamas River Area

34 Armstrong

Location: About 14 miles southeast of Estacada
Season: May–September
Sites: 12 basic sites; no hookups
Maximum length: 16 feet
Facilities: Tables, grills, vault toilets, drinking water
Fee per night: $$
Management: Mount Hood National Forest

Estacada–Clackamas River Area

	Hookup sites	Total sites	Maximum RV length	Hookups	Toilets	Showers	Drinking water	Dump station	Recreation	Fee	Can reserve
34 Armstrong		12	16		NF		•		FB	$$	•
35 Carter Bridge		15	28		NF				FBL	$$	
36 Fish Creek		24	16		NF		•		FB	$$	•
37 Hideaway Lake		9	16		NF				HFB	$$	
38 Indian Henry		86	36		F		•	•	HFB	$$	•
39 Kingfisher		23	16		NF		•		F	$$	•
40 Lake Harriet		13	30		NF		•		FBL	$$	•
41 Lazy Bend		21	16		F		•		FB	$$	•
42 Lockaby		30	16		NF		•		FBL	$$	•
43 Metzler County Park	46	70	35	WE	F	•	•	•	HSF	$$	•
44 Milo McIver State Park	44	53	50	WE	F	•	•	•	HFBLRC	$$	•
45 Promontory Park		58	35		F	•	•		FBL	$$-$$$	•
46 Raab		27	22		NF				SF	$$	•
47 Rainbow		17	16		NF		•		HF	$$	•
48 Ripplebrook		13	16		NF		•		F	$$	
49 Riverford		9	20		NF				F	$$	
50 Riverside		16	22		NF		•		HF	$$	•
51 Roaring River		19	16		NF		•		HF	$$	•
52 Shellrock Creek		7	16		NF				HF	$$	
53 Sunstrip		9	18		NF		•		FB	$$	•

Contact: (503) 630–6861; (877) 444–6777 for reservations; www.fs.fed.us/r6/mthood/recreation

Finding the campground: From Estacada, go 14.1 miles southeast on Oregon 224 to enter this camp on the right.

About the campground: Part of the Clackamas Wild and Scenic River line-up of campgrounds, this facility offers gravel site parking in a setting of young cedar and maple trees. It sits at the foot of a slope near a bridge and has a grassy bank for easy river access.

35 Carter Bridge

Location: About 14 miles southeast of Estacada
Season: Mid-May–September
Sites: 15 basic sites; no hookups
Maximum length: 28 feet
Facilities: Tables, grills, vault toilets; no drinking water
Fee per night: $$
Management: Mount Hood National Forest
Contact: (503) 630–6861; www.fs.fed.us/r6/mthood/recreation

Finding the campground: From Estacada, go 13.6 miles southeast on Oregon 224 to enter this camp on the left.

About the campground: Although it sits in a young forest of cedar, maple, and alder, this Clackamas River camp enjoys a nice amount of shade. The camp is just downstream from a whitewater launch site and, like most of its overnight counterparts, offers river fishing.

36 Fish Creek

Location: About 14 miles southeast of Estacada
Season: May–September
Sites: 24 basic sites; no hookups
Maximum length: 16 feet
Facilities: Tables, grills, vault toilets, drinking water
Fee per night: $$
Management: Mount Hood National Forest
Contact: (503) 630–6861; (877) 444–6777 for reservations; www.fs.fed.us/r6/mthood/recreation

Finding the campground: From Estacada, go 14.2 miles southeast on Oregon 224 and turn right on Fish Creek Road to enter the camp.

About the campground: This campground claims an attractive forested bench along the Clackamas River. Rhododendrons seasonally color the campground. For most visitors, fishing is the river's primary allure, with fly rods the chosen arsenal. Early in the year, kayaking and rafting bring their own following to the river.

37 Hideaway Lake

Location: About 41 miles southeast of Estacada, on Hideaway Lake
Season: Mid-June–September
Sites: 9 basic sites; no hookups
Maximum length: 16 feet
Facilities: Tables, grills, pit toilets; no drinking water
Fee per night: $$
Management: Mount Hood National Forest
Contact: (503) 630–6861; www.fs.fed.us/r6/mthood/recreation
Finding the campground: From Estacada, go 25 miles southeast on Oregon 224 and continue east on Forest Road 57 for another 7.4 miles. Turn left on FR 58, go 3.1 miles, and again turn left on FR 5830. Proceed 5.3 miles more, and turn left to reach the camp in 0.2 mile.
About the campground: This rustic camp, best suited for tents, provides access to an idyllic 12-acre lake tucked away in a hemlock-fir forest. Thirty feet deep, Hideaway Lake naturally produces both rainbow and brown trout. Because the thick vegetation limits shore access, inflatable fishing tubes and rafts serve anglers well. Hikers can trace the Shellrock Trail from the northwest shore of Hideaway Lake to Rock Lakes Basin Loop. This all-day hike or backpack visits additional, remote lakes, which offer solitude and fishing. Serene Lake is the largest of the hike-to lakes; stolen views along the trail stretch from Mount Jefferson to Washington's Mount Rainier. The blooms of beargrass and rhododendrons seasonally perk up the forest.

38 Indian Henry

Location: About 21 miles southeast of Estacada
Season: May–September
Sites: 86 basic sites; no hookups
Maximum length: 36 feet
Facilities: Tables, grills, flush toilets, drinking water, dump station
Fee per night: $$
Management: Mount Hood National Forest
Contact: (503) 630–6861; (877) 444–6777 for reservations; www.fs.fed.us/r6/mthood/recreation
Finding the campground: From Estacada, go 20.5 miles southeast on Oregon 224 and bear right on Forest Road 4620 just before the bridge. Continue 0.6 mile to enter the camp on the left; the Clackamas River Trail is on the right.
About the campground: This Clackamas River campground offers paved sites in a tall, old-growth forest of hemlock, cedar, and fir. Rotting logs, vine maples, and ferns contribute to the textured forest setting. Across from camp, you can access the 8-mile river trail; midway, a side spur visits the long plummet of Pup Falls. Fishing and rafting are primary river pursuits.

39 Kingfisher

Location: About 34 miles southeast of Estacada
Season: Late May–early September
Sites: 23 basic sites; no hookups
Maximum length: 16 feet
Facilities: Tables, grills, vault toilets, drinking water
Fee per night: $$
Management: Mount Hood National Forest
Contact: (503) 630–6861; (877) 444–6777 for reservations; www.fs.fed.us/r6/mthood/recreation
Finding the campground: From Estacada, go 25 miles southeast on Oregon 224 to its junction with Forest Roads 57 and 46. Bear right on FR 46, go 3.5 miles, and turn right onto FR 63. Go 3.5 miles more and turn right on FR 70 toward Bagby Hot Springs. Follow it 1.7 miles to reach this campground on the left.
About the campground: This forest campground sits along the Hot Springs Fork Collawash River and is the closest developed campground to Bagby Hot Springs. Beautiful old-growth firs and cedars and a vibrant midstory contribute to the invitation of camp. Gravel bars give anglers access to the river and their chosen sport.

40 Lake Harriet

Location: About 32 miles southeast of Estacada, on Lake Harriet
Season: May–September
Sites: 13 basic sites; no hookups
Maximum length: 30 feet
Facilities: Tables, grills, vault toilets, drinking water
Fee per night: $$
Management: Mount Hood National Forest.
Contact: (503) 630–6861; (877) 444–6777 for reservations; www.fs.fed.us/r6/mthood/recreation
Finding the campground: From Estacada, go 25 miles southeast on Oregon 224 to its junction with Forest Roads 57 and 46. Bear left on FR 57, go 6.3 miles, and turn left on gravel FR 4630. Go 1.1 miles more to reach campground.
About the campground: This campground occupies the alder and fir perimeter of a large, dirt parking flat where the Oak Grove Fork Clackamas River feeds into manmade Lake Harriet. The elongated reservoir sits at the foot of steep forested hillsides. A sandy boat ramp in the camp allows you to launch a rowboat or raft for fishing. No motors are allowed on the lake.

41 Lazy Bend

Location: About 9 miles southeast of Estacada
Season: May–September
Sites: 21 basic sites; no hookups
Maximum length: 16 feet
Facilities: Tables, grills, flush toilets, drinking water
Fee per night: $$
Management: Mount Hood National Forest
Contact: (503) 630–6861; (877) 444–6777 for reservations; www.fs.fed.us/r6 /mthood/recreation
Finding the campground: From Estacada, go 9.3 miles southeast on Oregon 224 to enter this camp on the right.
About the campground: On the Clackamas Wild and Scenic River, this campground has paved site parking in a rich setting of firs, maples, and alders. Cascaras, filberts, and vine maples fill out the midstory. The steep, forested slope across from camp adds to the naturalness of the setting. An informal riverside path heading upstream from camp serves anglers.

42 Lockaby

Location: 14 miles southeast of Estacada
Season: May–September
Sites: 30 basic sites; no hookups
Maximum length: 16 feet
Facilities: Tables, grills, vault toilets, drinking water
Fee per night: $$
Management: Mount Hood National Forest
Contact: (503) 630–6861; (877) 444–6777 for reservations; www.fs.fed.us/r6 /mthood/recreation
Finding the campground: From Estacada, go 14 miles southeast on Oregon 224. The campground is on the left.
About the campground: This campground is just upstream from a raft put-in site on the Clackamas River. It occupies a narrow forest corridor of cedars, maples, dogwoods, and alders. Several sites sit a few strides off the campground road but are close to the river. The Clackamas is a popular fishing water and provides a relaxing backdrop to a stay.

43 Metzler County Park

Location: About 6 miles southwest of Estacada
Season: May–September
Sites: 46 hookup sites, 24 basic sites; water and electric hookups
Maximum length: 35 feet
Facilities: Tables, barbecues, flush toilets, drinking water, showers, dump station, telephone, playground, ballfields, horseshoe pits
Fee per night: $$

Management: Clackamas County

Contact: (503) 353–4414, reservations accepted; www.co.clackamas.or.us/dtd /parks

Finding the campground: From the junction of Oregon 211 and OR 224 in south Estacada, go 3.7 miles south on OR 211, turn right (west) on South Tucker/South Springwater Road, and continue 0.6 mile. Turn left on Metzler Park Road to make a steep descent into the park. Turn right for the campground in 1.8 miles.

About the campground: Ideal for family getaways, this charming county park rests along Clear Creek, where three swimming holes keep campers cool in summer and brook trout provide sport for fishing enthusiasts. The basic sites, which sit closer to the creek, are rustic, shaded by cedar, fir, and maple trees. The hookup sites sit farther back in a younger woods. A nature trail, paired with a plant identification guide, suggests a stroll.

44 Milo McIver State Park

Location: About 4 miles west of Estacada

Season: Mid-March–October

Sites: 44 hookup sites, 9 basic sites; water and electric hookups

Maximum length: 50 feet

Facilities: Tables, grills, flush toilets, drinking water, showers, dump station, telephone, disc golf, boat launch, fish hatchery, picnic shelters

Fee per night: $$

Management: Oregon State Parks and Recreation Department

Contact: (503) 630–7150; (800) 452–5687 for reservations; www.oregonstate parks.org

Finding the campground: From the junction of Oregon 211 and OR 224 in Estacada, go 1 mile south on OR 211, turn right (west) on South Hayden Road, and proceed 1.3 miles. Turn right on South Springwater Road and go 1.2 miles to reach the park entrance on the right. Follow the signs into the campground.

About the campground: Along the Clackamas River, this large state park features both groomed and natural areas. Besides its developed, wooded campground, it has sweeping grassy picnic areas dotted by shade trees and riparian woods crisscrossed by hiking and equestrian trails. Wildlife sightings add to the enjoyment, while a bike path offers another way to see the park. The disc golf course covers a good-sized area, but fishing, boating, and rafting remain the key park draws.

45 Promontory Park

Location: 6 miles southeast of Estacada, at North Fork Reservoir

Season: Memorial Day weekend–September

Sites: 50 basic sites, 8 yomes (cross between tent and cabin); no hookups

Maximum length: 35 feet

Facilities: Tables, grills, flush toilets, drinking water, showers, camp store, playground, children's fishing pond, boat moorage, boat rental, launch, docks

Fee per night: $$, $$$ for yomes
Management: Portland General Electric
Contact: (503) 630–7229 for information and reservations; www.portland general.com/parks
Finding the campground: From the junction of Oregon 211 and OR 224 in south Estacada, go east on OR 224 for 6.1 miles and turn right. Make a quick left and follow signs through the park to the campground.
About the campground: This campground provides access to the 350-acre North Fork Reservoir, a popular place for boating and fishing, and to the 1-acre Small Fry Lake, a stocked fishing pond in which youngsters under 14 years old are allowed to catch up to 3 fish a day. The developed sites sit fairly close together in a forest of tall Douglas fir. A few sites overlook the steep bank to the long, narrow reservoir.

46 Raab

Location: About 29 miles southeast of Estacada
Season: Mid-May–early September
Sites: 27 basic sites; no hookups
Maximum length: 22 feet
Facilities: Tables, grills, vault toilets; no drinking water
Fee per night: $$
Management: Mount Hood National Forest
Contact: (503) 630–6861; (877) 444–6777 for reservations; www.fs.fed.us/r6 /mthood/recreation
Finding the campground: From Estacada, go 25 miles southeast on Oregon 224 to its junction with Forest Roads 57 and 46. Bear right on FR 46, go 3.5 miles, and turn right on FR 63. The campground is on the right in 0.7 mile.
About the campground: On a bluff above the Collawash River, this campground is framed by rhododendrons and tall firs and cedars. A wire-mesh fence separates the campground from the edge of the bluff; below are enticing green pools. If you follow the fence upstream, it leads to an outcrop overlooking a stretch of rushing river, but there is no access here. Farther upstream, a gravel bar provides river access.

47 Rainbow

Location: About 25 miles southeast of Estacada
Season: Mid-May–early September
Sites: 17 basic sites; no hookups
Maximum length: 16 feet
Facilities: Tables, grills, vault toilets, drinking water
Fee per night: $$
Management: Mount Hood National Forest
Contact: (503) 630–6861; (877) 444–6777 for reservations; www.fs.fed.us/r6 /mthood/recreation

Finding the campground: From Estacada, go 25 miles southeast on Oregon 224 to its junction with Forest Roads 57 and 46. Bear right on FR 46 to enter this campground on the right in less than 0.1 mile.

About the campground: This campground basks in the beauty of a multistory forest along the Oak Grove Fork Clackamas River, above its confluence with the main stem Clackamas River. The forest is visually rich with Douglas fir, cedar, moss-festooned bigleaf maple, vine maple, hazel, and an understory floral mosaic and varied shades of greens. Some sites rest along the river, but the soothing rush of the river current carries throughout camp. The Riverside Trail explores along both waterways and through old-growth forest, passing between Rainbow and Riverside campgrounds. Fishing is popular.

48 Ripplebrook

Location: About 26 miles southeast of Estacada
Season: Mid-May–early September
Sites: 13 basic sites; no hookups
Maximum length: 16 feet
Facilities: Tables, grills, vault toilets, drinking water
Fee per night: $$
Management: Mount Hood National Forest
Contact: (503) 630–6861; www.fs.fed.us/r6/mthood/recreation
Finding the campground: From Estacada, go almost 25 miles southeast on Oregon 224 and turn left to enter the campground. The turn is just before the junction of OR 224 and Forest Roads 57 and 46.

About the campground: This campground stretches for more than a quarter mile along the Oak Grove Fork Clackamas River. Due to its linear design, a number of sites offer fine river views. Douglas fir, cedar, and bigleaf maple trees shade the campsites; the understory explodes with greenery. Fishing or exploring the prized area hiking trails engage visitors.

49 Riverford

Location: About 29 miles southeast of Estacada
Season: Mid-May–early September
Sites: 5 basic sites, 4 walk-in tent sites; no hookups
Maximum length: 20 feet
Facilities: Tables, grills, vault toilets; no drinking water
Fee per night: $$
Management: Mount Hood National Forest
Contact: (503) 630–6861; www.fs.fed.us/r6/mthood/recreation
Finding the campground: From Estacada, go 25 miles southeast on Oregon 224 to its junction with Forest Roads 57 and 46. Bear right on FR 46 and go 3.6 miles to enter the campground on the right. (The campground entrance is 0.1 mile past the junction with FR 63.)

About the campground: This small, remote campground occupies a low bluff above the Clackamas Wild and Scenic River. Many of the sites offer river views, and a mixed age woods supplies shade. The pleasant retreat serves fishing enthusiasts. Off FR 63, you can locate the trailheads to Bagby Hot Springs and Bull of the Woods Wilderness.

50 Riverside

Location: About 28 miles southeast of Estacada
Season: Mid-May–early September
Sites: 11 basic sites, 5 walk-in tent sites; no hookups
Maximum length: 22 feet
Facilities: Tables, grills, vault toilets, drinking water
Fee per night: $$
Management: Mount Hood National Forest
Contact: (503) 630–6861; (877) 444–6777 for reservations; www.fs.fed.us/r6/mthood/recreation
Finding the campground: From Estacada, go 25 miles southeast on Oregon 224 to its junction with Forest Roads 57 and 46. Bear right on FR 46 and go 2.9 miles to enter the campground on right.
About the campground: This campground rests on a low bluff above the main stem Clackamas Wild and Scenic River. Some sites overlook the water, while others are wrapped in glorious forest. Grassy flats claim forest openings. The campground has a paved road and parking pads. Birds enliven the canopy with movement and song, and wily trout beckon anglers. The Riverside Trail, with its old-growth trees, invites a stroll.

51 Roaring River

Location: About 17 miles southeast of Estacada
Season: May–September
Sites: 19 basic sites; no hookups
Maximum length: 16 feet
Facilities: Tables, grills, vault toilets, drinking water
Fee per night: $$
Management: Mount Hood National Forest
Contact: (503) 630–6861; (877) 444–6777 for reservations; www.fs.fed.us/r6/mthood/recreation
Finding the campground: From Estacada, go 16.5 miles southeast on Oregon 224 to enter this camp on the left.
About the campground: This campground has access to two wild and scenic rivers: It sits across the road from the Clackamas River, while the picturesque Roaring River races along the campground's western edge. The facility primarily serves tent campers, with its sites tucked among the old-growth cedars and firs and moss-draped maples. The Roaring River Trail climbs away from camp; for fishing, the Clackamas River is the better bet.

52 Shellrock Creek

Location: About 33 miles southeast of Estacada
Season: Mid-June–early September
Sites: 7 basic sites; no hookups
Maximum length: 16 feet
Facilities: Tables, grills, vault toilets; no drinking water
Fee per night: $$
Management: Mount Hood National Forest
Contact: (503) 630–6861; www.fs.fed.us/r6/mthood/recreation
Finding the campground: From Estacada, go 25 miles southeast on Oregon 224 to its junction with Forest Roads 57 and 46. Bear left on FR 57, go 7.3 miles, and turn left on FR 58. Proceed 0.4 mile to enter the campground on the left.
About the campground: This small overnight facility is best suited for tent camping. It rests along picturesque Shellrock Creek in a forest of big firs and cedars, interspersed with yew trees and rhododendrons. Sites receive a mix of sun and shade. Parking is along the widened, gravel road shoulder; some sites have better tent flats than others. From this quiet camp, you may fish or hike the 0.5-mile Pacific Yew Trail, which starts near the bridge but can be overgrown.

53 Sunstrip

Location: About 17 miles southeast of Estacada
Season: May–September
Sites: 9 basic sites; no hookups
Maximum length: 18 feet
Facilities: Tables, grills, vault toilets, drinking water
Fee per night: $$
Management: Mount Hood National Forest
Contact: (503) 630–6861; (877) 444–6777 for reservations; www.fs.fed.us/r6 /mthood/recreation
Finding the campground: From Estacada, go 17.1 miles southeast on Oregon 224 to enter this camp on the right.
About the campground: This small Clackamas River campground is nestled in the shoreline forest of maple, fir, and hemlock. A few sites overlook the river. Across from camp rises a steep canyon slope. Fishing is the primary pursuit.

Olallie Lake Scenic Area

54 Camp Ten

Location: About 39 miles northeast of Detroit, on Olallie Lake
Season: Mid-June–September
Sites: 10 basic sites; no hookups
Maximum length: 16 feet
Facilities: Tables, grills, pit toilets; no drinking water
Fee per night: $$
Management: Mount Hood National Forest
Contact: (503) 630–6861; www.fs.fed.us/r6/mthood/recreation
Finding the campground: From Oregon 22 in Detroit, head northeast on Forest Road 46 for 25 miles and turn east on FR 4690. Follow it for 8.1 miles; the route changes to gravel after 6 miles. Turn right onto gravel FR 4220 for Olallie Lake Scenic Area. Go another 6.2 miles to enter the campground on the left.
About the campground: On the southwest shore of Olallie Lake, this campground has closely spaced sites in a forest of lichen-festooned mountain hemlock and spruce. Parking can be restrictive in some areas. A few sites overlook Olallie Lake, a beautiful, big high-mountain lake that pairs with an Olallie Butte view. A hiking trail encircles Olallie Lake but requires a walk along the road on the lake's west shore. The huckleberry bushes draw berry pickers in late summer. Fishing and nonmotorized boating keep campers on the go.

Olallie Lake Scenic Area

	Hookup sites	Total sites	Maximum RV length	Hookups	Toilets	Showers	Drinking water	Dump station	Recreation	Fee	Can reserve
54 Camp Ten		10	16		NF				HFB	$$	
55 Lower Lake		8	16		NF				HF	$	
56 Olallie Meadows		8	16		NF				HR	$	
57 Paul Dennis		19	16		NF			•	HFB	$–$$	
58 Peninsula		45	24		NF			•	HFB	$$	
59 Triangle Lake Equestrian Camp		8	30		NF				HR	$$	

55 Lower Lake

Location: About 38 miles northeast of Detroit, near Lower Lake
Season: Mid-June–September
Sites: 8 basic sites; no hookups
Maximum length: 16 feet
Facilities: Tables, grills, vault toilets; no drinking water
Fee per night: $
Management: Mount Hood National Forest
Contact: (503) 630-6861; www.fs.fed.us/r6/mthood/recreation
Finding the campground: From Oregon 22 in Detroit, head northeast on Forest Road 46 for 25 miles and turn east on FR 4690. Follow it for 8.1 miles; the route changes to gravel after 6 miles. Turn right onto gravel FR 4220 for Olallie Lake Scenic Area. Go another 4.5 miles to enter the campground on the right.
About the campground: In a mountain forest of spruce, fir, pine, and hemlock, this campground offers a quiet retreat. A talus slope abuts one site. From camp, a half-mile trail leads to the scenery, fishing, and huckleberry and blueberry patches at Lower Lake. From the fork in the trail beyond Lower Lake, you can walk 1 mile to Fish Lake, snuggled in a deep, treed basin. Or you can hike 3 miles to Red Lake, passing a string of lakes en route.

56 Olallie Meadows

Location: About 35 miles northeast of Detroit
Season: Mid-June–September
Sites: 7 basic sites, 1 cabin; no hookups
Maximum length: 16 feet
Facilities: Tables, grills, vault toilet; no drinking water
Fee per night: $
Management: Mount Hood National Forest
Contact: (503) 630-6861; www.fs.fed.us/r6/mthood/recreation
Finding the campground: From Oregon 22 in Detroit, head northeast on Forest Road 46 for 25 miles and turn east on FR 4690. Follow it for 8.1 miles; the route changes to gravel after 6 miles. Turn right onto gravel FR 4220 for Olallie Lake Scenic Area. The campground is on the left in another 1.4 miles.
About the campground: In a forest of lodgepole pine and spruce, you will find this campground and rustic cabin at the edge of picturesque Olallie Meadows, a rich, moist, textured meadow of grasses, wildflowers, and blueberries. You can sometimes spy deer or sandhill cranes in the lea. Gathered views include Olallie, Sisi, and Badger buttes. Horses may be tethered to horse trailers at camp, but the animals are not allowed in the meadow. The trail to Russ Lake begins at camp and passes two other mountain lakes along the way. Come prepared for mosquitoes.

57 Paul Dennis

Location: About 39 miles northeast of Detroit, on Olallie Lake
Season: Mid-June–September
Sites: 17 basic sites, 2 yurts; no hookups
Maximum length: 16 feet
Facilities: Tables, grills, vault toilets, drinking water
Fee per night: $–$$
Management: Mount Hood National Forest
Contact: (503) 630–6861; www.fs.fed.us/r6/mthood/recreation
Finding the campground: From Oregon 22 in Detroit, head northeast on Forest Road 46 for 25 miles and turn east on FR 4690. Follow it for 8.1 miles; the route changes to gravel after 6 miles. Turn right onto gravel FR 4220 for Olallie Lake Scenic Area. Go 5.2 miles more and turn left to reach camp in 0.25 mile.
About the campground: On the northeast shore of Olallie Lake, next door to rustic Olallie Lake Resort, a setting of lodgepole pines and mountain hemlocks enfolds this campground. Dwarf huckleberry and beargrass spread between the trees. Some sites overlook the big mountain lake, but all lie within easy access of the lake for fishing, nonmotorized boating, and admiring. A lakeshore trail nearly circles the lake and provides access to trails into Olallie Lake Scenic Area.

58 Peninsula

Location: About 40 miles northeast of Detroit, on Olallie Lake
Season: Mid-June–September
Sites: 39 basic sites, 6 walk-in tent sites; no hookups
Maximum length: 24 feet
Facilities: Tables, grills, vault toilets, drinking water
Fee per night: $$
Management: Mount Hood National Forest
Contact: (503) 630–6861; www.fs.fed.us/r6/mthood/recreation
Finding the campground: From Oregon 22 in Detroit, head northeast on Forest Road 46 for 25 miles and turn east on FR 4690. Follow it for 8.1 miles; the route changes to gravel after 6 miles. Turn right onto gravel FR 4220 for Olallie Lake Scenic Area. Reach the campground on the left in 6.6 miles.
About the campground: This campground occupies a high-elevation forest on a peninsula of beautiful, blue Olallie Lake. Some sites look out on the lake and the towering profile of Olallie Butte. Huckleberry picking, hiking, fishing, and quiet boating are favorite pastimes at and near camp. Part of the campground reflects the recovery since the fire of 2001.

59 Triangle Lake Equestrian Camp

Location: About 35 miles northeast of Detroit
Season: Mid-June–September
Sites: 8 basic sites; no hookups
Maximum length: 30 feet
Facilities: Tables, grills, vault toilets, water for horses, corrals; no drinking water
Fee per night: $$
Management: Mount Hood National Forest
Contact: (503) 630–6861; www.fs.fed.us/r6/mthood/recreation
Finding the campground: From Oregon 22 in Detroit, head northeast on Forest Road 46 for 25 miles and turn east on FR 4690. Follow it for 8.1 miles; the route changes to gravel after 6 miles. Turn right onto gravel FR 4220 for Olallie Lake Scenic Area. The campground is on the right in 2.1 miles.
About the campground: For the exclusive use of equestrians, this campground offers tranquil sites in a setting of lodgepole pines and mountain hemlocks. Long gravel parking pads accommodate both camp vehicles and horse trailers. Within Olallie Lake Scenic Area, equestrians find a variety of trails open to riding, but the short trail to shallow, marshy Triangle Lake is off-limits to horses. Fishing, quiet boating, and berry picking can fill out a stay.

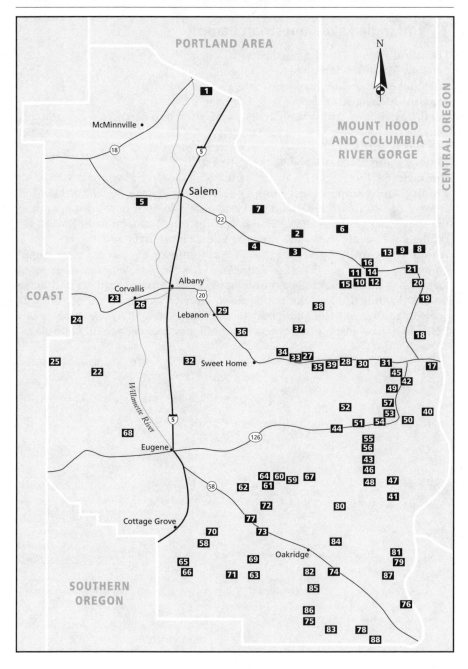

Willamette Valley and Western Cascades Slope

Between the Cascade Mountains and the Coast Range stretches the broad, fertile Willamette Valley fed by the Willamette River, which originates high in the snowy Cascades. The rich soil and mild climate of the Willamette Valley inspired thousands of families in the mid-1800s to make the grueling, 2,000-mile journey west on the Oregon Trail. The allure of fertile soil was the rival of gold, which fed the California gold rush at about the same time.

The valley is prime wildlife habitat; common sightings include Canada geese, ospreys, bald eagles, herons, deer, and the state animal—the beaver. The valley is also a critical migration and wintering spot on the Pacific Flyway. One of the best and most relaxing ways to watch wildlife is from a raft. The Willamette River was seemingly made for a lazy float trip. You may contact an outfitter, or pick up the *Willamette River Recreation Guide* from the Oregon State Parks and Recreation Department or a local visitor center. This brochure, complete with a river trail map, shows put-in and take-out spots, mileages, and approximate river flow and float times. Hiking trails offer another way to enjoy the valley scenery and wildlife, but learn what poison oak looks like and where it grows. Paved trails along river greenways serve cyclists, wheelchair users, exercise walkers, joggers, and families pushing baby strollers.

You need not get your hands dirty to share in the land's bounty. Roadside produce stands teem with baskets, lugs, and bins of fresh fruits, vegetables, and nuts. The many varieties astound and the tastes tantalize. But if you are a hands-on person, there are also plenty of u-pick farms. The Willamette Valley is noted for its fine berries and pinot noir grapes. Throughout the valley, award-winning wineries open their tasting rooms to the public.

Back roads will take you past covered bridges, river ferries, tulip fields, Christmas tree farms, golf courses, fishing waters, and blackberry brambles. At the heart of the valley, along the busy artery of Interstate 5, are the region's two major cities: Salem, the capital, and Eugene, a university town. Smaller farm and forest towns extend yesteryear charm.

The mild Willamette Valley climate allows year-round recreation, if you do not mind braving the occasional rainstorm. Winter visitors should have a full suit of rain gear and a sunny disposition. Summer days bask in sunlight, with temperatures climbing into the 90s, but humidity is seldom a problem.

This region also encompasses the western slope of the central Cascade Mountain Range, which makes up the Willamette River watershed. It brings together the spectacular scenery and recreational lineup of the upper

Willamette, Santiam, and McKenzie River drainages. Among the attractions are scenic byways, hiking trails, old-growth forest, sterling waterfalls, and prized waters for fishing, canoeing, speed boating, and waterskiing. Winter sports expand the offering. But whether you are working up a sweat or simply kicking back at camp, the mountain offering is top-notch.

The Cascades experience four distinct seasons, with the lower elevations remaining mild year-round. Winter rain typically claims the lower flanks, changing to snow before the passes and upper mountain reaches. Mixed conditions characterize spring and fall, and afternoon thunderstorms are possible in summer.

Salem Area

1 Champoeg State Park

Location: About 30 miles north of Salem
Season: Year-round
Sites: 79 hookup sites, 6 walk-in tent sites, 6 yurts, 6 cabins; water and electric hookups
Maximum length: 50 feet
Facilities: Tables, grills, flush toilets, drinking water, showers, dump station, telephone, dock, visitor center, museum, picnic pavilions, amphitheater for history pageant and other events
Fee per night: $$–$$$
Management: Oregon State Parks and Recreation Department
Contact: (503) 633–8170; (800) 452–5687 for reservations; www.oregonstateparks.org
Finding the campground: From exit 278 on Interstate 5, 5 miles south of Wilsonville, head west on Ehlen Road/Yergen Road. Go 3.6 miles and turn right on Case Road, which later merges into Champoeg Road (bearing left). Go 5.8 miles to enter the park on the right. The route is signed.
About the campground: This park captivates with Willamette Valley charm: sweeping green pastures, scenic oak groves, the sleepy Willamette River, and a comfortable, clean camp area. The park occupies the site where Oregon's first provisional government—the Northwest's first pro-American government—took flight. This area was also used as a Native American hunting and gathering camp, a fur-trading post, and a steamboat landing. Interpretive signs on the park grounds and the visitor center relate the tales. For the active, the park offers a 10-mile bicycle path, 1.5 miles of riverside hiking trail, fishing, and birding. The park is well located for exploring the valley backroads and visiting u-pick farms or for taking in the attractions of Portland: concerts, museums, shops, the Oregon Zoo, gardens, and more.

Salem Area

	Hookup sites	Total sites	Maximum RV length	Hookups	Toilets	Showers	Drinking water	Dump station	Recreation	Fee	Can reserve
1 Champoeg State Park	79	97	50	WE	F	•	•	•	HFBC	$$–$$$	•
2 Elkhorn Valley Recreation Site		24	18		NF		•		SF	$$	
3 Fisherman's Bend Recreation Site	21	52	40	W	F	•	•	•	HFBL	$$	•
4 John Neal Memorial Park		40	25		F		•		FBL	$$	
5 Polk County Fairgrounds	100	100	40	WE	F	•	•	•		$$	
6 Shady Cove		13	16		NF				HSF	$–$$	
7 Silver Falls State Park	47	113	60	WE	F	•	•	•	HSRC	$$–$$$	•

2 Elkhorn Valley Recreation Site

Location: About 30 miles east of Salem
Season: Mid-May–October
Sites: 24 basic sites; no hookups
Maximum length: 18 feet
Facilities: Tables, grills, vault toilets, drinking water
Fee per night: $$
Management: Salem District Bureau of Land Management
Contact: (503) 375-5646; www.or.blm.gov/salem
Finding the campground: From Oregon 22 at Mehama, 22 miles east of Salem, turn northeast onto North Fork Road/Forest Road 2209 for Little North Fork Recreation Area and go 8.4 miles to reach the campground on the left.
About the campground: This pleasant camp occupies an old-growth forest along the clear, blue-green Little North Fork Santiam River. Pastimes include relaxation, swimming, fishing, and walking short trails along the river. The camp is a jumping-off point to a host of area trails that follow the river, pass swimming holes, and lead into the prized forest and mountain settings of Opal Creek Scenic Recreation Area. A nearby golf course suggests an alternative means for whiling away the day.

3 Fisherman's Bend Recreation Site

Location: 28 miles east of Salem
Season: Mid-May–early October
Sites: 21 hookup sites, 29 basic sites, 2 cabins; water hookups
Maximum length: 40 feet
Facilities: Tables, grills, flush toilets, drinking water, showers, dump station, telephone, playground, ballfields, horseshoes, boat launch (drift boats or rafts), barrier-free trail and fishing dock for individuals with disabilities
Fee per night: $$
Management: Salem District Bureau of Land Management
Contact: (503) 375-5646; (877) 444-6777 for reservations; www.or.blm.gov/salem
Finding the campground: From Oregon 22, 28 miles east of Salem and 1.6 miles west of Mill City, turn south to enter the recreation site and camp.
About the campground: This large but friendly and welcoming camp and day-use area sits beside the North Santiam River, a popular waterway for fishing, rafting, and drift boating. The camp occupies a wooded flat, and the good-sized sites allow for comfort and privacy. A network of trails explores the riparian habitat. Great blue herons, mergansers, kingfishers, nighthawks, and ospreys travel the river corridor.

Barns dot the landscape in the fertile Willamette Valley.

Many Willamette Valley wineries offer tours to the public.

4   John Neal Memorial Park

Location: In Lyons, about 25 miles east of Salem
Season: Mid-April–mid-October
Sites: 40 basic sites; no hookups
Maximum length: 25 feet
Facilities: Tables, grills, flush toilets, drinking water, playground, ballfield, horseshoe pits, primitive launch for drift boat or raft
Fee per night: $$
Management: Linn County
Contact: (541) 967–3917; www.co.linn.or.us/parks
Finding the campground: From Oregon 22, 22 miles east of Salem and 7.7 miles west of Mill City, turn south on OR 226, go 0.9 mile, and continue east off OR 226 on Main Street for 0.5 mile. Turn left on Thirteenth Street to enter the park in 0.6 mile.
About the campground: Convenient for OR 22 travelers, this quiet, rustic camp claims a low bluff above the North Santiam River, a popular waterway for rafting and fishing. The sites dispersed through a natural forest of cedar, fir, maple, and alder have earthen parking.

5 Polk County Fairgrounds

Location: In Rickreall, about 11 miles southwest of Salem
Season: Year-round
Sites: 100 hookup sites, dry camping, tent camping on open lawn; water and electric hookups
Maximum length: 40 feet
Facilities: Flush toilets, drinking water, showers, dump station, playground
Fee per night: $$
Management: Polk County
Contact: (503) 623-3048
Finding the campground: From Salem, go 10 miles west on Oregon 22 and turn south on OR 99W. Go 0.8 mile, passing through Rickreall, to find the fairgrounds on the left.
About the campground: Within the parking lot for the main fairgrounds, you will find these paved and gravel sites. Power poles signal the hookup sites; tent camping is on the lawn. The area is shadeless but convenient for travelers and fairground attendees and participants. Next door is Nesmith County Park, with its picnic tables and inviting lawn and shade trees. Area wineries may suggest touring, starting with a tasting room across from the fairgrounds. The state tourism department puts out a winery tours brochure, available at individual wineries, chambers of commerce, and visitor centers. U-pick farms suggest another way to spend time.

6 Shady Cove

Location: About 41 miles east of Salem
Season: Year-round
Sites: 13 basic sites; no hookups
Maximum length: 16 feet
Facilities: Tables, grills, vault toilets; no drinking water
Fee per night: $-$$
Management: Willamette National Forest
Contact: (503) 854-3366; www.fs.fed.us/r6/willamette/recreation
Finding the campground: From Oregon 22 at Mehama, about 22 miles east of Salem, turn northeast at the sign for Little North Fork Recreation Area and go 19 miles on North Fork Road/Forest Road 2209 and FR 2207 to reach this camp at Shady Cove Bridge. The route begins paved, changing to gravel.
About the campground: Serving anglers and hikers, this camp sits on a richly forested flat above the Little North Santiam River at Shady Cove Bridge. Because the road into camp is twisting and sometimes rough, this facility is best suited for tent camping or small RVs. The Little North Fork Santiam River Trail is located across the river from camp, while other area trails enter the Opal Creek Scenic Recreation Area. A series of inviting green pools on the Little North Santiam River attracts swimmers to this canyon.

Falls at Silver Falls State Park.

7 Silver Falls State Park

Location: About 28 miles east of Salem
Season: Year-round
Sites: 47 hookup sites, 46 basic sites, 14 cabins, 6 horse campsites; water and electric hookups
Maximum length: 60 feet
Facilities: Tables, grills, flush toilets, drinking water, showers, dump station, telephone, nature center, play area, swimming pond, corrals at horse camp
Fee per night: $$-$$$
Management: Oregon State Parks and Recreation Department
Contact: (503) 873-8681; (800) 452-5687 for reservations; www.oregonstate parks.org
Finding the campground: From Oregon 22, 12 miles east of Salem, take the exit for Silver Falls State Park and follow OR 214 northeast for 15.5 miles to the park. OR 214 follows a weaving course, but signs mark the junctions.
About the campground: In the Cascade foothills along Silver Creek, you will find this picturesque family park that boasts 10 major waterfalls. You can visit each of the falls via the Trail of Ten Falls hiking loop, which offers unique perspectives as it passes above, below, and behind the droplet curtains. Falls viewing is also available from the picnic area, from the drive-to overlooks, or by walking short distances along the trail. Elsewhere, bicycle trails and horse trails explore the wooded park, with its areas of old growth and mature second growth. The tidy campground is set apart from the day-use bustle. The comfortable sites are easy to access, and campers can choose between sun or shade. Equestrians in the area are served by Howard Creek Horse Camp.

Detroit Lake Area

8 Breitenbush

Location: About 9 miles northeast of Detroit
Season: Maintained mid-May–late September
Sites: 30 basic sites; no hookups
Maximum length: 24 feet
Facilities: Tables, grills, vault toilets, drinking water
Fee per night: $$
Management: Willamette National Forest
Contact: (503) 854–3366; www.fs.fed.us/r6/willamette/recreation
Finding the campground: From Oregon 22 at the west end of Detroit, turn north on Forest Road 46 and go 9.1 miles to enter the camp on the right.
About the campground: Hemlocks, cedars, and vine maples envelop this attractive camp along the Breitenbush River. The pristine river is framed by overhanging trees and the greenery of its banks. Campers can fish or hike the nearby South Breitenbush Gorge Trail, which passes through old-growth forest and along a rocky chasm that pinches the South Fork into a fury of rushing water. The trailhead is off FR 4685, northeast of camp. The camp is also near the private, alternative-lifestyle Breitenbush Hot Springs.

9 Cleater Bend

Location: About 9 miles northeast of Detroit
Season: Maintained mid-May–late September
Sites: 9 basic sites; no hookups
Maximum length: 40 feet
Facilities: Tables, grills, vault toilets, drinking water

Detroit Lake Area

	Hookup sites	Total sites	Maximum RV length	Hookups	Toilets	Showers	Drinking water	Dump station	Recreation	Fee	Can reserve
8 Breitenbush		30	24		NF			•	HF	$$	
9 Cleater Bend		9	40		NF			•	HF	$$	
10 Cove Creek		63	40		F	•		•	SFBL	$$	
11 Detroit Lake State Recreation Area	178	311	60	WES	F	•		•	SFBL	$$–$$$	•
12 Hoover		37	40		F			•	HFSBL	$$–$$$	
13 Humbug		22	30		NF			•	HF	$$	
14 Santiam Flats		open	40		NF				FBL	$	
15 Southshore		30	30		NF			•	HFSBL	$$	
16 Upper Arm Recreation Area		5	20		NF				SFB		

Fee per night: $$

Management: Willamette National Forest

Contact: (503) 854–3366; www.fs.fed.us/r6/willamette/recreation

Finding the campground: From Oregon 22 at the west end of Detroit, turn north on Forest Road 46 and go 8.6 miles to enter the camp on the right.

About the campground: This small, compact Breitenbush River campground occupies a bend on the river where an island divides the flow. Sites are nestled in a lovely woodland setting of mixed conifers, alders, and rhododendrons. Campers can fish or take a hike along the South Breitenbush Gorge Trail (reached northeast of camp off FR 4685). Recreation at Detroit Lake is just minutes away.

10 Cove Creek

Location: About 6 miles south of Detroit, on Detroit Lake

Season: Mid-April–September

Sites: 63 basic sites; no hookups

Maximum length: 40 feet

Facilities: Tables, grills, flush toilets, drinking water, coin-operated showers, boat launch, dock

Fee per night: $$

Management: Willamette National Forest

Contact: (503) 854–3366; www.fs.fed.us/r6/willamette/recreation

Finding the campground: From Detroit, go 2.9 miles east on Oregon 22 and turn right (south) on Blowout Road/Forest Road 10, continuing 3.5 miles to enter the camp on the right.

About the campground: On the south shore of Detroit Lake, this large, comfortable campground offers great access to the reservoir's full lineup of fun: fishing, boating, swimming, sailing, waterskiing, and just relaxing beside the glistening water. The camp claims a gentle, evergreen-clad slope and offers paved roads and parking and running water amenities. For hiking, the Stahlman Point Lookout Trail begins off Blowout Road, 0.1 mile south of the campground turnoff.

11 Detroit Lake State Recreation Area

Location: 2 miles southwest of Detroit, on Detroit Lake

Season: March–early November

Sites: 178 full and partial hookup sites, 133 basic sites; water, electric, and sewer hookups

Maximum length: 60 feet

Facilities: Tables, grills, flush toilets, drinking water, showers, telephone, boat moorage, launch, dock, swimming beach, store

Fee per night: $$–$$$

Management: Oregon State Parks and Recreation Department

Contact: (503) 854–3346; (800) 452–5687 for reservations; www.oregonstate parks.org

Finding the campground: On Oregon 22, reach this campground on the north shore of Detroit Lake, 2 miles west of Detroit and 50 miles east of Salem.
About the campground: At this large, developed campground, welcoming fir-forested sites provide a base for recreation at Detroit Lake, a huge reservoir within the North Santiam River Canyon. Some sites overlook the water. Lake recreation includes everything from fishing to waterskiing, making the lake and the state park popular summer destinations.

12 Hoover

Location: About 4 miles southeast of Detroit, on Detroit Lake
Season: Mid-April–late September
Sites: 37 basic sites; no hookups
Maximum length: 40 feet
Facilities: Tables, grills, flush toilets, drinking water, boat launch, barrier-free trail, wheelchair-accessible fishing platforms and 200-foot-long pier
Fee per night: $$–$$$
Management: Willamette National Forest
Contact: (503) 854–3366; www.fs.fed.us/r6/willamette/recreation
Finding the campground: From Detroit, go east on Oregon 22 for 2.8 miles, turn right on Blowout Road/Forest Road 10, and go another 0.8 mile to find the camp entrance on the right.
About the campground: On the North Santiam River arm of Detroit Lake, a rich Douglas fir forest shades this campground, while the explosion of under-story greenery tantalizes the eye. Campsites are well spaced for privacy and comfort, but the water sports are likely to keep you away from camp. Fishing, boating, swimming, and waterskiing vie for your time. The 0.3-mile Hoover Nature Trail loops through the forest. The lower leg of the loop is wheelchair-accessible and leads to fishing platforms.

13 Humbug

Location: About 4 miles northeast of Detroit
Season: Maintained mid-May–late September
Sites: 22 basic sites; no hookups
Maximum length: 30 feet
Facilities: Tables, grills, vault toilets, drinking water
Fee per night: $$
Management: Willamette National Forest
Contact: (503) 854–3366; www.fs.fed.us/r6/willamette/recreation
Finding the campground: From Oregon 22 at the west end of Detroit, turn north on Forest Road 46 and go 4.4 miles to enter the campground on the right.
About the campground: At this Breitenbush River campground, you will find fairly spacious sites in a semi-open conifer forest rimmed by old-growth trees. The Humbug Flat Trail leaves the camp near site 9, passing above the river through bountiful rhododendrons and varied forest. Steep angler paths plunge toward fishing holes. The river flows clear and riffling over rounded

cobbles. Anglers can also try fishing from the dam, the shore, or a boat on Detroit Lake, a short drive to the south.

14   Santiam Flats

Location: About 3 miles east of Detroit, on Detroit Lake
Season: Maintained mid-April–late September
Sites: Anywhere from 20 to 100 basic sites; no hookups
Maximum length: 40 feet
Facilities: Some tables, chemical toilets, primitive boat launch; no drinking
water
Fee per night: $
Management: Willamette National Forest
Contact: (503) 854–3366; www.fs.fed.us/r6/willamette/recreation
Finding the campground: From Oregon 22, 2.5 miles east of Detroit, turn
south into this campground on the lake.
About the campground: This austere campground grew up around a flat
that had long been used by the public for camping and accessing Detroit Lake.
The sites still remain random, and the camp is best suited for self-contained
RVs. Santiam Flats can comfortably accommodate 30 to 40 units, but on holi-
day weekends the number often swells into the 100s. A few firs and shrubs remain, along with some shoreline willows. Despite the rough, potholed dirt
access, the campers keep coming. Their goal: to fish and boat Detroit Lake.

15   Southshore

Location: About 7 miles south of Detroit, on Detroit Lake
Season: Maintained mid-April–late September
Sites: 22 basic sites, 8 walk-in tent sites; no hookups
Maximum length: 30 feet
Facilities: Tables, grills, vault toilets, drinking water, boat launch, dock
Fee per night: $ $
Management: Willamette National Forest
Contact: (503) 854–3366; www.fs.fed.us/r6/willamette/recreation
Finding the campground: From Detroit, go 2.9 miles east on Oregon 22 and
turn right (south) on Blowout Road/Forest Road 10. Continue 4.2 miles to enter
this camp on the right.
About the campground: On the south shore of Detroit Lake—a huge reservoir
open to recreation—this campground occupies a shady mixed conifer forest. Together with its lush understory, the forest setting is almost as recommending as
the lake. All campsites have paved parking, though some sites are not as level as
others. Swimming, fishing, boating, waterskiing, and sailing keep lake-goers
happy. For hiking, the Stahlman Point Lookout Trail is not far from camp.

16 Upper Arm Recreation Area

Location: About 1 mile north of Detroit
Season: Year-round
Sites: 5 basic sites; no hookups
Maximum length: 20 feet
Facilities: Tables, pit or chemical toilets; no drinking water
Fee per night: None
Management: Willamette National Forest
Contact: (503) 854–3366; www.fs.fed.us/r6/willamette/recreation
Finding the campground: From Oregon 22 at the west side of Detroit, turn north on Forest Road 46 and go 0.9 mile to find this camp on the left.
About the campground: This compact, primitive camp sits on a forested flat above the Upper Breitenbush River arm of Detroit Lake. Vine maples and rhododendrons decorate the evergreen forest. Fires are prohibited, but campers may use their personal charcoal barbecues. A steep descent leads to the water, but this part of the reservoir recedes as summer wears on. Fishing, boating, and swimming are popular Detroit Lake pursuits.

Marion Forks Area

17   Big Lake and Big Lake West

Location: About 26 miles southeast of Marion Forks, on Big Lake
Season: May–October
Sites: 49 basic sites, 11 walk-in tent sites; no hookups
Maximum length: 35 feet
Facilities: Tables, grills, vault and flush toilets, drinking water, boat ramp
Fee per night: $$
Management: Willamette National Forest
Contact: (541) 822–3381; (877) 444–6777 for reservations; www.fs.fed.us/r6/willamette/recreation
Finding the campground: From U.S. Highway 20 at Santiam Pass, about 22 miles southeast of Marion Forks, turn south on Big Lake Road/Forest Road 2690 and go about 4 miles to these campgrounds.
About the campgrounds: The primary campground occupies the north shore of Big Lake, while the walk-in tent sites line the west shore. Big Lake is an aptly named natural lake below Hayrick and Hoodoo Buttes. Mount Washington adds to skyline views. Sites are nestled in a high-elevation forest of firs, hemlocks, and lodgepole pines. A few snags on the west shore have been carved with totems. The lake offers fishing, swimming, boating, and water-skiing, as well as canoeing along the scalloped shoreline. Area trails visit Patjens Lakes and Mount Washington Wilderness Area.

18   Big Meadows Horse Camp

Location: About 10 miles south of Marion Forks
Season: June–October
Sites: 9 basic sites; no hookups
Maximum length: 36 feet
Facilities: Tables, grills, vault toilets, drinking water, corrals, hitching posts, loading ramps, and spring-fed trough for stock watering

Marion Forks Area

	Hookup sites	Total sites	Maximum RV length	Hookups	Toilets	Showers	Drinking water	Dump station	Recreation	Fee	Can reserve
17 Big Lake and Big Lake West		60	35		F,NF		•		HFBL	$$	•
18 Big Meadows Horse Camp		9	36		NF		•		HR	$	
19 Marion Forks		15	24		NF		•		HF	$	
20 Riverside		37	24		NF		•		F	$	
21 Whispering Falls		16	30		F		•		F	$$	

Fee per night: $
Management: Willamette National Forest
Contact: (503) 854–3366; www.fs.fed.us/r6/willamette/recreation
Finding the campground: From Oregon 22, 27 miles east of Detroit and 5.6 miles west of Santiam Junction (the junction of OR 22 and U.S. Highway 20), turn north on Forest Road 2267. Go 0.9 mile and turn left on FR 2257 to enter the campground on the left in 0.5 mile.
About the campground: Established for equestrians, this campground rests in a welcoming forest of mixed firs, spruce, and mountain hemlock. Pole fencing defines the campground roadways and site turnouts. Each site is paired with a four-stall corral. Deer sometimes visit the vacant stalls, seeking out hay. Horse trails leave from camp. If you plan to enter Mount Jefferson Wilderness Area, be sure to obtain a wilderness permit. Huckleberry picking is a seasonal diversion.

19 Marion Forks

Location: In Marion Forks
Season: Maintained late May–late October
Sites: 15 basic sites; no hookups
Maximum length: 24 feet
Facilities: Tables, grills, vault toilets, drinking water
Fee per night: $
Management: Willamette National Forest
Contact: (541) 854–3366; www.fs.fed.us/r6/willamette/recreation
Finding the campground: The camp sits northeast off Oregon 22 at Marion Forks, 16 miles southeast of Detroit. A sign for the hatchery and forest camp marks the turn.
About the campground: Neighboring the Marion Forks Fish Hatchery, this quiet campground lines the south shore of sparkling Marion Creek. The sites have a rustic charm and are nicely shaded. The creek is not one for fishing, but you can cool your ankles here. Area trails lead to Independence Rock, Marion Lake, and the backcountry lakes and wilds of Mount Jefferson Wilderness Area.

20 Riverside

Location: About 3 miles north of Marion Forks
Season: Maintained late May–late September
Sites: 37 basic sites; no hookups
Maximum length: 24 feet
Facilities: Tables, grills, vault toilets, drinking water
Fee per night: $
Management: Willamette National Forest
Contact: (503) 854–3366; www.fs.fed.us/r6/willamette/recreation
Finding the campground: It is west off Oregon 22, 13.5 miles southeast of Detroit.

About the campground: In a full, multistory forest, this campground stretches along the shore of the North Santiam River. In spring, rhododendron and dogwood blooms dress up the midstory. Sparkling, clear, and green, the river courses over bedrock and seduces anglers. Some sites overlook the river; all sites have surfaced parking.

21 Whispering Falls

Location: About 8 miles northwest of Marion Forks
Season: Mid-April–September
Sites: 16 basic sites; no hookups
Maximum length: 30 feet
Facilities: Tables, grills, flush toilets, drinking water
Fee per night: $$
Management: Willamette National Forest
Contact: (503) 854-3366; www.fs.fed.us/r6/willamette/recreation
Finding the campground: It is west off Oregon 22, 8 miles southeast of Detroit.
About the campground: This forest campground offers a picturesque stay on the North Santiam River. It takes its name from the gentle-voiced tributary waterfall across the river from camp. A full forest and lush understory contribute to the beauty and privacy of the campsites. An abrupt bank separates much of the camp from the river, but the River Trail leads to a shoreline access for fishing and river admiring.

Corvallis Area

22 Alsea Falls Recreation Site

Location: About 29 miles southwest of Corvallis
Season: Mid-May–September
Sites: 16 basic sites; no hookups
Maximum length: 30 feet
Facilities: Tables, grills, vault toilets, drinking water
Fee per night: $$
Management: Salem District Bureau of Land Management
Contact: (503) 375-5646; www.or.blm.gov/salem
Finding the campground: From Corvallis, go 16 miles south on Oregon 99W and turn right (west) at the sign for Alpine and Alsea Falls. Drive 12.9 miles, passing through the town of Alpine, to reach the campground. The road is paved and graveled and follows part of the Alsea Falls National Back Country Byway.
About the campground: Mossy old stumps and moist pockets of skunk cabbage accent the forest of tall firs and alders that envelops this camp on the South Fork Alsea River. Sites are spacious and relaxing. From the bridge at camp, a trail heads down river a half mile to Alsea Falls. By extending the hike another mile, hikers can view Green Peak Falls: Continue downstream to McBee Park (a rustic campground), then hike upstream along Peak Creek to this unexpected waterfall. Green Peak Falls is 50 feet tall and twice as wide.

23 Benton Oaks RV Park and Campground

Location: In Corvallis
Season: Year-round
Sites: 28 hookup sites; open tent camping; water, electric, sewer, and cable hookups
Maximum length: 60 feet

Corvallis Area

	Hookup sites	Total sites	Maximum RV length	Hookups	Toilets	Showers	Drinking water	Dump station	Recreation	Fee	Can reserve
22 Alsea Falls Recreation Site		16	30		NF		•		HSF	$$	
23 Benton Oaks RV Park and Campground	28	28	60	WESC	F	•	•	•	HC	$$$	
24 Marys Peak		6	T		NF		•		H	$$	
25 Salmonberry County Park		20	40		F	•	•		FBL	$$	
26 Willamette Park		15	30		F		•		HSF	$	

Facilities: Flush toilets, drinking water, showers, dump station, laundry, telephone

Fee per night: $$$

Management: Benton County

Contact: (541) 766–6259; www.bentonoaks.com

Finding the campground: From U.S. Highway 20 at the west end of Corvallis, go north on Fifty-third Street for 1 mile to reach the fairgrounds on the left.

About the campground: This camping area at the fairgrounds exists primarily to serve fair participants during events, but it also provides travelers with a convenient base for exploring the Corvallis area. Among the attractions are the Willamette River, the valley u-pick farms, the William L. Finley National Wildlife Refuge, Oregon State University, and Peavy Arboretum. Sites have paved parking, some pull-through. Oaks nudge to the campground, and a neighboring farm opens views to the coastal hills.

24 Marys Peak

Location: About 25 miles southwest of Corvallis

Season: April–November, unless snow necessitates road closure

Sites: 6 tent sites; no hookups

Maximum length: Suitable for tents only

Facilities: Tables, grills, vault toilets, drinking water

Fee per night: $$

Management: Siuslaw National Forest

Contact: (541) 563–3211; www.fs.fed.us/r6/siuslaw/recreation

Finding the campground: From Oregon 34, 10 miles west of Philomath, turn north onto Marys Peak Road and proceed 9 miles to the campground entrance on the right.

About the campground: Just below the summit of Marys Peak, this tiny camp along Parker Creek occupies a semi-open stand of small noble firs. The Meadows Edge Trail skirts the campground to explore the fuller noble fir forest and open meadow of the upper mountain reaches. Other trails travel the east and north flanks of Marys Peak, which is the highest peak in the Coast Range. The mountain is noted for wildflowers, winter snowplay, and its views that stretch from the Pacific Ocean to the Cascades. The popular destination is still wild enough for deer and bobcat to be seen.

25 Salmonberry County Park

Location: About 30 miles southwest of Corvallis

Season: Mid-May–mid-October

Sites: 13 basic sites, 7 tent sites; no hookups

Maximum length: 40 feet

Facilities: Tables, grills, flush toilets, drinking water, showers, drift/car-top boat launch, barrier-free trail

Fee per night: $$

The Willamette Valley is noted for its fine grapes.

Management: Benton County
Contact: (541) 766–6871
Finding the campground: From Oregon 34, 6.4 miles west of Alsea and 32 miles east of Waldport, turn south on Salmonberry Road and go 0.3 mile to enter the park on the left.
About the campground: On an attractive flat above the quiet-flowing Alsea River, this campground has sites with gravel pads edging a large, central lawn. Alders shape the camp perimeter. Each site has been constructed to serve wheelchair users, with easy access to tables and grills. A 700-foot cinder-grade gravel trail provides a barrier-free access from the camp to the river. Fishing and drift boating are popular pursuits. This camp conveniently serves travelers passing between the Willamette Valley and the coast.

26 Willamette Park

Location: In Corvallis
Season: April–mid-November
Sites: 15 basic sites; no hookups
Maximum length: 30 feet
Facilities: Tables, fire rings, flush toilets, drinking water
Fee per night: $
Management: City of Corvallis
Contact: (541) 766–6918
Finding the campground: From Oregon 99W at the south end of Corvallis, turn east on Goodnight Avenue and follow the paved and graveled road 0.6 mile to the campground entrance on the left.
About the campground: This campground appeals to both the lazy and the active. It sits on a rise above the river day-use area of Willamette City Park, with its complement of fields, playgrounds, picnic areas, exercise trails, and natural valley woods. The campsites rim a broad, grassy flat with an evergreen edge, allowing campers to choose between sun or partial shade. The Willamette River flows broad, swift, and smooth. Blackberry brambles may entice you to risk the thorns for a tasty nibble.

Lebanon–Sweet Home Area

27 Cascadia State Park

Location: 14 miles east of Sweet Home
Season: March–October
Sites: 25 basic sites; no hookups
Maximum length: 35 feet
Facilities: Tables, grills, flush toilets, drinking water, horseshoe pits, sports field
Fee per night: $$
Management: Oregon State Parks and Recreation Department
Contact: (541) 854–3406; www.oregonstateparks.org
Finding the campground: It sits north off U.S. Highway 20, 14 miles east of Sweet Home.
About the campground: In the South Santiam River Valley, you will find this pleasant camp with paved roads and parking, ample lawn, and shade trees. Although the sites are fairly close together, they enjoy a natural habitat. Trout fishing on the river and hiking the 0.75-mile trail to Soda Creek Falls top the list of things to do. Foster Reservoir lies west of camp for boating and fishing; Menagerie Wilderness is east of the park for more serious hiking.

Lebanon–Sweet Home Area

	Hookup sites	Total sites	Maximum RV length	Hookups	Toilets	Showers	Drinking water	Dump station	Recreation	Fee	Can reserve
27 Cascadia State Park		25	35		F		•		HSF	$$	
28 Fernview		11	22		NF		•		HSF	$$	
29 Gill's Landing	21	22	60	WESCI	F	•	•	•	FBL	$$$	
30 House Rock		17	22		NF		•		HSF	$	
31 Lost Prairie		10	24		NF		•		H	$$	
32 Pioneer Park		10	35		NF		•			$$	
33 River Bend County Park	35	45	60	WE	F	•	•	•	SFB	$$	•
34 Sunnyside County Park	130	165	40	WE	F	•	•	•	SFBL	$$	•
35 Trout Creek		24	32		NF		•		HSF	$$	
36 Waterloo County Park	100	120	40	WE	F	•	•	•	SFBL	$$	•
37 Whitcomb Creek County Park		39	30		NF		•		SFBL	$$	
38 Yellowbottom		20	20		NF		•		HSF	$	
39 Yukwah		20	32		NF		•		HSF	$–$$	

28 Fernview

Location: 24 miles east of Sweet Home
Season: May–September
Sites: 11 basic sites; no hookups
Maximum length: 22 feet
Facilities: Tables, grills, vault toilets, drinking water
Fee per night: $$
Management: Willamette National Forest
Contact: (541) 367-5168; www.fs.fed.us/r6/willamette/recreation
Finding the campground: From Sweet Home, drive 24 miles east on U.S. Highway 20 and turn south into the campground.
About the campground: This campground on the south bank of the South Santiam River oozes with tranquility. A rich vine maple midstory creates an attractive canopy over the individual sites; towering hemlocks and firs deepen the shade. The South Santiam River consists of rushing stretches, deep pools for swimming or fishing, gravel bars, and outcrops. The campground is within easy reach of hiking trails to Rooster Rock (in the Menagerie Wilderness), House Rock, Iron Mountain, and the Old Santiam Wagon Road.

29 Gill's Landing

Location: In Lebanon
Season: Year-round
Sites: 21 hookup sites, 1 group tent site; water, electric, sewer, cable, and Internet hookups
Maximum length: 60 feet
Facilities: Tables, grills, flush toilets, drinking water, showers, dump station, boat launch, dock, swimming area, and playground; horseshoe pits, and ballfield at neighboring River Park
Fee per night: $$$
Management: City of Lebanon
Contact: (541) 451-7442
Finding the campground: From Main Street in the center of Lebanon, go east on Grant Street for 0.7 mile to reach this park.
About the campground: Opened in 2005, this relaxing park offers a pleasant stay beside the South Fork Santiam River. The full-service camp has developed parking spaces in a wooded setting. Grassy areas also welcome repose. Trails lead from the camp to the river for fishing access; the river boasts excellent trout, salmon, and steelhead fishing. Sand is brought in annually for the swimming area.

30 House Rock

Location: About 28 miles east of Sweet Home
Season: May–September
Sites: 17 basic sites; no hookups
Maximum length: 22 feet

Facilities: Tables, grills, vault toilets, drinking water
Fee per night: $
Management: Willamette National Forest
Contact: (541) 367–5168; www.fs.fed.us/r6/willamette/recreation
Finding the campground: From Sweet Home, drive 27 miles east on U.S. Highway 20 and turn south onto gravel Squaw Creek Road. Proceed about 1 mile to the campground.
About the campground: Bigleaf maples, alders, cedar, firs, and hemlocks weave a rich canopy of shade for this campground at the confluence of Squaw and Sheep Creeks. Because the sites lack long parking pads or pull-throughs, camping here is better suited to tents or small rigs. Fishing and area trails may coax guests away from the comfort of camp. House Rock, Old Santiam Wagon Road, Iron Mountain, and Rooster Rock are possible hikes in the area.

31 Lost Prairie

Location: 40 miles east of Sweet Home
Season: Late May–September
Sites: 4 basic sites, 6 walk-in tent sites; no hookups
Maximum length: 24 feet
Facilities: Tables, grills, vault toilets, drinking water
Fee per night: $$
Management: Willamette National Forest
Contact: (541) 367–5168; www.fs.fed.us/r6/willamette/recreation
Finding the campground: This campground sits south off U.S. Highway 20, 40 miles east of Sweet Home and 4.2 miles west of the junction of US 20 and Oregon 126.
About the campground: This campground enjoys a meadow and forest setting along Hackleman Creek. The walk-in sites are set back among the firs and spruce, just strides from the paved parking area. Wildflowers sprinkle the meadow. Just west of camp is the Hackleman Trail Old Growth Grove.

32 Pioneer Park

Location: In Brownsville
Season: Mid-April–mid-October
Sites: 4 basic sites, 6 walk-in tent sites; no hookups
Maximum length: 35 feet
Facilities: Tables, fire rings, chemical toilets (flush toilets in day-use area), drinking water, ballfields, horseshoe pits, dining pavilion, amphitheater
Fee per night: $$
Management: City of Brownsville
Contact: (541) 466–5666; www.ci.brownsville.or.us/park
Finding the campground: From the junction of Main Street and Park Avenue in Brownsville, go 0.1 mile west on Park Avenue to the campground.
About the campground: This rather informal camp sits at one end of the park in a grove of mature bigleaf maples. The park occupies a bend in the

Calapooya River and offers river access. Campers also have access to historic Brownsville, with its lovely old homes, museums, and antiques shops.

33 River Bend County Park

Location: About 9 miles east of Sweet Home
Season: April–November
Sites: 35 hookup sites, 10 basic sites; water and electric hookups
Maximum length: 60 feet
Facilities: Tables, grills, flush toilets, drinking water, showers, dump station, picnic shelter, softball field
Fee per night: $$
Management: Linn County
Contact: (541) 967–3917, reservations accepted; www.co.linn.or.us/parks
Finding the campground: From the junction of U.S. Highway 20 and Oregon 228 in Sweet Home, head east on US 20 for about 9 miles. The campground is north side of US 20 about 3 miles east of the Quartzville Road turnoff.
About the campground: Nestled in a bend on the South Santiam River, this camp, which opened in 2005, offers a relaxing and attractive stay in a woodsy setting. Sites are well spaced for privacy and have long, developed parking spurs. Plans call for the park campground to double in size in the next few years. Fishing and floating the river bend are popular entertainments. People can put in with their rafts or inner tubes at the upper end of the camp and take out at the lower end.

34 Sunnyside County Park

Location: About 7 miles northeast of Sweet Home
Season: April–November
Sites: 130 hookup sites, 35 basic sites; water and electric hookups
Maximum length: 40 feet
Facilities: Tables, grills, flush toilets, drinking water, showers, dump station, telephone, playground, boat dock, launch, moorage, fish-cleaning station, horseshoe pits, volleyball
Fee per night: $$
Management: Linn County
Contact: (541) 967–3917, reservations accepted; www.co.linn.or.us/parks
Finding the campground: From Sweet Home, go 5.5 miles east on U.S. Highway 20 and turn north on Quartzville Road, a BLM Back Country Byway, heading toward Green Peter Reservoir. Go 1.4 miles to enter the county park on the right.
About the campground: This tidy, attractive campground occupies a vast, trimmed lawn with cottonwoods and some planted pines and maples for pockets of shade. It sits between a forested ridge and Foster Reservoir and near a pair of big ponds with stark shores. The camp has paved roads and parking

pads and, despite its size, rolls out a fine welcome mat for your stay. Foster and Green Peter Reservoirs invite lake recreation. Blackberries bushes bordering Quartzville Road invite berry pickers to stain their fingers and perhaps collect enough for a pie.

35 Trout Creek

Location: 21 miles east of Sweet Home
Season: May–October
Sites: 24 basic sites; no hookups
Maximum length: 32 feet
Facilities: Tables, grills, vault toilets, drinking water
Fee per night: $$
Management: Willamette National Forest
Contact: (541) 367–5168; www.fs.fed.us/r6/willamette/recreation
Finding the campground: It is south off U.S. Highway 20, 21 miles east of Sweet Home.
About the campground: This South Santiam River campground offers swimming, fishing, and a pleasant stay in a natural woodland setting, but there is some road noise. Some of the sites overlook the river, while others offer great privacy. The multistory forest with its many dogwoods is especially appealing early in the camping season. Area trails enter Menagerie Wilderness or explore along Falls Creek to Soapgrass Mountain and Gordon Lakes. From the Trout Creek Trailhead, across the road from camp, a short spur leads to an elk viewing platform, while the main trail journeys into the wilderness to Rooster Rock.

36 Waterloo County Park

Location: About 9 miles northwest of Sweet Home
Season: Year-round
Sites: 100 hookup sites, 20 basic sites; water and electric hookups
Maximum length: 40 feet
Facilities: Tables, grills, flush toilets, drinking water, showers, dump station, playground, beach area, boat launch, shelter
Fee per night: $$
Management: Linn County
Contact: (541) 967–3917, reservations accepted; www.co.linn.or.us/parks
Finding the campground: From the junction of U.S. Highway 20 and Oregon 228 in Sweet Home, follow US 20 west for 8.4 miles and turn right (north) on Waterloo Drive at the sign for the park. Go 1 mile, passing through the community of Waterloo, and turn right into the park. The campground is at the end of the park road.
About the campground: This extensive riverside campground fronts the broad and glassy South Santiam River and enjoys a relaxing valley location. Sweeping lawns, shade-providing oaks and maples, and browsing deer lend to the idyllic scene. Cottonwoods grow along the river. The park offers room to

roam, but beware of poison oak. The river is open to boating, swimming, and fishing. Blackberry brambles hold tasty summer bites, if you can navigate the thorns.

37 Whitcomb Creek County Park

Location: About 17 miles northeast of Sweet Home, on Green Peter Reservoir
Season: Mid-April–Labor Day
Sites: 39 basic sites; no hookups
Maximum length: 30 feet
Facilities: Tables, grills, vault toilets, drinking water, boat dock, launch
Fee per night: $$
Management: Linn County
Contact: (541) 967-3917
Finding the campground: From Sweet Home, go 5.5 miles east on U.S. Highway 20 and turn north on Quartzville Road, a BLM Back Country Byway, heading toward Green Peter Reservoir. Go 11.1 miles and turn right into the county park. Go 0.6 mile more to enter the campground on the right; the boat ramp and picnic area are straight ahead.
About the campground: You will find this campground on the Whitcomb Creek Arm of Green Peter Reservoir, a popular place for speed boating, fishing, and swimming. In this terraced park, the spacious sites enjoy a deep forest shade; some sites are more level than others. Should the campground fill, owners of self-contained units can take advantage of dispersed camping along the widened road shoulder of the reservoir outside the park.

38 Yellowbottom

Location: About 29 miles northeast of Sweet Home
Season: Late May–mid-September
Sites: 20 basic sites; no hookups
Maximum length: 20 feet
Facilities: Tables, grills, vault toilets, drinking water
Fee per night: $
Management: Salem District Bureau of Land Management
Contact: (503) 375-5646; www.or.blm.gov/salem
Finding the campground: From Sweet Home, go 5.5 miles east on U.S. Highway 20 and turn north on Quartzville Road, a BLM Back Country Byway, heading toward Green Peter Reservoir. Go 23.7 miles and turn left into the campground.
About the campground: Set in a stand of magnificent old-growth trees interwoven with vine maples, rhododendrons, cascaras, and yews is this highly attractive campground. Across the road are a picnic area and an access trail to

Quartzville Creek, a wild and scenic waterway that engages with boulders, gravel bars, and gorgeous swimming holes. Sunbathing, swimming, fishing, and recreational gold panning are popular pursuits. At camp, Rhododendron Flat Loop offers a 1.2-mile hike.

39 Yukwah

Location: About 22 miles east of Sweet Home
Season: May–October
Sites: 20 basic sites; no hookups
Maximum length: 32 feet
Facilities: Tables, grills, vault toilets, drinking water, fishing platform
Fee per night: $–$$
Management: Willamette National Forest
Contact: (541) 367-5168; www.fs.fed.us/r6/willamette/recreation
Finding the campground: It is south off U.S. Highway 20, 21.5 miles east of Sweet Home.
About the campground: This neighbor to Trout Creek Campground (see campground 35) offers a similar stay on the South Santiam River, with perhaps a few stouter firs in camp. The forested sites radiate from the campground loop road, an arrangement that allows for plenty of privacy. A 0.25-mile trail provides river access.

Blue River–McKenzie Bridge Area

40 Alder Springs

Location: About 15 miles east of the community of McKenzie Bridge
Season: Late May–September
Sites: 6 tent sites; no hookups
Maximum length: Suitable for tents only
Facilities: Tables, grills, pit toilets; no drinking water
Fee per night: None
Management: Willamette National Forest
Contact: (541) 822-3381; www.fs.fed.us/r6/willamette/recreation
Finding the campground: From McKenzie Bridge, go 4.6 miles east on Oregon 126 and turn right (east) on OR 242 to find this campground on the left in 10.4 miles.

Blue River–McKenzie Bridge Area

	Hookup sites	Total sites	Maximum RV length	Hookups	Toilets	Showers	Drinking water	Dump station	Recreation	Fee	Can reserve
40 Alder Springs		6	T		NF				H		
41 Box Canyon Horse Camp		11	30		NF				HR		
42 Coldwater Cove		35	30		NF		•		HFBL	$$	•
43 Cougar Crossing		12	25		NF				HSFB	$$	
44 Delta		38	36		NF		•		HSFB	$$	
45 Fish Lake		7	30		NF		•		H	$	
46 French Pete		17	30		NF		•		HSF	$$	
47 Frissell Crossing		12	36		NF		•		HF	$$	
48 Homestead		7	25		NF				F		
49 Ice Cap		22	22		F		•		HFB	$$	
50 Limberlost		12	25		NF				F	$	
51 McKenzie Bridge		20	35		NF		•		FBL	$$	•
52 Mona		23	36		F		•		SFBL	$$	
53 Olallie		17	35		NF		•		HFBL	$$	•
54 Paradise		64	40		F		•		HFBL	$$	•
55 Slide Creek		16	25		NF		•		SFBL	$$	
56 Sunnyside		13	T		NF				SFB	$$	
57 Trail Bridge		26	45		F,NF		•		HFBL	$	

About the campground: On McKenzie Pass Scenic Byway, you will find this tiny camp in the firs opposite the trailhead to Linton Lake. Other trails in the area visit Proxy Falls and Scott Mountain. The byway, which passes between Three Sisters and Mount Washington Wilderness Areas, is a photographer's wonderland composed of striking images of lava, forest, lakes, and volcanoes. Dee Wright Observatory, a medieval-looking outpost atop a lava flow at McKenzie Pass, supplies a unique perspective on the neighborhood and is itself a photo subject.

41 Box Canyon Horse Camp

Location: About 30 miles southeast of the community of Blue River
Season: April–November, depending on snow
Sites: 11 basic sites; no hookups
Maximum length: 30 feet
Facilities: Tables, grills, vault toilets, corrals; no drinking water
Fee per night: None
Management: Willamette National Forest
Contact: (541) 822-3381; www.fs.fed.us/r6/willamette/recreation
Finding the campground: From the Blue River Junction on Oregon 126, drive east on OR 126 about 5 miles and turn south on Forest Road 19 (Aufderheide Forest Drive), heading toward Cougar Reservoir. In 0.2 mile, turn right to remain on FR 19. The camp is west off FR 19 in another 25.4 miles.
About the campground: This peaceful camp at the forested foot of Chucksney Mountain provides a pleasant overnight base for equestrians. Tall firs, rhododendrons, and ferns dress up the camp. Across the road is a historic guard station and an attractive meadow swath; interpretive panels along FR 19 introduce the area history. Trails from camp travel to Chucksney Mountain and into the Three Sisters Wilderness Area.

42 Coldwater Cove

Location: 18 miles northeast of the community of McKenzie Bridge, on Clear Lake
Season: Late May–mid-October
Sites: 35 basic sites; no hookups
Maximum length: 30 feet
Facilities: Tables, grills, vault toilets, drinking water, boat launch (nonmotorized boating)
Fee per night: $$
Management: Willamette National Forest
Contact: (541) 822-3381; (877) 444-6777 for reservations; www.fs.fed.us/r6/willamette/recreation
Finding the campground: From Oregon 126, 18 miles northeast of McKenzie Bridge, turn east at the sign for camp.
About the campground: This camp occupies the forested shore at the southeast corner of Clear Lake, a frigid, spring-fed natural lake at the head of

McKenzie Wild and Scenic River. A lava flow dotted by vine maples abuts the fir-shaded camp. Because of the sloping shore, some sites are more level than others. Ringing the lake, a superb trail visits Great Spring (source of the icy water), forest and flow, and rustic Clear Lake Resort, where rowboats may be rented. Another exceptional trail explores downstream along the exciting river, passing Sahalie and Koosah Falls, both of which have drive-to viewing areas. Fishing, rowing the length of the lake, and watching ospreys dive for fish are popular pastimes.

43 Cougar Crossing

Location: About 14 miles southeast of the community of Blue River, on Cougar Reservoir
Season: Year-round
Sites: 12 basic sites; no hookups
Maximum length: 25 feet
Facilities: Tables, grills, vault or chemical toilets; no drinking water
Fee per night: $$
Management: Willamette National Forest
Contact: (541) 822-3381; www.fs.fed.us/r6/willamette/recreation
Finding the campground: From the Blue River Junction on Oregon 126, drive east on OR 126 about 5 miles and turn south on Forest Road 19 (Aufderheide Forest Drive), heading toward Cougar Reservoir. In 0.2 mile, turn right to remain on FR 19. The camp is on the right in 9.3 miles, just after you cross the reservoir bridge.
About the campground: This small camp, which sits near the reservoir bridge and an information kiosk on Aufderheide Forest Drive, offers camping at the head of Cougar Reservoir. The sites have graveled parking and are open or partially shaded in a leafy setting dispersed with a few firs. Early in the year, the camp is actually on the reservoir. But as the lake water recedes in summer, the camp overlooks the stark reservoir basin and the South Fork McKenzie River. Reservoir recreation—boating, fishing, swimming, and waterskiing—as well as Terwilliger Hot Springs, a fee area 2.2 miles north of the camp on FR 19, fill out campers' itineraries.

44 Delta

Location: About 5 miles east of the community of Blue River
Season: Early May–late October
Sites: 38 basic sites; no hookups
Maximum length: 36 feet
Facilities: Tables, grills, vault toilets, drinking water
Fee per night: $$
Management: Willamette National Forest
Contact: (541) 822-3381; www.fs.fed.us/r6/willamette/recreation
Finding the campground: From the Blue River Junction on Oregon 126, drive east on OR 126 about 5 miles and turn south on Forest Road 19 (Aufder-

heide Forest Drive), heading toward Cougar Reservoir. Go 0.2 mile and turn right to reach the campground in another 0.9 mile.

About the campground: This quiet, old-growth forested campground occupies a delta formed by the main stem and the south fork of the McKenzie River. Firs, cedars, and hemlocks tower over camp, while enormous stumps, logs, dogwoods, and ferns add to the enchantment. The sites are spacious and well spaced. The barrier-free Delta Nature Trail begins at the end of the campground loop. Fishing, rafting on the McKenzie River, sightseeing along Aufderheide Scenic Drive, and boating on Cougar Reservoir are other diversions.

45 Fish Lake

Location: About 22 miles northeast of the community of McKenzie Bridge
Season: Late May–late September
Sites: 7 basic sites; no hookups
Maximum length: 30 feet
Facilities: Tables, grills, vault toilets, drinking water
Fee per night: $
Management: Willamette National Forest
Contact: (541) 822–3381; www.fs.fed.us/r6/willamette/recreation
Finding the campground: From the intersection of Oregon 22 and U.S. Highway 20/OR 126 (31.6 miles east of Detroit; 26 miles west of Sisters), go west on US 20/OR 126 and in 3.3 miles proceed left on OR 126 for Clear Lake. The campground is on the right in another 1.5 miles.
About the campground: Situated at the edge of seasonal Fish Lake and a lava flow, this campground is shaded by big cottonwoods and firs. As the summer sun dries up the lake, bald eagles feast on fish trapped in the small pools. By summer's end an expansive, grassy meadow has replaced the lake. The McKenzie River National Recreation Trail begins nearby, and Clear Lake, the McKenzie River, and Carmen Reservoir allow anglers to wet their fishing lines.

46 French Pete

Location: About 15 miles southeast of the community of Blue River
Season: Mid-May–mid-September
Sites: 17 basic sites; no hookups
Maximum length: 30 feet
Facilities: Tables, grills, vault toilets, drinking water
Fee per night: $$
Management: Willamette National Forest
Contact: (541) 822–3381; www.fs.fed.us/r6/willamette/recreation
Finding the campground: From the Blue River Junction on Oregon 126, drive east on OR 126 about 5 miles and turn south on Forest Road 19 (Aufderheide Forest Drive), heading toward Cougar Reservoir. In 0.2 mile, turn right to remain on FR 19. The camp is on the right in another 10.6 miles.
About the campground: In an old-growth setting along the South Fork McKenzie River, this linear campground is a gateway to the popular French Pete Trail. This canyon trail wins over hikers with its prized old growth and

sparkling creek. Engaging pools suggest a summer cool off. Other area trails explore peaks and drainages. You may also fish, recreate on Cougar Reservoir downstream from camp, and soak in Terwilliger Hot Springs, a fee area 3.5 miles to the north.

47 Frissell Crossing

Location: About 26 miles southeast of the community of Blue River
Season: Mid-May–mid-September
Sites: 12 basic sites; no hookups
Maximum length: 36 feet
Facilities: Tables, grills, vault toilets, drinking water
Fee per night: $$
Management: Willamette National Forest
Contact: (541) 822–3381; www.fs.fed.us/r6/willamette/recreation
Finding the campground: From the Blue River Junction on Oregon 126, drive east on OR 126 about 5 miles and turn south on Forest Road 19 (Aufderheide Forest Drive), heading toward Cougar Reservoir. In 0.2 mile, turn right to remain on FR 19. The camp is on the left in another 21 miles.
About the campground: This campground occupies an old-growth stand along the South Fork McKenzie River, just upstream from its confluence with the Roaring River. If you continue south past camp a short distance on FR 19, you will be able to view the Roaring River, a fast-plunging river of white bubbles fanning the lush greenery at its sides. The campground appeals to anglers, hikers, and camp "slugs." The ancient trees, lovely undergrowth, and hush of the river together shape a soothing backdrop for your stay. Trails lead upstream along the South Fork and a side creek.

48 Homestead

Location: About 22 miles southeast of the community of Blue River
Season: Year-round
Sites: 7 basic sites; no hookups
Maximum length: 25 feet
Facilities: Tables, grills, pit toilets; no drinking water
Fee per night: None
Management: Willamette National Forest
Contact: (541) 822–3381; www.fs.fed.us/r6/willamette/recreation
Finding the campground: From the Blue River Junction on Oregon 126, drive east on OR 126 about 5 miles and turn south on Forest Road 19 (Aufderheide Forest Drive), heading toward Cougar Reservoir. In 0.2 mile, turn right to remain on FR 19. The camp is on the right in 17.1 miles.
About the campground: A lovely old-growth stand of tall firs, cedars, and bigleaf maples weaves the cathedral for this linear campground along the South Fork McKenzie River; special fishing regulations apply. Gravel bars contribute to the river's character as it races past camp. Across the river, a steep canyon slope lends to the quiet and seclusion. Boulders outline the parking areas for the well-spaced sites.

49 Ice Cap

Location: 17 miles northeast of the community of McKenzie Bridge
Season: Late May–mid-September
Sites: 14 basic sites, 8 tent sites; no hookups
Maximum length: 22 feet
Facilities: Tables, grills, flush toilets, drinking water, waterfall viewing area
Fee per night: $$
Management: Willamette National Forest
Contact: (541) 822–3381; www.fs.fed.us/r6/willamette/recreation
Finding the campground: It is west off Oregon 126, 17 miles northeast of McKenzie Bridge.
About the campground: This camp in a fir-and-cedar woods along the McKenzie Wild and Scenic River provides access to the waterfall viewing platforms upstream from camp and to Carmen Reservoir downstream. The sites are spaced for comfort and privacy, but RVers may need to shop around for the most level site. Three viewpoints present the beauty and surge of 63-foot Koosah Falls; the equally impressive Sahalie Falls is a short hike farther upstream. Trails travel on both sides of the river, so you can also hike to the reservoir or Clear Lake or make a loop between the upper bridge and Carmen Reservoir. Fishing and quiet boating are available at the reservoir and Clear Lake, or you can fish the river.

50 Limberlost

Location: About 6 miles east of the community of McKenzie Bridge
Season: Late May–September
Sites: 12 basic sites; no hookups
Maximum length: 25 feet
Facilities: Tables, grills, vault toilets; no drinking water
Fee per night: $
Management: Willamette National Forest
Contact: (541) 822–3381; www.fs.fed.us/r6/willamette/recreation
Finding the campground: From McKenzie Bridge, go 4.6 miles east on Oregon 126 and turn right (east) on OR 242 to find the campground on the left in 1.4 miles.
About the campground: This cozy, rustic camp above Lost Creek sits at the lower end of McKenzie Pass Scenic Byway (OR 242). The entire byway is usually open by July and remains open through October, allowing for the viewing of fall colors. Lava flows, cinder cones, craters, and the magnificent presence of Three Sisters and Mount Washington, along with their respective wilderness areas, recommend the byway. Tall, straight trees enfold the closely spaced sites. Pockets of skunk cabbage accent the banks of the deep, clear creek. Area trails visit Proxy Falls, Linton Lake, and Scott Mountain and travel along the Upper McKenzie River.

51 McKenzie Bridge

Location: Less than 1 mile west of the community of McKenzie Bridge
Season: Late April–late September
Sites: 20 basic sites; no hookups
Maximum length: 35 feet
Facilities: Tables, grills, vault toilets, drinking water, primitive boat launch for drift boats and rafts
Fee per night: $$
Management: Willamette National Forest
Contact: (541) 822–3381; (877) 444–6777 for reservations; www.fs.fed.us/r6/willamette/recreation
Finding the campground: It is south off Oregon 126, 8.7 miles east of Blue River and 0.4 mile west of McKenzie Bridge.
About the campground: Campers here can enjoy the fun and relaxation afforded by the McKenzie River. The camp occupies a full, second-growth forest of firs, cedars, and western hemlocks, with a vibrant understory. Many sites overlook the river; all have gravel parking and are well spaced. River rafting, fishing, and reclining at camp are popular.

52 Mona

Location: About 7 miles northeast of the community of Blue River, on Blue River Reservoir
Season: Early May–mid-September
Sites: 23 basic sites; no hookups
Maximum length: 36 feet
Facilities: Tables, grills, flush toilets, drinking water, boat launch (en route to camp)
Fee per night: $$
Management: Willamette National Forest
Contact: (541) 822–3381; www.fs.fed.us/r6/willamette/recreation
Finding the campground: From the Blue River Junction on Oregon 126, go 2.7 miles east on OR 126 and turn north on Forest Road 15 for Blue River Reservoir. Go 3.8 miles, crossing over an arm of the reservoir, to follow the long entrance road into camp.
About the campground: This campground overlooks Blue River Reservoir from a forested plateau. A few old-growth monarchs rise among the otherwise second-growth trees. The camp is well laid out for comfort, with both pull-through and back-in camp spaces. Roads and parking are paved. The large lake is open to fishing, swimming, boating, and waterskiing.

53 Olallie

Location: 11 miles northeast of the community of McKenzie Bridge
Season: Late April–late October
Sites: 17 basic sites; no hookups

Maximum length: 35 feet
Facilities: Tables, grills, vault toilets, drinking water, boat launch (drift boat or raft)
Fee per night: $$
Management: Willamette National Forest
Contact: (541) 822-3381; (877) 444-6777 for reservations; www.fs.fed.us/r6 /willamette/recreation
Finding the campground: It is west off Oregon 126, 11 miles northeast of McKenzie Bridge.
About the campground: At the confluence of Olallie Creek and the McKenzie Wild and Scenic River sits this terraced camp. The sites are spacious and occupy a semi-open forest setting; several sites have river views. The McKenzie River National Recreation Trail travels the opposite shore and can be accessed off Deer Creek Road (Forest Road 2654), downstream from camp. Fishing, rafting, and drift boating are popular diversions.

54 Paradise

Location: About 4 miles east of the community of McKenzie Bridge
Season: May–late October
Sites: 64 basic sites; no hookups
Maximum length: 40 feet
Facilities: Tables, grills, flush toilets, drinking water, primitive boat launch for rafts
Fee per night: $$
Management: Willamette National Forest
Contact: (541) 822-3381; (877) 444-6777 for reservations; www.fs.fed.us/r6 /willamette/recreation
Finding the campground: From McKenzie Bridge, go 3.8 miles east on Oregon 126 and turn left to enter the campground.
About the campground: One of a handful of idyllic McKenzie River campgrounds, this facility serves rafters, anglers, and hikers. The McKenzie National Recreation Trail follows the wild and scenic river upstream some 24 miles to Clear Lake and its headwater spring, passing Sahalie and Koosah Falls en route. But if your time is limited and your feet are unwilling, you can also reach the lake and falls via OR 126. Sites have paved parking and sit in a rich, multistory old-growth forest.

55 Slide Creek

Location: About 15 miles southeast of the community of Blue River, on Cougar Reservoir
Season: Mid-May–late September
Sites: 16 basic sites; no hookups
Maximum length: 25 feet
Facilities: Tables, grills, pit toilets, drinking water, paved boat launch
Fee per night: $$

Management: Willamette National Forest
Contact: (541) 822–3381; www.fs.fed.us/r6/willamette/recreation
Finding the campground: From the Blue River Junction on Oregon 126, drive east on OR 126 about 5 miles and turn south on Forest Road 19 (Aufderheide Forest Drive), heading toward Cougar Reservoir. In 0.2 mile, bear right to remain on FR 19, following it another 9.3 miles. Upon crossing the reservoir bridge, turn left onto gravel FR 500, which heads north along the east shore. Go 1.4 miles to enter this camp on the left.
About the campground: This popular east-shore campground is located where Slide Creek feeds into Cougar Lake. The attractive, long green lake invites fishing, swimming, boating, and waterskiing. The canyon's ragged skyline and steep walls, rocky and forested, add to the setting. The campsites have developed, off-shoulder parking and are shaded by firs, maples, and dogwoods. Trailheads and a popular hot springs area lie within short drives of the camp.

56 Sunnyside

Location: About 15 miles southeast of the community of Blue River, on Cougar Reservoir
Season: Mid-May–mid-September
Sites: 13 tent sites; no hookups
Maximum length: Suitable for tents only
Facilities: Tables, grills, vault toilets; no drinking water
Fee per night: $$
Management: Willamette National Forest
Contact: (541) 822–3381; www.fs.fed.us/r6/willamette/recreation
Finding the campground: From the Blue River Junction on Oregon 126, drive east on OR 126 about 5 miles and turn south on Forest Road 19 (Aufderheide Forest Drive), heading toward Cougar Reservoir. In 0.2 mile, bear right to remain on FR 19, following it another 9.3 miles. Upon crossing the reservoir bridge, turn left on gravel FR 500 and proceed about 0.8 mile to enter this camp on the left. The entry road to the camp is steep.
About the campground: On the east shore of Cougar Reservoir, this improved dispersed camp offers gravel parking spurs, basic amenities, and shade for comfort. Typically, boaters will put in at Slide Creek Campground, just to the north, then moor their boats along shore here at Sunnyside. The lake invites fishing, swimming, boating, and waterskiing. Trailheads and a hot springs area are but short drives away.

57 Trail Bridge

Location: 13 miles northeast of the community of McKenzie Bridge, on Trail Bridge Reservoir
Season: Late April–late September
Sites: 26 basic sites; no hookups
Maximum length: 45 feet

Facilities: Tables, grills, flush and vault toilets, drinking water, boat launch
Fee per night: $
Management: Willamette National Forest
Contact: (541) 822–3381; www.fs.fed.us/r6/willamette/recreation
Finding the campground: It is west off Oregon 126, 13 miles northeast of McKenzie Bridge.
About the campground: This camp offers forested sites along Trail Bridge Reservoir, where the McKenzie River is harnessed for power generation. Additional RV camping is available on the open flat alongside the reservoir. This is an area where human influence overshadows the natural offering, but the reservoir offers fishing and boating. There is also convenient access to the McKenzie River National Recreation Trail and to the McKenzie Pass–Santiam Pass Scenic Byway, a loop drive following OR 126, U.S. Highway 20, and OR 242.

Eugene–Cottage Grove Area

58 Baker Bay

Location: About 7 miles east of Cottage Grove, on Dorena Lake
Season: April–October
Sites: 49 basic sites; no hookups
Maximum length: 40 feet
Facilities: Tables, grills, flush and vault toilets, drinking water, showers, dump station, telephone, boat rental, boat launch, dock, food concession
Fee per night: $$
Management: Lane County
Contact: (541) 942–7669; www.co.lane.or.us/parks
Finding the campground: From Interstate 5 at Cottage Grove, take exit 174 and go east on Row River Road for 4.4 miles. Bear right on the South Shore Road, following signs toward Dorena Lake, and in another 2.7 miles turn left for the camp.
About the campground: This campground and day-use recreation area faces Baker Bay, part of manmade Dorena Lake, which is contained in an attractive basin of rolling, wooded hills. The recreation area welcomes with lawn, shade trees, and an accent of charismatic big oaks. From the fir-and-oak grove of

Eugene–Cottage Grove Area	Hookup sites	Total sites	Maximum RV length	Hookups	Toilets	Showers	Drinking water	Dump station	Recreation	Fee	Can reserve
58 Baker Bay		49	40		F,NF	•	•	•	SFBL	$$	
59 Bedrock		19	20		NF		•		HF	$$	
60 Big Pool		5	T		NF		•		HF	$$	
61 Broken Bowl		16	20		F		•		HF	$$	
62 Cascara–Fall Creek State Recreation Site		47	45		NF		•	•	SFBL	$$	
63 Cedar Creek		8	16		NF				HSF	$	
64 Dolly Varden		5	T		NF		•		HF	$$	
65 Pine Meadows		92	40		F	•	•	•	FBL	$$	•
66 Primitive		15	40		NF		•		FBL	$	•
67 Puma		11	20		NF		•		HF	$$	
68 Richardson County Park	88	88	60	WE	F	•	•	•	SFBL	$$$	•
69 Rujada		11	22		F,NF		•		HF	$	
70 Schwartz		82	40		F	•	•	•	FB	$$	•
71 Sharps Creek Recreation Area		10	30		NF		•		SF	$	
72 Winberry		7	small		NF		•		HF	$	

camp, most sites offer lake glimpses. Because this is a bustling recreation water on summer weekends, midweek visits promise greater calm. Waterskiing, strolling along the shoreline, and taking a walk or bicycle ride on the nearby Row River Rail Trail are possible diversions.

59 Bedrock

Location: About 16 miles northeast of Lowell
Season: May–September
Sites: 13 basic sites, 6 tent sites; no hookups
Maximum length: 20 feet
Facilities: Tables, grills, vault toilets, drinking water
Fee per night: $$
Management: Willamette National Forest
Contact: (541) 937–2129; www.fs.fed.us/r6/willamette/recreation
Finding the campground: From Oregon 58, 13 miles east of Interstate 5 and 23 miles west of Oakridge, turn north on Jasper-Lowell Road and drive 2.8 miles, following the signs to Unity. Turn right on Big Fall Creek Road for Winberry and North Shore, go 0.4 mile, and bear left to remain on Big Fall Creek Road for another 13.8 miles. Enter the campground on the left.
About the campground: This camp along Fall Creek was touched by fire in 2003. Although the cathedral has been opened up, the vibrant growth of this forest is already erasing signs of the burn, and the new facilities have given the camp a facelift. Fall Creek National Recreation Trail, which can be accessed at the camp, allows for hikes along the creek in either direction. Nearby nature trails offer other exploration. Fishing and taking in the recreation at Fall Creek Reservoir are also available to campers.

60 Big Pool

Location: About 14 miles northeast of Lowell
Season: May–mid-September
Sites: 5 tent sites; no hookups
Maximum length: Suitable for tents only
Facilities: Tables, grills, vault toilets, drinking water
Fee per night: $$
Management: Willamette National Forest
Contact: (541) 937–2129; www.fs.fed.us/r6/willamette/recreation
Finding the campground: From Oregon 58, 13 miles east of Interstate 5 and 23 miles west of Oakridge, turn north on Jasper-Lowell Road and drive 2.8 miles, following the signs to Unity. Turn right on Big Fall Creek Road toward Winberry and North Shore, go 0.4 mile, and bear left to remain on Big Fall Creek Road. Proceed another 10.9 miles; the campground is on the right.
About the campground: Sandwiched between the road and Fall Creek, this tiny camp rests in a lush low-elevation Douglas fir forest. Fall Creek National Recreation Trail (NRT) travels the opposite shore of Fall Creek but can be easily accessed in either direction from camp. To the east, Johnny Creek and Clark Creek Nature Trails connect with the NRT and appeal in their own rights. You may also fish or take in the recreation at Fall Creek Reservoir.

61   Broken Bowl

Location: About 13 miles northeast of Lowell
Season: Late May–late September
Sites: 6 basic sites, 10 tent sites; no hookups
Maximum length: 20 feet
Facilities: Tables, grills, flush toilets, drinking water
Fee per night: $$
Management: Willamette National Forest
Contact: (541) 937–2129; www.fs.fed.us/r6/willamette/recreation
Finding the campground: From Oregon 58, 13 miles east of Interstate 5 and 23 miles west of Oakridge, turn north on Jasper-Lowell Road and drive 2.8 miles, following the signs to Unity. Turn right on Big Fall Creek Road toward Winberry and North Shore, go 0.4 mile, and bear left to remain on Big Fall Creek Road. Continue 10.2 miles to the campground.
About the campground: This campground and day-use area along Fall Creek has a lush, low-elevation setting of Douglas fir and western hemlock and provides visitors with access to Fall Creek National Recreation Trail, as well as waterplay in the creek. A paved trail from the day use leads to Fall Creek.

62   Cascara–Fall Creek State Recreation Site

Location: About 10 miles northeast of Lowell, on Fall Creek Reservoir
Season: Mid-May–early September
Sites: 42 basic sites, 5 walk-in tent sites; no hookups
Maximum length: 45 feet
Facilities: Tables, grills, vault toilets, drinking water, dump station, telephone, improved boat ramp, dock, security gate at night
Fee per night: $$
Management: Oregon State Parks and Recreation Department
Contact: (541) 937–1173; www.oregonstateparks.org
Finding the campground: From Oregon 58, 13 miles east of Interstate 5 and 23 miles west of Oakridge, turn north on Jasper-Lowell Road and drive 2.8 miles, following the signs to Unity. Turn right on Big Fall Creek Road toward Winberry and North Shore, go 0.4 mile, and bear left to remain on Big Fall Creek Road. Continue 7.2 miles and turn right on Peninsula Road. Proceed 0.3 mile to the campground entrance on the right.
About the campground: Along Fall Creek Reservoir, this comfortable camp tucked amid firs, alders, and a tangled understory offers sites that are either fully shaded or receive a mix of sun and shade. The sites have gravel parking and are well spaced for privacy. Campers enjoy convenient access to the reservoir for fishing and boating. A designated area serves swimmers.

63 Cedar Creek

Location: 23 miles east of Cottage Grove
Season: Mid-April–November
Sites: 8 basic sites; no hookups
Maximum length: 16 feet
Facilities: Tables, grills, vault toilets; no drinking water
Fee per night: $
Management: Umpqua National Forest
Contact: (541) 942–5591; www.fs.fed.us/r6/umpqua/recreation
Finding the campground: From Interstate 5 at Cottage Grove, take exit 174 and go east on Row River Road and Brice Creek Road for 23 miles. The camp is on the north side of Brice Creek Road.
About the campground: At the foot of the Calapooya Mountains, this small camp enjoys a rich, low-elevation forest and overlooks scenic Brice Creek, a clear stream punctuated by cascades and pools. A pedestrian bridge over the creek accesses the historic 5.5-mile Brice Creek Trail, which offers a fine tour along the creek and through old-growth stands; it is open to hiking and mountain bike riding. A spur and a loop option off the Brice Creek Trail add waterfall views on Trestle Creek, but these trails are open to hiking only. The pools of the creek may inspire you to swim or dance a fly line over to them.

64 Dolly Varden

Location: About 12 miles northeast of Lowell
Season: Late May–mid-September
Sites: 5 tent sites; no hookups
Maximum length: Suitable for tents only
Facilities: Tables, grills, vault toilets; no drinking water
Fee per night: $$
Management: Willamette National Forest
Contact: (541) 937–2129; www.fs.fed.us/r6/willamette/recreation
Finding the campground: From Oregon 58, 13 miles east of Interstate 5 and 23 miles west of Oakridge, turn north on Jasper-Lowell Road and drive 2.8 miles, following the signs to Unity. Turn right on Big Fall Creek Road toward Winberry and North Shore, go 0.4 mile, and bear left to remain on Big Fall Creek Road. Continue 9.7 miles to reach the campground.
About the campground: Like its counterparts farther upstream, this Fall Creek campground has a rich forest setting. It sits next to the lower trailhead for the 14-mile Fall Creek National Recreation Trail (NRT), which pursues the creek upstream, sometimes tracing the canyon slope. The NRT can be fragmented for more manageable short hikes, or you can walk the Johnny Creek and Clark Creek Nature Trails (both short drives east of camp). The recreation at Fall Creek Reservoir is also within a reasonable reach of camp.

65   Pine Meadows

Location: About 7 miles south of Cottage Grove, on Cottage Grove Lake
Season: Mid-May–early September
Sites: 92 basic sites; no hookups
Maximum length: 40 feet
Facilities: Tables, fire rings, flush toilets, drinking water, showers, dump station, telephone, playground, nearby boat launch
Fee per night: $$
Management: U.S. Army Corps of Engineers
Contact: (541) 942-5631; (877) 444-6777 for reservations
Finding the campground: From Interstate 5 south of Cottage Grove, take exit 170 and follow London Road south along the east side of the freeway for 3 miles. There turn left on Cottage Grove Reservoir Road and go another 2.5 miles to enter this camp on the right.
About the campground: This large, developed campground stretches along a fair piece of the eastern shore of Cottage Grove Lake, a large valley reservoir. The camp has a city park atmosphere, with lovely, groomed lawns and shading pines and firs. An open, grassy meadow extends between camp and the manmade lake. The campground has paved parking, with some pull-through sites available. The reservoir offers fishing, boating, and waterskiing, but late in the year, the water can be drawn down. Boaters obtain access at Wilson Creek Day Use, 0.6 mile south of camp.

66   Primitive

Location: About 8 miles south of Cottage Grove, on Cottage Grove Lake
Season: Mid-May–early September
Sites: 15 basic sites; no hookups
Maximum length: 40 feet
Facilities: Tables, fire rings, nonflush toilets, drinking water, nearby boat launch
Fee per night: $
Management: U.S. Army Corps of Engineers
Contact: (541) 942-5631; (877) 444-6777 for reservations.
Finding the campground: From Interstate 5 south of Cottage Grove, take exit 170 and follow London Road south along the east side of the freeway for 3 miles. Turn left on Cottage Grove Reservoir Road and go 3 miles to this camp on the right.
About the campground: These primitive campsites are scattered across a broad meadow dotted by trees and wildflowers on the east shore of Cottage Grove Lake. A few sites sit closer to the open, grassy shore. Geese, ducks, and herons are camp companions. The reservoir hosts fishing, boating, and waterskiing, with access obtained at Wilson Creek Day Use, 0.1 mile south of camp.

67 Puma

Location: About 18 miles northeast of Lowell
Season: May–September
Sites: 8 basic sites, 3 tent sites; no hookups
Maximum length: 20 feet
Facilities: Tables, grills, vault toilets, drinking water
Fee per night: $$
Management: Willamette National Forest
Contact: (541) 937–2129; www.fs.fed.us/r6/willamette/recreation
Finding the campground: From Oregon 58, 13 miles east of Interstate 5 and 23 miles west of Oakridge, turn north on Jasper-Lowell Road and drive 2.8 miles, following the signs to Unity. Turn right on Big Fall Creek Road toward Winberry and North Shore, go 0.4 mile, and bear left to remain on Big Fall Creek Road. Continue 15.4 miles to the campground.
About the campground: At this Fall Creek campground, the sites sit fairly close to one another, but the rich forest setting is appealing. Fall Creek National Recreation Trail leads hikers through the canyon, while the creek welcomes waterplay.

68 Richardson County Park

Location: About 20 miles northwest of Eugene, on Fern Ridge Lake
Season: Mid-April–mid-October
Sites: 88 hookup sites; water and electric hookups
Maximum length: 60 feet
Facilities: Tables, grills, flush toilets, drinking water, showers, dump station, telephone (at marina), playground (in day use), dock, launch, marina with 286 mooring slips, concession stand
Fee per night: $$$
Management: Lane County
Contact: (541) 682–2000; (541) 935–2005 for reservations; www.co.lane.or.us /parks
Finding the campground: From Oregon 126 at Veneta (about 15 miles west of Eugene), turn north on Territorial Road go 4.7 miles, and turn right on Clear Lake Road. The park is 0.2 mile ahead.
About the campground: Covering 157 acres on the northwest shore of Fern Ridge Lake (a large valley reservoir), this park has ample room to explore. The campground has a dual personality, with some sites in the valley trees and others spread across the groomed lawns dotted with planted conifers. You will find paved roads and parking pads, as well as several pull-through sites. The park has areas for sunning or resting in the shade, romping, swimming, boating, and fishing.

69 Rujada

Location: About 20 miles east of Cottage Grove
Season: Late May–September
Sites: 11 basic sites; no hookups
Maximum length: 22 feet
Facilities: Tables, grills, flush and vault toilets, drinking water, softball field and horseshoe pits at picnic area
Fee per night: $
Management: Umpqua National Forest
Contact: (541) 942–5591; www.fs.fed.us/r6/umpqua/recreation
Finding the campground: From Interstate 5 in Cottage Grove, take exit 174 and go east on Row River Road for 18.3 miles. Turn left on Layng Creek Road/Forest Road 17 and continue 1.8 miles to the campground and picnic area.
About the campground: Along Layng Creek sits this pleasant campground in a rich, varied forest with towering hemlocks and firs. The sites are roomy and well spaced, with tent pads and adequate parking. The 1.5-mile Swordfern Trail begins at the picnic area parking lot and travels through lovely forest along Layng Creek. By going 10.5 miles east of camp via FRs 17, 1790, 1702, 1702.728, and 1702.203, you will reach a half-mile trail to the 125-foot Moon Falls, which is tucked in an old-growth gallery.

70 Schwartz

Location: About 5 miles east of Cottage Grove
Season: Late April–late September
Sites: 82 basic sites; no hookups
Maximum length: 40 feet
Facilities: Tables, grills, flush toilets, drinking water, showers, dump station, playground, horseshoe pits
Fee per night: $$
Management: U.S. Army Corps of Engineers
Contact: (541) 942–5631; (877) 444–6777 for reservations
Finding the campground: From Interstate 5 in Cottage Grove, take exit 174 and go east on Row River Road for 4.4 miles. Bear right on South Shore Road, following the signs for Dorena Lake. Continue 0.4 mile to the camp.
About the campground: This quiet Row River Valley campground stretches below the dam of Dorena Lake. The river camp occupies a grassy meadow, with shading maples, firs, oaks, and cottonwoods. An ash swale contributes to the overall setting. The facility has paved roads and parking and convenient access to the fishing and boating on Dorena Lake. The area's Row River Rail Trail attracts hikers and bicyclists.

71 Sharps Creek Recreation Site

Location: About 18 miles southeast of Cottage Grove
Season: Mid-May–September
Sites: 10 basic sites; no hookups
Maximum length: 30 feet
Facilities: Tables, grills, vault toilets, drinking water (hand pump on Sharps Creek Road)
Fee per night: $
Management: Eugene District Bureau of Land Management
Contact: (541) 683–6600; www.edo.or.blm.gov
Finding the campground: From Interstate 5 in Cottage Grove, take exit 174 and go east on Row River Road for about 15 miles. Turn right (south) on Sharps Creek Road and proceed 3.2 miles to the camp entrance on the right.
About the campground: This small camp among tall, second-growth firs sits across the road from Sharps Creek and a handful of picnic sites atop the bluff. In this lightly traveled area, the camp remains relatively quiet; a neighboring field adds to its calm. Scenic Sharps Creek unites sparkling waters, gravel banks, and deep blue-green pools cupped in rocky outcrops. One particularly deep pool fashions a fine swimming hole. Sharps Creek is also open to recreational gold panning anytime but March 1 through May 31.

72 Winberry

Location: About 12 miles northeast of Lowell
Season: Mid-May–early September
Sites: 2 basic sites, 5 tent sites; no hookups
Maximum length: Small units only
Facilities: Tables, grills, vault toilets, drinking water, Adirondack-style shelters at a couple of sites
Fee per night: $
Management: Willamette National Forest
Contact: (541) 937–2129; www.fs.fed.us/r6/willamette/recreation
Finding the campground: From Oregon 58, 13 miles east of Interstate 5 and 23 miles west of Oakridge, turn north on Jasper-Lowell Road and drive 2.8 miles, following the signs to Unity. Turn right on Big Fall Creek Road toward Winberry and North Shore, go 0.4 mile, and turn right on Winberry Creek Road/Forest Road 1802. Proceed 9 miles to this camp on the right.
About the campground: Along the shore of crystalline Winberry Creek, this quiet camp is ideal for tenters. Tall firs and scenic bigleaf maples; an effusive understory of vine maple, hazel, thimbleberry, and cascara; and rustic Adirondack-style shelters are among its attributes. In the three-sided A-frame shelters, tiered bunks await the unrolling of sleeping bags. The camp offers fishing, and hiking is available nearby. A 1-mile trail leads to Station Butte (consult your Willamette National Forest map to locate the trailhead).

Oakridge Area

73 Black Canyon

Location: 6 miles west of Oakridge
Season: Late May–late September
Sites: 59 basic sites, 13 tent sites; no hookups
Maximum length: 44 feet
Facilities: Tables, grills, vault toilets, drinking water, boat ramp (for canoes and motor boats)
Fee per night: $$
Management: Willamette National Forest
Contact: (541) 937-2129; www.fs.fed.us/r6/willamette/recreation
Finding the campground: It is north off Oregon 58, 6 miles west of Oakridge and 22 miles east of Eugene.
About the campground: This camp claims a fir-cedar flat where the Middle Fork Willamette River bends to meet the upper end of Lookout Point Reservoir. The improved sites have level asphalt parking and enjoy the peace and shade that come from a mature forest setting. The designated tent sites have tent pads to ease the job of setting up camp. Rainbow and cutthroat trout chal-

Oakridge Area

		Hookup sites	Total sites	Maximum RV length	Hookups	Toilets	Showers	Drinking water	Dump station	Recreation	Fee	Can reserve
73	Black Canyon		72	44		NF		•		HSFBL	$$	
74	Blue Pool		25	20		NF				F	$$	
75	Campers Flat		5	18		NF		•		HF	$$	
76	Gold Lake		25	24		NF		•		HFBL	$$	
77	Hampton		4	36		NF		•		FBL	$	
78	Indigo Springs		3	18		NF				HF		
79	Islet		55	30		F,NF		•	•	HSBL	$$	
80	Kiahanie		19	24		NF		•		F	$$	
81	North Waldo		58	30		F,NF		•	•	HSBL	$$	
82	Packard Creek		35	28		NF		•		SFBL	$$	
83	Sacandaga		17	24		NF				HF	$	
84	Salmon Creek Falls		15	20		NF		•		SF	$$	
85	Sand Prairie		21	28		F,NF		•		HF	$$	
86	Secret		6	24		NF				SF	$$	
87	Shadow Bay		92	24		F,NF		•	•	HSBL	$$	
88	Timpanogas Lake		10	24		NF		•		HFB	$	

lenge the skills of anglers, while the Black Canyon Nature Trail offers a 1-mile interpretive walk through forest. Reservoir activities are boating, fishing, swimming, and waterskiing.

74 Blue Pool

Location: 9 miles east of Oakridge
Season: Mid-May–mid-September
Sites: 25 basic sites; no hookups
Maximum length: 20 feet
Facilities: Tables, grills, vault toilets; no drinking water
Fee per night: $$
Management: Willamette National Forest
Contact: (541) 782–2283; www.fs.fed.us/r6/willamette/recreation
Finding the campground: It is south off Oregon 58, 9 miles east of Oakridge.
About the campground: A mixed forest of fir, cedar, maple, and alder and a lush understory surround this campground. The well-spaced, private sites, some overlooking Salt Creek, have paved parking. Salt Creek provides a soothing backdrop and welcomes fishing. A 14-mile road trip upstream leads to the Salt Creek Falls Viewing Area, which features the 286-foot namesake waterfall, the second tallest in the state. At the developed viewing area, picnicking and hiking extend the recreation. Several paths double as cross-country ski trails in winter.

75 Campers Flat

Location: About 23 miles south of Oakridge
Season: Late May–mid-September
Sites: 5 basic sites; no hookups
Maximum length: 18 feet
Facilities: Tables, grills, pit toilets, drinking water
Fee per night: $$
Management: Willamette National Forest
Contact: (541) 782–2283; www.fs.fed.us/r6/willamette/recreation
Finding the campground: From Oregon 58, 2 miles east of Oakridge, turn south on Kitson Springs Road toward Hills Creek Reservoir, go 0.5 mile, and turn right on Forest Road 21. Follow it for 20 miles to enter the camp on the right.
About the campground: This small camp along the Middle Fork Willamette River features semi-open sites in a setting of cedars and cottonwoods. The river rushes past camp and shows sections of riffles and a deep pool bounded by rock outcroppings. Rainbow and cutthroat trout may tug at your fishing line here, so may suckers. An interpretive sign in camp identifies a portion of the old Oregon Central Military Wagon Road. Hikers can access the Middle Fork Trail near camp or pick up the 4.1-mile Youngs Rock Trail across the road from the camp entrance. The Youngs Rock Trail is popular with mountain bikers.

76 Gold Lake

Location: About 28 miles southeast of Oakridge, on Gold Lake
Season: Late May–mid-October
Sites: 25 basic sites; no hookups
Maximum length: 24 feet
Facilities: Tables, grills, vault toilets, drinking water, boat launch for nonmotorized boating, wheelchair-accessible canoe dock, picnic shelter
Fee per night: $$
Management: Willamette National Forest
Contact: (541) 782–2283; www.fs.fed.us/r6/willamette/recreation
Finding the campground: From Oregon 58, 26 miles east of Oakridge and 0.6 miles west of Willamette Pass, turn north on gravel Forest Road 500 and go 2 miles to the camp.
About the campground: This attractive, popular camp is found along Gold Lake, a 100-acre, 25-foot-deep mountain lake in an alpine forest setting of true fir, spruce, white pine, and mountain hemlock. Huckleberry and mountain ash further adorn camp and shore. The lake outlet has its own charm, with its deep-grass banks, alder clumps, and aquatic wildflowers. The outlet bridge bisects the camp, which has gravel parking, a few pull-through sites, and some lakeside sites. Only fly-fishing and nonmotorized boating are allowed on the lake. Trailheads at and near camp open the door to neighboring high lakes and peaks for anyone willing to put boot leather to the trail. Some paths double as cross-country ski trails.

77 Hampton

Location: 9 miles west of Oakridge, on Lookout Point Reservoir
Season: Late May–mid-September
Sites: 4 basic sites; no hookups
Maximum length: 36 feet
Facilities: Tables, grills, vault toilets, drinking water, boat launch
Fee per night: $
Management: Willamette National Forest
Contact: (541) 782–2283; www.fs.fed.us/r6/willamette/recreation
Finding the campground: It is north off Oregon 58, 9 miles west of Oakridge and 19 miles east of Eugene.
About the campground: This tiny facility exists primarily to put guests on Lookout Point Reservoir with a minimum of fuss. The camp is just off the highway, basic, and not very scenic. It does, however, have a launch for reservoir fishing, boating, and waterskiing.

78 Indigo Springs

Location: About 30 miles southeast of Oakridge
Season: Mid-May–October
Sites: 3 basic sites; no hookups
Maximum length: 18 feet
Facilities: Tables, fire rings, pit toilets; no drinking water
Fee per night: None
Management: Willamette National Forest
Contact: (541) 782-2283; www.fs.fed.us/r6/willamette/recreation
Finding the campground: From Oregon 58, 2 miles east of Oakridge, turn south on Kitson Springs Road toward Hills Creek Reservoir, go 0.5 mile, and turn right on Forest Road 21. Follow it for 27 miles to enter the camp on the left.
About the campground: Across FR 21 from the Middle Fork Willamette River, this tiny campground sits alongside Indigo Creek and a section of the old Oregon Central Military Wagon Road. It enjoys a rich conifer setting. From camp, a 500-foot trail loops around the headwater spring that gives birth to Indigo Creek. Campers can also take a few strides along the military wagon road before it becomes too overgrown. You may access the river or its companion trail on the other side of FR 21.

79 Islet

Location: About 36 miles east of Oakridge, on Waldo Lake
Season: Mid-June–September
Sites: 55 basic sites; no hookups
Maximum length: 30 feet
Facilities: Tables, grills, flush and pit toilets, drinking water, dump station (1 mile from camp), boat launch
Fee per night: $$
Management: Willamette National Forest
Contact: (541) 782-2283; www.fs.fed.us/r6/willamette/recreation
Finding the campground: From Oregon 58, 23 miles southeast of Oakridge, turn north on Forest Road 5897 toward Waldo Lake, go 11 miles, and continue left on FR 5898 toward North Waldo and Islet Campgrounds. Islet Campground is ahead 1.5 miles.
About the campground: This campground rests near the north end of Waldo Lake, a large, natural mountain lake acclaimed as one of the clearest lakes in the world. The sites sit back from the sandy shore in a forest of hemlocks and firs. Islet Point protrudes 0.1 mile into the lake and gives the camp its name. Benches at the end of the point welcome meditation and sunset gazing. The Shoreline Trail strings 1 mile between Islet and North Waldo Campgrounds. A longer trail system encircles the entire lake and branches off into Waldo Lake Wilderness. Canoeing and swimming further engage guests. Be sure to pack insect repellent because mosquitoes breed in the snowmelt pools along the lakeshore and can be bothersome from June to mid-August.

80   Kiahanie

Location: About 22 miles northeast of Oakridge
Season: Late May–late September
Sites: 19 basic sites; no hookups
Maximum length: 24 feet
Facilities: Tables, grills, vault toilets, drinking water
Fee per night: $$
Management: Willamette National Forest
Contact: (541) 782-2283; www.fs.fed.us/r6/willamette/recreation
Finding the campground: From Oregon 58 at the western outskirts of Oakridge, turn north at the sign for Westfir. From Westfir, go east on Aufderheide Memorial Drive/Forest Road 19 for 19.7 miles to enter this camp on the left.
About the campground: Along the scenic byway, this camp occupies a mostly uncut forest beside the North Fork Willamette Wild and Scenic River. The camp has a diverse canopy of fir, cedar, hemlock, yew, vine maple, alder, and bigleaf maple. Bountiful greenery, huge stumps, and the crystalline river complete the camp's welcome. The camp has gravel roads and parking and provides river access for fly-fishing. Native fish test the skills of anglers.

81   North Waldo

Location: About 35 miles east of Oakridge, on Waldo Lake
Season: Mid-June–mid-October
Sites: 58 basic sites; no hookups
Maximum length: 30 feet
Facilities: Tables, grills, flush and pit toilets, drinking water, dump station (near Islet Campground), boat launch
Fee per night: $$
Management: Willamette National Forest
Contact: (541) 782-2283; www.fs.fed.us/r6/willamette/recreation
Finding the campground: From Oregon 58, 23 miles southeast of Oakridge, turn north onto Forest Road 5897 toward Waldo Lake and go 11 miles. Continue left on FR 5898 toward North Waldo and Islet Campgrounds for 0.4 mile. Turn right on FR 5895 and travel 0.5 mile more to the camp.
About the campground: This popular camp rests in a high-elevation forest at the north end of Waldo Lake, a 10-square-mile natural lake, which lacks a permanent inlet. This helps make it one of the purest lakes in the world, although not great for fishing. The deep water off the camp's boat launch is perfect for sailboats. Hikers find trails starting from camp, including the 21-mile Waldo Lake Trail and the 1-mile Shoreline Trail to Islet Campground. Because mosquitoes can be annoying, pack repellent.

Waldo Lake.

82 Packard Creek

Location: About 9 miles southeast of Oakridge, on Hills Creek Reservoir
Season: Fully maintained late April–September
Sites: 35 basic sites; no hookups
Maximum length: 28 feet
Facilities: Tables, grills and barbecues, vault toilets, drinking water, boat launch, 2 fishing docks (1 barrier free), swimming area, sites with individual docks, 2 picnic shelters
Fee per night: $$
Management: Willamette National Forest
Contact: (541) 782-2283; www.fs.fed.us/r6/willamette/recreation
Finding the campground: From Oregon 58, 2 miles east of Oakridge, turn south on Kitson Springs Road toward Hills Creek Reservoir. Go 0.5 mile and turn right on Forest Road 21. Follow it 6 miles to the campground entrance on the left.
About the campground: This accommodating camp on Hills Creek Reservoir offers forested sites that sit fairly close together. But water sports are the primary draw, keeping visitors at the reservoir much of the day. Boating, fishing, swimming, and waterskiing are all popular. Expect the camp to fill on summer weekends and holidays. There is a short lakeshore trail at camp. Beware of poison oak when venturing off trails and roads.

83 Sacandaga

Location: About 27 miles south of Oakridge
Season: Late May–late September
Sites: 17 basic sites; no hookups
Maximum length: 24 feet
Facilities: Tables, grills or barbecues, pit toilets; no drinking water
Fee per night: $
Management: Willamette National Forest
Contact: (541) 782-2283; www.fs.fed.us/r6/willamette/recreation
Finding the campground: From Oregon 58, 2 miles east of Oakridge, turn south on Kitson Springs Road toward Hills Creek Reservoir. Go 0.5 mile and turn right on Forest Road 21. Follow it for 24.6 miles to the camp entrance on the right.
About the campground: This campground occupies a mixed forest on a bluff above the Middle Fork Willamette River. The rush of the river echoes through the canyon and contributes to the peacefulness of camp. A trail leads to a bench seat with a river canyon view. Other paths lead down to the river, should you want to fish or admire the water and rugged riverbank. For longer hikes, the Middle Fork Willamette Trail can be accessed from the entrance road into the camp.

84   Salmon Creek Falls

Location: About 5 miles east of Oakridge
Season: Late April–late September
Sites: 15 basic sites; no hookups
Maximum length: 20 feet
Facilities: Tables, grills, vault toilets, drinking water
Fee per night: $$
Management: Willamette National Forest
Contact: (541) 782–2283; www.fs.fed.us/r6/willamette/recreation
Finding the campground: From Oregon 58 at Oakridge, turn north at the light onto Crestview Street toward Rigdon Ranger Station and the Oakridge Business District. Go 0.2 mile and turn right on First Street, which becomes Forest Road 24. Travel 4.9 miles to enter this camp on the right.
About the campground: A full, mature forest of conifers and deciduous trees shrouds this camp above Salmon Creek and Salmon Creek Falls. A profuse woods flora adds to the loveliness of camp. Salmon Creek rushes through a tight canyon as it nears the falls and then cascades over 10-foot ledges and sloping bedrock. A misty green pools swirls at the base of the falls, with gravel-bar beaches located farther downstream. The viewing area for the falls is at the day-use area. Besides admiring and photographing the falls, you may fish, swim, or kayak.

85   Sand Prairie

Location: About 14 miles south of Oakridge
Season: Late May–mid-September
Sites: 21 basic sites; no hookups
Maximum length: 28 feet
Facilities: Tables, grills and barbecues, flush and vault toilets, drinking water
Fee per night: $$
Management: Willamette National Forest
Contact: (541) 782–2283; www.fs.fed.us/r6/willamette/recreation
Finding the campground: From Oregon 58, 2 miles east of Oakridge, turn south on Kitson Springs Road toward Hills Creek Reservoir. Go 0.5 mile and turn right on Forest Road 21. Follow it for 11 miles to enter the camp on the right.
About the campground: This campground along the Middle Fork Willamette River is nicely forested and has well-spaced sites for comfort. The setting blends towering evergreens and a leafy midstory; the dogwoods are especially pretty when in bloom. The camp marks the start of the 27-mile Middle Fork Trail, the river offers trout fishing, and the upper end of Hills Creek Reservoir is within a short drive of the camp.

86 Secret

Location: About 22 miles south of Oakridge
Season: Late May–mid-September
Sites: 6 basic sites; no hookups
Maximum length: 24 feet
Facilities: Tables, grills and barbecues, pit toilets; no drinking water
Fee per night: $$
Management: Willamette National Forest
Contact: (541) 782–2283; www.fs.fed.us/r6/willamette/recreation
Finding the campground: From Oregon 58, 2 miles east of Oakridge, turn
south on Kitson Springs Road toward Hills Creek Reservoir. Go 0.5 mile and
turn right on Forest Road 21. Follow it for 19 miles to enter the camp on the
right.
About the campground: This camp along the Middle Fork Willamette River
feels pleasantly isolated, and its handful of sites are nicely forested. The river's
riffles and deep pools draw anglers and summer visitors seeking a refreshing
dip. A nice pool is just upstream from camp. Cottonwoods reign along the
river.

87 Shadow Bay

Location: About 32 miles east of Oakridge, on Waldo Lake
Season: Late June–September
Sites: 92 basic sites; no hookups
Maximum length: 24 feet
Facilities: Tables, grills, flush and pit toilets, drinking water, dump station,
boat launch (0.5 mile from camp)
Fee per night: $$
Management: Willamette National Forest
Contact: (541) 782–2283; www.fs.fed.us/r6/willamette/recreation
Finding the campground: From Oregon 58, 23 miles southeast of Oakridge,
turn north onto Forest Road 5897 toward Waldo Lake. Go 6.6 miles and take
the left turn for Shadow Bay Campground, entering the campground in about
2 miles.
About the campground: On an attractive, large bay at the south end of
Waldo Lake, this camp occupies a moist forest that supports abundant foliage
but also provides habitat for pesky mosquitoes. Be sure to bring repellent. The
camp offers access to the Shoreline Trail, and it has a designated swimming
area. The sites rest in a mixed age forest set back from Waldo Lake, Shadow
Bay, and a small lily pond. Boats on the lake are restricted to a maximum
speed of 10 miles per hour.

88 Timpanogas Lake

Location: About 45 miles southeast of Oakridge, on Timpanogas Lake
Season: July–mid-October
Sites: 10 basic sites; no hookups
Maximum length: 24 feet
Facilities: Tables, grills, pit toilets, drinking water
Fee per night: $
Management: Willamette National Forest
Contact: (541) 782-2283; www.fs.fed.us/r6/willamette/recreation
Finding the campground: From Oregon 58, 2 miles east of Oakridge, turn south on Kitson Springs Road toward Hills Creek Reservoir. Go 0.5 mile and turn right on Forest Road 21. Follow FR 21 for 32 miles and turn left on FR 2154. Proceed another 10 miles or so to enter this camp on the left.
About the campground: Situated below the Cascade Crest in the Oregon Cascades Recreation Area, this camp is one of the most enchanting spots in the state, but it is guarded by mosquitoes until late summer. The spacious, well-forested sites sit near the lovely blue platter of Timpanogas Lake. Forest, meadow, and rugged slope rim the lake, which is open to nonmotorized boating and fishing. Trails explore the lakeshore and visit Indigo Lake, another high-mountain jewel along which pikas and pine martens dwell. Huckleberry bushes weighted with berries attract pickers, and photographers find plenty of subject matter.

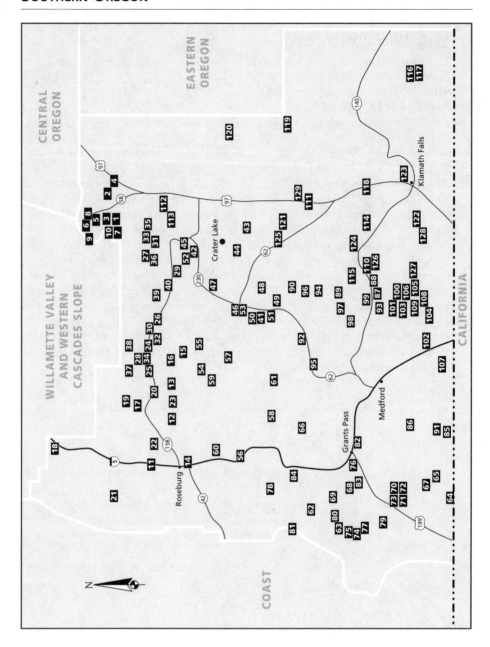

Southern Oregon

The southern region of the state features the spectacular Umpqua and Rogue River drainages, Crater Lake National Park, the wildlife havens of the Klamath Basin, and the rugged wilds and botanical diversity of the Siskiyou Mountains. It encompasses parts of six national forests: Siskiyou, Umpqua, Rogue River, Winema, Fremont, and Deschutes. Campers here will find superb opportunities for outdoor recreation and wildlife observation, but they will also be treated to cultural offerings, including the Shakespeare Festival in Ashland and Favell Museum in Klamath Falls.

This is "Jefferson State" country. For decades, the residents of southern Oregon and northern California have advocated the creation of a new state as a way to gain a stronger political voice. While they have not succeeded, they continue to maintain their separatist mindset. The major towns of this region are Roseburg, Grants Pass, Medford, Ashland, and Klamath Falls, but much of southern Oregon is lightly inhabited.

The weather can vary greatly in this diverse region. The southern valleys threaded by Interstate 5 typically have mild, wet winters punctuated by a few snowstorms that can close the freeway. Summers are hot and dry. The mountains experience four seasons, with some slopes harboring stubborn snowfields that linger well into summer. The Crater Lake area often has snow banks over 6 feet high when the summer travel season gets under way. Weather in the Klamath Basin is temperamental and varies from season to season. Winters can be relatively snow-free and cold or so snowbound that you need snowshoes or cross-country skis to enjoy it. Summers are generally warm and dry. Mosquitoes can be annoying, especially in the high lakes region and around the lakes and marshes of Klamath Basin.

Odell and Crescent Lakes Area

1 Contorta Flat

Location: About 11 miles southwest of the town of Crescent Lake, on Crescent Lake
Season: Mid-May–October
Sites: 25 basic sites; no hookups
Maximum length: 30 feet
Facilities: Tables, fire rings, vault toilets; no drinking water
Fee per night: $
Management: Deschutes National Forest
Contact: (541) 433–3200; www.fs.fed.us/r6/centraloregon/recreation
Finding the campground: From the small community of Crescent Lake on Oregon 58, turn south onto paved Forest Road 60. Go 2.3 miles, turn right to remain on FR 60, and continue another 7.7 miles. Turn left onto FR 280, following it 0.8 mile to the campground at road's end. The final few miles are on gravel.
About the campground: On the south shore of Crescent Lake, this campground occupies a flat of lodgepole pines. Views include Diamond Peak and Red Top Mountain. The lodgepole pines (*Pinus contorta*), which lend the area its name, grow tall and thin, offering little shade. Afternoon winds and early summer mosquitoes are common, but the area offers fishing, swimming, sailboarding, and sailing. Trails can be found in the nearby Diamond Peak Wilderness and Oregon Cascades Recreation Area.

Odell and Crescent Lakes Area	Hookup sites	Total sites	Maximum RV length	Hookups	Toilets	Showers	Drinking water	Dump station	Recreation	Fee	Can reserve
1 Contorta Flat		25	30		NF				SFB	$	
2 Crescent Creek		10	40		NF		•		F	$	
3 Crescent Lake		47	40		NF		•		HSFBL	$$	
4 Cy Bingham County Park		10	30		NF		•		FC	$	
5 Odell Creek		21	30		NF		•		SFB	$$	
6 Princess Creek		46	40		NF				SFBL	$$	
7 Spring		68	40		NF		•		HSFBL	$$	
8 Sunset Cove		20	40		NF		•		SFBL	$$	
9 Trapper Creek		32	40		NF		•		HSFBL	$$	
10 Whitefish Horse Camp		17	40		NF		•		HFBR	$$	•

2 Crescent Creek

Location: About 7 miles southeast of the town of Crescent Lake
Season: April–October
Sites: 10 basic sites; no hookups
Maximum length: 40 feet
Facilities: Tables, grills, pit toilets, drinking water
Fee per night: $
Management: Deschutes National Forest
Contact: (541) 433–3200; www.fs.fed.us/r6/centraloregon/recreation
Finding the campground: From Crescent Lake, drive 3.4 miles east on Oregon 58. Turn left onto Crescent Cutoff Road/Forest Road 61, go 3.3 miles, and turn right into camp. Because the sign for the campground is easy to miss, look for the entrance 0.1 mile past the intersection of FR 61 and FR 46.
About the campground: This lightly used camp claims a forest of lodgepole and ponderosa pines on a flat along Crescent Creek, a wild and scenic waterway. Bunchgrass, wildflowers, and arid shrubs spread between the sites. In this dry terrain, campers need to be extra careful with campfires. The creek flows deep and clear between banks of shrubs and willows, offering anglers a challenge. An access path leads from camp to creek.

3 Crescent Lake

Location: About 3 miles southeast of the town of Crescent Lake, on Crescent Lake
Season: Mid-May–October
Sites: 47 basic sites; no hookups
Maximum length: 40 feet
Facilities: Tables, grills, vault toilets, drinking water, boat launch, dock
Fee per night: $$
Management: Deschutes National Forest
Contact: (541) 433–3200; www.fs.fed.us/r6/centraloregon/recreation
Finding the campground: From the small community of Crescent Lake on Oregon 58, turn south onto paved Forest Road 60, go 2.3 miles, and turn right to remain on FR 60 another 0.4 mile. Turn left to enter the camp.
About the campground: At the north end of Crescent Lake sits this developed campground with paved interior roads and gravel parking. Firs and lodgepole pines shade the terraced camp. Some sites overlook the water; the upper sites may require more leveling. The lake is open to swimming, fishing, boating, sailing, sailboarding, and waterskiing. The Fawn Lake Trail starts off the campground entrance road.

4 Cy Bingham County Park

Location: In Crescent
Season: March–November
Sites: 10 basic sites; no hookups
Maximum length: 30 feet
Facilities: Some tables and grills, pit toilets, drinking water
Fee per night: $
Management: Klamath County
Contact: (541) 883–5121; www.co.klamath.or.us/ComDevelopment/Parks
Finding the campground: From U.S. Highway 97 in Crescent, head west on the Crescent Cutoff Road for 0.1 mile. Turn right and go a few hundred feet to the campground entrance on the left.
About the campground: Named for an early forester, this is a convenient, no-frills camp just off US 97 and close to the Little Deschutes River. The camp occupies a lodgepole pine flat. Logs outline the earthen sites, each of which has a table and/or grill. River access is across the road, and a bike path parallels the Crescent Cutoff Road.

5 Odell Creek

Location: About 2 miles north of the town of Crescent Lake, on Odell Lake
Season: April–October
Sites: 21 basic sites; no hookups
Maximum length: 30 feet
Facilities: Tables, grills, vault toilets, drinking water
Fee per night: $$
Management: Deschutes National Forest
Contact: (541) 433–3200; www.fs.fed.us/r6/centraloregon/recreation
Finding the campground: From Oregon 58, 1.9 miles west of the community of Crescent Lake and 5.4 miles east of Willamette Pass, turn south for the East Shore Odell Lake Access and enter the camp within 0.1 mile.
About the campground: This linear campground stretches along the east shore of Odell Lake, an enchanting, 6-mile-long natural lake with an outstanding fishery of trophy-sized Mackinaw, kokanee, and rainbow trout. Sites enjoy deep shade from a forest of fir and spruce. You can see Lakeview Mountain across the lake and Maiden Peak to the north. Although Odell Lake presents a full lineup of water sports, it receives less traffic than many lakes in the state. Odell Creek, the outlet at the edge of camp, is scenic in its own right. Across the creek from camp is a resort where boat rentals and other services are available. A trail to Fawn Lake begins near the resort.

6 Princess Creek

Location: About 6 miles northwest of the town of Crescent Lake, on Odell Lake
Season: Mid-May–October
Sites: 46 basic sites; no hookups
Maximum length: 40 feet
Facilities: Tables, grills, vault toilets, boat launch, dock; no drinking water
Fee per night: $$
Management: Deschutes National Forest
Contact: (541) 433–3200; www.fs.fed.us/r6/centraloregon/recreation
Finding the campground: It is south off Oregon 58, 5.6 miles northwest of Crescent Lake.
About the campground: This camp is spread along the north shore of Odell Lake. You can see Diamond Peak across the water. Great concentrations of hemlock, along with fir and spruce, shade the camp and protect it from the lake's notorious afternoon winds. The camp has a paved road, gravel parking, and comfortable sites, but it does get some traffic noise from OR 58 during the day. The lake is prized for its boating, fishing, and swimming. Bald eagles and ospreys also fish this 6-mile-long natural lake.

7 Spring

Location: About 9 miles southwest of the town of Crescent Lake, on Crescent Lake
Season: Mid-May–October
Sites: 68 basic sites; no hookups
Maximum length: 40 feet
Facilities: Tables, grills, vault toilets, drinking water, boat launch, dock
Fee per night: $$
Management: Deschutes National Forest
Contact: (541) 433–3200; www.fs.fed.us/r6/centraloregon/recreation
Finding the campground: From the community of Crescent Lake on Oregon 58, go south 2.3 miles on paved Forest Road 60 and turn right to remain on FR 60 for another 5.8 miles. Turn left and proceed 0.6 mile to enter camp.
About the campground: This is a developed campground on the south shore of Crescent Lake, a large lake on the outskirts of the Diamond Peak Wilderness. Sites have gravel parking and basic amenities and are partially shaded by lodgepole pines. Campers enjoy access to the lake for fishing, swimming, boating, waterskiing, sailboarding, and sailing and to Diamond Peak Wilderness for hiking. A trailhead 0.3 mile west of camp accesses the Oregon Cascades Recreation Area. Lake visitors should come prepared for mosquitoes at the start of summer.

8   Sunset Cove

Location: About 3 miles northwest of the town of Crescent Lake, on Odell Lake
Season: Mid-May–October
Sites: 20 basic sites; no hookups
Maximum length: 40 feet
Facilities: Tables, grills, vault toilets, drinking water, boat launch, dock, wheelchair-accessible jetty for fishing, fish-cleaning station
Fee per night: $$
Management: Deschutes National Forest
Contact: (541) 433–3200; www.fs.fed.us/r6/centraloregon/recreation
Finding the campground: It is south off Oregon 58, 4.7 miles east of Willamette Pass and 2.8 miles west of Crescent Lake Junction.
About the campground: This Odell Lake camp is situated in an evergreen forest punctuated by old-growth trees. Its location on the east shore provides front-row seating for sunset viewing, but it also puts you in the path of the strong afternoon winds if you venture out of tree cover. Nonetheless, the fishing, boating, swimming, and attractive setting overrule the wind factor, and sailboarders seem more than satisfied with the location's "drawback."

9   Trapper Creek

Location: About 9 miles northwest of the town of Crescent Lake, on Odell Lake
Season: June–October
Sites: 32 basic sites; no hookups
Maximum length: 40 feet
Facilities: Tables, grills, vault toilets, drinking water, boat launch, small dock
Fee per night: $$
Management: Deschutes National Forest
Contact: (541) 433–3200; www.fs.fed.us/r6/centraloregon/recreation
Finding the campground: From Oregon 58, 0.5 mile east of Willamette Pass and 7 miles west of Crescent Lake Junction, turn south on Odell Lake West Access Road/Forest Road 5810, go 2 miles, and turn left for the camp.
About the campground: On the west shore of Odell Lake, along pretty Trapper Creek, this camp is tucked in a fir and spruce forest, where huckleberries claim the understory. A paved road connects the sites, most of which have full shade and are protected from the wind. A few sites overlook Odell Lake, an enormous mountain lake that offers fine views, first-rate fishing, superb boating, and swimming. If you want a change of pace, the Yoran Lake Trail starts near camp.

10 Whitefish Horse Camp

Location: About 7 miles south of the town of Crescent Lake, near Crescent Lake
Season: Mid-May–October
Sites: 17 basic sites; no hookups
Maximum length: 40 feet
Facilities: Tables, grills, vault toilets, drinking water, corrals
Fee per night: $$
Management: Deschutes National Forest
Contact: (541) 433-3200; (877) 444-6777 for reservations; www.fs.fed.us/r6 /centraloregon/recreation
Finding the campground: From the community of Crescent Lake on Oregon 58, head south on paved Forest Road 60 for 2.3 miles. Turn right to remain on FR 60 and go another 4.4 miles to the campground entrance on the right.
About the campground: This camp is for the exclusive use of equestrians. It is highly functional, with both ample space between the sites and long, gravel parking pads. Corral size determines the difference in site pricing. The horse camp is set back in a lodgepole pine forest across the road from Crescent Lake, giving visitors the best of two worlds: the quiet of the forest and the recreation of the lake. Nearby day-use areas provide access to the lake. Horse trails leave camp to enter Diamond Peak Wilderness.

Roseburg Area

11 Amacher Park

Location: About 3 miles north of Roseburg
Season: April–October
Sites: 20 hookup sites, 10 tent sites; water, electric, and sewer hookups
Maximum length: 35 feet
Facilities: Tables, flush toilets, drinking water, showers, telephone, boat launch
Fee per night: $$
Management: Douglas County
Contact: (541) 957-7001; www.co.douglas.or.us/parks
Finding the campground: From Interstate 5, take exit 129 and head south along the east side of the freeway for 0.5 mile. Turn right to pass under the bridge supports and enter the park.
About the campground: Located along the North Umpqua River and below the freeway and a rail line is this attractive but somewhat noisy park. It has beautiful lawns and big shade trees, and the North Umpqua seldom disappoints anglers and boaters. Any swimming is at your own risk. Look for a beautiful myrtle grove near the day-use area.

Roseburg Area

	Hookup sites	Total sites	Maximum RV length	Hookups	Toilets	Showers	Drinking water	Dump station	Recreation	Fee	Can reserve
11 Amacher Park	20	30	35	WES	F	•	•		FBL	$$	
12 Cavitt Creek Recreation Site		10	30		NF		•		S	$	
13 Coolwater		7	24		NF		•		F	$	
14 Douglas County Fairgrounds RV Park	50	50	40	WE	F	•	•	•		$$$	
15 Hemlock Lake		13	35		NF				HFBL	$	
16 Lake in the Woods		11	35		F		•		HF	$	
17 Millpond Recreation Site		12	30		F,NF		•		SF	$	
18 Pass Creek County Park	30	40	42	WES	F	•	•		F	$$	
19 Rock Creek Recreation Site		17	30		NF		•		SF	$	
20 Susan Creek Recreation Site		31	30		F	•	•		HFB	$$	
21 Tyee		15	40		NF		•		SF	$	
22 Whistler's Bend Park		25	30		F,NF	•	•		HSFBL	$$	
23 Wolf Creek		8	30		F		•		HSF	$	

12 Cavitt Creek Recreation Site

Location: About 26 miles east of Roseburg
Season: Mid-May–early October
Sites: 10 basic sites; no hookups
Maximum length: 30 feet
Facilities: Tables, grills, vault toilets, drinking water
Fee per night: $
Management: Roseburg District Bureau of Land Management
Contact: (541) 440–4930; www.or.blm.gov/roseburg
Finding the campground: From Roseburg, drive 16.4 miles east on Oregon 138 to Glide. Turn south onto Little River Road (County Road 17). Go 6.6 miles and turn right onto Cavitt Creek Road. Pass through the covered bridge and continue another 3.2 miles to arrive at the campground.
About the campground: This popular, primitive campground sits above Cavitt Creek in a Douglas fir forest threaded with vine maples and ocean spray. A paved path links the camp with a day-use area and leads to a creek overlook and a stairway to an inviting swimming hole that is fed by a 5-foot cascade. The creek is closed to fishing. Spring wildflowers are varied and many.

Fishing in the North Umpqua River.

13   Coolwater

Location: About 33 miles east of Roseburg
Season: Late May–October
Sites: 7 basic sites; no hookups
Maximum length: 24 feet
Facilities: Tables, grills, vault toilets, drinking water
Fee per night: $
Management: Umpqua National Forest
Contact: (541) 496–3532; www.fs.fed.us/r6/umpqua/recreation
Finding the campground: From Roseburg, drive 16.4 miles east on Oregon 138 to Glide. Turn south onto Little River Road (County Road 17/Forest Road 27) and go 16.1 miles to this camp.
About the campground: This camp along the Little River enjoys a quiet setting of evergreens and maples. Camp guests may fish or frolic on the river or take the drive to Grotto Falls Trail: Across FR 27 from camp, take the marked turn for the falls on gravel FR 2703, go 4.3 miles, and turn left onto FR 2703.150. Go 2 miles more to reach the trailhead. This quarter-mile trail leads from clearcut to old-growth forest on its way to the 100-foot falls. The trail then wraps behind the falls to a grotto for protected viewing of the misty veil of water. Just 5.6 miles northwest of camp on Little River Road is a 1-mile trail through old-growth splendor to Wolf Creek Falls.

14   Douglas County Fairgrounds RV Park

Location: In Roseburg
Season: Year-round, except during the county fair the second week in August
Sites: 50 hookup sites; water and electric hookups
Maximum length: 40 feet
Facilities: Some tables, flush toilets, drinking water, showers, dump station, telephone
Fee per night: $$$
Management: Douglas County
Contact: (541) 440–4505
Finding the campground: From Interstate 5 at the south end of Roseburg, take exit 123 to reach the fairgrounds on the east side of the freeway.
About the campground: This clean, serviceable RV park is convenient for those attending fairground events and for travelers on I-5. Sites have gravel pads with lawn meridians on which to place your chair. A few mature trees provide shade, and the younger, planted trees promise more shade in the future. Also on the fairgrounds is the fine Douglas County Museum of History and Natural History.

15 Hemlock Lake

Location: About 47 miles east of Roseburg, on Hemlock Lake
Season: June–October
Sites: 13 basic sites; no hookups
Maximum length: 35 feet
Facilities: Tables, grills, vault toilets, boat launch; no drinking water
Fee per night: $
Management: Umpqua National Forest
Contact: (541) 496–3532; www.fs.fed.us/r6/umpqua/recreation
Finding the campground: From Roseburg, go 16.4 miles east on Oregon 138 to Glide. Turn south onto Little River Road (County Road 17/Forest Road 27) and follow the signs for Hemlock Lake. After 29.6 miles, turn right off FR 27 onto FR 2700.495 and go another 0.7 mile to the camp.
About the campground: You will find this pleasant campground on a fir-covered slope above the dam that forms Hemlock Lake. The manmade lake is the chief draw, inviting fishing and nonmotorized boating. If you prefer to hike, trails explore along the lake and visit Yellow Jacket Glade. Wildflower meadows and stands of old growth complement the trails.

16 Lake in the Woods

Location: About 42 miles east of Roseburg
Season: Late May–October
Sites: 11 basic sites; no hookups
Maximum length: 35 feet
Facilities: Tables, grills, flush toilets, drinking water
Fee per night: $
Management: Umpqua National Forest
Contact: (541) 496–3532; www.fs.fed.us/r6/umpqua/recreation
Finding the campground: From Roseburg, go 16.4 miles east on Oregon 138 to Glide. Turn south onto Little River Road (County Road 17/Forest Road 27) and go 26 miles to this camp on the right.
About the campground: This out-of-the-way camp offers a shady retreat in an old-growth forest at the edge of Lake in the Woods, a former swamp, horse pasture, and now lake. The shallow lake wears a cap of lilies and a ring of cat-tails, while rhododendron bushes decorate the forest. A restored historic cabin sits beside the lake. Seventy-foot Yakso Falls and 80-foot Hemlock Falls are only short hikes away.

17 Millpond Recreation Site

Location: About 27 miles northeast of Roseburg
Season: Mid-May–mid-October
Sites: 12 basic sites; no hookups
Maximum length: 30 feet
Facilities: Tables, grills, flush and vault toilets, drinking water, horseshoe pits, playing field, barrier-free trail along the creek, picnic pavilion

Fee per night: $
Management: Roseburg District Bureau of Land Management
Contact: (541) 440–4930; www.or.blm.gov/roseburg
Finding the campground: From Oregon 138, 22.4 miles east of Roseburg (about 6 miles east of Glide), turn left (northeast) onto Rock Creek Road and go 5 miles to the camp.
About the campground: The sites of this Rock Creek campground are distributed among second-growth trees and abundant groundcover. The riprap along the creek creates areas of deeper, faster water; there is one pool suitable for swimming. Rock Creek Fish Hatchery, near the junction of OR 138 and Rock Creek Road, is open year-round. You can view juvenile, fingerling, and brood fish, including chinook and coho salmon, steelhead, and rainbow trout.

18 Pass Creek County Park

Location: About 40 miles north of Roseburg
Season: Year-round
Sites: 30 hookup sites, 10 tent sites; water, electric, and sewer hookups
Maximum length: 42 feet
Facilities: Tables, grills, flush toilets, drinking water, showers, playground, laundry
Fee per night: $$
Management: Douglas County
Contact: (541) 957–7001; www.co.douglas.or.us/parks
Finding the campground: From exit 163 on Interstate 5, 10 miles south of Cottage Grove, follow frontage Curtin Park Road north along the west side of the freeway into the park.
About the campground: This clean, attractive, 23-acre park is sandwiched between Pass Creek and the freeway on the east and a rail line on the west. Sites have paved parking, and the shrub dividers contribute to privacy. Mature conifer and deciduous trees lend shade. A manmade pond is available for fishing; it supports crappie, bass, bluegill, and some trout. Geese make themselves at home at a small wildlife sanctuary in the park.

19 Rock Creek Recreation Site

Location: About 29 miles northeast of Roseburg
Season: Mid-May–October
Sites: 17 basic sites; no hookups
Maximum length: 30 feet
Facilities: Tables, grills, vault toilets, drinking water, site cabinets
Fee per night: $
Management: Roseburg District Bureau of Land Management
Contact: (541) 440–4930; www.or.blm.gov/roseburg
Finding the campground: From Oregon 138, 22.4 miles east of Roseburg (about 6 miles east of Glide), turn left (northeast) onto Rock Creek Road and go 6.6 miles to the camp entrance.
About the campground: This camp offers a relaxing stay along Rock Creek.

Second-growth firs and cedars join bigleaf maples and alders in providing shade for the sites, which are roomy and comfortable. Rock Creek flows wide and shallow, with a few deeper pools for wading. The camp is just a short drive from the Umpqua River, where you can hike, fly-fish, raft, kayak, or sightsee.

20 Susan Creek Recreation Site

Location: About 30 miles east of Roseburg
Season: May–October
Sites: 31 basic sites; no hookups
Maximum length: 30 feet
Facilities: Tables, grills, flush toilets, drinking water, showers, barrier-free trails, wildlife viewing platform
Fee per night: $$
Management: Roseburg District Bureau of Land Management
Contact: (541) 440–4930; www.or.blm.gov/roseburg
Finding the campground: It is south off Oregon 138, 29.5 miles east of Roseburg (12.5 miles east of Glide).
About the campground: This attractive, popular camp, which overlooks the North Umpqua River, was designed to be accessible and convenient for individuals with disabilities. The sites rest in a soothing setting of mature trees along the wild and scenic river, which is open to fly-fishing, rafting, and kayaking. A magnificent 79-mile trail follows the river from its headwaters high in the Cascades to the Swiftwater Trailhead, west of camp. At Susan Creek Recreation Site, short trails lead to the river and a watchable wildlife platform. Others link the camp to the day-use area, visit 50-foot Susan Creek Falls, and pass rock mounds left long ago by participants in an Indian rite of manhood.

21 Tyee

Location: About 23 miles northwest of Roseburg
Season: May–first week of October
Sites: 15 basic sites; no hookups
Maximum length: 40 feet
Facilities: Tables, grills, vault toilets, drinking water
Fee per night: $
Management: Roseburg District Bureau of Land Management
Contact: (541) 440–4930; www.or.blm.gov/roseburg
Finding the campground: From Interstate 5 at Sutherlin, take exit 136 and go west on Oregon 138 for 10.6 miles. Cross the river bridge and go 0.2 mile to Bullock Road. Turn right and follow Bullock Road 0.3 mile to the campground on the right.
About the campground: On a plateau above the Umpqua River, a day-use area divides the campground. A mix of fir, cedar, maple, vine maple, and dogwood lend full shade. Leafy shrubs contribute privacy to the already well-spaced sites. A paved path travels the length of the rim and offers views of the

river, while stairs descend to a river access. Although regulations prohibit trout fishing, anglers still find sport, and the camp is quiet and restful.

22 Whistler's Bend Park

Location: About 15 miles northeast of Roseburg
Season: Year-round
Sites: 23 basic sites, 2 yurts; no hookups
Maximum length: 30 feet
Facilities: Tables, grills, flush and chemical toilets, drinking water, showers, playground (at day-use area), boat launch
Fee per night: $$
Management: Douglas County
Contact: (541) 673–4863; www.co.douglas.or.us/parks.asp
Finding the campground: From Roseburg, go east on Oregon 138 for 12 miles and turn left (north) onto Whistler's Park Road. Go 2.7 miles to enter the county park and follow the signs to the camp.
About the campground: This 148-acre park tucked in a bend of the North Umpqua River provides campers with ample room to roam. Because it is managed as a wildlife refuge, the park also offers opportunities to watch birds and wildlife, including the rare Columbia white-tailed deer. Nestled at the foot of a hill, the rustic camp blends with its oak woodland and riverbank setting. The parking is paved. In spring, camas and iris adorn the natural grasses. The river captivates with it blue-green clarity and recreation. As always, be sure to check current fishing regulations. A river trail invites exercise, but beware of poison oak when exploring.

23 Wolf Creek

Location: About 28 miles east of Roseburg
Season: Mid-May–September
Sites: 8 basic sites; no hookups
Maximum length: 30 feet
Facilities: Tables, grills, flush toilets, drinking water (volleyball, horseshoe pits, and playing field at day-use area)
Fee per night: $
Management: Umpqua National Forest
Contact: (541) 496–3532; www.fs.fed.us/r6/umpqua/recreation
Finding the campground: From Roseburg, go 16.4 miles east on Oregon 138 to Glide. Then head south on Little River Road (County Road 17/Forest Road 27) and go 11.7 miles to enter this camp on the right.
About the campground: This campground along the Little River offers closely spaced sites in a second-growth forest. A nature trail makes a loop through the mixed tree setting; you can access it at the camp or via the bridge over the river at the day-use area. If you drive 1.2 miles west of camp, you can walk the 1-mile Wolf Creek Trail, which crosses the crescent-shaped bridge over the Little River to tour a classic low-elevation forest en route to Wolf Creek Falls. The trail halts at an outcrop with an impressive view of the 80-foot upper-falls segment; below the viewpoint is the lower chute.

Steamboat–Lemolo Lake Area

24 | Apple Creek

Location: About 5 miles east of Steamboat
Season: Late May–October
Sites: 8 basic sites; no hookups
Maximum length: 22 feet
Facilities: Tables, grills, pit toilets; no drinking water
Fee per night: $
Management: Umpqua National Forest
Contact: (541) 496–3532; www.fs.fed.us/r6/umpqua/recreation
Finding the campground: It is south off Oregon 138, 4.5 miles east of Steamboat and 25.5 miles east of Glide.
About the campground: This campground rests on a forested bench below OR 138 and along the prized North Umpqua River. The camp is shaded by a mix of conifer and deciduous trees and has a luxuriant understory. Hikers will find the Panther Trailhead for the 79-mile North Umpqua National Recreation

Steamboat–Lemolo Lake Area

	Hookup sites	Total sites	Maximum RV length	Hookups	Toilets	Showers	Drinking water	Dump station	Recreation	Fee	Can reserve
24 Apple Creek		8	22		NF				HF	$	
25 Bogus Creek		15	35		F		•		SFBL	$	
26 Boulder Flat		11	24		NF				HSFBL	$	
27 Bunker Hill		8	small		NF				HFB	$	
28 Canton Creek		5	22		F		•		S	$	
29 Clearwater Falls		9	25		NF					$	
30 Eagle Rock		25	30		NF		•		HF	$	
31 East Lemolo		15	22		NF				FBL	$	
32 Horseshoe Bend		24	35		F		•		HSFBL	$$	
33 Inlet		13	25		NF				HFB	$	
34 Island		7	20		NF				SFB	$	
35 Kelsay Valley Trailhead Camp		16	20		NF				HFR	$	
36 Poole Creek		59	35		NF		•		HSFBL	$	
37 Scaredman Creek Recreation Site		9	25		NF				S		
38 Steamboat Falls		10	20		NF				S		
39 Toketee Lake		32	30		NF				HFBL	$	
40 Whitehorse Falls		5	25		NF					$	

Trail just west of the campground turnoff: Follow Forest Road 4714 south across the river bridge to the trailhead. The trail both follows the river and climbs to the upper canyon.

25 Bogus Creek

Location: 4 miles west of Steamboat
Season: Late May–mid-October
Sites: 15 basic sites; no hookups
Maximum length: 35 feet
Facilities: Tables, grills, flush toilets, drinking water, raft launch
Fee per night: $
Management: Umpqua National Forest
Contact: (541) 496–3532; www.fs.fed.us/r6/umpqua/recreation
Finding the campground: It is north off Oregon 138, 4 miles west of Steamboat and about 17 miles east of Glide.
About the campground: Across OR 138 from the North Umpqua River and a public river access, this campground sits in a restful forest setting beside Bogus Creek. Douglas firs dominate the landscape, and the sites are well spaced for comfort. The river is within easy striking distance for rafting, kayaking, and fly-fishing. About a mile west is the Wright Creek Trailhead for the North Umpqua National Recreation Trail.

26 Boulder Flat

Location: 16 miles east of Steamboat
Season: Late May–mid-September
Sites: 11 basic sites; no hookups
Maximum length: 24 feet
Facilities: Tables, grills, vault toilets, raft launch; no drinking water
Fee per night: $
Management: Umpqua National Forest
Contact: (541) 496–3532; www.fs.fed.us/r6/umpqua/recreation
Finding the campground: It is north off Oregon 138, 16 miles east of Steamboat and 37 miles east of Glide.
About the campground: This camp, with its well-spaced sites, occupies a fir and maple flat on the North Umpqua River across from the Boulder Creek confluence. There is direct access to the river for fishing and rafting. The camp also lies within reach of the North Umpqua National Recreation Trail (accessed via Marsters Bridge to the west or near Soda Springs Dam 2 miles to the east) and the Boulder Creek Trail (also reached near Soda Springs Dam).

27 Bunker Hill

Location: About 60 miles east of Glide, on Lemolo Lake
Season: Mid-May–October
Sites: 8 basic sites; no hookups
Maximum length: Small units only
Facilities: Tables, grills, pit toilets; no drinking water
Fee per night: $
Management: Umpqua National Forest
Contact: (541) 498–2531; www.fs.fed.us/r6/umpqua/recreation
Finding the campground: From Oregon 138, 54 miles east of Glide, turn north onto Forest Road 2610 (Birds Point Road), signed for Lemolo Lake. Go 3 miles to a junction and proceed straight on FR 2610 for another 2.5 miles. Turn right onto FR 2612, go 0.6 mile, and turn right to enter the camp.
About the campground: Below forested Bunker Hill on the northwest shore of manmade Lemolo Lake sits this small, rustic campground ideally suited for tents. You may spot bald eagles soaring over camp. Fishing and hiking are popular pastimes here; boating access is available elsewhere on the lake. Look for the North Umpqua National Recreation Trail near the intersection of FR 2610 and FR 2612. OR 138 is part of the Rogue–Umpqua Scenic Byway, should you get the itch to sightsee.

28 Canton Creek

Location: Less than 1 mile northeast of Steamboat
Season: Mid-May–mid-October
Sites: 5 basic sites; no hookups
Maximum length: 22 feet
Facilities: Tables, grills, flush toilets, drinking water
Fee per night: $
Management: Umpqua National Forest
Contact: (541) 496–3532; www.fs.fed.us/r6/umpqua/recreation
Finding the campground: From Oregon 138 in Steamboat, 21 miles east of Glide, go 0.3 mile north on Forest Road 38 (Steamboat Creek Road). The campground is on the right.
About the campground: This small, lightly used campground is best suited for tent camping. It occupies a low bluff above Steamboat Creek near the Canton Creek confluence and is a popular place to swim in summer. Firs, maples, alders, and cedars shade the sites. A day-use area claims the upper end of the camp, and a memorial honors three Douglas County law enforcement officers who lost their lives in a helicopter crash nearby. Both Steamboat and Canton Creeks are closed to angling to protect spawning steelhead and salmon, but the North Umpqua River is open for catch-and-release fly-fishing. Steamboat Falls, upstream from the camp via FR 38, is worth visiting and photographing; in the fall, look for spawning chinooks.

29 Clearwater Falls

Location: About 52 miles east of Glide
Season: June–October
Sites: 9 basic sites; no hookups
Maximum length: 25 feet
Facilities: Tables, grills, vault or pit toilets; no drinking water
Fee per night: $
Management: Umpqua National Forest
Contact: (541) 498–2531; www.fs.fed.us/r6/umpqua/recreation
Finding the campground: The western half of the campground sits south off Oregon 138, 51.5 miles east of Glide. The eastern half is reached by traveling another 1.2 miles east on OR 138, turning right (south) on FR 4785, then heading right (west) on Trap Creek Loop. Enter the campground in 0.8 mile.
About the campground: Parted by Clearwater Creek and its waterfall, this campground and its day-use area offer forest relaxation and falls viewing. The western campsites occupy a slope of old-growth Douglas firs and mountain hemlocks and have better access to the waterfall viewing. The eastern sites are more open, sitting along the quiet water at the head of the falls. Because of some awkward approaches, the campground is best suited for small units and tent camping. Mossy boulders and logs accentuate sparkling Clearwater Falls. From OR 138, you can reach additional falls, as well as trails and Toketee, Lemolo, and Diamond Lakes.

30 Eagle Rock

Location: About 12 miles east of Steamboat
Season: Late May–mid-September
Sites: 25 basic sites; no hookups
Maximum length: 30 feet
Facilities: Tables, grills, vault toilets, drinking water
Fee per night: $
Management: Umpqua National Forest
Contact: (541) 496–3532; www.fs.fed.us/r6/umpqua/recreation
Finding the campground: It is north off Oregon 138, 11.5 miles east of Steamboat and 32.5 miles east of Glide.
About the campground: This camp on the North Umpqua Wild and Scenic River has paved roads and parking. Sites are well spaced along a forested flat; some are fully shaded by firs, while others receive a mixture of sun and shade. The landmark outcrop known as Eagle Rock overlooks this part of the river. Hikers can access the North Umpqua National Recreation Trail at Marsters Bridge to the west. OR 138 serves up a scenic river drive for those who prefer to save the boot leather.

31 East Lemolo

Location: About 60 miles east of Glide, on Lemolo Lake
Season: Mid-May–October
Sites: 15 basic sites; no hookups
Maximum length: 22 feet
Facilities: Tables, grills, vault toilets, primitive boat launch; no drinking water
Fee per night: $
Management: Umpqua National Forest
Contact: (541) 498–2531; www.fs.fed.us/r6/umpqua/recreation
Finding the campground: From Oregon 138, 54 miles east of Glide, turn north onto Forest Road 2610 toward Lemolo Lake. Go 3 miles and turn right onto FR 2614. Go 2.2 miles, turn left onto gravel FR 2614.430, and proceed 0.3 mile to the camp at road's end.
About the campground: This camp overlooks the east shore of Lemolo Lake, a reservoir harnessing the North Umpqua River. The earthen sites are tucked among tightly clustered lodgepole pines. Because the camp is small, most sites offer views of the lake; some are right on the lakeshore. Forested Bunker Hill is visible across the water. Boating is a popular pastime, as is fishing for kokanee and rainbow and brown trout.

32 Horseshoe Bend

Location: About 8 miles east of Steamboat
Season: Late May–late September
Sites: 24 basic sites; no hookups
Maximum length: 35 feet
Facilities: Tables, grills, flush toilets, drinking water, raft put-in
Fee per night: $$
Management: Umpqua National Forest
Contact: (541) 496–3532; www.fs.fed.us/r6/umpqua/recreation
Finding the campground: From Oregon 138, 7.5 miles east of Steamboat, turn south at the sign for Horseshoe Bend Campground, Raft Launch, and North Umpqua Trail. Go 0.1 mile and turn right onto Forest Road 4750. Drive another 0.8 mile to the camp.
About the campground: This facility consists of three camp flats: Beaver, Deer, and Otter. Deer Flat is for groups and must be reserved in advance. For wheelchair-accessible sites and accommodations, go to Beaver Flat. The single-party campsites have paved parking and are nestled in the woods along the North Umpqua River. The riffles and pools of the river invite fishing, hiking, and rafting. You will find a river access trail in Otter Flat. From the Horseshoe Bend Raft Put-in, it is a 2- to 3-hour float to Gravel Bin Takeout, 6.7 miles downstream. The North Umpqua National Recreation Trail follows the river on the opposite shore; you can access it by backtracking 0.8 mile on FR 4750 and driving across the one-lane bridge to the trailhead.

33 Inlet

Location: About 60 miles east of Glide, on Lemolo Lake
Season: Mid-May–October
Sites: 13 basic sites; no hookups
Maximum length: 25 feet
Facilities: Tables, grills, vault toilets; no drinking water
Fee per night: $
Management: Umpqua National Forest
Contact: (541) 498–2531; www.fs.fed.us/r6/umpqua/recreation
Finding the campground: From Oregon 138, 54 miles east of Glide, turn north onto Forest Road 2610 toward Lemolo Lake. Go 3 miles to a junction and turn right onto FR 2614. Go 2.6 miles more to the camp entrance on the right.
About the campground: This camp sits across the road from the east shore of Lemolo Lake at the point where the North Umpqua River feeds into the reservoir. Lupine and paintbrush adorn the floor of the lodgepole pine forest. The camp has gravel roads and parking and offers convenient lake access for fishing. The North Umpqua National Recreation Trail passes nearby.

34 Island

Location: 1 mile east of Steamboat
Season: Year-round
Sites: 7 basic sites; no hookups
Maximum length: 20 feet
Facilities: Tables, grills, vault toilets; no drinking water
Fee per night: $
Management: Umpqua National Forest
Contact: (541) 496–3532; www.fs.fed.us/r6/umpqua/recreation
Finding the campground: It is south off Oregon 138, 1 mile east of Steamboat.
About the campground: This camp is cut into a slope between OR 138 and the North Umpqua Wild and Scenic River, a blue-ribbon fly-fishing stream that has attracted the likes of author Zane Grey. Firs, maples, dogwoods, and the song of the river add to the camp's appeal. When river levels are adequate, you can make a 2- to 3-hour float trip between Horseshoe Bend Raft Put-in (6.5 miles east on OR 138) and Gravel Bin Raft Takeout (0.2 mile west of camp).

35 Kelsay Valley Trailhead Camp

Location: About 62 miles east of Glide
Season: Mid-May–September
Sites: 16 basic sites; no hookups
Maximum length: 20 feet
Facilities: Tables, grills, vault toilets, corral, hitching posts; no drinking water
Fee per night: $
Management: Umpqua National Forest

Contact: (541) 498–2531; www.fs.fed.us/r6/umpqua/recreation
Finding the campground: From Oregon 138, 56 miles east of Glide, turn north onto gravel Forest Road 60 (Windigo Pass Road). Go 4.5 miles, turn right onto red-dirt FR 6000.958, and follow it 1.5 miles to the camp and trailhead. You bypass a 2-site camp en route.
About the campground: This camp is designed to serve both families and equestrian campers. Several site spurs are long enough to accommodate horse trailers. The camp rests in a lodgepole pine forest on the outskirts of a wildflower-spangled high meadow threaded by Bradley Creek, a tributary of the North Umpqua River. Hiker/horse trails travel the area. If you follow the North Umpqua Trail upstream, you will eventually reach the river's headwaters, Maidu Lake, on the Cascade Crest. Come prepared for mosquitoes.

36 Poole Creek

Location: About 58 miles east of Glide, on Lemolo Lake
Season: Mid-May–October
Sites: 59 basic sites; no hookups
Maximum length: 35 feet
Facilities: Tables, grills, vault toilets, drinking water, boat launch, dock
Fee per night: $
Management: Umpqua National Forest
Contact: (541) 498–2531; www.fs.fed.us/r6/umpqua/recreation
Finding the campground: From Oregon 138, 54 miles east of Glide, turn north onto Forest Road 2610 toward Lemolo Lake. Go 3 miles to a junction and proceed straight on FR 2610 for another mile to the campground entrance on the right.
About the campground: This camp sits in a dry forest of lodgepole pines, Shasta red firs, and mountain hemlocks on the western shore of Lemolo Lake, which captures the North Umpqua River as it descends from the Cascade Crest. Boating is a chief draw, as is fishing for kokanee and trout: eastern brook, rainbow, and German brown. Hiking trails and a designated swimming beach provide other diversions. Waterskiing is allowed on part of the lake.

37 Scaredman Creek Recreation Site

Location: About 4 miles north of Steamboat
Season: Maintained May–October
Sites: 9 basic sites; no hookups
Maximum length: 25 feet
Facilities: Tables, grills, pit toilets; no drinking water
Fee per night: None
Management: Roseburg District Bureau of Land Management
Contact: (541) 440–4930; www.or.blm.gov/roseburg
Finding the campground: From Oregon 138 at Steamboat, 21 miles east of Glide, head northeast on Forest Road 38 (Steamboat Creek Road) for 0.5 mile and turn left onto Canton Creek Road. Go another 3.5 miles to enter this camp on the right.

About the campground: You will find this quiet camp in a tall stand of Douglas firs along Canton Creek, downstream from the confluence with Scaredman Creek. Although Canton Creek is closed to fishing, the creek's beauty still engages as it riffles over gravel beds and pinches into green pools. This camp is ideal for escaping civilization or exploring the North Umpqua River corridor.

38　Steamboat Falls

Location: About 6 miles northeast of Steamboat
Season: June–November
Sites: 10 basic sites; no hookups
Maximum length: 20 feet
Facilities: Tables, grills, vault toilets; no drinking water
Fee per night: None
Management: Umpqua National Forest
Contact: (541) 496–3532; www.fs.fed.us/r6/umpqua/recreation
Finding the campground: From Oregon 138 in Steamboat, 21 miles east of Glide, go northeast 5.5 miles on Forest Road 38 (Steamboat Creek Road). Turn right onto FR 3810 and continue another 0.6 mile to the camp entrance.
About the campground: This campground lines a forested bench along Steamboat Creek at Steamboat Falls, a dazzling, multidirectional, tiered waterfall that spans the 70- to 100-foot breadth of the creek. A fish ladder helps salmon bypass the falls as they migrate upstream. Because the creek is a critical spawning ground for salmon and steelhead, it and its tributaries are closed to fishing.

39　Toketee Lake

Location: About 43 miles east of Glide, on Toketee Lake
Season: Year-round, weather permitting
Sites: 32 basic sites; no hookups
Maximum length: 30 feet
Facilities: Tables, grills, pit toilets, boat launch, dock; no drinking water
Fee per night: $
Management: Umpqua National Forest
Contact: (541) 498–2531; www.fs.fed.us/r6/umpqua/recreation
Finding the campground: From Oregon 138, 41 miles east of Glide, turn north onto Forest Road 34 (Toketee-Rigdon Road). Go 0.3 mile, turn left to remain on FR 34, and go another 1.2 miles to the campground entrance on the right.
About the campground: This restful camp is located along the upper North Umpqua River, where it feeds into manmade Toketee Lake. The river resembles a sparkling, creek-sized ribbon as it races past camp. Cedars and alders frame the waterway and shade the campsites. The camp has gravel roads and earthen parking, as well as an adjacent boat launch. Campers can boat and fish the reservoir. The North Umpqua National Recreation Trail passes next to

camp, and the Toketee Lake Trail can be found along FR 34, 0.5 mile south of the camp entrance.

40 Whitehorse Falls

Location: About 48 miles east of Glide
Season: June–October
Sites: 5 basic sites; no hookups
Maximum length: 25 feet
Facilities: Tables, grills, vault toilets; no drinking water
Fee per night: $
Management: Umpqua National Forest
Contact: (541) 498–2531; www.fs.fed.us/r6/umpqua/recreation
Finding the campground: It is north off Oregon 138, 48 miles east of Glide.
About the campground: This tiny, lightly used campground rests in a stand of old-growth Douglas firs above the Clearwater River and Whitehorse Falls. Rhododendrons and chinquapins complement the towering trees. At the camp's small picnic area, a viewing platform overlooks the 12-foot falls. A stair-step series of small cascades precedes the falls, and a deep, tranquil pool collects the plummeting water before it continues downstream. Additional falls along OR 138 may suggest outings, as will Toketee, Lemolo, and Diamond Lakes.

Crater Lake–Diamond Lake Area

41 Abbott Creek

Location: About 10 miles north of Prospect
Season: Mid-May–October
Sites: 25 basic sites; no hookups
Maximum length: 40 feet
Facilities: Tables, grills, pit toilets, drinking water
Fee per night: $$
Management: Rogue River National Forest
Contact: (541) 560–3400; www.fs.fed.us/r6/rogue-siskiyou
Finding the campground: From Oregon 62, 6.2 miles north of Prospect and 6.3 miles south of the junction of OR 62 and OR 230, turn west on Forest Road 68 and go 3.6 miles to reach the camp on the left.
About the campground: This camp flat beside Abbott Creek presents a mosaic of open meadow, clustered shrubs, and pocket groves of pines, firs, and deciduous trees. There are sites to appeal to the sun seeker, the shade lover, and even the undecided. The camp is quiet and rustic and offers access to the creek at several points. Because the creek is small, youngsters can fish and explore without getting into too much trouble.

Crater Lake–Diamond Lake Area

	Hookup sites	Total sites	Maximum RV length	Hookups	Toilets	Showers	Drinking water	Dump station	Recreation	Fee	Can reserve
41 Abbott Creek		25	40		NF		•		F	$$	
42 Broken Arrow		148	35		F	•	•	•	HSFBLC	$	
43 Crater Lake National Park: Lost Creek		16	T		NF		•			$$	
44 Crater Lake National Park: Mazama		200	30		F	•	•	•	H	$$	
45 Diamond Lake		240	35		F	•	•	•	HSFBLC	$$	•
46 Farewell Bend		61	40		F		•		HF	$$	
47 Hamaker		10	30		NF		•		HF	$$	
48 Huckleberry Mountain		25	25		NF		•				
49 Mill Creek		10	25		NF				F	$	
50 Natural Bridge		17	40		NF				HF	$	
51 River Bridge		10	30		NF				HF	$	
52 Thielsen View		60	35		NF		•		HSFBLC	$	
53 Union Creek		74	30		NF		•		HF	$$	

42 Broken Arrow

Location: On Diamond Lake
Season: Late May–September
Sites: 148 basic sites; no hookups
Maximum length: 35 feet
Facilities: Tables, grills, flush toilets, drinking water, showers, dump station, barrier-free facilities
Fee per night: $
Management: Umpqua National Forest
Contact: (541) 498–2531; www.fs.fed.us/r6/umpqua/recreation
Finding the campground: From Oregon 138, 80 miles east of Roseburg, turn west on Diamond Lake Loop/Forest Road 4795 for the north entry to Diamond Lake Recreation Area. At 0.3 mile keep left and continue for another 2.9 miles. There, turn right for the south shore attractions, reaching Broken Arrow on the left in 0.5 mile.
About the campground: Tucked away from shore in the lodgepole pines, this camp shared by humans, jays, and golden-mantled squirrels sits at the southeastern corner of Diamond Lake. The center of activity is the natural lake, which covers more than 3,000 acres. It offers year-round fun, taking you from goggles and swimsuits to snowshoes and mittens. During the camping season, swimming, boating, and fishing for rainbow trout are all popular. Five boat ramps serve lake users. Next to camp, South Shore Picnic Area has a designated swimming beach. A paved pedestrian-and-bicycle trail travels the shoreline, and nearby hiking trails lead to Teal and Horse Lakes, Silent Creek, and Mount Bailey.

43 Crater Lake National Park: Lost Creek

Location: About 3 miles southeast of Crater Lake
Season: July–mid-October
Sites: 16 tent sites; no hookups
Maximum length: Suitable for tents only
Facilities: Tables, grills, vault toilets, drinking water
Fee per night: $$
Management: National Park Service
Contact: (541) 594–3100; www.nps.gov/crla
Finding the campground: From the Rim Drive junction at the south end of Crater Lake, near Crater Lake National Park Headquarters, follow the rim loop counterclockwise. Go about 8 miles on East Rim Drive, turn right toward the Pinnacles and Lost Creek Campground, and continue 3 miles to the camp entrance on the right.
About the campground: Next to Sand Creek Canyon, en route to the Pinnacles, this campground threaded by Lost Creek occupies a quiet, shady stand of lodgepole pines. While the camp is removed from the main bustle, it is still within easy reach of the 33-mile Rim Drive, with its viewpoints, trailheads, and sightseeing opportunities. The camp is also just a short drive from the Pin-

Wizard Island in Crater Lake.

nacles, an intriguing canyon of sandcastle-like volcanic fumaroles, which beg to be visited and photographed. The Pinnacles are one of nature's art galleries.

44 Crater Lake National Park: Mazama

Location: About 4 miles south of Crater Lake
Season: Mid-June–mid-October
Sites: 200 basic sites; no hookups
Maximum length: 30 feet
Facilities: Tables, grills, flush toilets, drinking water, showers, dump station, laundry, telephone, food service
Fee per night: $$
Management: National Park Service
Contact: (541) 594–3100; www.nps.gov/crla
Finding the campground: This camp is reached east off the south entrance road to Crater Lake National Park, 0.1 mile north of the south entrance station off Oregon 62 and 3.5 miles south of Rim Drive. The park's vehicle entry fee is good for 7 days.

About the campground: On a plateau of lodgepole pines above the pictur-esque, deeply eroded drainage of Annie Creek sits this campground at the gateway to Crater Lake National Park. Crater Lake was formed some 7,700 years ago when the ancient volcano Mount Mazama collapsed and filled with water to form the deepest lake in the United States and one of the clearest lakes in the world. The 33-mile Rim Drive explores the crater, with stops for hikes, sightseeing, and photography. The lake's color explores lovely and un-common shades of blue. From camp, the Annie Creek Trail descends to the wildflower-spangled banks of Annie Creek. Other park trails top the caldera peaks for panoramic views of the caldera, lake, and Cascades. A narrated boat tour (a fee attraction) leaves from Cleetwood Cove. To board the boat, you must hike 1.1 miles and descend 700 feet in elevation from the rim trailhead to the cove.

45 Diamond Lake

Location: On Diamond Lake
Season: Mid-May–October
Sites: 240 basic sites; no hookups
Maximum length: 35 feet
Facilities: Tables, grills, flush toilets, drinking water, showers, dump station, barrier-free facilities, 2 boat ramps, fish-cleaning station, visitor information station (across road from camp)
Fee per night: $$
Management: Umpqua National Forest
Contact: (541) 498–2531; (877) 444–6777 for reservations; www.fs.fed.us/r6/umpqua/recreation
Finding the campground: From Oregon 138, 80 miles east of Roseburg, turn west on Diamond Lake Loop/Forest Road 4795 for the north entry to Diamond Lake Recreation Area. At 0.3 mile keep left and continue for another 2.2 miles to enter camp.
About the campground: Just off the Rogue–Umpqua Scenic Byway, along the east shore of 3,000-acre Diamond Lake, you will find this camping "me-tropolis." It is surrounded by the Mount Thielsen Wilderness, Oregon Cas-cades Recreation Area, and the Umpqua National Forest. Recreation on the lake includes fishing, swimming, and boating. A paved pedestrian-and-bicycle trail travels the lakeshore, and the local hiking options range from short na-ture trails to the interstate Pacific Crest National Scenic Trail. A full-service lakeside resort with boat and sports equipment rentals is just a short hop away.

46 Farewell Bend

Location: About 12 miles north of Prospect
Season: Mid-May–October
Sites: 61 basic sites; no hookups
Maximum length: 40 feet
Facilities: Tables, grills, flush toilets, drinking water, playground

Fee per night: $$
Management: Rogue River National Forest
Contact: (541) 560–3400; www.fs.fed.us/r6/rogue-siskiyou
Finding the campground: It is west off Oregon 62, 12.2 miles north of Prospect and 0.3 mile south of the junction of OR 62 and OR 230.
About the campground: This pleasant, popular campground is contained by a scenic bend of the Upper Rogue River. A few pine trees rise among the Douglas firs and hemlocks of camp. The sites have trampled earthen floors, but the perimeters burst with greenery. The river courses over bedrock, except where a gorge squeezes it into a 4- to 5-foot-wide chute near sites 20 and 21. The campground is ideal for relaxing at the river or for sightseeing, with Crater Lake National Park, Diamond Lake Recreation Area, and the Upper Rogue River–Union Creek country all nearby. Superior hiking trails follow Union Creek and the Upper Rogue River. You may want to take a drive along OR 62 in late spring or early summer to see the dogwood blooms, a signature of the area.

47 Hamaker

Location: About 26 miles north of Prospect
Season: Mid-May–October
Sites: 10 basic sites; no hookups
Maximum length: 30 feet
Facilities: Tables, grills, vault toilets, drinking water
Fee per night: $$
Management: Rogue River National Forest
Contact: (541) 560–3400; www.fs.fed.us/r6/rogue-siskiyou
Finding the campground: From the junction of Oregon 62 and OR 230, 12.5 miles north of Prospect, head north on OR 230 for 12.2 miles. Turn right (east) onto gravel Forest Road 6530, go 0.6 mile, and bear right on FR 6530.900. Proceed another 0.8 mile to the camp.
About the campground: This idyllic campground occupies a forested bench overlooking the Rogue Wild and Scenic River as it threads out of Crater Lake National Park. Gorgeous, old-growth Shasta red firs and Douglas firs rise above camp. The setting is perfect for lounging, but anglers in pursuit of wily trout can try their luck negotiating the shrubs of the riverbanks. Hikers might check out a segment of the Upper Rogue Trail, which pursues this prized waterway downstream from Crater Rim Viewpoint (north on OR 230) to Lost Creek Reservoir (southwest of Prospect). Reach the trail upstream from camp at the barricaded river bridge that is open to pedestrians only.

48 Huckleberry Mountain

Location: About 22 miles northeast of Prospect
Season: Mid-June–October
Sites: 25 basic sites; no hookups
Maximum length: 25 feet

Facilities: Tables, fire rings, vault toilets, drinking water (although sometimes not available until July)

Fee per night: None

Management: Rogue River National Forest

Contact: (541) 560–3400; www.fs.fed.us/r6/rogue-siskiyou

Finding the campground: From the junction of Oregon 62 and OR 230, 12.5 miles north of Prospect, head east on OR 62 for 5.7 miles. Turn south on gravel Forest Road 60 at the sign for the campground near milepost 63. Follow FR 60, which is narrow, winding, and steep, for 4.2 miles to enter the camp.

About the campground: This rustic mountaintop camp is best suited to small units because its access road is so steep and narrow. The sites are widespread for ample privacy, but they lack formal parking. Old-growth Shasta red firs, meadows of false hellebore, and huckleberry flats compose the setting. In late summer, as the berries ripen, you may encounter folks with buckets swinging from their belts and blue stains on their fingertips. Altogether, the camp offers a serene, picturesque retreat that also appeals to wildlife.

Ancient Douglas fir.

49 Mill Creek

Location: About 3 miles north of Prospect
Season: Mid-May–October
Sites: 10 basic sites; no hookups
Maximum length: 25 feet
Facilities: Tables, grills, vault toilets; no drinking water
Fee per night: $
Management: Rogue River National Forest
Contact: (541) 560–3400; www.fs.fed.us/r6/rogue-siskiyou
Finding the campground: From Prospect, go 2 miles north on Oregon 62. Turn right (east) onto Forest Road 6200.030, go 1 mile, and turn left onto FR 6200.035 to enter camp.
About the campground: This tiny, creekside camp is set among old-growth firs, with a midstory tangle of dogwood, maple, and chinquapin. It offers a quiet base from which to explore the Upper Rogue River Area.

50 Natural Bridge

Location: About 10 miles north of Prospect
Season: Mid-May–October
Sites: 17 basic sites; no hookups
Maximum length: 40 feet
Facilities: Tables, grills and rock fireplaces, vault toilets; no drinking water
Fee per night: $
Management: Rogue River National Forest
Contact: (541) 560–3400; www.fs.fed.us/r6/rogue-siskiyou
Finding the campground: From Oregon 62, about 10 miles north of Prospect and 2.8 miles south of the junction of OR 62 and OR 230, head west on Forest Road 6200.300 toward Natural Bridge, go 0.4 mile, and bear right for the campground. Left leads to the parking for Natural Bridge Viewpoint.
About the campground: Set back from OR 62, this quiet campground covers a large forested flat along the Rogue River. It offers spacious sites, many of them riverside. Firs, pines, hemlocks, and dogwoods shade the camp. Fishing, hiking, and sightseeing along the Rogue River lure guests. The Rogue Gorge Trail passes through camp, while the Upper Rogue National Recreation Trail traces the opposite bank of the Rogue River. You can access the Upper Rogue Trail via the footbridge to Natural Bridge Viewpoint. The viewpoint is worth the short walk to see the spectacular basalt gorge, where a lava tube swallows the river whole, only to spit it out 200 feet downstream.

51 River Bridge

Location: About 5 miles north of Prospect
Season: Mid-May–October
Sites: 10 basic sites; no hookups
Maximum length: 30 feet
Facilities: Tables, grills, vault toilets; no drinking water

Fee per night: $
Management: Rogue River National Forest
Contact: (541) 560–3400; www.fs.fed.us/r6/rogue-siskiyou
Finding the campground: From Prospect, go 4 miles north on Oregon 62. Turn left (west) onto gravel Forest Road 6210 and go 0.9 mile to the camp entrance on the right.
About the campground: This small camp occupies a forest flat set back from the Rogue Wild and Scenic River, where it takes a wide bend. Tall firs and hemlocks, along with a leafy midstory, create nearly full shade. The river and Upper Rogue National Recreation Trail are just steps away from your RV or tent. Riffles occasionally break the glassy surface of the river. A lava outcrop reveals a ropelike pattern and allows for bank fishing.

52 Thielsen View

Location: On Diamond Lake
Season: Mid-May–mid-October
Sites: 60 basic sites; no hookups
Maximum length: 35 feet
Facilities: Tables, grills, vault toilets, drinking water, boat ramps
Fee per night: $
Management: Umpqua National Forest
Contact: (541) 498–2531; www.fs.fed.us/r6/umpqua/recreation
Finding the campground: From Oregon 138, 80 miles east of Roseburg, turn west onto Diamond Lake Loop/Forest Road 4795 for the north entrance to Diamond Lake Recreation Area. At 0.3 mile, go right and continue for another 3 miles to the camp.
About the campground: At the foot of Mount Bailey on the west shore of Diamond Lake, this campground offers a comfortable stay and a magnificent view of Mount Thielsen. The campsites rest in a mixed forest of pine and fir. Historically, the lake has been stocked annually, and the blue expanse offers ample room to troll. Bicyclists can ride an 11-mile paved trail around the lake, while hikers can choose from a plethora of destinations in Mount Thielsen Wilderness, Oregon Cascades Recreation Area, and Umpqua National Forest.

53 Union Creek

Location: In the community of Union Creek, about 11 miles north of Prospect
Season: Mid-May–October
Sites: 74 basic sites; no hookups
Maximum length: 30 feet
Facilities: Tables, grills, vault toilets, drinking water
Fee per night: $$
Management: Rogue River National Forest
Contact: (541) 560–3400; www.fs.fed.us/r6/rogue-siskiyou
Finding the campground: It is west off Oregon 62, 11.2 miles north of Prospect and 1.3 miles south of the junction of OR 62 and OR 230.

About the campground: This engaging camp straddles Union Creek at its confluence with the Upper Rogue River. The sites are well spaced, cozy, and private. Trails explore both banks of the creek and the east shore of the river, but to access the Upper Rogue National Recreation Trail on the west shore, you will need to drive 1.5 miles south to Natural Bridge Campground and Viewpoint Parking, where there is a pedestrian bridge over the river. Hiking, fishing, sightseeing, and nature study are area pursuits. Among the outstanding features are old-growth trees, dogwood blooms, and dramatic unions of volcanic outcrop and clear, racing water.

Myrtle Creek Area

54 Boulder Creek

Location: About 50 miles east of the town of Myrtle Creek
Season: May–October
Sites: 8 basic sites; no hookups
Maximum length: 22 feet
Facilities: Tables, grills, pit toilets; no drinking water
Fee per night: $
Management: Umpqua National Forest
Contact: (541) 825–3201; www.fs.fed.us/r6/umpqua/recreation
Finding the campground: From Oregon 227 in Tiller, go northeast on South Umpqua River Scenic Route/Forest Road 28 for 13.6 miles. The camp entrance is on the right.
About the campground: This campground rests in a full conifer-maple forest along the South Umpqua River. Boulder Creek flows into the river at the upper end of camp; paths to the river are a little rough but passable. They allow you to view the river and cool your ankles, but the river is closed to fishing. Waterfalls farther upstream might be worth a visit: Campbell Falls is 0.8 mile northeast, while South Umpqua Falls is 6.1 miles northeast.

55 Camp Comfort

Location: About 60 miles east of the town of Myrtle Creek
Season: May–October
Sites: 5 basic sites; no hookups
Maximum length: 22 feet

Myrtle Creek Area

	Hookup sites	Total sites	Maximum RV length	Hookups	Toilets	Showers	Drinking water	Dump station	Recreation	Fee	Can reserve
54 Boulder Creek		8	22		NF				S	$	
55 Camp Comfort		5	22		NF				S	$	
56 Charles V. Stanton County Park	20	40	45	WES	F	•	•	•	FBL	$$	•
57 Cover		7	22		NF					$	
58 Devils Flat		3	22		NF				H	$	
59 Dumont Creek		5	16		NF				S	$	
60 Millsite RV Park	11	11	50	WESC	F	•	•	•		$$	
61 Threehorn		5	22		NF					$	

Facilities: Tables, grills, vault toilets; no drinking water
Fee per night: $
Management: Umpqua National Forest
Contact: (541) 825-3201; www.fs.fed.us/r6/umpqua/recreation
Finding the campground: From Oregon 227 at Tiller, go northeast on South Umpqua River Scenic Route/Forest Road 28 for 26 miles. The camp entrance is on the right.
About the campground: This attractive camp is nestled in a grove of old-growth trees. Sugar pines, firs, hemlocks, and cedars scratch the sky, as rhododendrons and vine maples fill out the midstory. A steep slope separates the camp from the South Umpqua River, but you can reach the river via the 0.25-mile, barrier-free Camp Comfort Trail. Because the end of this trail is relatively steep and topped with loose gravel, wheelchair users will probably want to turn around sooner. The trail leads through lovely woods, offers river overlooks, and ends where the Castle Rock and Black Rock Forks combine to form the river. Downstream from the confluence is a swimming hole, but be careful of the rock ledges along the sides of the pool. You can also take a 6.3-mile drive downstream to view South Umpqua Falls, a combination bedrock waterslide and broken-ledge chute.

56 Charles V. Stanton County Park

Location: About 8 miles south of the town of Myrtle Creek; 2 miles north of Canyonville
Season: Year-round
Sites: 20 hookup sites, 20 basic sites; water, electric, and sewer hookups
Maximum length: 45 feet
Facilities: Tables, barbecues (at nonhookup sites only), flush toilets, drinking water, showers, dump station, telephone, playground, gravel-bar boat launch
Fee per night: $$
Management: Douglas County
Contact: (541) 957-7001, reservations accepted; www.co.douglas.or.us/parks
Finding the campground: From Interstate 5 southbound, take exit 101 and go 1 mile south along the frontage road on the east side of the freeway to the park. From I-5 northbound, take exit 99 and go 1 mile north on the east frontage road.
About the campground: Along the South Umpqua River on the east side of I-5 is this attractive 22-acre campground shaded by mature firs and oaks. The lower camp flat contains the nonhookup sites and is closer to the river. All sites have paved parking. Beyond the camp are open lawns for those who want to romp or play. Fishing is popular.

57 Cover

Location: About 50 miles east of the town of Myrtle Creek
Season: May–October
Sites: 7 basic sites; no hookups
Maximum length: 22 feet

Facilities: Tables, grills, vault toilets; no drinking water
Fee per night: $
Management: Umpqua National Forest
Contact: (541) 825–3201; www.fs.fed.us/r6/umpqua/recreation
Finding the campground: From Oregon 227 at Tiller, go northeast on South Umpqua River Scenic Route for 5 miles, then continue east on Forest Road 29 for about 12 miles to reach the camp.
About the campground: This camp along Jackson Creek offers sites in a semi-open setting of Douglas firs and bigleaf maples, with alders growing toward the creek. Tiny Jackson Creek is a scenic complement to your stay, as it courses over bedrock and gravel beds. Just 2 miles west of camp is the World's Largest Sugar Pine.

58 Devils Flat

Location: About 40 miles southeast of the town of Myrtle Creek
Season: May–October
Sites: 3 basic sites; no hookups
Maximum length: 22 feet
Facilities: Tables, grills, vault toilets; no drinking water
Fee per night: $
Management: Umpqua National Forest
Contact: (541) 825–3201; www.fs.fed.us/r6/umpqua/recreation
Finding the campground: From Interstate 5, take the Azalea exit (exit 88), and go east on County Road 36 (Cow Creek Road) for 17 miles to reach this camp on the left.
About the campground: Just upstream from Cow Creek Falls, at the foot of a steep slope, you will find this reduced-services, little-used camp opposite the historic Devils Flat Guard Station, where a circa 1915 ranger cabin and a horse barn still stand. The camp has a gravel road and open grassy sites ringed by cedars. From the guard station, you can access the Cow Creek Falls and Devils Flat Trails. Because the camp is just 10 miles upstream from Galesville Reservoir (which captures Cow Creek), you can participate in the reservoir recreation, as well.

59 Dumont Creek

Location: About 45 miles east of the town of Myrtle Creek
Season: May–October
Sites: 5 basic sites; no hookups
Maximum length: 16 feet
Facilities: Tables, grills, pit toilets; no drinking water
Fee per night: $
Management: Umpqua National Forest
Contact: (541) 825–3201; www.fs.fed.us/r6/umpqua/recreation
Finding the campground: From Oregon 227 at Tiller, go northeast on South Umpqua River Scenic Route/Forest Road 28 for 11.6 miles to enter the camp on the right.

About the campground: This small camp occupies a forest flat of second-growth firs above the South Umpqua River. When making your way to the river, be alert for poison oak. At the upstream end of camp, where the river spills through fingers of basalt, is a deep, inviting swimming hole. Because of the riverbed cobbles intermixed with the sand, you may want to wade or swim in sneakers. At the downstream end of camp, Dumont Creek empties into the river. For the protection of wild fish, the river and its tributaries are closed to fishing.

60 Millsite RV Park

Location: In the city of Myrtle Creek
Season: Year-round
Sites: 11 hookup sites, a few tent sites (as available); water, electric, sewer, and cable hookups
Maximum length: 50 feet
Facilities: Tables, flush toilets, drinking water, showers, dump station, telephone, ballfield
Fee per night: $$
Management: City of Myrtle Creek
Contact: (541) 863–3171
Finding the campground: From Interstate 5, take exit 108 and go east into Myrtle Creek. At the west end of town, turn right (south) onto Northwest Fourth Avenue and proceed 0.2 mile to this RV park at the far edge of the city park.
About the campground: This is a tidy, convenient little oasis on the I-5 corridor. The sites have paved parking, grassy meridians with tables, and the open park at their back. Campers can choose between sun or partial shade. But trains passing on a track close to the park can rattle you from your slumber.

61 Threehorn

Location: About 50 miles southeast of the town of Myrtle Creek
Season: Late May–October
Sites: 5 basic sites; no hookups
Maximum length: 22 feet
Facilities: Tables, grills, pit toilets; no drinking water
Fee per night: $
Management: Umpqua National Forest
Contact: (541) 825–3201; www.fs.fed.us/r6/umpqua/recreation
Finding the campground: It is east off Oregon 227, 13 miles south of Tiller and 14.7 miles north of Shady Cove.
About the campground: This small, primitive campground is tucked in a stand of big, attractive sugar pines, cedars, and firs just off OR 227. It offers a relaxing, shady stay or a convenient overnight stop for people traveling this isolated highway. Sites have gravel parking; some are more level than others.

Grants Pass–Cave Junction Area

62 | Alameda County Park

Location: About 25 miles northwest of Grants Pass
Season: Year-round
Sites: 25 basic sites; no hookups
Maximum length: 40 feet

Grants Pass–Cave Junction Area

	Hookup sites	Total sites	Maximum RV length	Hookups	Toilets	Showers	Drinking water	Dump station	Recreation	Fee	Can reserve
62 Alameda County Park		25	40		NF		•	•	FBL	$$	
63 Big Pine		12	40		NF		•	•	H	$	
64 Bolan Lake		12	15		NF				HSFBL	$	
65 Cave Creek		18	small		NF		•		H	$$	
66 Elderberry Flat		9	30		NF				O		
67 Grayback		39	40		F		•	•	F	$$	
68 Griffin County Park	14	18	40	WES	F	•	•	•	FBL	$$–$$$	•
69 Indian Mary County Park	68	92	40	WES	F	•	•	•	FBL	$$–$$$	•
70 Lake Selmac County Park: Eagle Loop		14	T		NF		•		SFB	$$	
71 Lake Selmac County Park: Heron and Teal Loops		20	T		NF		•		HSFBL	$$	
72 Lake Selmac County Park: Mallard Loop	14	32	40	WES	F	•	•	•	HSFBLR	$$–$$$	•
73 Lake Selmac County Park: Osprey Loop	23	36	40	WES	F	•	•	•	SFBL	$$–$$$	•
74 Sam Brown		29	35		NF	•	•		H	$	
75 Sam Brown Horse Camp		7	40		NF		•		HR	$	
76 Schroeder County Park	29	31	40	WES	F	•	•		SFBL	$$–$$$	•
77 Secret Creek		4	T		NF					$	
78 Skull Creek		5	30		NF				F		
79 Spalding Pond		4	T		NF		•		F	$	
80 Tin Can		4	small		NF				H	$	
81 Tucker Flat Recreation Site		8	small		NF				HF		
82 Valley of the Rogue State Park	146	173	75	WE	F	•	•	•	HF	$$	•
83 Whitehorse County Park	8	44	40	WE	F	•	•		SFBL	$$	•
84 Wolf Creek County Park	19	35	30	WE	NF		•	•	H	$$	

Facilities: Some tables and grills, vault toilets, drinking water (except during cold spells), dump station, boat ramp
Fee per night: $$
Management: Josephine County
Contact: (541) 474–5285; www.co.josephine.or.us/parks
Finding the campground: From Interstate 5 north of Grants Pass, take exit 61 and go 3.6 miles northwest to Merlin. From there, proceed west for 14.3 miles on Merlin–Galice Road, passing through Galice, to reach this county campground on the right.
About the campground: This primitive, informal campground occupies a large flat along the Rogue Wild and Scenic River. Random oaks and ponderosa pines along with a few madrones shade the flat. The understory is grassy (dirt where more trampled). This is a popular fishing and summer river recreation site. Camp guests can take advantage of the many outfitter trips for rafting or fishing or the shuttle services offered along Merlin–Galice Road. Superb riverside hiking trails lie within short drives of camp.

63 Big Pine

Location: About 30 miles west of Grants Pass
Season: May–October
Sites: 12 basic sites; no hookups
Maximum length: 40 feet
Facilities: Tables, grills and barbecues, vault toilets, drinking water, dump station, playground, horseshoe pits
Fee per night: $
Management: Siskiyou National Forest
Contact: (541) 471–6500; www.fs.fed.us/r6/rogue-siskiyou
Finding the campground: From Interstate 5 north of Grants Pass, take exit 61 and go 3.6 miles northwest to Merlin. From there, proceed west 8.6 miles on Merlin–Galice Road and turn south onto Forest Road 25 toward Big Pine and Briggs Valley. Go 11.9 miles more. The campground is on the right.
About the campground: Stretched across a forested flat along the banks of Myers Creek is this fine family campground. Some magnificent firs and pines tower above the camp, while vine maples and filberts fill out the midstory. The campsites have earthen parking, and a rustic split-rail fence frames the camp meadow. You can follow a nature trail to explore the forest and visit the area's champion ponderosa pine. Big Pine shoots 250 feet skyward and has a diameter of almost 6 feet. Also from camp, spur trails lead to the longer trails that traverse the valleys of Taylor and Briggs Creeks.

64 Bolan Lake

Location: About 30 miles southeast of Cave Junction
Season: July–October
Sites: 12 basic sites; no hookups
Maximum length: 15 feet

Facilities: Some tables and fire rings, pit and vault toilets; no drinking water
Fee per night: $
Management: Siskiyou National Forest
Contact: (541) 592–4000; www.fs.fed.us/r6/rogue-siskiyou
Finding the campground: From the junction of U.S. Highway 199 and Oregon 46 in Cave Junction, go south on US 199 for 6.4 miles and turn east on Waldo Road (a scenic byway), heading toward Takilma and Happy Camp. Go 4.8 miles to a four-way intersection and proceed straight; the road name changes to Happy Camp Road. Continue another 12.4 miles and turn left at a sign for the campground, now on gravel Forest Road 4812. Go 4.1 miles to a three-way junction and proceed straight for Bolan Lake on unlabeled FR 040. Remain on FR 040 as it skirts below the north face of Bolan Mountain to enter the camp in 1.6 miles.
About the campground: This primitive campground is spread along the northern half of 15-acre Bolan Lake, a cold, deep mountain lake that occupies a forest and meadow at the foot of Bolan Mountain. The campground is beautiful and, despite its remoteness, very popular on weekends. A small gravel beach, trout fishing, and nonmotorized boating are the lake attractions. Trails from camp explore the lakeshore and ascend to Bolan Mountain Lookout.

65   Cave Creek

Location: About 15 miles east of Cave Junction
Season: Mid-May–mid-September
Sites: 18 basic sites; no hookups
Maximum length: No trailers or large RVs
Facilities: Tables, vault toilets, drinking water
Fee per night: $$
Management: Siskiyou National Forest
Contact: (541) 592–4000; www.fs.fed.us/r6/rogue-siskiyou
Finding the campground: From the junction of U.S. Highway 199 and Oregon 46 at Cave Junction, go east on OR 46/Forest Road 46 for 15.3 miles to the campground entrance on the right. (No trailers may proceed past Grayback Campground, which is 11.1 miles east of Cave Junction.)
About the campground: Along Cave Creek stretches this linear, open-forest campground that provides convenient access to Oregon Caves National Monument (reached via trail or road). The monument offers guided underground tours and has fine nature trails that tie into the more extensive trail network of the region. A record-size Douglas fir is one of the hiking destinations. The cool of the cave is especially inviting on hot summer days.

66   Elderberry Flat

Location: About 35 miles northeast of Grants Pass
Season: May–September
Sites: 9 basic sites; no hookups
Maximum length: 30 feet

Facilities: Tables, grills, vault toilets; no drinking water
Fee per night: None
Management: Bureau of Land Management
Contact: (541) 770–2200; www.or.blm.gov/medford/recreationsites
Finding the campground: From the city of Rogue River, go north on East Evans Creek Road for 18 miles and turn left onto West Fork Evans Creek Road. Continue another 9 miles to this campground.
About the campground: This out-of-the-way campground serves motorcycle and off-highway-vehicle enthusiasts, so you can expect it to be loud and dusty. A forest of firs and hemlocks shades the sites.

67 Grayback

Location: About 11 miles east of Cave Junction
Season: Mid-May–September, weather permitting
Sites: 39 basic sites; no hookups
Maximum length: 40 feet
Facilities: Tables, barbecues, flush toilets, drinking water, dump station
Fee per night: $$
Management: Siskiyou National Forest
Contact: (541) 592–4000; www.fs.fed.us/r6/rogue-siskiyou
Finding the campground: From the junction of U.S. Highway 199 and Oregon 46 at Cave Junction, go east on OR 46/Forest Road 46 for 11.1 miles to the campground entrance on the right. No trailers may proceed past Grayback Campground.
About the campground: This campground occupies a mixed, multistoried forest of firs, dogwoods, madrones, filberts, and yews. It is contained within a bend of Sucker Creek at its confluence with Grayback Creek. The barrier-free Grayback Interpretive Trail offers views of Sucker Creek and leads to a falls-viewing platform. The campground lies en route to Oregon Caves National Monument and is within an easy drive of a couple of wineries of the Illinois Valley.

68 Griffin County Park

Location: About 7 miles west of Grants Pass
Season: Year-round, but water is shut off during cold spells
Sites: 14 hookup sites, 4 tent sites; water, electric, and sewer hookups
Maximum length: 40 feet
Facilities: Tables, grills, flush toilets, drinking water, showers, dump station, telephone, playground, boat ramp
Fee per night: $$–$$$
Management: Josephine County
Contact: (541) 474–5285, reservations accepted; www.co.josephine.or.us/parks

Finding the campground: From the intersection of U.S. Highway 199 and Riverbanks Road south of Grants Pass, go northwest on Riverbanks Road for 6 miles and turn right at the sign for Griffin Park. Drive 1 mile to the park entrance on the left.

About the campground: You will find this lovely tree-shaded campground on a gentle slope along the south bank of the Rogue River. Lower sites overlook a broad gravel bar to the acclaimed scenic and recreational waterway; fishing, rafting, and swimming are among the enticements. Ospreys nest on the far shore, and swallows circle overhead and dart after flies rising from the water's surface.

69 Indian Mary County Park

Location: About 15 miles northwest of Grants Pass
Season: Year-round, but water is shut off during cold spells
Sites: 68 hookup sites, 24 basic sites; water, electric, and sewer hookups
Maximum length: 40 feet
Facilities: Tables, grills, flush toilets, drinking water, showers, dump station, telephone, playground, horseshoe pits, volleyball, disc golf, boat ramp
Fee per night: $$–$$$
Management: Josephine County
Contact: (541) 474–5285, reservations accepted; www.co.josephine.or.us /parks
Finding the campground: From Interstate 5 north of Grants Pass, take exit 61 and go 3.6 miles northwest to Merlin. From there, proceed west 6.7 miles more on Merlin–Galice Road to reach the campground on the right.

About the campground: This showplace campground on the Rogue River offers sweeping, tidy grounds and great river access. Its three camping areas are spread across a tree-shaded grassy flat. The tall native pines, oaks, and maples, along with the various planted trees, make reclining at camp inviting, but a full range of river recreation and family activities are right at your elbow. You can be as lazy or as active as you wish.

70 Lake Selmac County Park: Eagle Loop

Location: About 23 miles southwest of Grants Pass, on Lake Selmac
Season: Year-round
Sites: 14 tent sites; no hookups
Maximum length: Suitable for tents only
Facilities: Tables, grills, pit toilets, drinking water (except during cold weather)
Fee per night: $$
Management: Josephine County
Contact: (541) 474–5285; www.co.josephine.or.us/parks
Finding the campground: From U.S. Highway 199, 20 miles south of Grants Pass and 7 miles north of Cave Junction, turn east on Lakeshore Drive, go 2

miles, and bear left to stay on Lakeshore Drive for another 0.6 mile. Turn right on McMullin Creek Road, then take a quick right turn off it. At the junction just ahead, turn right for Eagle Loop.

About the campground: One of five campground loops on 160-acre Lake Selmac, this tent-camping area occupies a wooded plateau above the lake. A steep 50-foot slope separates the lakeshore from the camp, but a couple of sites overlook the water. There is nearby access for boating (10 miles per hour maximum) and swimming. Bass, crappie, and trout may tug at your fishing lines.

71 Lake Selmac County Park: Heron and Teal Loops

Location: About 23 miles southwest of Grants Pass, on Lake Selmac
Season: Year-round
Sites: 5 tent sites at Heron, 15 tent sites at Teal; no hookups
Maximum length: Suitable for tents only
Facilities: Both loops: tables, grills, pit toilets, drinking water (except during cold weather); Teal Loop: boat launch, dock, fish-cleaning station
Fee per night: $$
Management: Josephine County
Contact: (541) 474–5285; www.co.josephine.or.us/parks
Finding the campgrounds: From U.S. Highway 199, 20 miles south of Grants Pass and 7 miles north of Cave Junction, turn east on Lakeshore Drive, go 2 miles, and bear right on Reeves Creek Road. Go 0.8 mile, bear left on South Shore Road, and go 0.2 mile to Heron Loop or 0.4 mile to Teal Loop.
About the campgrounds: Among the campground loops on Lake Selmac, these two tent areas occupy a plateau of firs, pines, and madrones. Some sites offer parking above the lake with a table right on shore. You can see rolling, wooded hills across the lake. Fishing, boating, swimming, and hiking occupy campers. Watch for ospreys, swans, and coots. A grassy spit at each of the camps gives shore anglers a casting edge.

72 Lake Selmac County Park: Mallard Loop

Location: About 23 miles southwest of Grants Pass, on Lake Selmac
Season: Year-round, but water is shut off during cold spells
Sites: 14 hookup sites, 12 basic sites, 6 horse sites; water, electric, and sewer hookups
Maximum length: 40 feet
Facilities: Tables, grills, flush toilets, drinking water, showers, dump station, telephone, playground, ballfield, boat launch, corrals at horse sites
Fee per night: $$–$$$
Management: Josephine County
Contact: (541) 474–5285, reservations accepted; www.co.josephine.or.us /parks
Finding the campground: From U.S. Highway 199, 20 miles south of Grants Pass and 7 miles north of Cave Junction, turn east on Lakeshore Drive, go 2 miles, and bear left to stay on Lakeshore Drive for another 0.6 mile. Turn right

on McMullin Creek Road and take a quick right turn off it. At the next junction, proceed straight 0.5 mile to Mallard.

About the campground: One of five campground loops on 160-acre Lake Selmac, this loop offers a choice of grassy or wooded sites set back from the lake. You will find a horse staging area and trails leaving camp, as well as the various lake recreations: boating (10 miles per hour maximum); fishing for bass, crappie, and trout; and swimming. Lake Selmac sits in a pretty wooded basin.

73 Lake Selmac County Park: Osprey Loop

Location: About 23 miles southwest of Grants Pass
Season: Year-round, but water is shut off during cold spells
Sites: 23 hookup sites, 13 basic sites; water, electric, and sewer hookups
Maximum length: 40 feet
Facilities: Tables, grills, flush toilets, drinking water, showers, dump station, telephone, playground, boat launch, fishing dock
Fee per night: $$-$$$
Management: Josephine County
Contact: (541) 474-5285, reservations accepted; www.co.josephine.or.us /parks
Finding the campground: From U.S. Highway 199, 20 miles south of Grants Pass and 7 miles north of Cave Junction, turn east on Lakeshore Drive, go 2 miles, and bear right on Reeves Creek Road. Go 0.5 mile to reach Osprey Loop on the right.
About the campground: Occupying a gentle, wooded slope, this campground is separated from Lake Selmac by Reeves Creek Road. The glimmer of the lake is nonetheless a vital part of the camp ambience, and guests may boat, fish, or swim. Ospreys sometimes circle over Lake Selmac, giving credence to the loop's name. The shady setting of camp provides a welcome retreat from the fun in the sun.

74 Sam Brown

Location: About 30 miles west of Grants Pass
Season: May-October
Sites: 29 basic sites; no hookups
Maximum length: 35 feet
Facilities: Tables, grills, vault toilets, drinking water, picnic shelters, solar showers
Fee per night: $
Management: Siskiyou National Forest
Contact: (541) 471-6500; www.fs.fed.us/r6/rogue-siskiyou
Finding the campground: From Interstate 5 north of Grants Pass, take exit 61 and go 3.6 miles northwest to Merlin. From there, proceed west 8.6 miles on Merlin-Galice Road. Turn left (south) on Forest Road 25 toward Big Pine and Briggs Valley and continue 12.8 miles more. Turn right on FR 2512, go 0.3 mile, and enter the campground on the left.

About the campground: The campsites are arranged in two loops at the perimeter of a fenced meadow: Loop A is forested; loop B is sunnier, occupying the lower meadow toward the creek. The sites have gravel parking and are well spaced for privacy and comfort. The trails that follow Briggs, Taylor, and Dutchy Creeks can all be accessed at or near camp.

75 Sam Brown Horse Camp

Location: About 30 miles west of Grants Pass
Season: May–October
Sites: 7 basic sites; no hookups
Maximum length: 40 feet
Facilities: Tables, grills, vault toilets, drinking water, corral at each site
Fee per night: $
Management: Siskiyou National Forest.
Contact: (541) 471–6500; www.fs.fed.us/r6/rogue-siskiyou
Finding the campground: From Interstate 5 north of Grants Pass, take exit 61 and go 3.6 miles northwest to Merlin. From there, proceed west 8.6 miles on Merlin–Galice Road. Turn left (south) on Forest Road 25 toward Big Pine and Briggs Valley and continue 12.8 miles. Turn right on FR 2512, go 0.1 mile, and again turn right to reach the horse camp in 0.2 mile.
About the campground: This accommodating horse camp occupies a semi-open forest flat, giving campers and their animals plenty of space and convenient access to the area's multiple-use trails. Taylor, Dutchy, and Briggs Creeks all have companion trails to explore. The rustic corrals blend with the setting.

76 Schroeder County Park

Location: On the western outskirts of Grants Pass
Season: Year-round, but water is shut off during cold spells
Sites: 29 hookup sites, 2 tent sites; water, electric, and sewer hookups
Maximum length: 40 feet
Facilities: Tables, grills, flush toilets, drinking water, showers, telephone, playground, ballfields and courts, boat launch
Fee per night: $$–$$$
Management: Josephine County
Contact: (541) 474–5285, reservations accepted; www.co.josephine.or.us /parks
Finding the campground: From the junction of U.S. Highway 199 and Oregon 99 in southern Grants Pass, go 0.9 mile south on US 199 and turn right (west) onto Redwood Avenue. Follow it 1.4 miles, turn right onto Willow Lane (signed for the park), and continue 0.8 mile to the enter the park.
About the campground: This pleasant campground sits on a tree-shaded flat above a day-use area that actually fronts the Rogue River. The camp offers paved sites, tall oaks, groomed lawns, some privacy hedges, and mature cottonwoods along the river. Ducks and squirrels sometimes enliven the camp.

Fishing, swimming, and boating are the primary onsite activities, but the park sits within easy reach of the urban attractions of Grants Pass.

77   Secret Creek

Location: About 33 miles west of Grants Pass
Season: Spring–fall
Sites: 4 tent sites; no hookups
Maximum length: Suitable for tents only
Facilities: Some tables and fire rings, vault toilet; no drinking water
Fee per night: $
Management: Siskiyou National Forest
Contact: (541) 471-6500; www.fs.fed.us/r6/rogue-siskiyou
Finding the campground: From Interstate 5 north of Grants Pass, take exit 61 and go 3.6 miles northwest to Merlin. From there, proceed west 8.6 miles on Merlin–Galice Road. Turn left (south) onto Forest Road 25 toward Big Pine and Briggs Valley, go 15.3 miles, and make a left turn followed by a quick right into this campground.
About the campground: This tiny, forested campground is tucked along pretty Secret Creek. Because the sites are closely spaced, the parking is sharply angled, and there are no turnarounds, this camp is strictly for tent camping. The trails along Taylor and Briggs Creeks might bring on the urge to explore, and the Secret Way Trail begins near camp.

78   Skull Creek

Location: About 11 miles northwest of Glendale
Season: Year-round
Sites: 5 basic sites; no hookups
Maximum length: 30 feet
Facilities: Tables, fire rings, vault toilet; no drinking water
Fee per night: None
Management: Medford District Bureau of Land Management
Contact: (541) 618-2200; www.or.blm.gov/medford
Finding the campground: When coming from the north on Interstate 5, take exit 103 and head west 2.5 miles toward Riddle and take the bypass around town to follow Cow Creek BLM Back Country Byway in another 3 miles. Once on the byway, travel 29.5 miles southwest along Cow Creek to find the marked turn for this recreation site. The camp is just up the slope to the right. When coming from the south on Interstate 5, take exit 80, proceed into Glendale, and take Brown Road to Reuben County Road, heading west. This road eventually becomes the byway. Find the marked campground turnoff (a left), 13.5 miles from the exit.
About the campground: Along Cow Creek Back Country Byway, these few sites dot a rise above and across the road from Cow Creek. The sites have level gravel parking pads, and views sweep the neighboring ridges and their mosaics of mixed age trees. The camp is popular with hunters, and the sur-

rounding countryside has a rich mining legacy. At the Cow Creek Gold Panning Area, reached by going northwest on the byway from camp, you can swill your pan for color.

79 Spalding Pond

Location: About 28 miles southwest of Grants Pass
Season: May–October
Sites: 4 tent sites; no hookups
Maximum length: Suitable for tents only
Facilities: Tables, fire rings, compost toilets, drinking water, barrier-free path and fishing docks
Fee per night: $
Management: Siskiyou National Forest
Contact: (541) 471–6500; www.fs.fed.us/r6/rogue-siskiyou
Finding the campground: From U.S. Highway 199, 16 miles south of Grants Pass and 12 miles north of Cave Junction, take paved Forest Road 25 northwest toward Onion Mountain Lookout. Follow this curvy, single-lane road for 7.2 miles and turn left onto unlabeled, gravel FR 2524 (Spalding Mill Road); avoid FR 243. Go 4.3 miles on FR 2524, turn right onto FR 045, and proceed 0.7 mile to the camp.
About the campground: Central to the camp is heart-shaped Spalding Pond, which reflects the green of the surrounding forest as well as the dry slopes dotted with manzanitas. This pond was created to serve Spalding Mill (1933–1936) and later expanded by the Forest Service to its present 3-acre size. The sites are well spaced through the evergreen forest; from them you can see the pond and hear the burble of Soldier Creek. A barrier-free trail leads partway around the pond and accesses fishing docks.

80 Tin Can

Location: About 20 miles west of Grants Pass
Season: Year-round
Sites: 4 basic sites; no hookups
Maximum length: Best suited for tents and pickup campers
Facilities: Tables, grills, vault toilets; no drinking water
Fee per night: $
Management: Siskiyou National Forest
Contact: (541) 471–6500; www.fs.fed.us/r6/rogue-siskiyou
Finding the campground: From Interstate 5 north of Grants Pass, take exit 61, go 3.6 miles northwest to Merlin, and from there, proceed west 8.6 miles on Merlin–Galice Road. Turn left (south) onto Forest Road 25 toward Big Pine and Briggs Valley and go 5 miles to reach this campground on the left.
About the campground: This tiny campground is best suited for tent and pickup camping because of the tight parking angles and lack of turnarounds. It sits along crystalline Taylor Creek and is nestled in a vibrant woods of firs,

pines, dogwoods, and vine maples. In spring, giant trilliums adorn the forest floor, while the dogwoods flaunt their blooms at eye level. Fish weirs partition Taylor Creek and create artificial cascades. A footbridge spans the waterway, linking the camp to Taylor Creek Trail, which leads both up- and downstream from Tin Can.

81 Tucker Flat Recreation Site

Location: About 60 miles northwest of Grants Pass
Season: Year-round, as long as roads are accessible
Sites: 8 basic sites; no hookups
Maximum length: Best suited for tents and pickup campers
Facilities: Some tables, grills or fire rings, pit toilets; no drinking water
Fee per night: None
Management: Medford District Bureau of Land Management
Contact: (541) 618–2200; www.or.blm.gov/medford
Finding the campground: From Interstate 5 north of Grants Pass, take exit 61, go 3.6 miles northwest to Merlin, and proceed west on Merlin–Galice Road for 18.2 miles, passing through Galice to Grave Creek. There, cross the Rogue River and bear left on the Grave Creek–Marial BLM Back Country Byway. (Be sure to request a byway brochure from the Medford District Office to help you navigate the BLM roads.) Follow the byway for 33 miles and bear right past Rogue River Ranch to enter this campground. Watch for byway signs at junctions, especially 20 miles into the tour, where the route drops back into the canyon. It is also advisable to call the BLM about the road conditions before attempting this drive.
About the campground: Although a bit difficult to reach, this out-of-the-way recreation site provides a pleasant, primitive camping experience in the Wild Rogue Country. The camp flat above Mule Creek is shaded by fir, tan oak, and live oak. From camp, the Mule Creek Trail heads upstream and eventually meets the Panther Ridge Trail for a skyline tour of the Wild Rogue Wilderness. You can access the acclaimed Rogue River Trail in the vicinity of Rogue River Ranch, just a short hike away. The ranch is on the National Register of Historic Places and is open for viewing. Fishing, swimming, and wildlife watching also keep campers busy.

82 Valley of the Rogue State Park

Location: About 10 miles southeast of Grants Pass
Season: Year-round
Sites: 146 full or partial hookup sites, 21 basic sites, 6 yurts; water and electric hookups
Maximum length: 75 feet
Facilities: Tables, grills, flush toilets, drinking water, showers, dump station, telephone, playground, horseshoe pits, boat launch, meeting hall
Fee per night: $ $

Management: Oregon State Parks and Recreation Department

Contact: (541) 582–1118; (800) 452–5687 for reservations; www.oregon stateparks.org

Finding the campground: From Interstate 5, south of the city of Rogue River, take exit 45. Locate the state park north of the rest area here.

About the campground: Although you may hear the drone of freeway traffic, this long, sprawling, attractive campground borders a scenic mile on the Rogue River. Altogether, the state park claims a 3-mile stretch of river and offers ample recreational access. The campsites are spacious with paved parking. Native pines, oaks, and cedars, along with a variety of landscape trees, contribute to the shade and beauty of camp. You can fish, boat, or walk the 1.1-mile River Edge Trail. You can even arrange for a shuttle pickup at the park for a jet boat tour.

83 Whitehorse County Park

Location: About 7 miles west of Grants Pass

Season: Year-round, but water is shut off during cold spells

Sites: 8 hookup sites, 36 basic sites; water and electric hookups

Maximum length: 40 feet

Facilities: Tables, some barbecues and grills, flush toilets, drinking water, showers, telephone, playground, horseshoe pits, volleyball, paved boat ramp

Fee per night: $$

Management: Josephine County

Contact: (541) 474–5285, reservations accepted; www.co.josephine.or.us/parks

Finding the campground: From Sixth Street in Grants Pass, go west on G Street, which later becomes Upper River Road and then Lower River Road, to enter the park in 7.3 miles.

About the campground: This fine campground sits on a gentle, wooded hillside above the north bank of the Rogue River. A day-use area claims the lower portion of the park, closer to the river. Attractive lawn and ponderosa pines and oaks lend character to the camp, while cottonwoods grow toward the river. Since the park is also a bird sanctuary, naturalists will enjoy the companionship of herons, geese, ospreys, wood ducks, and songbirds. Fishing, rafting, swimming, and riverside nature walks keep visitors delightfully busy.

84 Wolf Creek County Park

Location: In the community of Wolf Creek, about 20 miles north of Grants Pass

Season: Year-round, but water is shut off during cold spells

Sites: 19 hookup sites, 16 basic sites; water and electric hookups

Maximum length: 30 feet

Facilities: Tables, grills, pit toilets, drinking water, dump station, playground, disc golf, baseball field, horseshoe pits

Fee per night: $$

Management: Josephine County

Contact: (541) 474–5285; www.co.josephine.or.us/parks

Finding the campground: From Interstate 5, take exit 76 and head west into the town of Wolf Creek. From there, follow the signs for the park, which lies at the end of Main Street, 0.3 mile past the historic Wolf Creek Tavern (or Wolf Creek Inn).

About the campground: This quiet, wooded campground sits just outside the small town of Wolf Creek. The town's historic Inn, a state heritage site, was a stagecoach stop on the Oregon–California line. The campsites are snuggled among the tall firs, pines, and madrones and have earthen parking. A full green understory helps to ensure privacy. Only an intermittent train whistle or a big game at the ballfield disturbs the quiet. A foot trail leads from camp to a viewpoint and the summit of London Peak.

Wolf Creek Inn.

Medford Area

85 Applegate Lake Recreation Areas

Location: About 30 miles southwest of Medford, on Applegate Reservoir
Season: Mid-May–October
Sites: 7 RV spaces at Hart-tish; 30 total walk-in tent sites at Hart-tish, Carberry, and Watkins; no hookups
Maximum length: 40 feet
Facilities: Tables, grills, flush toilets (Hart-tish), vault toilets (walk-in camps), drinking water (all), boat launch (Hart-tish)
Fee per night: $$ (Hart-tish); $ (walk-in camps)
Management: Rogue River National Forest
Contact: (541) 899–3888; www.fs.fed.us/r6/rogue-siskiyou
Finding the campgrounds: From Jacksonville, take Oregon 238 west toward Grants Pass, going 7.4 miles to Ruch. Turn south onto Applegate Road toward Applegate Dam and Star Ranger Station. Go 14.5 miles to the reservoir: Hart-tish, Watkins, and Carberry Recreation Areas dot the west shore; French Gulch is across Applegate Dam on Forest Road 1075.

Medford Area

	Hookup sites	Total sites	Maximum RV length	Hookups	Toilets	Showers	Drinking water	Dump station	Recreation	Fee	Can reserve
85 Applegate Lake Recreation Areas		37	40		F,NF		•		HSFBL	$–$$	
86 Cantrall–Buckley County Park		30	25		NF	•	•		SF	$$	
87 Doe Point		30	32		F		•		HSFB	$$	
88 Fish Lake		17	32		F		•		HSFBL	$$	
89 Fourbit Ford		7	20		NF		•		F	$$	
90 Imnaha		4	20		NF				H	$	
91 Jackson		12	T		F		•		SF	$	
92 Joseph Stewart State Park	148	197	80	WE	F	•	•	•	HSFBLC	$$	
93 North Fork		9	24		NF		•		HF	$	
94 Parker Meadows		8	25		NF		•			$	
95 Rogue Elk County Park	15	35	35	WE	F,NF	•	•	•	SFBL	$$	
96 South Fork		6	18		NF		•		HF	$	
97 Whiskey Spring		36	30		NF		•		H	$	
98 Willow Lake Recreation Area	37	70	25	WES	F,NF	•	•	•	SFBL	$$–$$$	
99 Willow Prairie Horse Camp		10	40		NF		•		HR	$	

About the campgrounds: These camps serve visitors to Applegate Reservoir and the surrounding mountains. Fishing and boating (10 miles per hour maximum) are popular draws, especially when the reservoir is high. But the area also boasts superb hiking trails. The Collings Mountain Trail offers a challenging skyline hike and bypasses a trap built for Bigfoot. Other trails wander the reservoir shore or introduce the region's mining past. For each of the camps, parking is in an open lot, with tables and amenities just strides away.

86 Cantrall–Buckley County Park

Location: About 18 miles southwest of Medford
Season: Year-round
Sites: 30 basic sites; no hookups
Maximum length: 25 feet
Facilities: Tables, barbecues, vault toilets, drinking water, coin-operated showers (at day-use area), playground, volleyball, horseshoe pits
Fee per night: $$
Management: Jackson County
Contact: (541) 774–8183; www.jacksoncountyparks.com
Finding the campground: From Oregon 238, 25 miles east of Grants Pass, 8.5 miles west of Jacksonville, turn south on Hamilton Road and go 1 mile to enter the campground on the right.
About the campground: In an 89-acre woodland of pines, oaks, madrones, and firs sits this county park complex with 1.75 miles of Applegate River frontage. The rustic camp claims a knoll above the river; its companion day-use area is open only on weekends and holidays. Deer are common here, and birding is popular. Trout fishing and swimming will keep you entertained, or you may want to head east into historic Jacksonville. This town traces its origins to the placer gold discoveries of 1851–1852. It retains its old-town charm, and its museums and shops welcome strolling.

87 Doe Point

Location: About 38 miles east of Medford, on Fish Lake
Season: May–mid-October
Sites: 25 basic sites, 5 walk-in tent sites; no hookups
Maximum length: 32 feet
Facilities: Tables, grills, flush toilets, drinking water
Fee per night: $$
Management: Rogue River National Forest
Contact: (541) 552–2900; www.fs.fed.us/r6/rogue-siskiyou
Finding the campground: From Oregon 140, 37.5 miles east of Medford and 6.5 miles west of Lake of the Woods, turn south at the sign for Doe Point Campground on Forest Road 810 and go 0.5 mile to enter camp.
About the campground: This attractive camp fronts the north shore of Fish Lake, a big, sparkling mountain lake enlarged by a dam on the North Fork Lit-

tle Butte Creek. The sites are well spaced and shaded by firs. Across the lake rises Brown Mountain (elevation 7,311 feet). This shield volcano and the lava flow it produced are among the most recent in the Cascades. Brown Mountain Lava Field covers 13 square miles and measures 250 feet thick. If you hike the Fish Lake Trail to the Pacific Crest Trail and walk south along the PCT, you can visit the outskirts of the lava field or traverse it. Fishing and swimming keep most guests at the lake.

88 Fish Lake

Location: About 39 miles east of Medford, on Fish Lake
Season: May–mid-October
Sites: 17 basic sites; no hookups
Maximum length: 32 feet
Facilities: Tables, grills, flush toilets, drinking water, boat launch, dock, fish-cleaning building
Fee per night: $$
Management: Rogue River National Forest
Contact: (541) 552–2900; www.fs.fed.us/r6/rogue-siskiyou
Finding the campground: From Oregon 140, 38 miles east of Medford and 6 miles west of Lake of the Woods, turn south for Fish Lake, go 0.6 mile, and bear right to enter camp.
About the campground: This comfortable camp is on the north shore of Fish Lake, a scenic mountain lake enlarged by a dam. The natural lake was only a third this size. Across the lake, you can view volcanic Brown Mountain. Fish Lake is open to fishing, swimming, and boating (10 miles per hour maximum or self-propelled). Along its shore is the Fish Lake Trail, which ultimately connects with the Pacific Crest Trail for longer hikes. Sites have paved or earthen parking and double-wide spaces for trailers. Ospreys and eagles commonly soar overhead.

89 Fourbit Ford

Location: About 34 miles northeast of Medford
Season: Mid-May–October
Sites: 7 basic sites; no hookups
Maximum length: 20 feet
Facilities: Tables, grills, vault toilets, drinking water
Fee per night: $$
Management: Rogue River National Forest
Contact: (541) 865–2700; www.fs.fed.us/r6/rogue-siskiyou
Finding the campground: From Oregon 140, 26 miles east of Medford, go 6 miles north on County Road 821 to Forest Road 3065. From Butte Falls, travel 10 miles south on CR 821 to FR 3065. Turn east and follow FR 3065 for 1.4 miles to enter the camp on the left; the final 1.1 miles are on gravel.
About the campground: This pleasant campground overlooks Fourbit Creek. Pines and firs shade the camp, which sits in a meadow. The campsites are well

spaced but have relatively short parking spurs. You can fish in the creek, but this is mainly a spot to retreat from daily concerns and enjoy the surroundings.

90 Imnaha

Location: About 60 miles northeast of Medford
Season: Mid-May–October
Sites: 4 basic sites; no hookups
Maximum length: 20 feet
Facilities: Tables, grills, pit toilets; no drinking water
Fee per night: $
Management: Rogue River National Forest
Contact: (541) 865–2700; www.fs.fed.us/r6/rogue-siskiyou
Finding the campground: From Prospect, go east on Butte Falls–Prospect Road for 2.8 miles. Turn left onto Bessie Creek Road/Forest Road 37, go 8.2 miles, and turn left into camp. All but the last mile is paved.
About the campground: Near Imnaha Guard Station, this tiny camp sits at the edge of a meadow. Paths lead to a big fir and Imnaha Springs; the creek that emerges from the springs threads past camp. The fir has a 7-foot diameter and could easily feel at home among California's sequoia redwoods. At the far side of the guard station, a gate opens to a boardwalk and path leading to an enchanting, hummocky meadow flat drained by the silver rivulets of Imnaha Springs. Mosses, wildflowers, and clumps of aquatic vegetation contribute to the captivating mosaic. En route to camp, you will have passed the Middle Fork Rogue Trail, which enters Sky Lakes Wilderness.

91 Jackson

Location: About 25 miles southwest of Medford
Season: May–September
Sites: 12 tent sites; no hookups
Maximum length: Suitable for tents only
Facilities: Tables, barbecues, flush toilets, drinking water
Fee per night: $
Management: Rogue River National Forest
Contact: (541) 899–3888 www.fs.fed.us/r6/rogue-siskiyou
Finding the campground: From Jacksonville, take Oregon 238 west toward Grants Pass. Go 7.4 miles to Ruch and turn south onto Applegate Road toward Applegate Dam and Star Ranger Station. Go 9.5 miles and turn right to enter this campground.
About the campground: Primarily for tent campers, this campground offers a central parking area and walk-to sites along the Applegate River. Pines, cedars, and madrones lend shade. Swimming is at your own risk. Hiking and the recreational opportunities created by Applegate Reservoir are close by. Nearby McKee Covered Bridge makes a nice photo opportunity.

McKee Covered Bridge.

92 Joseph Stewart State Park

Location: About 35 miles northeast of Medford, on Lost Creek Reservoir
Season: Mid-April–late October
Sites: 148 hookup sites, 49 basic sites; water and electric hookups
Maximum length: 80 feet
Facilities: Tables, grills, flush toilets, drinking water, showers, dump station, telephone, playground, store, marina, boat rental, boat launch, dock
Fee per night: $$
Management: Oregon State Parks and Recreation Department
Contact: (541) 560–3334; www.oregonstateparks.org
Finding the campground: It is north off Oregon 62, 10 miles southwest of Prospect and about 35 miles northeast of Medford.
About the campground: In Rogue River Country, along the southeast shore of Lost Creek Reservoir stretches this attractive, developed park, with a

sweeping groomed lawn, young pines, and some leafy shade trees. Lost Creek Reservoir captures the Rogue, creating a wonderful playground for swimming, fishing, boating, and sailing. Where the river flows free, rafting extends the to-do list. Hiking the area trails or cycling a 6-mile bike path provides a different lake perspective. Cole M. Rivers Fish Hatchery, near the Lost Creek dam, is the largest hatchery in the state and is open for touring.

93 North Fork

Location: About 37 miles east of Medford
Season: Late April–mid-November
Sites: 9 basic sites; no hookups
Maximum length: 24 feet
Facilities: Tables, grills, vault toilets, drinking water
Fee per night: $
Management: Rogue River National Forest
Contact: (541) 552-2900; www.fs.fed.us/r6/rogue-siskiyou
Finding the campground: From Oregon 140, 36 miles east of Medford and 8 miles west of Lake of the Woods, turn south on Forest Road 37 to reach the camp on the right in 0.5 mile. Or, from Dead Indian Memorial Road 23.4 miles east of Ashland, turn north on FR 37 and go 7.2 miles to reach the camp on the left.
About the campground: On North Fork Little Butte Creek, the outlet of Fish Lake, this camp offers a rustic camping experience. The North Fork flows broad and clear between grassy banks. A tall, rich fir forest with chinquapin understory and the outskirts of Brown Mountain Lava Field contribute to the setting. The parking spaces are gravel, but only one site offers pull-through parking. By hiking the Fish Lake Trail, you can reach the dam in 0.6 mile, a resort in 3 miles, and the Pacific Crest Trail in 5 miles. Fish Lake (accessible by trail or road) offers fishing, boating, and swimming.

94 Parker Meadows

Location: About 70 miles northeast of Medford
Season: August–October
Sites: 8 basic sites; no hookups
Maximum length: 25 feet
Facilities: Tables, grills, vault toilets, drinking water, Adirondack shelter
Fee per night: $
Management: Rogue River National Forest
Contact: (541) 865-2700; www.fs.fed.us/r6/rogue-siskiyou
Finding the campground: From Prospect, go east on Butte Falls–Prospect Road for 2.8 miles and turn left onto Bessie Creek Road/Forest Road 37, which begins paved but changes to gravel. Continue 20 miles and turn right onto an unmarked gravel road to enter camp in 0.25 mile.

About the campground: This isolated camp rests in a forest of big firs and hemlocks with a huckleberry understory. Although it has the amenities of a basic forest camp, the location has a wilderness feeling about it. Nature and wildlife are right at your doorstep. The rustic A-frame shelter is at site 9. Not far from camp is the trail along the South Fork Rogue River that leads into Sky Lakes Wilderness.

95 Rogue Elk County Park

Location: About 25 miles northeast of Medford
Season: Mid-April–mid-October
Sites: 15 hookup sites, 20 tent sites; water and electric hookups
Maximum length: 35 feet
Facilities: Tables, barbecues, flush and vault toilets, drinking water, showers, dump station, telephone, playground, boat launch
Fee per night: $$
Management: Jackson County
Contact: (541) 774-8183; www.jacksoncountyparks.com
Finding the campground: It is south off Oregon 62, 4.8 miles northeast of Shady Cove.
About the campground: This shaded and landscaped camp fronts the Rogue River downstream from Lost Creek Reservoir. The overflow tent area occupies a more natural forest setting. The Rogue entertains and enchants with fishing, boating, and swimming.

96 South Fork

Location: About 45 miles east of Medford
Season: Mid-May–October
Sites: 6 basic sites; no hookups
Maximum length: 18 feet
Facilities: Tables, grills, vault toilets, drinking water
Fee per night: $
Management: Rogue River National Forest
Contact: (541) 865-2700; www.fs.fed.us/r6/rogue-siskiyou
Finding the campground: Start from the town of Butte Falls, which is reached some 30 miles northeast of Medford via signed routes off OR 62 or off OR 140. At 1 mile east of Butte Falls, turn north onto Butte Falls–Prospect Road, go 8.5 miles, and turn right onto Lodgepole Road/Forest Road 34. Continue 7.3 miles more to enter the camp on the right.
About the campground: This campground occupies a pine- and fir-covered bench above the road and the South Fork Rogue River. Half a mile east of camp, near the junction of FR 37 and FR 34, you can access the South Fork Rogue River Trail. Other trails in the area venture into Sky Lakes Wilderness.

97 Whiskey Spring

Location: About 32 miles east of Medford
Season: Mid-May–October
Sites: 36 basic sites; no hookups
Maximum length: 30 feet
Facilities: Tables, grills, vault toilets, drinking water
Fee per night: $
Management: Rogue River National Forest
Contact: (541) 865–2700; www.fs.fed.us/r6/rogue-siskiyou
Finding the campground: From Oregon 140, 26 miles east of Medford, go 6 miles north on County Road 821 to Forest Road 3065. From Butte Falls, travel 10 miles south on CR 821 to FR 3065. Turn east and follow FR 3065 for 0.3 mile to enter the camp on the left.
About the campground: This campground occupies a large flat of pine trees, with a few cedars and firs sprinkled through the ranks. RVers will find several long gravel parking pads, as well as some pull-through sites. Adjacent to camp is a spring-fed beaver pond and Whiskey Creek, a trout stream. In season, spring peepers enliven the night forest; other times it is an owl sounding. Squirrels, deer, beavers, woodpeckers, and wood ducks can be spied. A 1-mile, barrier-free trail with a cinder surface skirts the beaver pond, Whiskey Creek, and Whiskey Spring, while touring a rich woodland seasonally decorated with colorful wildflowers.

98 Willow Lake Recreation Area

Location: About 35 miles east of Medford, on Willow Lake
Season: April–October
Sites: 37 full or partial hookup sites, 29 tent sites, 4 cabins; water, electric, and sewer hookups
Maximum length: 25 feet
Facilities: Tables, grills, flush and vault toilets, drinking water, showers (at beach), dump station, telephone, boat rentals, launch, dock, fish-cleaning station, store, restaurant
Fee per night: $$–$$$
Management: Jackson County
Contact: (541) 774–8183; www.jacksoncountyparks.com
Finding the campground: From Oregon 140, 26 miles east of Medford, go 8 miles north on County Road 821 to Willow Lake Road. From the town of Butte Falls, go 8 miles south on CR 821 to Willow Lake Road. Turn west and follow Willow Lake Road 0.4 mile to the recreation area.
About the campground: This campground-resort complex occupies more than 900 acres on the west shore of Willow Lake, a large reservoir rimmed by

forest. Cross-lake views find Mount McLoughlin. This is a busy place: Swimming, fishing, and canoeing are popular, and a section of the lake is set aside for waterskiing. The RV area features sites with gravel or earthen parking. The tent area claims a mildly rolling, pine-clad slope, with some sites overlooking the water.

99 Willow Prairie Horse Camp

Location: About 29 miles east of Medford
Season: Maintained from mid-May–September
Sites: 10 basic sites; no hookups
Maximum length: 40 feet
Facilities: Tables, grills, vault toilets, drinking water, corrals
Fee per night: $
Management: Rogue River National Forest
Contact: (541) 865–2700; www.fs.fed.us/r6/rogue-siskiyou
Finding the campground: From Oregon 140, 26 miles east of Medford and 8 miles west of Lake of the Woods, turn north on County Road 821, heading for Butte Falls. Go 1.6 miles and turn left on Forest Road 3738. Go another 1.2 miles and bear left on FR 3735 to enter camp on the right in 0.2 mile.
About the campground: This fine horse camp sits next to a prairie meadow threaded by the West Branch Willow Creek. Douglas and grand firs supply shade to the well-spaced sites, which are both accommodating and comfortable. Horse trails allow you to explore from camp. The meadow, a reclaimed beaver pond, now has a new population of beavers, which are again raising the water level. Buttercup, lupine, and false hellebore add a touch of color to the soggy area. Overlooking the lea is the restored Willow Prairie Cabin, which is on the National Register of Historic Places; an antler door handle provides admittance.

Ashland Area

100 Beaver Dam

Location: About 25 miles northeast of Ashland
Season: Mid-May–mid-October
Sites: 4 basic sites; no hookups
Maximum length: 20 feet
Facilities: Tables, grills, pit toilets; no drinking water
Fee per night: $
Management: Rogue River National Forest
Contact: (541) 552–2900; www.fs.fed.us/r6/rogue-siskiyou
Finding the campground: From Ashland, go 23.4 miles east on Dead Indian Memorial Road. Turn left (north) onto paved Forest Road 37, go 1.4 miles, and turn right into camp.
About the campground: This small, primitive campground occupies a forest of Douglas fir, grand fir, lodgepole pine, and spruce along the willow-lined banks of Beaver Dam Creek. It serves as a quiet retreat. For streamside exploration and trout fishing, a foot trail links this camp to Daley Creek Campground (see next entry) and continues about 2 miles beyond. Howard Prairie and Hyatt Lakes are a short drive southwest from the camp.

Ashland Area

	Hookup sites	Total sites	Maximum RV length	Hookups	Toilets	Showers	Drinking water	Dump station	Recreation	Fee	Can reserve
100 Beaver Dam		4	20		NF				HF	$	
101 Daley Creek		6	18		NF				HF	$	
102 Emigrant Lake Recreation Area	32	74	50	WES	F	•	•	•	SFBL	$$–$$$	•
103 Howard Prairie Resort	185	255	40	WES	F	•	•	•	SFBL	$$–$$$	
104 Hyatt Lake Recreation Site		54	35		F	•	•	•	HFBL	$$	
105 Klum Landing		32	25		F	•	•		SFBL	$$	
106 Lily Glen Horse Camp		25	30		NF		•		FR	$$	
107 Mount Ashland		6	T		NF				H		
108 Wildcat		12	20		NF				FBL	$	
109 Willow Point		40	35		NF		•		HSFBL	$$	

101 Daley Creek

Location: About 25 miles northeast of Ashland
Season: Early May–mid-November
Sites: 6 basic sites; no hookups
Maximum length: 18 feet
Facilities: Tables, grills, vault toilets; no drinking water
Fee per night: $
Management: Rogue River National Forest
Contact: (541) 552–2900; www.fs.fed.us/r6/rogue-siskiyou
Finding the campground: From Ashland, go 23.4 miles east on Dead Indian Memorial Road. Turn left (north) onto paved Forest Road 37, go 1.6 miles, and turn left into camp.
About the campground: This quiet hideaway occupies a slight knoll at the confluence of Beaver Dam and Daley Creeks. It rests in a mixed forest and has two sites set aside for wheelchair users. Beaver Dam Trail links this camp to Beaver Dam Campground (see above) and allows for a couple of miles of exploring along Beaver Dam Creek. Both creeks are wonderfully clear with a series of small pools. Along the banks, grassy openings between the willows provide access to the pools.

102 Emigrant Lake Recreation Area

Location: About 4 miles southeast of Ashland, on Emigrant Lake
Season: Mid-March–mid-October
Sites: 32 hookup sites, 42 basic sites; water, electric, and sewer hookups
Maximum length: 50 feet
Facilities: Tables, grills, flush toilets, drinking water, showers, dump station, telephone, playground, ballfield, horseshoe pits, waterslide, boat rental, 2 boat ramps, food concession
Fee per night: $$–$$$
Management: Jackson County
Contact: (541) 774–8183, reservations recommended; www.jacksoncounty parks.com
Finding the campground: From Interstate 5 in Ashland, take exit 14 and go southeast on Oregon 66 for 3.2 miles. Turn left at the sign for Emigrant Lake Recreation Area and continue about a mile to the camp entrance on the left.
About the campground: This campground with paved site parking occupies an oak-studded, grassy hillside above popular Emigrant Lake, a large, horseshoe-shaped reservoir hugged by arid valley foothills. Recreational opportunities center on the lake, where you can swim, boat, fish, sail, water-ski, and sailboard. A waterslide is open Memorial Day through Labor Day; there is a fee to use it.

103 Howard Prairie Resort

Location: About 22 miles east of Ashland, on Howard Prairie Lake
Season: Mid-April–October
Sites: 185 RV hookup sites, 70 tent sites, RV rentals; water, electric, and sewer hookups
Maximum length: 40 feet
Facilities: Tables, flush toilets, drinking water, showers, laundry, dump station, marina, boat rental, camp store, restaurant
Fee per night: $$–$$$
Management: Jackson County (operated by concessionaire)
Contact: (541) 774–8183 or (541) 482–1979; www.jacksoncountyparks.com
Finding the campground: From Ashland, go 19 miles east on Dead Indian Memorial Road toward Lake of the Woods. Turn south on Hyatt Prairie Road and proceed 3.2 miles to enter the resort on left.
About the campground: The camping areas surround the large, bustling, full-service resort/marina complex. An attractive shoreline forest contains the camp, successfully keeping the woodland mystique while providing comfort and convenience. Rainbow trout fishing, hiking, and sailing are popular pastimes.

104 Hyatt Lake Recreation Site

Location: About 20 miles east of Ashland, on Hyatt Lake
Season: Late April–October
Sites: 30 basic sites in the main overnight area, 17 drive-in tent sites, 7 walk-in tent sites; no hookups
Maximum length: 35 feet
Facilities: Tables, grills and barbecues, flush toilets, drinking water, showers, dump station, telephone, playground, volleyball, horseshoe pits, 2 boat launches, dock, fish-cleaning station, boat trailer parking
Fee per night: $$
Management: Medford District Bureau of Land Management
Contact: (541) 618–2200; www.or.blm.gov/medford
Finding the campground: From Oregon 66, 17 miles east of Ashland and 44 miles west of Klamath Falls, turn north on East Hyatt Road at the sign for the reservoir. Go 3 miles and proceed straight for the recreation site as the main road curves left and becomes Hyatt Prairie Road. In 0.1 mile, turn left for Hyatt Lake Recreation Site.
About the campground: This star in the portfolio of BLM campgrounds occupies a gentle, forested slope above Hyatt Lake, a popular boating and fishing reservoir. Mount McLoughlin looms to the north. Ospreys sometimes dive for fish. The sites are mostly shaded by Douglas firs and grand firs. The Pacific Crest Trail passes through the area not far from camp.

105 Klum Landing

Location: About 27 miles east of Ashland, on Howard Prairie Lake
Season: Mid-April–October
Sites: 32 basic sites; no hookups
Maximum length: 25 feet
Facilities: Tables, grills, flush toilets, drinking water, showers, boat launch, playground
Fee per night: $$
Management: Jackson County
Contact: (541) 774–8183; www.jacksoncountyparks.com
Finding the campground: From Ashland, drive 19 miles east on Dead Indian Memorial Road. Turn right (south) onto Hyatt Prairie Road, go 4.6 miles, and turn left onto Howard Prairie Dam Road. Drive 3 miles farther to reach the camp on the left.
About the campground: This primitive campground spreads across 156 acres of a pine- and fir-forested slope at the southern end of Howard Prairie Lake, a big, elongated reservoir that offers swimming, fishing, and boating. The campsites are well shaded, a welcome change from the sun-drenched lake. Because all sites are back-ins and some have difficult approaches, this campground is inappropriate for large RV units. The Pacific Crest Trail offers hiking.

106 Lily Glen Horse Camp

Location: About 20 miles east of Ashland, on Howard Prairie Lake
Season: Mid-April–October
Sites: 25 basic sites; no hookups
Maximum length: 30 feet
Facilities: Tables, grills, vault toilets, drinking water, corrals
Fee per night: $$
Management: Jackson County
Contact: (541) 774–8183; www.jacksoncountyparks.com
Finding the campground: From Ashland, drive 20 miles east on Dead Indian Memorial Road. Turn right (south) to enter camp. (The turn is 1 mile east of Hyatt Prairie Road.)
About the campground: This camp occupies a flat shaded by ponderosa pines along the shallow north end of Howard Prairie Reservoir. While boating is popular on much of the lake, there is no launch here. Because of that, this camp extends a quieter stay. A rustic barn and water tower contribute to the atmosphere of camp. You can access horse trails nearby, and fishing is popular.

107 Mount Ashland

Location: About 20 miles south of Ashland
Season: Late June–October
Sites: 6 basic sites; no hookups
Maximum length: Best suited for tents
Facilities: Tables, barbecues, pit toilets; no drinking water
Fee per night: None
Management: Rogue River National Forest
Contact: (541) 552–2900; www.fs.fed.us/r6/rogue-siskiyou
Finding the campground: From Interstate 5 south of Ashland, take exit 6 and head west, following the signs to Mount Ashland. Go 0.7 mile, turn right on Mount Ashland Road/Forest Road 20, and follow it for 9.3 miles to reach the campground. The final 0.4 mile is on gravel; the campground is 0.7 mile past the ski area.
About the campground: The campsites—primarily walk-in sites—radiate from both sides of FR 20. Campers enjoy the spectacular high-elevation tapestry of the south flank of Mount Ashland: clusters of big-diameter firs, alpine meadows, grassland, and rocky jumbles. Views from the camp are of the rocky crest of Mount Ashland to the north and the snowy crown of 14,000-foot Mount Shasta (in California) to the south. You may spy grouse, juncos, and jays. This camp is close to the Pacific Crest National Scenic Trail, which follows the crest of the Siskiyou Mountains here.

108 Wildcat

Location: About 22 miles east of Ashland, on Hyatt Lake
Season: Late April–October
Sites: 12 basic sites; no hookups
Maximum length: 20 feet
Facilities: Tables, grills, vault toilets, horseshoe pits, boat launch; no drinking water
Fee per night: $
Management: Medford District Bureau of Land Management
Contact: (541) 618–2200; www.or.blm.gov/medford
Finding the campground: From Oregon 66, 17 miles east of Ashland, 44 miles west of Klamath Falls, turn north on East Hyatt Road at the sign for the reservoir. Go 3 miles and proceed straight on East Hyatt Road as the main road curves left and becomes Hyatt Prairie Road. Go another 2 miles to Wildcat.
About the campground: Campers will enjoy ample shoreline at this small campground that sits on a forested peninsula stretching into Hyatt Lake. Ponderosa pines rise among the mixed firs of camp, creating partial to full shade. The road through camp and site parking are all gravel. Fishing, boating, hiking, and relaxing are the main diversions.

109 Willow Point

Location: About 24 miles east of Ashland, on Howard Prairie Lake
Season: Mid-April–October
Sites: 40 basic sites; no hookups
Maximum length: 35 feet
Facilities: Tables, grills, vault toilets, drinking water, boat launch, fish-cleaning station
Fee per night: $$
Management: Jackson County
Contact: (541) 774–8183; www.jacksoncountyparks.com
Finding the campground: From Ashland, head east 19 miles on Dead Indian Memorial Road. Turn right (south) onto Hyatt Prairie Road, go 4.6 miles, and turn left onto Howard Prairie Dam Road. Go 0.5 mile to the campground entrance on the left.
About the campground: Situated on 59 acres along Willow Creek and the southwest shore of Howard Prairie Lake is this forested campground with views of Mount McLoughlin. Fishing, boating, swimming, and sailing are the primary draws of the area, but the Pacific Crest National Scenic Trail passes at the south end of the reservoir for anyone interested in hiking.

Klamath Falls–Klamath Basin Area

110 Aspen Point

Location: About 35 miles northwest of Klamath Falls, on Lake of the Woods
Season: Late May–mid-September
Sites: 61 basic sites; no hookups
Maximum length: 40 feet
Facilities: Tables, grills, flush toilets, drinking water, dump station, boat launch, boat rentals nearby
Fee per night: $$
Management: Winema National Forest
Contact: (541) 885-3400; (877) 444-6777 for reservations; www.fs.fed.us/r6 /frewin

Klamath Falls–Klamath Basin Area	Hookup sites	Total sites	Maximum RV length	Hookups	Toilets	Showers	Drinking water	Dump station	Recreation	Fee	Can reserve
110 Aspen Point		61	40		F		•	•	HSFBL	$$	•
111 Collier Memorial State Park	50	68	60	WES	F	•	•	•	HF	$$	
112 Corral Springs		6	40		NF						
113 Digit Point		64	30		F,NF		•	•	HSFBL	$	
114 Eagle Ridge Park		6	30		NF		•		FBL		
115 Fourmile Lake		25	22		NF		•		HSFBL	$$	
116 Gerber Reservoir: North		18	35		NF		•	•	SFBL	$	
117 Gerber Reservoir: South		26	40		NF		•	•	SFBL	$	
118 Hagelstein Park		10	30		F		•		FBL	$	
119 Head of the River		5	40		NF				F		
120 Jackson Creek		12	25		NF				F		
121 Jackson F. Kimball State Recreation Site		10	45		NF				F	$	
122 Keno Recreation Area		25	35		F	•	•	•	SFBL	$$	
123 Klamath County Fairgrounds	12	12	40	WES	F	•	•			$$	
124 Odessa Creek		5	20		NF				FBL		
125 Scott Creek		6	20		NF						
126 Sunset		67	40		F		•		HSFBL	$$	•
127 Surveyor Recreation Site		5	25		NF						
128 Topsy Recreation Site		15	40		NF		•		FBL	$	
129 Williamson River		10	30		NF		•		F	$	

Finding the campground: From Oregon 140, 34 miles west of Klamath Falls and 44 miles east of Medford, turn south onto Forest Road 3704, go 0.7 mile, and turn right for the campground.

About the campground: This forested campground occupies the northeast shore of Lake of the Woods, a lovely mountain lake that invites swimming, casting a fishing line, trolling along shore, or sailing the lake's length. Brown Mountain and Mount McLoughlin punctuate the skyline. Trails in the area follow the shoreline, lead to neighboring lakes, and meet up with the Pacific Crest Trail.

111 Collier Memorial State Park

Location: 5 miles north of Chiloquin
Season: Mid-April–late October
Sites: 50 hookup sites, 18 basic sites; water, electric, and sewer hookups
Maximum length: 60 feet
Facilities: Tables, grills, flush toilets, drinking water, showers, dump station, telephone, logging museum, pioneer village, gift shop, 4-corral primitive horse camp
Fee per night: $$
Management: Oregon State Parks and Recreation Department
Contact: (541) 783-2471; www.oregonstateparks.org
Finding the campground: It is east off U.S. Highway 97, 5 miles north of Chiloquin and 30 miles north of Klamath Falls.
About the campground: An open-air logging museum and the Spring Creek–Williamson River confluence are the headline attractions at this park in the Klamath Basin. The closely spaced sites are nestled in a second-growth forest of ponderosa and lodgepole pines; bitterbrush and currant bushes dot the needle-strewn forest floor. The camp is located above the Williamson River, across US 97 from Spring Creek and the logging museum. A pedestrian underpass allows for safe passage between the camp and the day-use area. Fishing, hiking the short trails along Spring Creek, and wandering the red cinder paths among the museum exhibits are activities to pursue in the park. Not far from here, Agency and Upper Klamath Lakes beckon with boating, canoeing, fishing, and birding.

112 Corral Springs

Location: About 5 miles north of Chemult
Season: Mid-May–mid-October
Sites: 6 basic sites; no hookups
Maximum length: 40 feet
Facilities: Tables, grills, vault toilets; no drinking water
Fee per night: None
Management: Winema National Forest
Contact: (541) 365-7001; www.fs.fed.us/r6/frewin
Finding the campground: From U.S. Highway 97, 2.8 miles north of Che-

mult and 5.3 miles south of the junction of US 97 and Oregon 58, turn west onto gravel Forest Road 9774 and go 2 miles to enter this camp on the right.

About the campground: This improved campground has gravel roads and long, gravel parking spaces. It is set in a lodgepole pine forest with small meadow clearings. It offers a quiet retreat or a traveler's stop and lies along the historic Old Klamath Trail, which was used by Native Americans and early explorers. Early in the year, come prepared for mosquitoes.

113 Digit Point

Location: About 13 miles west of Chemult, on Miller Lake
Season: Mid-June–September
Sites: 64 basic sites; no hookups
Maximum length: 30 feet
Facilities: Tables, grills, flush and vault toilets, drinking water, dump station, boat ramp
Fee per night: $
Management: Winema National Forest
Contact: (541) 365-7001; www.fs.fed.us/r6/frewin
Finding the campground: From U.S. Highway 97, 1 mile north of Chemult, turn west onto gravel Forest Road 9772 and go 12 miles to enter this camp on the right.

About the campground: More than a mile above sea level, this campground claims a broad peninsula on the southwest shore of Miller Lake, an attractive natural lake on the eastern side of the Cascade Crest. Mixed conifers frame the sites and provide shade. A fine 4-mile trail rings the lake, offering a chance to view wildlife. Boating, fishing, and swimming are popular. From the west end of the Miller Lakeshore Trail, hikers can take a spur to the Pacific Crest National Scenic Trail or cross over the crest to Maidu Lake. The latter is the head of the North Umpqua Wild and Scenic River and marks the start of the North Umpqua National Recreation Trail. Come prepared for mosquitoes at these high lakes.

114 Eagle Ridge Park

Location: About 22 miles northwest of Klamath Falls
Season: Year-round
Sites: 6 basic sites; no hookups
Maximum length: 30 feet
Facilities: Tables, fire rings, pit toilets, drinking water, boat launch, dock
Fee per night: None
Management: Klamath County
Contact: (541) 883-5121; www.co.klamath.or.us/comdevelopment/park_locations.htm
Finding the campground: From the junction of U.S. Highway 97 and Oregon 140 at Klamath Falls, head west on OR 140 for 17.2 mile and turn right (east) for the park. Follow the park and wildlife viewing signs along a gravel route for 4.4 miles to reach the camp.

About the campground: On Shoalwater Bay on Upper Klamath Lake, this camp occupies a small, open flat at the western foot of the pine-and-juniper-clad Eagle Ridge. The sites have basic amenities and gravel parking, but bring your own shade source. At night, the lapping of the lake against the shore enables a tranquil sleep. By day, the lake invites fishing, boating, and bird watching for eagles, grebes, cormorants, and geese. Although the road beyond the camp is unsuitable for trailers and passenger vehicles, you can hike or mountain bike along it for 2 miles to the tip of the peninsula, where you will find additional birding and fishing, as well as views of the lake, Pelican Butte, and Mountain Lakes Wilderness.

115 Fourmile Lake

Location: About 40 miles northwest of Klamath Falls, on Fourmile Lake
Season: Mid-June–October
Sites: 25 basic sites; no hookups
Maximum length: 22 feet
Facilities: Tables, grills, vault toilets, drinking water, boat ramp
Fee per night: $$
Management: Winema National Forest
Contact: (541) 885–3400; www.fs.fed.us/r6/frewin
Finding the campground: From Oregon 140, 34.6 miles west of Klamath Falls, turn north on gravel Forest Road 3661. Follow it 5.5 miles to Fourmile Lake and the campground.
About the campground: The sites are distributed among the lodgepole pines on the shore of Fourmile Lake, which has been enlarged by a small dam. A few sites overlook the water and the attractive lake basin. This area is a gateway to the Sky Lakes Wilderness; a single trailhead serves as the jumping-off point. Trout fishing, swimming, and boating engage guests at camp.

116 Gerber Reservoir: North

Location: About 45 miles east of Klamath Falls, on Gerber Reservoir
Season: Mid-May–late September
Sites: 18 basic sites; no hookups
Maximum length: 35 feet
Facilities: Tables, grills, vault toilets, drinking water, dump station, boat launch, dock, fish-cleaning station
Fee per night: $
Management: Lakeview District Bureau of Land Management
Contact: (541) 883–6916; www.or.blm.gov/lakeview/recreation
Finding the campground: From Klamath Falls, go 18 miles east on Oregon 140 to Dairy, turn right onto OR 70, and go 7 miles southeast to Bonanza. From there, bear right on East Langell Valley Road, go another 10.5 miles, and turn left onto Gerber Road. Proceed 8.1 miles and turn right toward Gerber Reservoir Recreation Site. You will reach a junction in 0.6 mile. Keep left and go another 0.6 mile to this campground.

About the campground: Tucked among the ponderosa pines and scraggly junipers is this popular BLM camp on the western shore of Gerber Reservoir, which was created to provide irrigation. Sites near the water are more closely spaced. You may see waterfowl, bald eagles, and ospreys. The potholes northwest of the reservoir attract other birds, including sandhill cranes. Bass, crappie, catfish, and perch are among the game fish here, and the lake is popular with boaters. During World War II, the U.S. military used an island in this reservoir for bombing practice. Today, ospreys and pelicans are the only bombers of Gerber Reservoir.

117 Gerber Reservoir: South

Location: About 45 miles east of Klamath Falls, on Gerber Reservoir
Season: Mid-May–late September
Sites: 26 basic sites; no hookups
Maximum length: 40 feet
Facilities: Tables, grills, vault toilets, drinking water, dump station, boat launch, fish-cleaning station
Fee per night: $
Management: Lakeview District Bureau of Land Management
Contact: (541) 883–6916; www.or.blm.gov/lakeview/recreation
Finding the campground: From Klamath Falls, go 18 miles east on Oregon 140 to Dairy, turn right onto OR 70, and go 7 miles southeast to Bonanza. From there, bear right on East Langell Valley Road, go another 10.5 miles, and turn left onto Gerber Road. Proceed 8.1 miles and turn right toward Gerber Reservoir Recreation Site. You will reach a junction in 0.6 mile. Go right 0.4 mile to this campground.
About the campground: Gerber Reservoir is a 3,830-acre playground for water-loving campers. Fishing, swimming, boating, and birding are all popular. Near the dam, this camp is generally quieter and has roomier sites set farther back from shore than its northern counterpart. Ponderosa pines supply the shade, while a basalt-studded, sage prairie fans out from camp. Watch the skies for bald eagles, which nest at the north end of the lake.

118 Hagelstein Park

Location: About 10 miles north of Klamath Falls
Season: Year-round, but only self-contained RVs October–March
Sites: 10 basic sites; no hookups
Maximum length: 30 feet
Facilities: Tables, grills, flush toilets, drinking water, boat launch, dock
Fee per night: $
Management: Klamath County
Contact: (541) 883–5121; www.co.klamath.or.us/comdevelopment/park_locations.htm
Finding the campground: It is east off U.S. Highway 97, 10 miles north of the junction of US 97 and Oregon 39 at the north end of Klamath Falls, 15 miles south of Chiloquin.

About the campground: This campground sits beside a small, spring-fed pond and inlet of Upper Klamath Lake. Yellow wildflowers emblazon the juniper- and basalt-covered slope of Naylox Mountain, which overshadows the camp. The camp layout includes groomed lawns, site amenities, and natural trees and shrubs for partial shade. Parking is on the gravel shoulder of the camp road. Swallows nest under the pond footbridge, and schools of fish can sometimes be seen. The camp makes an attractive base and provides boating access to Upper Klamath Lake, where anglers can vie for the prized rainbow trout.

119 Head of the River

Location: About 30 miles northeast of Chiloquin
Season: Maintained from May–September
Sites: 5 basic sites; no hookups
Maximum length: 40 feet
Facilities: Tables, grills, pit toilets; no drinking water
Fee per night: None
Management: Winema National Forest
Contact: (541) 885–3424; www.fs.fed.us/r6/frewin
Finding the campground: From Chiloquin, head northeast on Sprague River Highway for 5.4 miles and turn left onto paved Williamson River Road. Follow it for 7.6 miles and turn left to remain on Williamson River Road for another 16.8 miles. Turn left onto dirt Forest Road 4648, go 0.4 mile, and turn left to enter the camp.
About the campground: This small campground is tucked away in a lodgepole pine forest beside the spring at the head of the Williamson River, an acclaimed crystalline water with a prized trout fishery downstream. Pole fencing defines the road and sites of camp; egresses in the fence provide access to the headwater and its river. Ponderosa pines cluster at the river's head, while clumps of aquatic plants dress the spring in striking contrast to the dried grasses of the forest floor. The camp provides a quiet retreat, putting you in the company of deer, mergansers, kingfishers, and songbirds. In fall, the camp serves as a hunter's base.

120 Jackson Creek

Location: About 48 miles northeast of Chiloquin
Season: Maintained June–September
Sites: 12 basic sites; no hookups
Maximum length: 25 feet
Facilities: Tables, grills, pit toilets; no drinking water
Fee per night: None
Management: Winema National Forest
Contact: (541) 365–7001; www.fs.fed.us/r6/frewin
Finding the campground: From U.S. Highway 97, 24 miles south of Chemult and 21 miles north of Chiloquin, turn east on Silver Lake Road (County

676), go 22 miles, and turn right on cinder Forest Road 49 at the sign for the campground. Go another 4.6 miles and turn left on FR 4900.740 to enter the campground in 0.3 mile.

About the campground: This primitive, out-of-the-way campground is housed among ponderosa pines on a flat beside alder-lined Jackson Creek. A few old-growth pines tower above the dense stand of young trees. Wildflowers sprinkle the creekside meadows. Hunting, fishing, relaxing, cross-country skiing, and watching for deer and antelope can entertain camp guests.

121 Jackson F. Kimball State Recreation Site

Location: About 18 miles northwest of Chiloquin
Season: Mid-April–late October
Sites: 10 basic sites; no hookups
Maximum length: 45 feet
Facilities: Tables, grills, pit toilets; no drinking water
Fee per night: $
Management: Oregon State Parks and Recreation Department
Contact: (541) 783–2471; www.oregonstateparks.org
Finding the campground: From the junction of U.S. Highway 97 and Oregon 62, about 3 miles south of Chiloquin, go west on OR 62 for 12.5 miles and turn right on Sun Mountain Road. Proceed 3 miles to reach the park entrance on the left.

About the campground: This primitive campground occupies a wooded flat at the headwater of Wood River, a spellbinding spring-launched river with water so turquoise that the Crayola® company would kill for the color. Aspens and a few ponderosa pines intersperse the firs and lodgepole pines of camp. Because parking is on the gravel road shoulder, with the site tables and grills a few strides away, the camp is better suited for tenting. You may spy a beaver lodge on the riverbank. Seasonally, you should come prepared for mosquitoes. From camp, you can venture out to Fort Klamath Museum, Crater Lake National Park, or the Pacific Crest Trail.

122 Keno Recreation Area

Location: In Keno, about 11 miles southwest of Klamath Falls
Season: Memorial Day–mid-September
Sites: 25 basic sites; no hookups
Maximum length: 35 feet
Facilities: Tables, grills, flush toilets, drinking water, showers, dump station, playground, boat launch, dock
Fee per night: $$
Management: Pacific Power Company
Contact: (541) 498–2531; www.pacificpower.net
Finding the campground: From the junction of U.S. Highway 97 and Oregon 66 in southwest Klamath Falls, go west on OR 66 for 9.8 miles. Turn right at the sign for Keno Recreation Area at the west end of Keno. Go 0.7 mile on gravel road to enter the camp.

About the campground: This campground rests on a low, broad knoll above a Klamath River reservoir in a pleasant setting of pine, juniper, sage, bitterbrush, and bunchgrass. Beyond camp stretches an arid prairie inhabited by quail and jackrabbits. You may fish, boat, water-ski, watch birds, and swim at a designated site. Near the dam, cormorants commonly line up on the boom. Elsewhere, white pelicans, great blue herons, egrets, night herons, ospreys, swallows, and ducks may cause you to raise your binoculars.

123 Klamath County Fairgrounds

Location: In Klamath Falls
Season: Year-round
Sites: 12 hookup sites; water, electric, and sewer hookups
Maximum length: 40 feet
Facilities: Flush toilets, drinking water, showers, telephone, playground (across street)
Fee per night: $$
Management: Klamath County
Contact: (541) 883–3796; www.kcfairgrounds.org
Finding the campground: It is east off Sixth Street, at the corner of Altamont Drive and South Sixth Street in Klamath Falls. Arrange your stay at the fairgrounds office.
About the campground: In an open field at the north end of the fairgrounds is this designated overnight area for RVs, where you simply back up against a fence to the hookup post. Although not fancy or aesthetic, the sites serve visitors on the go, whether they are involved with fair events or taking in the museums, country music, and natural and historical attractions of Klamath Falls. No dogs are allowed between July 10 and 30.

124 Odessa Creek

Location: About 23 miles northwest of Klamath Falls
Season: April–November, depending on snow
Sites: 5 basic sites; no hookups
Maximum length: 20 feet
Facilities: Tables, grills, vault toilets, primitive boat launch; no drinking water
Fee per night: None
Management: Winema National Forest
Contact: (541) 885–3400; www.fs.fed.us/r6/frewin
Finding the campground: From the junction of U.S. Highway 97 and Oregon 140 in Klamath Falls, go west on OR 140 for 21.8 miles and turn right (northeast) onto Forest Road 3639. Drive another 0.8 mile into the camp.
About the campground: Where Odessa Creek empties into Upper Klamath Lake, you will find this small, primitive camp among the ponderosa pines and thick understory of aspen, dogwood, wild rose, cherry, and other flowering shrubs. The sites have earthen parking and provide a front-row seat to the marshy channels and areas of open water for birding, fishing, canoeing, and

A toad blends into the forest floor.

boating. You may spot bald eagles, beavers, kingfishers, grebes, frogs, deer, and water snakes. The trout fishing is renowned, with 5- and 6-pounders not uncommon.

125 Scott Creek

Location: About 25 miles south of Chemult
Season: Maintained June–September
Sites: 6 basic sites; no hookups
Maximum length: 20 feet
Facilities: Tables, grills, vault toilets; no drinking water
Fee per night: None
Management: Winema National Forest
Contact: (541) 365–7001; www.fs.fed.us/r6/frewin
Finding the campground: From U.S. Highway 97, about 25 miles south of Chemult and 20 miles north of Chiloquin, head west on gravel West Boundary Road (Forest Road 66). Go 3 miles and turn right on Sun Mountain Road. Go 0.6 mile and turn left on FR 2310. Proceed 2.1 miles to FR 060 and turn left. Go 0.2 mile more to the campground.

About the campground: Pretty Scott Creek flows alongside this rustic campground set among the ponderosa pines and white firs. This is a campground for lounging and catching up with your reading.

126 Sunset

Location: About 35 miles northwest of Klamath Falls, on Lake of the Woods
Season: Late May–late September
Sites: 67 basic sites; no hookups
Maximum length: 40 feet
Facilities: Tables, grills, flush toilets, drinking water, boat launch, docks, boat rental nearby
Fee per night: $$
Management: Winema National Forest
Contact: (541) 885-3400; (877) 444-6777 for reservations; www.fs.fed.us/r6 /frewin
Finding the campground: From Oregon 140, 33 miles west of Klamath Falls, 45 miles east of Medford, turn south on Dead Indian Memorial Highway, go 2.5 miles, and turn right to enter the camp.
About the campground: This popular campground on the east side of Lake of the Woods allows you to escape to the cool shade of the firs and pines when you are not out on the lake fishing, swimming, and boating. Mount McLoughlin can be seen from shore. The 1-mile Sunset Trail links the camp and Rainbow Bay. Longer trails in the vicinity lead to Fourmile Lake and its entourage of smaller lakes. Hard-core hikers can journey into wilderness.

127 Surveyor Recreation Site

Location: About 30 miles west of Klamath Falls
Season: Mid-May–Labor Day weekend
Sites: 5 basic sites; no hookups
Maximum length: 25 feet
Facilities: Tables, grills, vault toilets; no drinking water
Fee per night: None
Management: Lakeview District Bureau of Land Management
Contact: (541) 883-6916; www.or.blm.gov/lakeview/recreation
Finding the campground: From the junction of U.S. Highway 97 and Oregon 66 in southwest Klamath Falls, go west on OR 66 for 15.7 miles. Turn right on the paved Keno Access Road (BLM 39-7E-31) for Buck Lake and Spencer Creek. Go 14.1 miles and turn left for the camp. Or, from Dead Indian Memorial Road, 0.5 mile east of Howard Prairie Lake, turn south on Keno Access Road and go 13 miles before turning right into camp.
About the campground: This primitive camp is an ideal place for quiet reflection. It is tucked in an old-growth fir setting. Logs are scattered across the forest floor, which is covered by ferns and the delicate blossoms of prince's pine, starflower, and trillium. The camp has dirt roads and parking and gets light use.

128 Topsy Recreation Site

Location: About 16 miles southwest of Klamath Falls
Season: Mid-May–Labor Day weekend
Sites: 15 basic sites; no hookups
Maximum length: 40 feet
Facilities: Tables, grills, vault toilets, drinking water, boat launch, barrier-free dock and fishing pier
Fee per night: $
Management: Lakeview District Bureau of Land Management
Contact: (541) 883–6916; www.or.blm.gov/lakeview/recreation
Finding the campground: From the junction of U.S. Highway 97 and Oregon 66 in southwest Klamath Falls, go west on OR 66 for 15.3 miles. Turn left onto gravel Topsy Road as you reach John C. Boyle Reservoir. Follow the signs about 1 mile to the camp entrance on the right.
About the campground: This terraced camp is both pretty and functional, blending into its natural pine setting above John C. Boyle Reservoir. All sites have level gravel parking pads, but some also offer tent platforms. From almost anywhere in camp, you can admire the sparkling water. You can watch birds and wildlife right from your lawn chair; an osprey nest overlooks shore. Crappie, bass, catfish, and panfish tug at the lines of anglers, and the reservoir is open to boating.

129 Williamson River

Location: About 7 miles north of Chiloquin
Season: Mid-May–November
Sites: 10 basic sites; no hookups
Maximum length: 30 feet
Facilities: Tables, grills, pit toilets, drinking water
Fee per night: $
Management: Winema National Forest
Contact: (541) 885–3424; www.fs.fed.us/r6/frewin
Finding the campground: From Chiloquin, go about 5 miles north on U.S. Highway 97 and turn right (east) onto Forest Road 9730 for the Collier and Williamson River Campgrounds. Keep left at the Collier Campground turnoff, going 1.3 miles on FR 9730, a wide, improved surface road. Turn right and go another 0.4 mile to the camp.
About the campground: At a distance from US 97, this quiet campground occupies a bench above the Williamson River. Ponderosa and lodgepole pines surround the sites, and dry-land shrubs dot the forest floor. Here, the river is shallow, flowing over waving mats of algae. Willows and grass claim the bank below the camp, while sage is dominant on the opposite shore. This camp offers convenient access to neighboring Collier Memorial State Park, as well as to the sights, sounds, and stops of the Klamath Basin–Upper Klamath Lake Area.

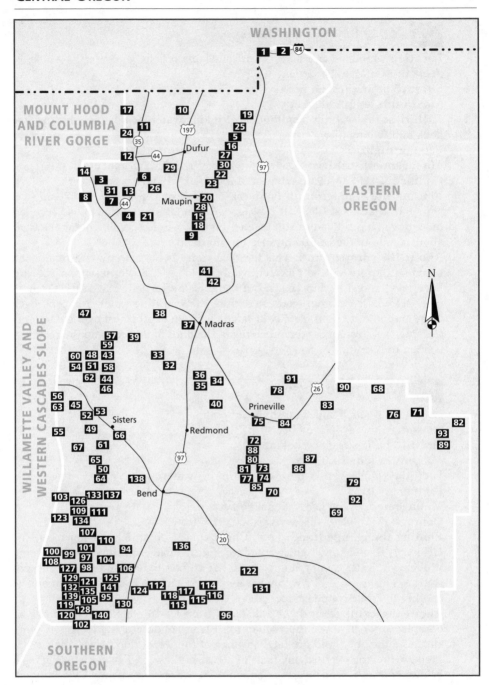

Central Oregon

Central Oregon includes the eastern slopes of the Central Cascades and the High Lava Plains, which spread out from Bend. The east-central Cascades serve up such outstanding features as the Metolius Wild and Scenic River, the Three Sisters, Mount Bachelor, Tam McArthur Rim, and the Cascade Lakes Area.

Within the High Lava Plains, you will find the Deschutes Wild and Scenic River, Newberry National Volcanic Monument, and Crooked River National Grassland. You can visit ghost towns, rock climb at Smith Rock State Park, hunt for thundereggs in Ochoco National Forest, go speedboating at Cove Palisades, fish at area reservoirs, and stargaze at Pine Mountain Observatory.

The tourist-oriented communities of Bend and Sisters, along with several ranching towns and the river-floating mecca of Maupin, serve travelers.

The Cascade Range, that snowcapped chain of volcanoes that partitions the state and dominates the skyline in much of Central Oregon, was named by noted botanist David Douglas. Two stages of volcanic activity shaped these mountains. The younger volcanoes occur in the eastern part of the range. Their dry slopes support ponderosa and lodgepole pines and western larches.

The High Lava Plains feature a textured mosaic of sagebrush and native bunchgrass, juniper and pine forests, lava flows and lava-tube caves, obsidian ridges, cinder cones, and caldera lakes. Newberry Volcano, a shield volcano in the center of the state, covers a larger area than any other volcano in Oregon.

Golden and bald eagles, peregrine falcons, ospreys, and nighthawks favor these rugged plains, as do bluebirds and western tanagers. The larcenous gray jay is often a companion in the Cascades.

Given the diversity of the region, you should expect a variety of weather. The Cascades host downhill and cross-country skiing in winter and offer partially shaded trails and cool mountain lakes in summer. Do not be deceived by the dusty lodgepole pine forests; snowmelt can create ponds that breed mosquitoes, sometimes in hordes. Be sure to keep a supply of insect repellent handy.

Weather on the arid plains varies from crisp, chilly days in winter to baking temperatures in summer. Outdoor activities are generally possible year-round, with caving, rock climbing, hiking, mountain biking, and horseback riding among the more popular pursuits. Snowmobiling and ice fishing fill out the winter calendar at Newberry National Volcanic Monument. Throughout Central Oregon, both in the mountains and on the high plains, summertime visitors should be prepared for afternoon thunderstorms.

Rufus Area

1 Giles French Park

Location: Just northeast of Rufus
Season: Year-round
Sites: Open camping; no hookups
Maximum length: 40 feet
Facilities: Flush toilets, drinking water, boat launch
Fee per night: None
Management: U.S. Army Corps of Engineers
Contact: (541) 296–1181 or (541) 298–7650; www.nwp.usace.army.mil
Finding the campground: From Interstate 84, about 25 miles east of The Dalles, take exit 109 for Rufus and follow the frontage road on the north side of the freeway east for 0.5 mile to the campground.
About the campground: This combination campground and day-use area stretches for 1.7 miles along the Columbia River between the boat launch and John Day Dam. A steep slope plunges from the camp to the rocky riverbank. Overnight parking is allowed on the large gravel- or asphalt-surfaced lots, while tent camping is allowed on the grass. Shade trees are a few steps away, and wind is common in the gorge. Shad and sturgeon fishing, bounty fishing for northern pike minnow, boating, and visiting John Day Dam and its fish-viewing windows keep campers on the go.

2 Le Page Park

Location: About 5 miles northeast of Rufus
Season: April–October
Sites: 22 hookup sites, open tent camping; water and electric hookups
Maximum length: 40 feet
Facilities: Flush toilets, drinking water, dump station, boat launch, docks
Fee per night: $$
Management: U.S. Army Corps of Engineers
Contact: (541) 296–1181 or (541) 298–7650; www.nwp.usace.army.mil

Rufus Area

	Hookup sites	Total sites	Maximum RV length	Hookups	Toilets	Showers	Drinking water	Dump station	Recreation	Fee	Can reserve
1 Giles French Park		open	40		F		•		FBL		
2 Le Page Park	22	22	40	WE	F		•	•	SFBL	$$	

Finding the campground: It is off Interstate 84 at exit 114.

About the campground: This landscaped park overlooks the John Day River just as it meets the harnessed Columbia River above John Day Dam. The camp provides boaters and anglers with convenient access to the water, and 3 miles up the John Day River, an 8-site, boat-to camp is available for overnight stays. Black locust trees give some shade to the RV spaces, which directly overlook the water. Tenters can pitch their shelters anywhere on the grass. A beach area serves swimmers.

Dufur–Maupin Area

3 Barlow Crossing

Location: About 17 miles southeast of Government Camp
Season: June–October
Sites: 6 basic sites; no hookups
Maximum length: Small units only due to road conditions
Facilities: Tables, grills, vault toilets; no drinking water
Fee per night: $$
Management: Mount Hood National Forest
Contact: (541) 352–6002; www.fs.fed.us/r6/mthood/recreation
Finding the campground: From Oregon 35 at the White River crossing, 2 miles south of the Mount Hood Meadows ski area and 5 miles north of the junction of U.S. Highway 26 and OR 35, follow Forest Road 48 southeast for 8.8 miles, turn right (west) on FR 43, and go 0.6 mile. There turn right on narrow, dirt Old Barlow Road/FR 3530 to reach the camp in 0.2 mile. Turn right, followed by a second right to locate the sites. (*NOTE:* Old Barlow Road is closed from December 15 to April 1 and requires four-wheel-drive beyond the camp turnoff.)
About the campground: In the fall, hunters use this quiet, rustic camp, which is situated in a forest of firs and lodgepole pines above 10-foot-wide Barlow Creek, just upstream from its confluence with the White River. The sites have pretty log tables, but the parking is undefined; one site sits at creek level. Steller's jays color and animate camp. Nearby interpretive signs tell the story of Barlow Road, an overland segment of the Oregon Trail that linked the Columbia River Gorge to the Willamette Valley. This difficult route allowed pioneers to avoid a treacherous voyage down the Columbia River. Early pioneers cached supplies near here in 1845.

4 Bear Springs

Location: About 24 miles southwest of Maupin
Season: Late May–September
Sites: 21 basic sites; no hookups
Maximum length: 32 feet
Facilities: Tables, grills, vault toilets, drinking water
Fee per night: $$
Management: Mount Hood National Forest
Contact: (541) 467–2291; www.fs.fed.us/r6/mthood/recreation
Finding the campground: From Oregon 216, 4 miles east of its junction with U.S. Highway 26 and 24 miles west of Maupin, turn south at the sign for the campground. Go 0.1 mile to the camp entrance on the right.
About the campground: Above the headwaters of Indian Creek, you will find this pleasant forest campground, which has a paved road and gravel parking. Many of the sites are better suited for tents or small RV units because of

Dufur–
Maupin Area

	Hookup sites	Total sites	Maximum RV length	Hookups	Toilets	Showers	Drinking water	Dump station	Recreation	Fee	Can reserve
3 Barlow Crossing		6	small		NF				F	$$	
4 Bear Springs		21	32		NF		•			$$	
5 Beavertail Recreation Site		15	40		NF		•		FBL	$–$$	
6 Bonney Crossing		8	16		NF				HF	$$	
7 Clear Creek Crossing		7	16		NF				HO	$$	
8 Clear Lake		28	32		NF		•		FBL	$$	
9 Devil's Canyon Recreation Site		4	T		NF				FB	$–$$	
10 Dufur City Park	10	10	40	WES	F	•	•	•	F	$–$$	
11 Eightmile Crossing		21	30		NF				HC	$$	
12 Fifteenmile Forest Camp		3	16		NF				H	$$	
13 Forest Creek		8	16		NF				F	$$	
14 Frog Lake		33	22		NF		•		HFBL	$$	•
15 Harpham Flat Recreation Site		9	25		NF				FBL	$–$$	
16 Jones Canyon Recreation Site		8	40		NF				FB	$–$$	
17 Knebal Springs Horse Camp		8	22		NF				HR	$$	
18 Long Bend Recreation Site		4	25		NF				FB	$–$$	
19 Macks Canyon Recreation Site		17	40		NF		•		HFBLC	$–$$	
20 Maupin City Park	25	47	40	WES	F	•	•		FBL	$$–$$$	
21 McCubbins Gulch		7	25		NF				O	$$	
22 Oak Springs Recreation Site		6	40		NF				FB	$–$$	
23 Oasis Recreation Site		10	40		NF				FB	$–$$	
24 Pebble Ford		3	16		NF				H	$$	
25 Rattlesnake Canyon Recreation Site		8	40		NF				FB	$–$$	
26 Rock Creek Reservoir		33	18		NF		•		HSFBL	$$	•
27 Twin Springs Recreation Site		7	40		NF				FB	$–$$	
28 Wapinitia Recreation Site		6	25		NF				FBL	$–$$	
29 Wasco County Fairgrounds: Hunt RV Park	120	270	60	WE	F	•	•	•		$$	•
30 White River Recreation Site		3	40		NF				FB	$–$$	
31 White River Station		6	small		NF				F	$$	

the spur size and parking access; there is one pull-through site. Grand firs, Douglas firs, and ponderosa pines shade this compact camp. Bring a good book and settle in.

5 Beavertail Recreation Site

Location: About 21 miles north of Maupin
Season: Year-round
Sites: 15 basic sites; no hookups
Maximum length: 40 feet
Facilities: Tables, vault toilets, drinking water, drift boat/raft launch
Fee per night: $–$$
Management: Prineville District Bureau of Land Management
Contact: (541) 416–6700; www.or.blm.gov/prineville
Finding the campground: From the junction of U.S. Highway 197 and Oregon 216 East at Tygh Valley (7 miles north of Maupin), go east on OR 216, crossing the Deschutes River at Sherars Bridge in 7 miles. Proceed another 1.1

Camping along the Deschutes River.

miles east and turn left (north) onto gravel Deschutes River Access Road, a BLM Back Country Byway. Go 9.6 miles to this camp on the left.

About the campground: This camp rests on a grassy bench at a bend in the Deschutes River. It offers campers convenient access to superb fishing and river floating (a boater's pass is required for the river). A few trees provide spotty shade. Across the river you can see a steep canyon wall. In this fragile, arid canyon, fires and smoking are prohibited from June 1 to October 15.

6 Bonney Crossing

Location: About 17 miles west of Tygh Valley
Season: May–mid-October
Sites: 8 basic sites; no hookups
Maximum length: 16 feet
Facilities: Tables, grills, vault toilets; no drinking water
Fee per night: $$
Management: Mount Hood National Forest
Contact: (541) 467-2291; www.fs.fed.us/r6/mthood/recreation
Finding the campground: From the junction of U.S. Highway 197 and Oregon 216 East at Tygh Valley (7 miles north of Maupin), go west 6 miles on Tygh Valley and Wamic Market Roads to Wamic. From there, continue west for another 6 miles on Rock Creek Dam Road/Forest Road 48. Turn right (north) onto FR 4810, go 2 miles, and turn right again onto FR 4811. Go 1.2 miles, turn right onto dirt FR 2710, and go 1.7 miles to the camp.
About the campground: This small campground rests in a transition forest along Badger Creek as it drains out of Badger Creek Wilderness. Douglas firs, oaks, and ponderosa pines contribute to the aesthetics of camp. The creek is captivating and clear. On the north bank look for the Badger Creek Trail, which follows the scenic waterway upstream into the wilderness for prized solitude. You may spot wild turkeys in the grasslands.

7 Clear Creek Crossing

Location: About 29 miles west of Maupin
Season: May–September
Sites: 7 basic sites; no hookups
Maximum length: 16 feet
Facilities: Tables, grills, vault toilets; no drinking water
Fee per night: $$
Management: Mount Hood National Forest
Contact: (541) 467-2291; www.fs.fed.us/r6/mthood/recreation
Finding the campground: From Oregon 216, 2 miles east of its junction with U.S. Highway 26 and 26 miles west of Maupin, turn north on Forest Road 2130 at the sign for the campground. Go 3 miles and turn right to enter the camp. Watch out for free-ranging cattle.
About the campground: You will find this campground on Clear Creek within McCubbins Gulch Off-Highway-Vehicle Area, downstream from the Mc-

Cubbins Gulch diversion. The campsites occupy a mild slope in a setting of mature firs; logs outline the roadway and sites. Clear Creek is aptly named. The log footbridge that spans the creek leads to Clear Creek Trail, a 5-mile-long link between this camp and the rustic Keeps Mill Campground. OHV trails can be accessed off FR 2130; look for them while en route to camp.

8   Clear Lake

Location: About 11 miles southeast of Government Camp
Season: Late May–early September
Sites: 28 basic sites; no hookups
Maximum length: 32 feet
Facilities: Tables, grills, vault toilets, drinking water, boat launch
Fee per night: $$
Management: Mount Hood National Forest
Contact: (541) 352–6002; (877) 444–6777 for reservations; www.fs.fed.us/r6 /mthood/recreation
Finding the campground: From Government Camp, go southeast on U.S. Highway 26 for 9.5 miles, turn right onto Forest Road 2630, and go 1.1 miles to the camp entrance.
About the campground: Located on a slope above Clear Lake and shaded by firs and mountain hemlocks, this campground can fill up on summer weekends. All sites have gravel parking, some have pull-throughs, and some have tree-filtered lake views. Chinquapins, kinnikinnick, and rhododendrons grow in the sunny forest openings. Boating (10 miles per hour maximum) and fishing fill out campers' days. There are opportunities to hike beyond the camp.

9   Devil's Canyon Recreation Site

Location: About 5 miles south of Maupin
Season: Year-round
Sites: 4 tent sites; no hookups
Maximum length: Suitable for tents only
Facilities: Tables, pit toilets; no drinking water
Fee per night: $–$$
Management: Prineville District Bureau of Land Management
Contact: (541) 416–6700; www.or.blm.gov/prineville
Finding the campground: From the Deschutes River bridge on U.S. Highway 197 in Maupin, go south on US 197 for 0.2 mile and turn right at the BLM sign for Upper River Access. Drive 5 miles to reach this camp on the right.
About the campground: This primitive campground occupies a sagebrush flat and offers views of a scenic bend in the Deschutes River. A butte rises across the river. Red-winged blackbirds, orioles, mergansers, ducks, swallows, and geese visit the area. Fishing and boating are popular. You will find a launch at Wapinitia Recreation Site, 2 miles downstream. Fires and smoking are prohibited from June 1 to October 15.

10 Dufur City Park

Location: In Dufur
Season: March–October
Sites: 10 hookup sites, some tent camping; water, electric, and sewer hookups
Maximum length: 40 feet
Facilities: Flush toilets, drinking water, showers, dump station, playground, volleyball, horseshoe pits, ballfield, swimming pool
Fee per night: $–$$
Management: City of Dufur
Contact: (541) 467-2349
Finding the campground: The campground is at the south end of the city of Dufur; follow signs for the park.
About the campground: At this pleasant city park, camping is available at the edge of the playing fields. The camp rests along Fifteenmile Creek, which offers fishing and nurtures the fully grown trees that provide shade. The camp is a convenient base from which to explore historic Dufur, a quaint farming and ranching community, and the Columbia River Gorge is only minutes away.

11 Eightmile Crossing

Location: About 17 miles west of Dufur
Season: June–mid-October
Sites: 21 basic sites; no hookups
Maximum length: 30 feet
Facilities: Tables, grills, vault toilets; no drinking water
Fee per night: $$
Management: Mount Hood National Forest
Contact: (541) 467-2291; www.fs.fed.us/r6/mthood/recreation
Finding the campground: From U.S. Highway 197, take the exit for Dufur and at the south end of town, head west on Dufur Valley Road/Forest Road 44. Follow it for 17 miles and turn right (north) on FR 4430 to enter the campground on the right in 0.3 mile. From Oregon 35, 16 miles northeast of Government Camp, 26 miles south of Hood River, turn east on FR 44 and go 9.8 miles to reach FR 4430. Proceed north to the camp.
About the campground: You will find this quiet camp in a mixed age conifer forest along the upper reaches of Eightmile Creek. The sites are comfortably spaced and fully or partially shaded. At the camp is a trailhead for the 6.2-mile, hike or bike Eightmile Loop Trail. A half-mile, barrier-free trail pursues Eightmile Creek downstream to Lower Eightmile Forest Camp. As an alternative place to stay, Lower Eightmile Forest Camp (also called Lower Crossing Campground) has three closely spaced sites (16-foot maximum length) with fee and similar facilities. You can reach it by going 0.5 mile east on FR 44 from its junction with FR 4430 and then 1 mile north on FR 4440.

12 Fifteenmile Forest Camp

Location: About 23 miles southwest of Dufur
Season: June–mid-October
Sites: 3 basic sites; no hookups
Maximum length: 16 feet
Facilities: Tables, grills, vault toilets; no drinking water
Fee per night: $$
Management: Mount Hood National Forest
Contact: (541) 467-2291; www.fs.fed.us/r6/mthood/recreation
Finding the campground: From U.S. Highway 197, take the exit for Dufur; at the south end of town, head west on Dufur Valley Road/Forest Road 44 and go 18.5 miles. Turn south on FR 4420 for Flag Point Lookout, go 2.1 miles, and proceed another 1.9 miles south on FR 2730 to reach this campground on the left. When arriving from Oregon 35, go 8.3 miles east on FR 44 and turn south on FR 4420, following the remaining directions to camp.
About the campground: This closely grouped trio of sites occupies an open stand of huge ponderosa pines along Fifteenmile Creek. Across the creek is the Badger Creek Wilderness; this camp is a gateway to the wilderness trail system. Riffling Fifteenmile Creek cuts a deep drainage at the camp.

13 Forest Creek

Location: About 25 miles west of Tygh Valley
Season: Late May–October
Sites: 8 basic sites; no hookups
Maximum length: 16 feet
Facilities: Tables, grills, vault toilets; no drinking water
Fee per night: $$
Management: Mount Hood National Forest
Contact: (541) 467-2291; www.fs.fed.us/r6/mthood/recreation
Finding the campground: From the junction of Oregon 216 East and U.S. Highway 197 at Tygh Valley, head west on Tygh Valley and Wamic Market Roads for 6 miles to Wamic. From there, continue west on Rock Creek Dam Road/Forest Road 48 for 18 miles, turn left (south) on gravel FR 4885, go 1 mile, and turn left on FR 3530 to enter the camp in 0.2 mile. The road beyond the camp is not maintained for passenger cars.
About the campground: Historically a wayside stop for pioneers, this small, quiet camp sits among ponderosa pines, hemlocks, cedars, spruce, and firs. It rests along Forest Creek on Old Barlow Road, part of the Oregon Trail. Barlow was an overland toll road that allowed pioneers to bypass the treacherous voyage on the Columbia River to reach the Willamette Valley's fertile farmland.

14 Frog Lake

Location: About 8 miles southeast of Government Camp
Season: Late May–mid-September
Sites: 33 basic sites; no hookups
Maximum length: 22 feet
Facilities: Tables, grills, vault toilets, drinking water, boat launch
Fee per night: $$
Management: Mount Hood National Forest.
Contact: (541) 352–6002; (877) 444–6777 for reservations; www.fs.fed.us/r6/mthood/recreation
Finding the campground: From Government Camp, go southeast on U.S. Highway 26 for 7 miles and turn left on Forest Road 2610 to enter this camp in 0.5 mile.
About the campground: This popular campground occupies a forest of hemlocks and firs along the shore of quiet Frog Lake. You can see Mount Hood peeking over the trees, especially from the south end of the day-use area. The camp is a fine base for outdoor recreation: You can fish or take your nonmotorized boat out on the lake or hike nearby trails to Frog Lake Buttes and Twin Lakes. You also have easy access to the Pacific Crest National Scenic Trail.

15 Harpham Flat Recreation Site

Location: About 4 miles south of Maupin
Season: Year-round
Sites: 9 basic sites; no hookups
Maximum length: 25 feet
Facilities: Tables, vault toilets, boat launch; no drinking water
Fee per night: $-$$
Management: Prineville District Bureau of Land Management
Contact: (541) 416–6700; www.or.blm.gov/prineville
Finding the campground: From the Deschutes River bridge on U.S. Highway 197 in Maupin, go south on US 197 for 0.2 mile and turn right at the BLM sign for Upper River Access. Drive 3.5 miles to reach the campground entrance on the right.
About the campground: Adjacent to a popular raft put-in, this campground bustles with activity. It occupies a broad, sunny flat where the river canyon broadens; campers should bring a good shade source and ample water. Fishing, boating, rafting, and sightseeing keep Deschutes River campers returning again and again. Fires and smoking are prohibited from June 1 to October 15.

16 Jones Canyon Recreation Site

Location: About 19 miles north of Maupin
Season: Year-round
Sites: 8 basic sites; no hookups
Maximum length: 40 feet

Facilities: Tables, vault and pit toilets, boat launch (downstream at Beavertail); no drinking water
Fee per night: $-$$
Management: Prineville District Bureau of Land Management
Contact: (541) 416-6700; www.or.blm.gov/prineville
Finding the campground: From the junction of U.S. Highway 197 and Oregon 216 East at Tygh Valley (7 miles north of Maupin), go east on OR 216, crossing the Deschutes River at Sherars Bridge in 7 miles. Continue east another 1.1 miles, turn left (north) on gravel Deschutes River Access Road, a BLM Back Country Byway, and go 7.7 miles to reach this camp on the left.
About the campground: Tall clumps of sagebrush isolate the sites of this treeless camp above the Deschutes River, just downstream from Jones Canyon. The camp has fine river canyon views, world-class fishing, and nearby access for boating and rafting. The Deschutes is a prized wild and scenic river. Boaters must secure permits and should find out where and when motorized boats are permissible. River otters can sometimes be spied. Fires and smoking are prohibited from June 1 to October 15.

17 Knebal Springs Horse Camp

Location: About 25 miles west of Dufur
Season: June–October
Sites: 8 basic sites; no hookups
Maximum length: 22 feet
Facilities: Tables, fire rings, vault toilets, horse-loading ramp, hitching rail, corrals, trough; no drinking water
Fee per night: $$
Management: Mount Hood National Forest
Contact: (541) 467-2291; www.fs.fed.us/r6/mthood/recreation
Finding the campground: From Forest Road 44, 21.7 miles west of Dufur (at the south end of town) and 5.1 miles east of Oregon 35, turn north on the paved FR 17, go 0.5 mile, and bear right on FR 1720. Go 2.6 miles more to enter the campground via gravel FR 150 on the right. Be alert for the turnoff.
About the campground: This serviceable, comfortable campground is intended for use by equestrian campers only. The campsites are partially shaded by firs, pines, and larches. Trail 474, the Knebal Springs Trail, passes the camp and connects with other horse trails in the area. The springs at camp are fenced.

18 Long Bend Recreation Site

Location: About 5 miles south of Maupin
Season: Year-round
Sites: 4 basic sites; no hookups
Maximum length: 25 feet
Facilities: Tables, vault toilets; no drinking water
Fee per night: $-$$

Management: Prineville District Bureau of Land Management
Contact: (541) 416–6700; www.or.blm.gov/prineville
Finding the campground: From the Deschutes River bridge on U.S. Highway 197 in Maupin, go south on US 197 for 0.2 mile and turn right at the BLM sign for Upper River Access. Drive another 4.4 miles to reach the campground entrance on the right.
About the campground: This linear camp claims a narrow strip of shoreline along the Deschutes River. White alders line the riverbank, and hackberry grows at the upper edge of the camp. Across the river you can see cliffs, rims, and an active rail line. The Deschutes River provides fishing and boating, but strong undercurrents make swimming dangerous. Fires and smoking are prohibited from June 1 to October 15.

19 Macks Canyon Recreation Site

Location: About 29 miles north of Maupin
Season: Year-round
Sites: 17 basic sites; no hookups
Maximum length: 40 feet
Facilities: Tables, vault toilets, drinking water, boat launch
Fee per night: $–$$
Management: Prineville District Bureau of Land Management
Contact: (541) 416–6700; www.or.blm.gov/prineville
Finding the campground: From the junction of U.S. Highway 197 and Oregon 216 East at Tygh Valley (7 miles north of Maupin), go east on OR 216, crossing the Deschutes River at Sherars Bridge in 7 miles. Continue another 1.1 miles east and turn left (north) on gravel Deschutes River Access Road, a BLM Back Country Byway. Go 17 miles to reach this camp.
About the campground: This camp occupies a site where prehistoric Indian tribes wintered in pit houses more than 2,000 years ago. Present-day campers are similarly attracted to the mostly open river flat because of its convenient access to the Deschutes River and superb fishing and boating. The abandoned railroad grade on this side of the canyon serves hikers and bicyclists. It extends from the north end of the camp downstream to Deschutes River State Recreation Area. The trail offers fine river views and occasional river access, but beware of rattlesnakes in the rocky reaches and off trail. Fires and smoking are prohibited June 1 to October 15; boaters should familiarize themselves with river rules.

20 Maupin City Park

Location: In Maupin
Season: Year-round
Sites: 25 hookup sites, 22 tent sites; water, electric, and sewer hookups
Maximum length: 40 feet
Facilities: Tables, flush toilets, drinking water, showers, telephone, fee docking and launch, community building with kitchen for rent; no campfires

Fee per night: $$–$$$
Management: City of Maupin
Contact: (541) 395–2252
Finding the campground: The park is off Bakeoven Road in Maupin, on the east shore of the Deschutes River.
About the campground: Across the bridge from Maupin, this city park provides a lovely overnight camping facility. The hookup sites have concrete two-tracks on which to park, lawn, the shade of locust trees, and superb river views. You can reach the tent area by crossing a footbridge over Bakeoven Creek. The tent sites are on a big, open lawn edged by locusts and alders; there is shade late in the day. A grain elevator on the opposite side of Bakeoven Road adds to the rural atmosphere. Geese browse the park lawn in the morning. This is a fine place to relax, watch the rafters float by, join in a river trip yourself, or fish, boat, or sightsee.

21 McCubbins Gulch

Location: About 24 miles southwest of Maupin
Season: May–September
Sites: 7 basic sites; no hookups
Maximum length: 25 feet
Facilities: Tables, grills, vault toilets; no drinking water
Fee per night: $$
Management: Mount Hood National Forest
Contact: (541) 467–2291; www.fs.fed.us/r6/mthood/recreation
Finding the campground: From Oregon 216, 5 miles east of its junction with U.S. Highway 26 and 23 miles west of Maupin, turn north on Forest Road 2110 at the sign for the campground. Go 1.1 miles, turn right on gravel FR 230, and continue another 0.3 mile to the campground entrance on the right.
About the campground: This off-highway-vehicle (OHV) campground claims a mild slope and flat along McCubbins Gulch, a diversion of Clear Creek. The silt-bottomed stream flows along the lower edge of camp. A bridge across it leads to one of the OHV trails in the area; others start near the camp entrance. The camp floor is somewhat rolling, rutted, and barren, but the tall firs and pines are pleasant. Dust and noise are part of the deal, so if you are not an OHV enthusiast, avoid this camp.

22 Oak Springs Recreation Site

Location: About 4 miles north of Maupin
Season: Year-round
Sites: 6 basic sites; no hookups
Maximum length: 40 feet
Facilities: Tables, vault toilets; no drinking water
Fee per night: $–$$
Management: Prineville District Bureau of Land Management
Contact: (541) 416–6700; www.or.blm.gov/prineville

Finding the campground: From U.S. Highway 197 in Maupin, go east on Bakeoven Road to Deschutes River Access Road. Turn left (north) and proceed downstream 4 miles to the campground entrance on the left.

About the campground: This camp on the Deschutes River has a central, gravel parking area with tables set up around it. At the south end of camp, a basalt outcrop grades to the river. A few residences dot the opposite arid slope, while Oak Springs provide a splash of uncharacteristic green. Fishing, boating, rafting, and relaxing are the pursuits of campers. Undercurrents in the river make swimming dangerous. Fires and smoking are prohibited from June 1 to October 15.

23 Oasis Recreation Site

Location: About 1 mile north of Maupin
Season: Year-round
Sites: 10 basic sites; no hookups
Maximum length: 40 feet
Facilities: Tables, vault toilets; no drinking water
Management: Prineville District Bureau of Land Management
Fee per night: $–$$
Contact: (541) 416–6700; www.or.blm.gov/prineville
Finding the campground: From U.S. Highway 197 in Maupin, go east on Bakeoven Road to Deschutes River Access Road. Turn left (north) and proceed 1.2 miles downstream to the campground entrance on the left.

About the campground: One of the larger BLM camps along the Lower Deschutes River, Oasis occupies a long stretch of shore. Native grasses grow in the camp, while sagebrush grows at the periphery and willows and alders along the bank. Here, the canyon lacks the wild and rocky disposition it reveals farther downstream, but the river still hosts boating and fishing and captivates onlookers. For whitewater excitement, schedule a float trip with one of the outfitters in Maupin. Fires and smoking are prohibited from June 1 to October 15.

24 Pebble Ford

Location: About 18 miles west of Dufur
Season: May–mid-October
Sites: 3 basic sites; no hookups
Maximum length: 16 feet
Facilities: Tables, grills, vault toilets; no drinking water
Fee per night: $$
Management: Mount Hood National Forest
Contact: (541) 467–2291; www.fs.fed.us/r6/mthood/recreation
Finding the campground: From Forest Road 44, 17.5 miles west of Dufur (at the south end of town) and 9.3 miles east of Oregon 35, turn south on the gravel road indicated for the campground and continue 0.1 mile to the entrance.

About the campground: In a setting of firs, cedars, and ponderosa pines, this small campground straddles a tributary; a footbridge links the camp halves. Sites have gravel parking, and most have tables and grills. Trails explore the surrounding forest.

25 Rattlesnake Canyon Recreation Site

Location: About 23 miles north of Maupin
Season: Year-round
Sites: 8 basic sites; no hookups
Maximum length: 40 feet
Facilities: Tables, vault toilets, boat launch (upstream at Beavertail); no drinking water
Fee per night: $-$$
Management: Prineville District Bureau of Land Management
Contact: (541) 416–6700; www.or.blm.gov/prineville
Finding the campground: From the junction of U.S. Highway 197 and Oregon 216 East at Tygh Valley (7 miles north of Maupin), go east on OR 216, crossing the Deschutes River at Sherars Bridge in 7 miles. Continue east another 1.1 miles and turn left (north) on gravel Deschutes River Access Road, a BLM Back Country Byway. Go 10.5 miles to this camp on the left.
About the campground: This camp occupies a mild bench above the Deschutes Wild and Scenic River. Its sites blend into the expanse of sagebrush and rabbitbrush. Trees grow closer to the river, a cliff overlooks camp, and a tableland sits across the river. Fishing, boating, and rafting are the primary diversions. The river canyon funnels various birds past camp; bats may be active at dusk. Boaters should familiarize themselves with river rules. Undercurrents make swimming dangerous, and fires and smoking are prohibited June 1 to October 15.

26 Rock Creek Reservoir

Location: About 13 miles west of Tygh Valley, on Rock Creek Reservoir
Season: Mid-April–early October
Sites: 33 basic sites; no hookups
Maximum length: 18 feet
Facilities: Tables, grills, vault toilets, drinking water, boat ramp (nonmotorized boats only)
Fee per night: $$
Management: Mount Hood National Forest
Contact: (541) 467–2291; (877) 444–6777 for reservations; www.fs.fed.us/r6/mthood/recreation
Finding the campground: From the junction of Oregon 216 East and U.S. Highway 197 at Tygh Valley, head west on Tygh Valley and Wamic Market Roads for 6 miles to Wamic. From there, continue west on Rock Creek Dam Road/Forest Road 48 for 6.5 miles, turn right (west) on FR 4820, go 0.2 mile, and turn right on FR 120. Go another 0.2 mile to the camp.

About the campground: You will find this camp on the south side of the dam that captures Rock Creek and creates the reservoir. A picnic area is on the north side. Oaks and small ponderosa pines grow in the basin. The lake offers trout fishing, swimming, and silent boating.

27 Twin Springs Recreation Site

Location: About 16 miles north of Maupin
Season: Year-round
Sites: 7 basic sites; no hookups
Maximum length: 40 feet
Facilities: Tables, vault toilets; no drinking water
Fee per night: $-$$
Management: Prineville District Bureau of Land Management
Contact: (541) 416-6700; www.or.blm.gov/prineville
Finding the campground: From the junction of U.S. Highway 197 and Oregon 216 East at Tygh Valley (7 miles north of Maupin), go east on OR 216, crossing the Deschutes River at Sherars Bridge in 7 miles. Continue east another 1.1 miles and turn left (north) on gravel Deschutes River Access Road, a BLM Back Country Byway. Go 4 miles to this camp on the left.
About the campground: This shadeless camp occupies a low, sagebrush-covered plateau above the Deschutes River. Basalt cliffs rise across the river. The railroad track that traverses the opposite shore represents the victor in a battle to see which railroad would serve the canyon. The abandoned grade on this side is used now by hikers and bicyclists; you can access the grade at Macks Canyon, at the north end of Deschutes River Access Road. Fishing, boating, and rafting are the river pursuits; undercurrents make swimming dangerous. Fires and smoking are prohibited from June 1 to October 15.

28 Wapinitia Recreation Site

Location: About 3 miles south of Maupin
Season: Year-round
Sites: 6 basic sites; no hookups
Maximum length: 25 feet
Facilities: Tables, vault toilets, boat launch; no drinking water
Fee per night: $-$$
Management: Prineville District Bureau of Land Management
Contact: (541) 416-6700; www.or.blm.gov/prineville
Finding the campground: From the Deschutes River bridge on U.S. Highway 197 in Maupin, go south on US 197 for 0.2 mile and turn right at the BLM sign for Upper River Access. Drive 3 miles to the campground entrance on the right.
About the campground: This campground fronts the Deschutes River where bald, rounded ridges shape the canyon. Junipers dot the opposite slope, and white alders edge the river. Fishing, boating, rafting, and enjoying the remote canyon quiet are reasons to visit. Fires and smoking are prohibited from June 1 to October 15.

29 | Wasco County Fairgrounds: Hunt RV Park

Location: In Tygh Valley
Season: May–November
Sites: 120 hookup sites, 150 tent sites; water and electric hookups
Maximum length: 60 feet
Facilities: Flush toilets, drinking water, showers, dump station, telephone, horse stalls for rent
Fee per night: $$
Management: Wasco County
Contact: (541) 483–2288, reservations accepted
Finding the campground: From the junction of U.S. Highway 197 and Oregon 216 East at Tygh Valley (7 miles north of Maupin), go west on Tygh Valley Road for 0.3 mile and turn right onto Main Street. Follow it for 0.1 mile and turn right onto Fairgrounds Road. Follow Fairgrounds Road 1.8 miles to arrive at the fairgrounds and Hunt RV Park.
About the campground: You will find this pleasant wayside on a flat surrounded by the bald, rolling hills of the Plateau Country. Mature trees shade the camp's groomed lawns. When events are not taking place at the fairgrounds, the camp can be quite restful. Otherwise, you will find a bustling mini-village of RVs and tents.

30 | White River Recreation Site

Location: About 5 miles north of Maupin
Season: Year-round
Sites: 3 basic sites; no hookups
Maximum length: 40 feet
Facilities: Tables, vault toilets; no drinking water
Fee per night: $–$$
Management: Prineville District Bureau of Land Management
Contact: (541) 416–6700; www.or.blm.gov/prineville
Finding the campground: From U.S. Highway 197 in Maupin, head east on Bakeoven Road to Deschutes River Access Road. Turn left (north) and proceed 5.2 miles downriver to the campground entrance on the left.
About the campground: This camp has a gravel parking area partitioned into marked spaces; tables paired with the sites occupy the lot's perimeter. Sagebrush and a few riverside alders are the only vegetation on this otherwise open flat. Like the other camps of the Deschutes River corridor, this one serves up breathtaking river and canyon views and great fishing. The White River confluence is across the Deschutes River from camp. Maupin is the base for several river-running outfitters, should you seek a livelier look at the Deschutes. Fires and smoking are prohibited from June 1 to October 15.

31 White River Station

Location: About 18 miles southeast of Government Camp
Season: May–October
Sites: 6 basic sites; no hookups
Maximum length: Small units only due to narrow, bumpy entry road
Facilities: Tables, grills, vault toilets; no drinking water
Fee per night: $$
Management: Mount Hood National Forest
Contact: (541) 467–2291; www.fs.fed.us/r6/mthood/recreation
Finding the campground: From Oregon 35 at the White River crossing, 2 miles south of the Mount Hood Meadows ski area, 5 miles north of the junction of U.S. Highway 26 and OR 35, follow Forest Road 48 southeast for 8.8 miles and turn right (west) on FR 43 for 0.6 mile. Turn left on narrow, dirt Old Barlow Road/FR 3530 to reach the camp on the left in 1.2 miles. Old Barlow Road is closed from December 15 to April 1.
About the campground: First used by pioneers on the Oregon Trail, this quiet camp occupies a semi-open flat along the White River. A few big firs rise among the lodgepole pines, while alders and cottonwoods grow beside the river. The sites are roomy and widely spaced; they have log tables and undefined parking. Interpretive signs introduce the history of the area. The White River originates from glaciers on Mount Hood and rolls turbulent, cloudy, and fast past the camp.

Madras–Redmond Area

32 The Cove Palisades State Park: Crooked River

Location: About 10 miles southwest of Madras, about 25 miles northwest of Redmond
Season: Year-round
Sites: 91 hookup sites; water and electric hookups
Maximum length: 60 feet
Facilities: Tables, grills, flush toilets, drinking water, showers, dump station, telephone, boat launch (at day-use area)
Fee per night: $$
Management: Oregon State Parks and Recreation Department
Contact: (541) 546–3412; (800) 452–5687 for reservations; www.oregonstate parks.org
Finding the campground: From U.S. Highway 97/26 in Madras, take Culver Highway southwest at the sign for Cove Palisades and go 7.1 miles. Turn right (west) onto Gem Lane and follow the signs for the state park through a series of turns to reach this campground on the left in 2.5 miles. From Redmond, go north on US 97 for 16 miles, turn left (west) at the sign for the park, and continue to follow the park signs another 8.5 miles to enter this campground on the left.

Madras–Redmond Area

	Hookup sites	Total sites	Maximum RV length	Hookups	Toilets	Showers	Drinking water	Dump station	Recreation	Fee	Can reserve
32 The Cove Palisades State Park: Crooked River	91	91	60	WE	F	•	•	•	SFBL	$$	•
33 The Cove Palisades State Park: Deschutes River	87	184	60	WES	F	•	•		HSFBL	$$–$$$	•
34 Haystack		24	30		F,NF	•			FBL	$	
35 Haystack Reservoir: South Shore		20	T		NF				FB		
36 Haystack Reservoir: West Shore		25	30		NF				FBL		
37 Jefferson County Fairgrounds	65	65	60	WESC	F	•	•	•		$$	•
38 Pelton Park	28	72	40	E	F	•	•		SFBL	$$–$$$	•
39 Perry South		63	40		NF		•		SFBL	$$	
40 Skull Hollow		40	25		NF						
41 South Junction Recreation Site		7	T		NF				F	$–$$	
42 Trout Creek Recreation Site		21	25		NF				HFBLC	$–$$	

About the campground: This campground claims a high plateau above the Crooked River Arm of Lake Billy Chinook. Although it lacks a lake overlook, the campground provides views of Mount Jefferson and Three Fingered Jack. The flat is landscaped with lawn and trees for some shade, and the sites have paved parking. For lake recreation, just take the short drive downhill into the core of the park. The turnoff for the marina and restaurant is a mile from the camp. The day-use boat launch, picnic area, and swimming area are 1.1 miles away.

33 The Cove Palisades State Park: Deschutes River

Location: About 14 miles southwest of Madras, 29 miles northwest of Redmond
Season: May–September
Sites: 87 hookup sites, 94 basic sites, 3 cabins and houseboats; water, electric, and sewer hookups
Maximum length: 60 feet

Lake Billy Chinook at Cove Palisades State Park.

Facilities: Tables, grills, flush toilets, drinking water, showers, telephone, store, playground, boat launch (at day-use area), fish-cleaning station
Fee per night: $$–$$$
Management: Oregon State Parks and Recreation Department
Contact: (541) 546–3412; (800) 452–5687 for reservations; www.oregonstate parks.org
Finding the campground: From U.S. Highway 97/26 in Madras, take Culver Highway southwest at the sign for Cove Palisades and go 7.1 miles. Turn right (west) onto Gem Lane and follow the signs for the state park through a series of turns to reach this campground on the left in 7 miles. From Redmond, go north on US 97 for 16 miles, turn left (west) at the sign for the park, and continue to follow the signs another 13 miles to the campground.
About the campground: This campground occupies a canyon near the Deschutes River Arm of Lake Billy Chinook. Native junipers, along with locusts, cottonwoods, and willows, shade the developed camp. Nature trails lead to Ship Rock and to the day-use swimming area. A longer hiking trail climbs to and then traverses the summit plateau of The Peninsula, which overlooks the camp. This landmark, shaped by the Deschutes and Crooked River Arms of Lake Billy Chinook, dishes up fine views of the lake and another area landmark, The Island. You can access the lake at the park's day-use areas on either side of the camp. Billy Chinook is one of the state's premier recreational waters for boating, fishing, swimming, and waterskiing.

34 Haystack

Location: About 12 miles south of Madras; 22 miles north of Redmond, on Haystack Reservoir
Season: Mid-May–September
Sites: 24 basic sites; no hookups
Maximum length: 30 feet
Facilities: Tables, grills, flush and vault toilets, drinking water, boat launch, covered picnic tables (at Haystack Reservoir)
Fee per night: $
Management: Crooked River National Grassland
Contact: (541) 475–9272; www.fs.fed.us/r6/centraloregon/recreation
Finding the campground: From U.S. Highway 97, 8 miles south of Madras and 18 miles north of Redmond, turn east onto Jericho Lane, go 1.2 miles, and turn right onto Haystack Road. Continue 2.1 miles to reach the campground entrance road. Follow it left for 0.5 mile to the camp.
About the campground: This campground is on a juniper- and sagebrush-covered slope above the east shore of Haystack Reservoir. It has paved roads and parking and presents views of Haystack and Juniper Buttes, Mount Jefferson, and the surrounding high desert and distant Cascades. Because of the wind and sun, keep the sunscreen handy. The lake is regularly stocked with fish. Sailboards, boats, and geese ply the sun-spangled water.

35 | Haystack Reservoir: South Shore

Location: About 10 miles south of Madras and 20 miles north of Redmond, on Haystack Reservoir
Season: Year-round
Sites: 20 tent sites; no hookups
Maximum length: Small rigs recommended
Facilities: Chemical toilets; no drinking water
Fee per night: None
Management: Crooked River National Grassland
Contact: (541) 475-9272; (541) 416-6640; www.fs.fed.us/r6/centraloregon/recreation
Finding the campground: From U.S. Highway 97, 8 miles south of Madras and 18 miles north of Redmond, turn east onto Jericho Lane, go 1.2 miles, and turn right onto Haystack Road. Continue 1.1 miles to reach this camp on the left.
About the campground: This dry-weather camp consists of a maze of rough dirt roads and primitive overnight spots scattered across the gentle, juniper-dotted south slope of Haystack Reservoir. This area is better suited for tent camping; the west shore better serves RVs. RVers who choose to use the South Shore Campground should avoid times of heavy rain and mud. Seen to the north is Mount Hood, to the west is Mount Jefferson. As the reservoir recedes in summer, visitors drive across the growing beach (dry lakebed) to reach the open water for their fun and sport. The lake attracts boaters, anglers, sail-boarders, and swimmers.

36 | Haystack Reservoir: West Shore

Location: About 10 miles south of Madras and 20 miles north of Redmond, on Haystack Reservoir
Season: Year-round
Sites: 25 primitive RV sites; no hookups
Maximum length: 30 feet
Facilities: Vault toilets, paved boat launch; no drinking water
Fee per night: None
Management: Crooked River National Grassland
Contact: (541) 475-9272; (541) 416-6640; www.fs.fed.us/r6/centraloregon/recreation
Finding the campground: From U.S. Highway 97, 8 miles south of Madras and 18 miles north of Redmond, turn east onto Jericho Lane, go 1.2 miles, and turn right onto Haystack Road. Continue 0.6 mile to reach this camp on the left.
About the campground: This camp claims a narrow strip of shoreline on the west side of Haystack Reservoir. Views from the camp are of the arid, juniper-dotted hills; the open expanse of the Crooked River National Grassland; and Haystack and Juniper Buttes. The camp is basically an undeveloped parking lot, but it makes up for that with lake access for boating, fishing, and sail-boarding.

37 Jefferson County Fairgrounds

Location: In Madras
Season: Year-round
Sites: 65 hookup sites; water, electric, sewer, and cable hookups
Maximum length: 60 feet
Facilities: Tables, flush toilets, drinking water, showers, dump station, telephone
Fee per night: $$
Management: Jefferson County
Contact: (541) 325–5050, reservations accepted
Finding the campground: From U.S. Highway 97/26 at the south end of Madras, turn west onto Fairgrounds Road, go 0.1 mile, and turn right toward the RV camp entrance.
About the campground: This RV camp occupies an open, gravel flat at the eastern edge of the Jefferson County Fairgrounds. It offers a clean, orderly layout, with a table at each site, and it is highly convenient for event participants or attendees. Make reservations well in advance. The open lawn adjacent to the RV spaces welcomes repose.

38 Pelton Park

Location: About 13 miles northwest of Madras, on Lake Simtustus
Season: Late April–September
Sites: 28 hookup sites, 36 basic sites, 8 yomes; electric hookups
Maximum length: 40 feet
Facilities: Tables, fire rings, flush toilets, drinking water, showers, laundry, telephone, camp store, snack bar, volleyball, horseshoe pits, swimming area, boat rental, moorage, launch, fish-cleaning station, community kitchen for rent
Fee per night: $$–$$$
Management: Portland General Electric
Contact: (541) 475–0517; (503) 464–8515 for reservations; www.portland general.com/parks
Finding the campground: From the junction of U.S. Highway 97 and US 26 West in Madras, go north on US 26W for 9.4 miles and turn left at Pelton Junction onto Pelton Dam Road. Continue 3.3 miles to enter the park on the right.
About the campground: This campground and its accompanying day-use area occupy half a mile of the Lake Simtustus shore for a full lineup of wet fun. The canyon junipers provide welcome shade. Across the water, you can see a basalt-rimmed canyon wall. The camp has paved parking, dry lawns, picturesque junipers, and a few natural boulders and outcrops. Some sites overlook the lake, and plans call for more of the sites to have electricity. Much of Lake Simtustus has a maximum boat speed of 10 miles per hour, but there is an area designated for speed craft. Kokanee, steelhead, rainbow and brown trout, and smallmouth bass make for excellent fishing and, later, dining. You will need both a valid state fishing license and a Warm Springs Indian Reservation license; you can buy the latter at the camp store.

39 Perry South

Location: About 30 miles southwest of Madras, on Lake Billy Chinook
Season: May–September
Sites: 59 basic sites, 4 walk-in tent sites; no hookups
Maximum length: 40 feet
Facilities: Tables, grills, vault toilets, drinking water, boat launch, dock, fish-cleaning station
Fee per night: $$
Management: Deschutes National Forest
Contact: (541) 549–7700; www.fs.fed.us/r6/centraloregon/recreation
Finding the campground: From U.S. Highway 97/26 in Madras, take Culver Highway southwest at the sign for Cove Palisades and go 7.1 miles. Turn right (west) onto Gem Lane and follow the signs for the state park through a series of turns, remaining on the main road to and through the park. Eventually, the route becomes Forest Road 64. After going 20.3 miles from the Culver Highway turnoff, you will come to the junction of FR 64 and FR 1170; stay on FR 64 and drive another 2.5 miles to reach camp. (Carrying a Deschutes National Forest map can help you track your progress.)
About the campground: This camp straddles FR 64 in a narrow draw above the Metolius River Arm of Lake Billy Chinook. A dry forest houses the camp; at the lower camp, you will find some big pines and a spring. The lower camp also sits closer to the lake, but the upper camp is the quieter retreat. Boating, swimming, fishing, and waterskiing entertain guests. You must have both a state license and a Warm Springs tribal license to fish the Metolius River Arm of Lake Billy Chinook. Nesting bald eagles are treated to a mandated quiet on this part of the lake until April 15 each year. By the time the campground opens in May, the success of their nests is secured; keep an eye on the skies for the regal birds.

40 Skull Hollow

Location: About 13 miles northeast of Redmond
Season: Year-round
Sites: 40 basic sites; no hookups
Maximum length: 25 feet
Facilities: Vault toilets; no drinking water
Fee per night: None
Management: Crooked River National Grassland
Contact: (541) 475–9272; www.fs.fed.us/r6/centraloregon/recreation
Finding the campground: From Redmond, drive 3 miles north on U.S. Highway 97 and turn right (east) at the sign for O'Neil and Lone Pine. Follow O'Neil Road for 4.8 miles, turn left onto Lone Pine Road, and continue another 5.3 miles. Turn left onto Forest Road 5710, go 0.1 mile, and turn left to enter the camp.
About the campground: This amazing camp, seemingly in the middle of nowhere and possessing little to recommend it, blossoms into a tent city on

weekends. The reason is Smith Rock State Park to the southwest, a world-renowned rock climbing area on the Crooked River. The camp also lies within easy reach of the Gray Butte Trail for hiking and mountain biking, the Endurance Trail for horseback riding, and the wide-open spaces of the Crooked River National Grassland. A loop road and vault toilets alone define this minimalist camp on the juniper-dotted sage-grassland. In this fragile, dry landscape, pay heed to fire restrictions and use common sense when parking: Use established turnouts and avoid vegetated areas.

41 South Junction Recreation Site

Location: About 36 miles north of Madras
Season: Year-round
Sites: 7 tent sites; no hookups
Maximum length: Suitable for tents only
Facilities: Tables, pit toilets; no drinking water
Fee per night: $–$$
Management: Prineville District Bureau of Land Management
Contact: (541) 416–6700; www.or.blm.gov/prineville
Finding the campground: From the junction of U.S. Highway 197 and US 97 at Shaniko Junction (21 miles south of Maupin; 26 miles north of Madras), go west on South Junction Road, which begins paved and becomes gravel. Follow it 9.2 miles to a fork, bear right, and go another 0.4 mile to enter the camp via a narrow dirt road.
About the campground: Located on the east shore of the Deschutes River, across from Warm Springs Indian Reservation and the Warm Springs River confluence, these campsites are well spaced among the juniper and sagebrush of the grassland slope. Each site features a shade tree or two. The river, a strong enticement to anglers and daydreamers, is 0.1 mile from camp, across a BLM fence and a railroad track. A stile allows for an easy passage over the fence; be alert when crossing the tracks. Fires and smoking are prohibited from June 1 to October 15.

42 Trout Creek Recreation Site

Location: About 16 miles north of Madras
Season: Year-round
Sites: 21 basic sites; no hookups
Maximum length: 25 feet
Facilities: Tables, vault toilets, boat launch; no drinking water
Fee per night: $–$$
Management: Prineville District Bureau of Land Management
Contact: (541) 416–6700; www.or.blm.gov/prineville
Finding the campground: From Madras, go 3 miles north on U.S. Highway 97. Turn left onto Cora Lane and then immediately left again onto Clark Drive. Proceed 8 miles to Gateway (the road name changes en route). In Gateway, turn right onto Clemmens Drive toward Trout Creek. Drive 4.3 miles, passing

through a narrow tunnel with 14-foot clearance and down a steep gravel road to the base of the canyon. Turn left and continue 0.3 mile to the recreation site. The road is not recommended for trailers.

About the campground: This recreation site occupies a pretty canyon along the Deschutes River. Sites claim a broad flat of native grasses, sagebrush, and rabbitbrush, with a light sprinkling of junipers. In this sun-drenched canyon, the juniper-shaded sites are quickly snapped up. Just downstream looms an impressive butte. An abandoned railroad grade, now a multiple-use trail, journeys upstream to Mecca Flat, offering views of, and occasional access to, the river. Fishing and boating are popular. Fires and smoking are prohibited from June 1 to October 15.

Sisters Area

43 | Allen Springs

Location: About 20 miles northwest of Sisters
Season: April–October
Sites: 13 basic sites, 4 walk-in tent sites; no hookups
Maximum length: 30 feet
Facilities: Tables, grills, vault toilets, drinking water (in season)
Fee per night: $$

Sisters Area

	Hookup sites	Total sites	Maximum RV length	Hookups	Toilets	Showers	Drinking water	Dump station	Recreation	Fee	Can reserve
43 Allen Springs		17	30		NF		•		HF	$$	
44 Allingham		10	40		NF		•	•	HF	$$	
45 Blue Bay		25	40		NF		•		HFBL	$$	•
46 Camp Sherman		15	35		NF		•		HF	$$	
47 Candle Creek		4	20		NF				HF	$$	
48 Canyon Creek		4	20		NF				HF		
49 Cold Springs		23	40		NF		•		H	$$	
50 Driftwood		17	20		NF				HSFB	$$	
51 Gorge		18	40		NF		•		HF	$$	
52 Graham Horse Camp		13	40		NF		•		HR	$$	
53 Indian Ford		25	40		NF		•			$$	
54 Jack Creek		11	40		NF				HR		
55 Lava Camp Lake		10	20		NF				HF		
56 Link Creek		33	40		NF		•		HSFBL	$$	•
57 Lower Bridge		12	25		NF		•		HF	$$	
58 Pine Rest		8	T		NF		•		HF	$$	
59 Pioneer Ford		20	40		NF		•		HF	$$	
60 Sheep Springs Horse Camp		10	40		NF		•		HR	$$	•
61 Sisters Cow Camp Horse Camp		5	40		NF				HR	$$	
62 Smiling River		38	40		NF		•		HF	$$	
63 South Shore		39	30		NF		•		HSFBL	$$	•
64 Three Creek Lake		10	20		NF				HSFB	$$	
65 Three Creek Meadow		20	40		NF				HFR	$$	
66 Three Sisters Overnight Park		60	40		F		•	•		$$	
67 Whispering Pines Horse Camp		9	30		NF				HR	$$	

Camping near the Metolius River.

Management: Deschutes National Forest
Contact: (541) 549–7700; www.fs.fed.us/r6/centraloregon/recreation
Finding the campground: From Sisters, go west on U.S. Highway 20 for 9.3 miles, turn right (north) onto paved Forest Road 14, and follow it for 11.1 miles to the campground entrance on the left.
About the campground: One of a string of choice family campgrounds along the Metolius Wild and Scenic River, this camp occupies a bend of the river. Sites typically rest among the fir, cedar, and ponderosa pine trees, except the walk-in sites, which occupy a meadow at the downstream end of the camp. Because river trails trace both banks, you can fashion a 6-mile loop hike between Lower Bridge (downstream) and the bridge at Wizard Falls Fish Hatchery (upstream). Fly-fishing lines often dance over the stunning water, while geese dwell in the quiet afforded by the bend.

44　Allingham

Location: About 16 miles northwest of Sisters
Season: May–September
Sites: 10 basic sites; no hookups
Maximum length: 40 feet
Facilities: Tables, grills, vault toilets, drinking water, dump station
Fee per night: $$
Management: Deschutes National Forest
Contact: (541) 549–7700; www.fs.fed.us/r6/centraloregon/recreation
Finding the campground: From Sisters, go west on U.S. Highway 20 for 9.3 miles, turn right (north) onto paved Forest Road 14, and follow it for 6 miles. Turn left onto FR 1419 at the sign that reads TO CAMP SHERMAN, go 0.2 mile, and turn right onto paved FR 900, which is signed for campgrounds. Go 0.7 mile to reach this camp on the left.
About the campground: This Metolius River campground has several pull-through sites and is well suited for RVs and large trailers. Ponderosa pines and bitterbrush set the stage for your stay. Views are of the glassy river, its green banks, and the cabins on the opposite shore. Fly-fishing, hiking the trails, and visiting the Camp Sherman fish-feeding platform or Wizard Falls Fish Hatchery are area pursuits.

45　Blue Bay

Location: About 14 miles northwest of Sisters, on Suttle Lake
Season: Mid-April–late September
Sites: 25 basic sites; no hookups
Maximum length: 40 feet
Facilities: Tables, grills, vault toilets, drinking water, boat launch, fish-cleaning station
Fee per night: $$
Management: Deschutes National Forest
Contact: (541) 549–7700; (877) 444–6777 for reservations; www.fs.fed.us/r6/centraloregon/recreation
Finding the campground: From U.S. Highway 20, 13 miles west of Sisters, 6.5 miles east of Santiam Pass, turn south onto paved Forest Road 2070 toward Suttle and Blue Lakes (the east access road). Go 1 mile to the campground entrance on the right.
About the campground: In a select-cut forest of firs and ponderosa pines, this campground offers semi-sunny sites along the south shore of Suttle Lake, a big, natural lake that boasts a full range of lake recreation. Vine maples claim the lower story. The campground has paved roads and gravel parking pads, some of which are pull-throughs. Entertainment here includes boating, fishing, waterskiing, and hiking the 3.25-mile Shoreline Trail. Elsewhere on the lake, you will find suitable swimming areas. Most days, boaters and anglers must contend with a strong afternoon wind.

46 Camp Sherman

Location: About 16 miles northwest of Sisters
Season: April–October
Sites: 15 basic sites; no hookups
Maximum length: 35 feet
Facilities: Tables, grills, vault toilets, drinking water, picnic shelter
Fee per night: $$
Management: Deschutes National Forest
Contact: (541) 549–7700; www.fs.fed.us/r6/centraloregon/recreation
Finding the campground: From Sisters, go west on U.S. Highway 20 for 9.3 miles, turn right (north) onto paved Forest Road 14, and follow it for 6 miles. Turn left onto FR 1419 at the sign that reads TO CAMP SHERMAN, go 0.2 mile, and turn right onto paved FR 900 (signed for campgrounds). Go 0.2 mile to reach this camp on the left.
About the campground: This campground occupies a flat of mixed age ponderosa pines; the mature pines parade reddish yellow trunks. A grassy meadow extends to the river, while bitterbrush claims the roadside. Wildflower-decorated islands and banks contribute to the charm of the river. Relaxing, birding, hiking, fly-fishing, and sightseeing are among the pastimes here.

47 Candle Creek

Location: About 16 miles northwest of Sisters
Season: April–October
Sites: 4 basic sites; no hookups
Maximum length: 20 feet
Facilities: Tables, grills, vault toilets; no drinking water
Fee per night: $$
Management: Deschutes National Forest
Contact: (541) 549–7700; www.fs.fed.us/r6/centraloregon/recreation
Finding the campground: From Sisters, go west on U.S. Highway 20 for 9.3 miles, turn right (north) onto paved Forest Road 14, and follow it for 13.6 miles to Lower Bridge, where the road becomes gravel and its name changes to FR 12. Go another mile on FR 12 and turn right onto FR 980. Proceed 1.5 miles to the campground.
About the campground: This peaceful campground sits on a forested bluff above the Metolius River at the Candle Creek confluence. Alders and vine maples grow along the swift waterway, which is open to catch-and-release fishing. You can access the West Metolius Trail from camp; it leads along the river.

48   Canyon Creek

Location: About 18 miles northwest of Sisters
Season: April–September
Sites: 4 basic sites; no hookups
Maximum length: 20 feet
Facilities: Tables, grills, vault toilets; no drinking water
Fee per night: None
Management: Deschutes National Forest
Contact: (541) 549–7700; www.fs.fed.us/r6/centraloregon/recreation
Finding the campground: From Sisters, go west on U.S. Highway 20 for 9.3 miles, turn right (north) onto paved Forest Road 14, and follow it for 2.6 miles. Turn left onto FR 1419 at the sign for Camp Sherman, go 1.3 miles, and pro-

The Metolius River Trail affords continuous river views.

ceed straight on FR 1420, following the signs for Sheep Springs Horse Camp. Follow FR 1420 for 4 miles (the road eventually becomes gravel), turn right onto FR 1420.400, and go 0.7 mile to the campground.

About the campground: At the convergence of Canyon Creek and the Metolius River, you will find this small, pleasant campground in a setting of ponderosa pines, bitterbrush, and bunchgrass. At the end of the campground loop, the West Metolius Trail departs on a 9-mile journey down the river to Candle Creek. You will enjoy spectacular scenes of sun-gilded riffles, channels, and deep pools; grassy islands showy with wildflowers; families of geese and mergansers; nesting ospreys; and the dancing lines of the fly anglers. The color of the river ranges from icy blue to satiny black.

49 Cold Springs

Location: 4 miles west of Sisters
Season: April–September
Sites: 23 basic sites; no hookups
Maximum length: 40 feet
Facilities: Tables, grills, vault toilets, drinking water
Fee per night: $$
Management: Deschutes National Forest
Contact: (541) 549–7700; www.fs.fed.us/r6/centraloregon/recreation
Finding the campground: From the junction of U.S. Highway 20 and Oregon 242 at the west end of Sisters, go west on OR 242 for 4 miles to reach this camp.

About the campground: Lovely ponderosa pines and an aspen grove create a soothing setting for your stay. There are both pull-through and back-in gravel parking spurs. Spring Trail begins near the campground entrance and leads a quarter of a mile through mixed woods and across a spring to a lava outcrop. You can scramble to the top of the outcrop for a new perspective on the area or follow an old jeep trail away from the site to extend your journey. The area is particularly appealing in early October, when the aspens turn yellow and jet-black ravens pass between the trees. Birding is popular here.

50 Driftwood

Location: About 16 miles southwest of Sisters, on Three Creek Lake
Season: July–mid-September
Sites: 17 basic sites; no hookups
Maximum length: 20 feet
Facilities: Tables, grills, vault toilets; no drinking water
Fee per night: $$
Management: Deschutes National Forest
Contact: (541) 549–7700; www.fs.fed.us/r6/centraloregon/recreation
Finding the campground: From U.S. Highway 20 in Sisters, turn south at the sign for Three Creek Lake onto South Elm, which later becomes Forest Road 16. Go 15.7 miles to the campground entrance on the right. The final 1.6 miles are on gravel.

About the campground: On the north shore of Three Creek Lake, you will find this campground in a forest of lodgepole and whitebark pines and true firs. Half of the sites are pull-in; parking for the remaining sites is along the widened road shoulder. The campsites are strung along the shore of this shimmering manmade lake at the foot of Tam McArthur Rim. Drift logs ring the lake, hinting at the camp's name. The sites receive only partial shade, and you should come prepared for mosquitoes. Fishing, nonmotorized boating, and hiking the trails to Tam McArthur Rim and Little Three Creek Lake engage guests.

51 Gorge

Location: About 17 miles northwest of Sisters
Season: May–September
Sites: 18 basic sites; no hookups
Maximum length: 40 feet
Facilities: Tables, grills, vault toilets, drinking water
Fee per night: $$
Management: Deschutes National Forest
Contact: (541) 549-7700; www.fs.fed.us/r6/centraloregon/recreation
Finding the campground: From Sisters, go west on U.S. Highway 20 for 9.3 miles, turn right (north) onto paved Forest Road 14, and follow it for 6 miles. Turn left on FR 1419 at the sign pointing to Camp Sherman, go 0.2 mile, and turn right onto paved FR 900 (signed for campgrounds). Go 1.8 miles to reach this camp on the left.
About the campground: This Metolius River campground occupies a ponderosa pine flat, with bitterbrush growing in the understory. Sites are partially sunny, and a number of them offer pull-through parking, which will appeal to visitors with larger rigs. The banks of the Metolius here are grassy, and fly-fishing is the order of the day.

52 Graham Horse Camp

Location: About 7 miles northwest of Sisters
Season: May–October
Sites: 13 basic sites; no hookups
Maximum length: 40 feet
Facilities: Tables, grills, pit toilets, drinking water, central partitioned corral, horse-loading chute, corrals at 4 sites, hitching rails
Fee per night: $$
Management: Deschutes National Forest
Contact: (541) 549-7700; www.fs.fed.us/r6/centraloregon/recreation
Finding the campground: From the junction of U.S. Highway 20 and Oregon 242 at the west end of Sisters, go 4 miles west on US 20 and turn left onto gravel Forest Road 1012 toward the Cold Springs Cut-off and Graham Corral. Go 1 mile, turn right onto FR 1012.300, and go another mile. Turn right onto FR 340 and go 0.6 mile to the camp.

About the campground: Along the lengthy Metolius–Windigo National Recreation Trail, this horse camp occupies the site where numerous roundups were held from the late 1800s to the early 1900s. Here, sheep and cows that ranged the Cache Mountain–Metolius River area were gathered and counted. The central corral seen and used today re-creates the historic scene. Present-day campers enjoy a spacious facility in a beautiful setting of ponderosa pines and bitterbrush. To the north above the treetops, you may glimpse Black Butte.

53 Indian Ford

Location: About 6 miles northwest of Sisters
Season: May–September
Sites: 25 basic sites; no hookups
Maximum length: 40 feet
Facilities: Tables, grills, vault toilets, drinking water
Fee per night: $$
Management: Deschutes National Forest
Contact: (541) 549-7700; www.fs.fed.us/r6/centraloregon/recreation

Black Butte summit.

Finding the campground: From Sisters, go 5.6 miles west on U.S. Highway 20, turn right onto Forest Road 11, and immediately make a right turn into the camp.

About the campground: This camp sits beside a narrow creek in a tranquil setting of big ponderosa pines, aspens, bunchgrass, and sagebrush. The ford at this location was mentioned in the journals of 19th-century explorer John C. Fremont. The camp is convenient for through travelers on US 20. You can watch birds right at your site, but there is traffic noise. With this camp as a base, you can hike to the top of Black Butte or fly-fish the Metolius Wild and Scenic River. The frontier village of Sisters holds a different appeal, with its galleries and boutiques.

54 Jack Creek

Location: About 17 miles northwest of Sisters
Season: May–October
Sites: 11 basic sites; no hookups
Maximum length: 40 feet
Facilities: Tables, grills and fire rings, vault toilets; no drinking water
Fee per night: None
Management: Deschutes National Forest
Contact: (541) 549-7700; www.fs.fed.us/r6/centraloregon/recreation
Finding the campground: From Sisters, go west on U.S. Highway 20 for 12 miles, turn right (north) onto paved Forest Road 12, and follow it for 4.4 miles. Turn left onto FR 1230, go 0.6 mile, cross a bridge, and turn left onto FR 1232. Go another 0.2 mile to reach the campground entrance on the left.

About the campground: This campground has a random, informal layout, with tables and grills hinting at the site locations. Big, impressive pines rise above camp, but the primary attraction is Jack Creek, one of the prettiest creeks in the country. Cold and crystalline, Jack Creek originates from a spring and wends its way around islands and under logs dressed in mosaics of fern, giant lupine, grass, and young trees. A trail leads upstream from the camp to the spring, Head of Jack Creek. The hike is worthwhile; every few strides reveals a scene worth photographing. Near the FR 1230 bridge, you can access the Metolius–Windigo Trail, a long-distance trail. Jack Creek is closed to angling.

55 Lava Camp Lake

Location: About 14 miles southwest of Sisters
Season: May–October
Sites: 10 basic sites; no hookups
Maximum length: 20 feet
Facilities: Tables, grills, vault toilets; no drinking water
Fee per night: None
Management: Deschutes National Forest
Contact: (541) 549-7700; www.fs.fed.us/r6/centraloregon/recreation

Finding the campground: From the junction of U.S. Highway 20 and Oregon 242 at the west end of Sisters, go west on OR 242 for 14 miles and turn left onto red-cinder Forest Road 900. Go 0.4 mile to the camp, bypassing a parking lot for the Pacific Crest Trail.

About the campground: You will find this rustic camp just off McKenzie Pass Scenic Highway (OR 242) next to tiny, mud-bottomed Lava Camp Lake. The sites rest on a terrace above the lake and along the shoreline in a mixed forest of lodgepole pines, mountain hemlocks, and firs. Half a mile west on OR 242, Dee Wright Observatory serves up fine views of the Three Sisters and Mount Washington Wilderness Areas, the Cascade volcanoes, and the mosaic of forest and lava flow. The fortress-like observatory, constructed of volcanic rock and perched atop a crusty flow, itself, makes a good photo subject. The arrangement of its open-air windows allows you to pinpoint landmarks. The twisting scenic highway presents additional wilderness views, as well as access to the Pacific Crest and a host of other trails. In the fall, the red blush of the vine maples suggests a drive.

56 Link Creek

Location: About 15 miles northwest of Sisters, on Suttle Lake
Season: April–September
Sites: 33 basic sites; no hookups
Maximum length: 40 feet
Facilities: Tables, grills, vault toilets, drinking water (in season), boat dock, launch, fish-cleaning station
Fee per night: $$
Management: Deschutes National Forest
Contact: (541) 549–7700; (877) 444–6777 for reservations; www.fs.fed.us/r6 /centraloregon/recreation
Finding the campground: From U.S. Highway 20, 13 miles west of Sisters and 6.5 miles east of Santiam Pass, turn south onto paved Forest Road 2070 toward Suttle and Blue Lakes (the east access road). Go 2.3 miles to the campground entrance on the right.
About the campground: This campground sits next to Link Creek on the southwest shore of Suttle Lake. Mixed pines and firs tower above the camp, while sticky laurel bushes grow in the more open areas. The campground has paved roads, and the sites feature either gravel or paved parking pads, some of them pull-throughs. Several sites overlook the huge natural lake. Boating, fishing, waterskiing, swimming, and hiking the 3.25-mile Shoreline Trail keep campers entertained. Afternoon winds commonly wash over the lake. In the fall, look for kokanee spawning in Link Creek.

57   Lower Bridge

Location: About 23 miles northwest of Sisters
Season: April–October
Sites: 12 basic sites; no hookups
Maximum length: 25 feet
Facilities: Tables, grills, vault toilets, drinking water
Fee per night: $$
Management: Deschutes National Forest
Contact: (541) 549–7700; www.fs.fed.us/r6/centraloregon/recreation
Finding the campground: From Sisters, go west on U.S. Highway 20 for 9.3 miles, turn right (north) onto paved Forest Road 14, and follow it for 13.5 miles to this campground. The entrance is on the right as you arrive at Lower Bridge.
About the campground: This pleasant, shady camp sits downstream from Lower Bridge (Bridge 99), on the stretch of water where fishing with flies and barbless lures is allowed. Fishing on the Metolius Wild and Scenic River is catch-and-release only to protect wild fish. The sites occupy a terraced forest slope above the river. Western tanagers sometimes decorate the tree branches. Foot trails trace the riverbanks in both directions. Upstream, a 6-mile loop hike is possible, crossing the river on the bridge at Wizard Falls Fish Hatchery.

58   Pine Rest

Location: About 17 miles northwest of Sisters
Season: April–October
Sites: 8 tent sites; no hookups
Maximum length: Suitable for tents only
Facilities: Tables, grills, vault toilets, drinking water (in season), picnic shelter
Fee per night: $$
Management: Deschutes National Forest
Contact: (541) 549–7700; www.fs.fed.us/r6/centraloregon/recreation
Finding the campground: From Sisters, go west on U.S. Highway 20 for 9.3 miles, turn right (north) onto paved Forest Road 14, and follow it for 6 miles. Turn left onto FR 1419 at the sign for Camp Sherman, go 0.2 mile, and turn right onto paved FR 900 (signed for campgrounds). Go 1.5 miles to reach this camp on the left.
About the campground: For tent campers, this area extends a pleasant stay along the Metolius River. Sites are spread across a shrub and meadow flat beneath ponderosa pines, firs, and larches. On the opposite shore, a few cabins overlook the river. The rustic stone and log picnic shelter is an attractive camp structure. You may well want to try your hand at fly-fishing.

Head of the Metolius River.

59 Pioneer Ford

Location: About 22 miles northwest of Sisters
Season: May–October
Sites: 18 basic sites, 2 walk-in sites; no hookups
Maximum length: 40 feet
Facilities: Tables, grills, vault toilets, drinking water, picnic shelter
Fee per night: $$
Management: Deschutes National Forest
Contact: (541) 549-7700; www.fs.fed.us/r6/centraloregon/recreation
Finding the campground: From Sisters, go west on U.S. Highway 20 for 9.3 miles, turn right (north) onto paved Forest Road 14, and follow it for 12.6 miles to this campground on the left.
About the campground: Part of the Metolius River lineup of popular family campgrounds, Pioneer Ford provides convenient access to fly-fishing, riverside trails, the Wizard Falls Fish Hatchery, and the Head of the Metolius (the originating spring for this spectacular river). The sites occupy an attractive flat of cedars, firs, and pines.

60 Sheep Springs Horse Camp

Location: About 22 miles northwest of Sisters
Season: May–October
Sites: 10 basic sites; no hookups
Maximum length: 40 feet
Facilities: Tables, grills, pit toilets, drinking water (creek for livestock), 40 box stalls (4 per site)
Fee per night: $$
Management: Deschutes National Forest
Contact: (541) 549-7700; (877) 444-6777 for reservations (which are required); www.fs.fed.us/r6/centraloregon/recreation
Finding the campground: From U.S. Highway 20, 12 miles west of Sisters, 7.5 miles east of Santiam Pass, turn north onto Forest Road 12, and follow it for 7.9 miles. (FR 12 begins paved but becomes gravel.) Turn left onto FR 1260, go 1.1 miles, and turn right onto FR 1260.200. Go another 1.3 miles to the campground entrance on the right.
About the campground: Set aside for the exclusive use of people camping with horses, this campground extends a pleasant, quiet stay in a forest of ponderosa pines and mixed firs. A pole fence separates the camp from Sheep Springs Meadow. Across the road from the camp is the Metolius–Windigo Trail, on which long-distance rides are possible. Deer seeking stray wisps of hay sometimes venture into camp.

61 Sisters Cow Camp Horse Camp

Location: About 4 miles southwest of Sisters
Season: May–October
Sites: 5 basic sites; no hookups
Maximum length: 40 feet
Facilities: Tables, grills, pit toilets, spring water for horses only, large central corral, loading ramp; no drinking water
Fee per night: $$
Management: Deschutes National Forest
Contact: (541) 549-7700; www.fs.fed.us/r6/centraloregon/recreation
Finding the campground: From Sisters, go west on Oregon 242 for 1.3 miles and turn left (southwest) onto Forest Road 15, a paved and gravel route. Follow it for 2.4 miles and turn left to enter the camp in 0.2 mile.
About the campground: Located on a broad, grassy flat with mature ponderosa pines, the sites of this horse camp encircle a large, partitioned corral. In the 1920s, this camp was a cattle roundup and shipping site; hence the awkward name. The long-distance Metolius–Windigo Trail passes camp.

62 Smiling River

Location: About 17 miles northwest of Sisters
Season: May–October
Sites: 38 basic sites; no hookups
Maximum length: 40 feet
Facilities: Tables, grills, vault toilets, drinking water (in season)
Fee per night: $$
Management: Deschutes National Forest
Contact: (541) 549-7700; www.fs.fed.us/r6/centraloregon/recreation
Finding the campground: From Sisters, go west on U.S. Highway 20 for 9.3 miles, turn right (north) onto paved Forest Road 14, and follow it for 6 miles. Turn left onto FR 1419 at the sign for Camp Sherman, go 0.2 mile, and turn right onto paved FR 900 (signed for campgrounds). Go 1 mile to reach this camp on the left.
About the campground: Of the string of Metolius River camps, this one is well suited for large RVs and trailers. It has many pull-through sites and offers attractive riverside stays beneath some lovely ponderosa pines. Across the river are some privately owned cabins and a beautiful meadow. Standing hip-deep in the river, fly-fishers tempt wild fish with their dancing lines and arsenal of flies.

63 South Shore

Location: About 14 miles northwest of Sisters, on Suttle Lake
Season: April–September
Sites: 39 basic sites; no hookups
Maximum length: 30 feet

Facilities: Tables, grills, vault toilets, drinking water, boat dock, launch, fish-cleaning station
Fee per night: $$
Management: Deschutes National Forest
Contact: (541) 549–7700; (877) 444–6777 for reservations; www.fs.fed.us/r6/centraloregon/recreation
Finding the campground: From U.S. Highway 20, 13 miles west of Sisters, 6.5 miles east of Santiam Pass, head south on paved Forest Road 2070 toward Suttle and Blue Lakes (the east access road). Go 1.1 miles to this campground on the right.
About the campground: On the south shore of Suttle Lake—a huge natural lake in a scenic, tree-lined basin—this campground offers the full gamut of water fun. The midday sun can pierce through the canopy of tall firs and big ponderosa pines, but generally campsites enjoy good shade throughout the day. There are paved roads through the camp and gravel or paved parking pads. Lakeside sites are snapped up quickly. Boating, fishing, waterskiing, and swimming, as well as hiking the 3.25-mile Shoreline Trail and just relaxing at camp, should keep everyone in the family happy. To escape having to battle the afternoon winds, shore anglers will want to rise early.

64　Three Creek Lake

Location: 16 miles southwest of Sisters, on Three Creek Lake
Season: July–mid-September
Sites: 10 basic sites; no hookups
Maximum length: 20 feet
Facilities: Tables, grills, vault toilets; no drinking water
Fee per night: $$
Management: Deschutes National Forest
Contact: (541) 549–7700; www.fs.fed.us/r6/centraloregon/recreation
Finding the campground: From U.S. Highway 20 in Sisters, go south at the sign for Three Creek Lake on South Elm, which later becomes Forest Road 16. Go 16 miles to the campground. The final 1.9 miles are on gravel.
About the campground: Sandwiched between Three Creek Lake and Tam McArthur Rim, this campground sits in the shadow of the towering rim in a setting of firs, mountain hemlocks, and lodgepole pines. Clark's nutcrackers may visit the treetops. Wildflowers speckle the grassy lakeshore. This popular camp offers quiet lake recreation and superb hiking to the top of Tam McArthur Rim, from which there are dizzying views and access to Broken Top. Mosquitoes can be annoying. A tiny, rustic store near the camp entrance sells tackle and bait and rents rowboats.

65 Three Creek Meadow

Location: About 15 miles southwest of Sisters
Season: June–mid-September
Sites: 11 basic sites, adjacent horse camp with 9 sites; no hookups
Maximum length: 40 feet
Facilities: Tables, grills, vault toilets, corrals at horse camp; no drinking water
Fee per night: $$
Management: Deschutes National Forest
Contact: (541) 549-7700; www.fs.fed.us/r6/centraloregon/recreation
Finding the campground: From U.S. Highway 20 in Sisters, head south at the sign for Three Creek Lake on South Elm, which later becomes Forest Road 16. Go 14.7 miles to enter the family campground, 14.9 miles to enter the horse camp. The final mile is not paved.
About the campground: This campground duo sits among the lodgepole pines on the fringe of Three Creek Meadow. Wildflowers often dress the meadow, and deep, sparkling streams thread through it. Tam McArthur Rim looms to the south, retaining its snow for much of the year. It makes for a striking view, at times with a halo of clouds. At the camp, shade is limited, and mosquitoes can be a bother. An open flat serves large camping rigs. Hiking, horseback riding, and fishing engage visitors. The shops, galleries, and eateries of Sisters may lure you back to town.

66 Three Sisters Overnight Park

Location: In Sisters
Season: Mid-April–mid-October
Sites: 60 basic sites, some hike/bike-in sites; no hookups
Maximum length: 40 feet
Facilities: Tables, fire pits, flush toilets, drinking water, dump station, telephone
Fee per night: $$
Management: City of Sisters
Contact: (541) 549-6022; www.ci.sisters.or.us/overnightpark
Finding the campground: The camp is on the south side of U.S. Highway 20 at the east end of Sisters, just west of the junction of US 20 and Oregon 126 East.
About the campground: This campground occupies a scenic pine flat on the east shore of Squaw Creek; a day-use area claims the west shore. Beneath the big pines, you will find lawn or natural vegetation. The park is convenient for travelers and a fine base from which to explore Sisters, a picturesque frontier-character village that is perfect for strolling; galleries, shops, and eateries invite you inside. Sisters is at the heart of one of the state's highly prized recreational areas. From camp you can easily get to Bend, Smith Rock State Park, Tam McArthur Rim, the Metolius River, the McKenzie River, McKenzie Pass, and the Three Sisters and Mount Washington Wilderness Areas.

67 Whispering Pines Horse Camp

Location: About 10 miles southwest of Sisters
Season: Mid-May–mid-October
Sites: 9 basic sites; no hookups
Maximum length: 30 feet
Facilities: Tables, grills, vault toilets, 4-horse corrals; no drinking water
Fee per night: $$
Management: Deschutes National Forest
Contact: (541) 549-7700; www.fs.fed.us/r6/centraloregon/recreation
Finding the campground: From Sisters, go west on Oregon 242 for 5.7 miles and turn left (south) onto gravel Forest Road 1018 toward Whispering Pines. Continue 4.3 miles and turn left onto FR 1520. Drive another 0.2 mile to the campground entrance on the left.
About the campground: This equestrian camp has a meadow floor with an open stand of mature ponderosa pines and a punctuation of clustered firs. The sites are large, comfortable, and functional. Trout Creek flows past the camp. Contact the Sisters Ranger District about horse trails in the area.

Prineville Area

68 Allen Creek Horse Camp

Location: About 44 miles east of Prineville
Season: May–September
Sites: 5 basic sites; no hookups
Maximum length: 24 feet
Facilities: Tables, grills, vault toilet, corrals; no drinking water
Fee per night: None
Management: Ochoco National Forest
Contact: (541) 416–6500; www.fs.fed.us/r6/centraloregon/recreation
Finding the campground: From Prineville, go east on U.S. Highway 26 about 17 miles and bear right (northeast) on Ochoco Creek Road/Forest Road 22. Follow it 27 miles to enter the camp on the right.
About the campground: The campground is set up to serve people camping with horses. It claims an attractive ponderosa pine forest along picturesque Allen Creek. The rustic corrals blend with the setting, and the old roads leading from the camp invite exploration. Water is available for your stock, but you will need to bring water for your own drinking and cooking.

69 Antelope Flat Reservoir

Location: About 44 miles southeast of Prineville, on Antelope Flat Reservoir
Season: May–September
Sites: 25 basic sites; no hookups
Maximum length: 30 feet
Facilities: Tables, grills, vault toilets, boat launch, drinking water
Fee per night: $
Management: Ochoco National Forest
Contact: (541) 416–6500; www.fs.fed.us/r6/centraloregon/recreation
Finding the campground: From the junction of Main Street and U.S. Highway 26 in Prineville, go east on US 26 for 1 mile and turn right (south) toward Paulina on North Combs Flat Road (Paulina Highway). Go 30.2 miles, turn right onto gravel Forest Road 17, and stay on it. After 10.1 miles, FR 17 turns left onto FR 16, only to quickly veer right away from it. The campground is 2.8 miles farther on FR 17.
About the campground: This campground occupies a dry forest setting of ponderosa pines, junipers, and bunchgrass above Antelope Flat Reservoir. Canoes and fishing boats ply the lake, which is rimmed by low dusky hills clad in pine and sage. Sites have defined parking, with the sites closer to the water tending to be more closely spaced. Paths lead to shore and to a boat ramp. The camp is generally relaxing, unless it is a bad mosquito season.

Prineville Area

	Hookup sites	Total sites	Maximum RV length	Hookups	Toilets	Showers	Drinking water	Dump station	Recreation	Fee	Can reserve
68 Allen Creek Horse Camp		5	24		NF				FR		
69 Antelope Flat Reservoir		25	30		NF		•		FBL	$	
70 Big Bend Recreation Site		15	25		NF				FBL	$–$$	
71 Big Springs		5	20		NF						
72 Castle Rock Recreation Site		6	35		NF				F	$	
73 Chimney Rock Recreation Site		16	24		NF		•		HF	$	
74 Cobble Rock Recreation Site		15	25		NF				F	$	
75 Crook County RV Park	81	92	40	WESC	F	•	•	•	F	$$$	•
76 Deep Creek		6	24		NF				F	$	
77 Devil's Post Pile Recreation Site		7	25		NF				F	$	
78 Dry Creek Horse Camp		5	small		NF				HR		
79 Elkhorn		4	24		NF						
80 Lone Pine Recreation Site		8	25		NF				F	$	
81 Lower Palisades Recreation Site		15	35		NF				F	$	
82 Mud Springs		6	20		NF				HR		
83 Ochoco Forest Camp		6	24		NF		•		HF	$$	
84 Ochoco Lake Crook County Park		22	35		F		•		FBL	$$	
85 Poison Butte Recreation Site		5	T		NF				F	$	
86 Prineville Reservoir State Park (main campground)	45	73	54	WES	F	•	•		SFBL	$$–$$$	•
87 Prineville Reservoir State Park: Jasper Point	30	30	30	WE	NF		•		SFBL	$$	•
88 Stillwater Recreation Site		10	35		NF				F	$	
89 Sugar Creek		17	24		NF		•			$	
90 Walton Lake		31	30		NF		•		HSFBL	$$	
91 Wildcat		17	30		NF		•		HF	$	
92 Wiley Flat		5	24		NF						
93 Wolf Creek		10	20		NF					$	

70 Big Bend Recreation Site

Location: 19 miles south of Prineville
Season: Year-round
Sites: 15 basic sites; no hookups
Maximum length: 25 feet
Facilities: Tables, fire rings, vault toilets, nearby boat launch (at Prineville Reservoir); no drinking water
Fee per night: $–$$
Management: Prineville District Bureau of Land Management
Contact: (541) 416–6700; www.or.blm.gov/prineville
Finding the campground: From U.S. Highway 26 in Prineville, head south on Main Street/Oregon 27, the Lower Crooked River BLM Back Country Byway, and proceed 19 miles to the turnoff for the camp.
About the campground: At this Crooked River recreation site below Prineville Reservoir, the camping spots sit among the junipers, and visitors have easy access to the river for fishing and to the reservoir (1.2 miles upstream) for both fishing and boating. The reservoir looks its best when it is full, blue, and reflecting its arid surroundings. Fires and smoking are prohibited from June 1 to October 15.

71 Big Springs

Location: About 55 miles east of Prineville
Season: May–October
Sites: 5 basic sites; no hookups
Maximum length: 20 feet
Facilities: A few tables and crude fire rings, pit toilets; no drinking water
Fee per night: None
Management: Ochoco National Forest
Contact: (541) 477–6900; www.fs.fed.us/r6/centraloregon/recreation
Finding the campground: From Prineville, go east on U.S. Highway 26 about 17 miles and bear right (northeast) on Ochoco Creek Road/Forest Road 22. Follow it 8 miles to the Ochoco Ranger Station. From there, go east on FR 42 for 28 miles and turn left onto FR 4270. Go 1.5 miles more and turn left onto FR 100 to reach the camp in another 0.1 mile.
About the campground: At this primitive camp, you can recline in a mixed setting of pine forest and meadow and enjoy nature's peace. Wildflowers decorate the meadow, but there are very few parking options for large units when the meadow periphery is wet. The camp's remote locale serves hunters well.

72 Castle Rock Recreation Site

Location: About 12 miles south of Prineville
Season: Year-round
Sites: 6 basic sites; no hookups
Maximum length: 35 feet
Facilities: Tables, grills, vault toilets; no drinking water

Fee per night: $
Management: Prineville District Bureau of Land Management
Contact: (541) 416–6700; www.or.blm.gov/prineville
Finding the campground: From U.S. Highway 26 in Prineville, head south on Main Street/Oregon 27, the Lower Crooked River BLM Back Country Byway, for 12.3 miles to reach the camp.
About the campground: Where the Crooked River Canyon broadens, you will find this camp, which is a little drier and sunnier than its upstream counterparts. Here, the west canyon wall is arid with a ragged rim; the east canyon wall parades exciting rock features. A single pull-through site accommodates large units. Fishing is popular. Fires and smoking are prohibited from June 1 to October 15.

73 Chimney Rock Recreation Site

Location: 16 miles south of Prineville
Season: Year-round
Sites: 16 basic sites; no hookups
Maximum length: 24 feet
Facilities: Tables, vault toilets, drinking water, fishing dock for individuals with disabilities
Fee per night: $
Management: Prineville District Bureau of Land Management
Contact: (541) 416–6700; www.or.blm.gov/prineville
Finding the campground: From U.S. Highway 26 in Prineville, head south on Main Street/Oregon 27, the Lower Crooked River BLM Back Country Byway, and proceed 16 miles to the camp on the right.
About the campground: A fishing dock is center stage at this campground on the Crooked Wild and Scenic River. RVers typically prefer the upstream end of the camp, which has a broad gravel lot for easy parking. The sites downstream tend to be fairly short, although a few near the turnaround loop are fine for RVs. Swallows nest in the cliffs across the river, and Chimney Rock looms above the camp. You may choose to lace on your hiking boots for a closer look at the camp's namesake; the trailhead sits across the road from camp. The Rim Trail travels 1.4 miles and gains 500 feet to reach the saddle of Chimney Rock. From this lofty perspective, you can admire the Central Cascades, the Crooked River, the camp, and the stunning river canyon. Fires and smoking are prohibited from June 1 to October 15.

74 Cobble Rock Recreation Site

Location: 17 miles south of Prineville
Season: Year-round
Sites: 15 basic sites; no hookups
Maximum length: 25 feet

The Crooked Wild and Scenic River.

Facilities: Tables, grills, vault toilets; no drinking water
Fee per night: $
Management: Prineville District Bureau of Land Management
Contact: (541) 416-6700; www.or.blm.gov/prineville
Finding the campground: From U.S. Highway 26 in Prineville, head south on Main Street/Oregon 27, the Lower Crooked River BLM Back Country Byway, and proceed 17 miles to the camp.
About the campground: This campground on the Crooked River has gravel roads and defined road shoulder or pullout parking. Although fire rings are provided, a strict ban on fires and smoking is in effect from June 1 to October 15 to protect this fragile, dry canyon. The camp has a dotting of junipers, and a few ponderosa pines grow near the river. Views include nearby Chimney Rock, columnar buttes and crests, and a palisades just across the river from the camp. When the fish are not biting, you can hike the Rim Trail to Chimney Rock. The trailhead is 1 mile north, across OR 27 from Chimney Rock Recreation Site (see above).

75 Crook County RV Park

Location: In Prineville
Season: Year-round
Sites: 81 hookup sites, 9 tent sites, 2 cabins; water, electric, sewer, and cable hookups
Maximum length: 40 feet
Facilities: Flush toilets, drinking water, showers, dump station, telephone, playground at nearby Crooked River Park
Fee per night: $$$
Management: Crook County
Contact: (541) 447-2599; (800) 609-2599 for reservations
Finding the campground: From U.S. Highway 26 in Prineville, head south on Main Street/Oregon 27 at the sign for the fairgrounds. Go 0.5 mile and turn left to enter the RV park.
About the campground: This comfortable RV park is ideal for campers attending fairground events or sightseeing in Prineville. It has formal tent pads and long, paved parking spaces. The young trees in camp have yet to provide much shade, but there are some big cottonwoods and weeping willows in the neighborhood. OR 27 is a Bureau of Land Management Back Country Byway, serving up a scenic drive along the Lower Crooked River. Crooked River Park, across the road from the camp, has a playground and offers fishing.

76 Deep Creek

Location: About 50 miles east of Prineville
Season: May–September
Sites: 6 basic sites; no hookups
Maximum length: 24 feet
Facilities: Tables, grills, vault toilet; no drinking water

Fee per night: $
Management: Ochoco National Forest
Contact: (541) 416–6500; www.fs.fed.us/r6/centraloregon/recreation
Finding the campground: From Prineville, go east on U.S. Highway 26 about 17 miles and bear right (northeast) on Ochoco Creek Road/Forest Road 22. Follow it 8 miles to the Ochoco Ranger Station. From there, go east on FR 42 for 24 miles and turn right into the camp.
About the campground: Located along the North Fork Crooked River near its confluence with Deep Creek, this rustic camp boasts many big yellow-bellied pines. The sites enjoy a mix of sun and shade, and most have tables and grills. The river calls to anglers, while the casual rock collector can usually discover an agate or two among the cobbles on shore.

77 Devil's Post Pile Recreation Site

Location: About 18 miles south of Prineville
Season: Year-round
Sites: 7 basic sites; no hookups
Maximum length: 25 feet
Facilities: Tables, grills, vault toilets; no drinking water
Fee per night: $
Management: Prineville District Bureau of Land Management
Contact: (541) 416–6700; www.or.blm.gov/prineville
Finding the campground: From U.S. Highway 26 in Prineville, head south on Main Street/Oregon 27, the Lower Crooked River BLM Back Country Byway, and proceed 17.5 miles to the camp.
About the campground: This camp along the byway is tucked among the junipers at a bend in the Crooked River. It has back-in and pull-through sites. Camp guests while away their time fishing, relaxing, and admiring the canyon setting. Fires and smoking are prohibited from June 1 to October 15.

78 Dry Creek Horse Camp

Location: About 17 miles northeast of Prineville
Season: Mid-April–November
Sites: 5 basic sites; no hookups
Maximum length: Tents and small RV units
Facilities: Tables, grills, pit toilet, corrals; no drinking water
Fee per night: None
Management: Ochoco National Forest
Contact: (541) 416–6500; www.fs.fed.us/r6/centraloregon/recreation
Finding the campground: From Prineville, go east on U.S. Highway 26 for 9 miles and turn left onto Mill Creek Road/Forest Road 33. Go 5 miles, turn left onto FR 3370, and continue another 2.4 miles. Turn left onto FR 200 and go 0.1 mile to the camp. The road into the camp is not suitable for large RVs.
About the campground: Established for the equestrian camper, this facility offers convenient, serviceable sites in a forest of pines and firs near Brennan

Palisades. There are rustic pole corrals and split-rail fences. Dry Creek is across the road, as is the Giddy-Up-Go Trail, a 12-mile loop ride.

79 Elkhorn

Location: About 38 miles southeast of Prineville
Season: May–September
Sites: 4 basic sites; no hookups
Maximum length: 24 feet
Facilities: Tables, some grills, pit toilets; no drinking water
Fee per night: None
Management: Ochoco National Forest
Contact: (541) 416–6500; www.fs.fed.us/r6/centraloregon/recreation
Finding the campground: From the Paulina Highway, 33 miles east of Prineville, 23 miles west of Paulina, head south on gravel Drake Creek Road/Forest Road 16. Go 4.5 miles to this campground on the left. Although the turnoff may be unmarked, the camp is visible from FR 16.
About the campground: Encircled by a rail fence, this small rustic camp occupies a pine and meadow setting. Arnica and wild roses add seasonal color to the meadow. Hunters and agate collectors sometimes make use of this peaceful outpost.

80 Lone Pine Recreation Site

Location: About 14 miles south of Prineville
Season: Year-round
Sites: 8 basic sites; no hookups
Maximum length: 25 feet
Facilities: Tables, grills, vault toilets; no drinking water
Fee per night: $
Management: Prineville District Bureau of Land Management
Contact: (541) 416–6700; www.or.blm.gov/prineville
Finding the campground: From U.S. Highway 26 in Prineville, head south on Main Street/Oregon 27, the Lower Crooked River BLM Back Country Byway, and proceed 14.3 miles to the camp.
About the campground: This is one of several BLM camps on the east bank of the Crooked River. Lone Pine primarily has a juniper setting, but a ponderosa pine here and there lends credence to the camp's name. The canyon crest shapes a lovely skyline. The sites have defined parking, and there is direct fishing access from camp. Fires and smoking are prohibited from June 1 to October 15.

81 Lower Palisades Recreation Site

Location: About 15 miles south of Prineville
Season: Year-round
Sites: 15 basic sites; no hookups

Maximum length: 35 feet
Facilities: Tables, fireplaces, vault toilets, 2 small fishing docks for individuals with disabilities; no drinking water
Fee per night: $
Management: Prineville District Bureau of Land Management
Contact: (541) 416–6700; www.or.blm.gov/prineville
Finding the campground: From U.S. Highway 26 in Prineville, head south on Main Street/Oregon 27, the Lower Crooked River BLM Back Country Byway, and proceed 15.3 miles to this riverside camp.
About the campground: This is one of the more developed campgrounds along the Crooked Wild and Scenic River and the byway. The sites are well spaced and have good river access, and the junipers create at least some shade at each site. Across the river from the camp rise bulging, cobbled palisade cliffs. A barrier-free trail accesses the fishing docks. Along the river corridor, a ban on smoking and fires is in effect from June 1 to October 15.

82 Mud Springs

Location: About 87 miles east of Prineville
Season: June–October
Sites: 5 basic sites, 1 horse campsite; no hookups
Maximum length: 20 feet
Facilities: Tables, vault toilets, horse corrals; no drinking water
Fee per night: None
Management: Ochoco National Forest
Contact: (541) 477–6900; www.fs.fed.us/r6/centraloregon/recreation
Finding the campground: From Paulina (56 miles southeast of Prineville), go east on County Road 112 (the Paulina Highway toward Suplee) for 4.2 miles. Turn left onto gravel CR 113, which becomes Forest Road 58 and later changes to gravel. Travel 20 miles and turn left onto FR 5840. Go another 6 miles, turn right onto FR 5840.400, and proceed 0.7 mile to the camp.
About the campground: This serene but primitive campground on the southeast flank of Wolf Mountain will appeal to the escapist. It enjoys a setting of big meadows and big pines and allows campers to spread out. False hellebore, widow grass, buttercup, wyethia, violet, and larkspur color the meadow. Trail 821, the South Prong Trail, provides hiker/horse access to Black Canyon Wilderness. Hunters use this camp in the fall.

83 Ochoco Forest Camp

Location: About 25 miles northeast of Prineville
Season: Mid-May–September
Sites: 6 basic sites; no hookups
Maximum length: 24 feet
Facilities: Tables, grills, vault toilet, drinking water, log picnic shelter
Fee per night: $$
Management: Ochoco National Forest

Contact: (541) 416–6500; www.fs.fed.us/r6/centraloregon/recreation
Finding the campground: From Prineville, go east on U.S. Highway 26 about 17 miles, bear right onto paved Ochoco Creek Road/Forest Road 22, and proceed 8 miles to this campground, which is adjacent to Ochoco Ranger Station.
About the campground: This quiet little camp sits beside pretty Ochoco Creek, which cuts a deep groove through a brushy meadow as it meanders past camp. Ponderosa pines and alders frame the sites and are interspersed with native grasses and shrubs. Across the road from the camp starts the Lookout Mountain Trail, which leads past magnificent old-growth ponderosa pines and through grasslands decorated with springtime irises to attain a superb Ochoco Forest vantage.

84 Ochoco Lake Crook County Park

Location: 7 miles east of Prineville
Season: April–October
Sites: 22 basic sites, some hike/bike sites; no hookups

Ponderosa pines frame the head of Lookout Mountain Trail.

Maximum length: 35 feet
Facilities: Tables, grills, flush toilets, drinking water, boat launch, fish-cleaning station
Fee per night: $$
Management: Crook County
Contact: (541) 447-1209
Finding the campground: From Prineville, go east on U.S. Highway 26 for 7 miles to reach the park on the right.
About the campground: This park features groomed lawns shaded by junipers on a slope above Ochoco Reservoir, which is open for recreation. Fishing and boating are the chief attractions. Arid, juniper-dotted tablelands and hills shape the basin and view. Blacktop trails allow short strolls along the lake.

85 Poison Butte Recreation Site

Location: About 18 miles south of Prineville
Season: Year-round
Sites: 5 tent sites; no hookups
Maximum length: Small rigs only
Facilities: Tables, fire rings, vault toilets; no drinking water
Fee per night: $
Management: Prineville District Bureau of Land Management
Contact: (541) 416-6700; www.or.blm.gov/prineville
Finding the campground: From U.S. Highway 26 in Prineville, head south on Main Street/Oregon 27, the Lower Crooked River BLM Back Country Byway, and go 18.2 miles to the camp.
About the campground: This is one of the smaller camps along the Crooked River. Like the others, it is set in a juniper forest, but some big ponderosa pines loom across the river. The river here slows, broadens, and grows shallow enough that anglers can often wade across it. White rocks and grassy banks complement the green water, and geese and herons may favor the site with a visit. Fires and smoking are prohibited from June 1 to October 15.

86 Prineville Reservoir State Park (Main Campground)

Location: About 16 miles southeast of Prineville, on Prineville Reservoir
Season: Year-round
Sites: 45 full or partial hookup sites, 23 basic sites, 5 cabins; water, electric, and sewer hookups
Maximum length: 54 feet
Facilities: Tables, grills, flush toilets, drinking water, showers, telephone, boat launch, docks, fish-cleaning station
Fee per night: $$-$$$
Management: Oregon State Parks and Recreation Department
Contact: (541) 447-4363; (800) 452-5687 for reservations; www.oregonstate parks.org

Finding the campground: From the junction of Main Street and U.S. Highway 26 in Prineville, go east on US 26 for 1 mile, turn right (south) onto North Combs Flat Road, and follow it for 1.2 miles. Turn right onto Juniper Canyon Road and continue 13 miles to a junction. Head right and drive 0.7 mile more to reach the main campground.

About the campground: This developed camp is located on a juniper canyon slope above Prineville Reservoir. Some sites overlook the water, and most receive a mix of sun and shade. Noise from the speedboats and Jet Skis carries across the water, but these recreational activities are among the reasons folks come to the park. Fishing and swimming are two of the quieter pursuits. Big Island adds to views of this vast, sparkling lake.

87 Prineville Reservoir State Park: Jasper Point

Location: About 18 miles southeast of Prineville, on Prineville Reservoir
Season: Mid-April–mid-October
Sites: 30 partial hookup sites; water and electric hookups
Maximum length: 30 feet
Facilities: Tables, grills, vault toilets, drinking water, boat launch
Fee per night: $$
Management: Oregon State Parks and Recreation Department
Contact: (541) 447–4363; (800) 452–5687 for reservations; www.oregonstate parks.org
Finding the campground: From the junction of Main Street and U.S. Highway 26 in Prineville, go east on US 26 for 1 mile, turn right (south) onto North Combs Flat Road, and follow it for 1.2 miles. Turn right onto Juniper Canyon Road and continue 13 miles to a junction. Bear left and go another 2.5 miles to Jasper Point.

About the campground: Set apart from the more developed portion of the state park, this camp claims another sun-basked, juniper-studded slope above Prineville Reservoir. It offers direct access to the lake for fishing, boating, waterskiing, and Jet Skiing. The lake boasts excellent fishing, and in this hot climate, swimming is popular.

88 Stillwater Recreation Site

Location: About 13 miles south of Prineville
Season: Year-round
Sites: 10 basic sites; no hookups
Maximum length: 35 feet
Facilities: Tables, grills, vault toilets; no drinking water
Fee per night: $
Management: Prineville District Bureau of Land Management
Contact: (541) 416–6700; www.or.blm.gov/prineville
Finding the campground: From U.S. Highway 26 in Prineville, head south on Main Street/Oregon 27, the Lower Crooked River BLM Back Country Byway, and go 13.2 miles to the camp.

About the campground: Along the scenic byway and a slow stretch of the

Crooked River, you will find this camp cradled between canyon walls of differing character: one rock, the other juniper-grassland. Fishing and water play may engage you, though probably not at the same time. To protect the arid canyon habitat, a ban on fires and smoking is in effect from June 1 to October 15.

89 Sugar Creek

Location: About 70 miles east of Prineville
Season: May–October
Sites: 17 basic sites; no hookups
Maximum length: 24 feet
Facilities: Tables, grills, vault toilets, drinking water, barrier-free trail to creek
Fee per night: $
Management: Ochoco National Forest
Contact: (541) 477–6900; www.fs.fed.us/r6/centraloregon/recreation
Finding the campground: From Paulina (56 miles southeast of Prineville), go east on County Road 112 (the Paulina Highway toward Suplee). Go 4.2 miles and turn left onto gravel CR 113/Forest Road 58. Continue 8.5 miles to the campground entrance on the right.
About the campground: You will find this relaxing campground in an attractive forest of ponderosa pines on the banks of Sugar Creek. The warbling of songbirds and the telegraphic knocking of woodpeckers are likely to accompany your stay here. Bald eagles have a winter roost nearby. Split-rail fences add charm to the scene, and a barrier-free trail allows for creek viewing.

90 Walton Lake

Location: About 32 miles northeast of Prineville, on Walton Lake
Season: Late May–late September
Sites: 31 basic sites; no hookups
Maximum length: 30 feet
Facilities: Tables, grills, vault toilet, drinking water, boat ramp (electric motors permitted but no gas motors), swimming area, barrier-free fishing pier
Fee per night: $$
Management: Ochoco National Forest
Contact: (541) 416–6500; www.fs.fed.us/r6/centraloregon/recreation
Finding the campground: From Prineville, go east on U.S. Highway 26 about 17 miles, bear right on paved Ochoco Creek Road/Forest Road 22, and proceed another 15 miles, following the signs to locate this campground.
About the campground: This popular campground is located along the shore of Walton Lake, a former mountain meadow that was transformed into a quiet mountain lake by a small earthen dam. Campsites dot the ponderosa pine forest on the north and south shores; site parking is either on the roadside or on spurs. The lake is stocked with trout three times each summer, so the fishing

is usually pretty good. Quiet boating, swimming, hiking the lakeside trail, watching the antics of otter or muskrat, and just relaxing in camp are other potential activities. The camp also holds a trailhead for the Round Mountain National Recreation Trail, for a more challenging hike.

91 Wildcat

Location: About 19 miles northeast of Prineville
Season: May–September
Sites: 17 basic sites; no hookups
Maximum length: 30 feet
Facilities: Tables, grills, vault toilets, drinking water
Fee per night: $
Management: Ochoco National Forest
Contact: (541) 416–6500; www.fs.fed.us/r6/centraloregon/recreation
Finding the campground: From Prineville, go east on U.S. Highway 26 for 9 miles and turn left (north) onto Mill Creek Road/Forest Road 33. Drive another 10.4 miles to the campground entrance on the right. Part of the route is on gravel.
About the campground: Firs and ponderosa pines shade this East Fork Mill Creek campground, which is a gateway to Mill Creek Wilderness. The East Fork is your guide upstream into the wilderness, a wildflower showcase with areas of recovered burn, thriving forest, and the intriguing forked monolith of Twin Pillars. The trail crisscrosses the sparkling East Fork several times. Although there are often logs or stones, you may still have to ford the creek on occasion. Another fine rock destination is Steins Pillar. To reach its trailhead, go 4 miles south from camp on FR 33, turn east onto FR 500, and go 2 miles. Steins Pillar is a 350-foot-tall, free-standing column of pinkish stone streaked with black.

92 Wiley Flat

Location: About 44 miles southeast of Prineville
Season: May–September
Sites: 5 basic sites; no hookups
Maximum length: 24 feet
Facilities: Tables, some grills, pit toilets; no drinking water
Fee per night: None
Management: Ochoco National Forest
Contact: (541) 416–6500; www.fs.fed.us/r6/centraloregon/recreation
Finding the campground: From the Paulina Highway, 33 miles east of Prineville, 23 miles west of Paulina, turn south on gravel Drake Creek Road/Forest Road 16 and go 10.4 miles. Turn right onto FR 400 and follow the rough road 0.8 mile into the camp.
About the campground: Although this out-of-the-way camp can accommodate large vehicles, the rocky access road promises a rattling ride, and the dirt roads within the camp are impassable in wet weather. The headwater spring

of Wiley Creek sends a silver thread through this quiet meadow dotted with mixed age pines. Arnica, wild strawberry, wild geranium, violet, and cinquefoil are among the meadow wildflowers. Birds, filtered sunlight, and the rich vanilla scent of pines can contribute to the relaxing atmosphere. In the fall, hunters frequent this area.

93 Wolf Creek

Location: About 70 miles east of Prineville
Season: May–November
Sites: 10 basic sites; no hookups
Maximum length: 20 feet
Facilities: Tables, grills, vault toilets; no drinking water
Fee per night: $
Management: Ochoco National Forest
Contact: (541) 477–6900; www.fs.fed.us/r6/centraloregon/recreation
Finding the campground: From Paulina (56 miles southeast of Prineville), go east on County Road 112 (the Paulina Highway toward Suplee) for 4.2 miles. Turn left onto gravel CR 113/Forest Road 58 and continue 7.2 miles to the junction of FR 58 and FR 42. Turn left onto FR 42 and go 1.7 miles. Enter the campground upon crossing the Wolf Creek bridge.
About the campground: A rustic, zigzagging rail fence wraps around this campground, which sits beside Wolf Creek in a meadow dotted with ponderosa pines. The murmur of the small, attractive creek is soothing.

Bend Area

94 Big River

Location: About 22 miles southwest of Bend
Season: April–October
Sites: 9 basic sites, 2 tent sites; no hookups
Maximum length: 26 feet
Facilities: Tables, grills, vault toilet, boat launch; no drinking water
Fee per night: $
Management: Deschutes National Forest
Contact: (541) 383–4000; www.fs.fed.us/r6/centraloregon/recreation
Finding the campground: From U.S. Highway 97, 17.5 miles south of Bend, 4.9 miles north of the turnoff for La Pine State Recreation Area, turn west for Fall River on Forest Road 42 (labeled Vandevert Road and then South Century Drive). Go 4.6 miles to the camp.
About the campground: Shaded by lodgepole and small ponderosa pines, this camp overlooks a slow stretch of the Deschutes River. A few shrubs intersperse the grasses and needle mat of the forest floor. The dirt access road can be rutted, so take it easy when entering camp. Fishing is the main attraction here. The boat ramp is on the opposite side of FR 42.

95 Bull Bend

Location: About 37 miles southwest of Bend
Season: April–October
Sites: 12 basic sites; no hookups
Maximum length: 30 feet
Facilities: Tables, grills, vault toilets, boat launch; no drinking water
Fee per night: $
Management: Deschutes National Forest
Contact: (541) 383–4000; www.fs.fed.us/r6/centraloregon/recreation
Finding the campground: From U.S. Highway 97 at Wickiup Junction, 27 miles south of Bend, go west on County Road 43 for 8 miles. Turn left (south) onto gravel Forest Road 4370 and continue 1.5 miles to the camp.
About the campground: This camp occupies a piney peninsula in a horseshoe bend of the Deschutes River. Bitterbrush and currant grow beneath the trees. Fishing, swimming, canoeing, and rafting are popular pursuits. You can fashion a short float trip around the camp peninsula by putting in at the upstream end of the river bend and taking out downstream.

96 China Hat

Location: About 65 miles southeast of Bend
Season: April–November
Sites: 14 basic sites; no hookups
Maximum length: 30 feet

Bend Area

	Hookup sites	Total sites	Maximum RV length	Hookups	Toilets	Showers	Drinking water	Dump station	Recreation	Fee	Can reserve
94 Big River		11	26		NF				FBL	$	
95 Bull Bend		12	30		NF				SFBL	$	
96 China Hat		14	30		NF		•				
97 Cow Meadow		21	26		NF				FBL	$	
98 Crane Prairie		140	30		NF		•		FBL	$$	
99 Cultus Corral Horse Camp		11	30		NF		•		R	$	
100 Cultus Lake		55	25		NF		•		HSFBL	$$	
101 Deschutes Bridge		12	30		NF		•		F	$	
102 East Davis		10	40		NF		•		FB	$	
103 Elk Lake		21	25		NF		•		HSFBL	$$	
104 Fall River		10	25		NF				F	$	
105 Gull Point		79	30		F,NF		•	•	FBL	$$	
106 La Pine State Recreation Area	137	145	85	WES	F	•	•	•	HSFBL	$$	•
107 Lava Lake		43	30		NF		•		HFBL	$$	
108 Little Cultus		10	30		NF		•		HFBL	$	
109 Little Fawn		20	30		NF		•		HFBL	$	
110 Little Lava Lake		12	26		NF		•		FBL	$	
111 Mallard Marsh		15	25		NF				FBL	$	
112 McKay Crossing		10	26		NF				HF	$	
113 Newberry NVM: Chief Paulina Horse Camp		14	26		NF				HFBR	$$	
114 Newberry NVM: Cinder Hill		110	30		F,NF		•		HFBL	$$	
115 Newberry NVM: East Lake		29	26		F,NF		•		HSFBL	$$	
116 Newberry NVM: Hot Springs		50	26		NF		•		HFBL	$$	
117 Newberry NVM: Little Crater		50	30		NF		•		HFBL	$$	
118 Newberry NVM: Paulina Lake		69	30		NF		•		HFBL	$$	
119 North Davis Creek		17	25		NF		•		FBL	$	
120 North Lava Flow		25	25		NF				FBL	$	
121 North Twin		19	30		NF		•		HSFBL	$	
122 Pine Mountain		12	30		NF						
123 Point		9	25		NF				HSFBL	$	
124 Prairie		16	30		NF		•		HF	$$	
125 Pringle Falls		7	25		NF				FB	$	
126 Quinn Meadow Horse Camp		24	30		NF		•		HR	$$	•
127 Quinn River		41	30		NF		•		HFBL	$$	

Bend Area (continued)

	Hookup sites	Total sites	Maximum RV length	Hookups	Toilets	Showers	Drinking water	Dump station	Recreation	Fee	Can reserve
128 Reservoir		28	30		NF				FBL	$	
129 Rock Creek		31	30		NF		•		FBL	$	
130 Rosland	5	11	40	WES	F		•	•	F	$$	
131 Sand Spring		5	25		NF				O		
132 Sheep Bridge		18	30		NF		•		FBL	$	
133 Soda Creek		10	25		NF				F		
134 South		23	26		NF				FBL	$	
135 South Twin		24	26		F,NF		•		HSFBL	$$	
136 Swamp Wells Horse Camp		6	25		NF				HOR		
137 Todd Creek Horse Camp		8	30		NF				R	NWF Pass	
138 Tumalo State Park	23	90	44	WES	F	•	•		SF	$$–$$$	•
139 West South Twin		24	30		F,NF		•		HSFBL	$$	
140 Wickiup Butte		10	25		NF				FBL	$	
141 Wyeth		4	25		NF				FB	$	

Facilities: Tables, grills, vault toilets, drinking water
Fee per night: None
Management: Deschutes National Forest
Contact: (541) 383–4000; www.fs.fed.us/r6/centraloregon/recreation
Finding the campground: From U.S. Highway 97 at La Pine (about 30 miles south of Bend), head east on Forest Road 22. Go 26.4 miles, turn left (north) onto FR 18, and continue 5.9 miles to the camp entry road on the left.
About the campground: This primitive camp sits south of its namesake peak in a forest that has been greatly thinned to eliminate an insect infestation. The camp offers solitude and bird watching and serves the fall hunter. En route to camp, you will pass South Ice Cave; it is north off FR 22, 1.2 miles west of the intersection with FR 18.

97 Cow Meadow

Location: About 47 miles southwest of Bend, on Crane Prairie Reservoir
Season: May–mid-October
Sites: 21 basic sites; no hookups
Maximum length: 26 feet
Facilities: Tables, grills, vault toilets, boat launch; no drinking water
Fee per night: $
Management: Deschutes National Forest
Contact: (541) 383–4000; www.fs.fed.us/r6/centraloregon/recreation

Finding the campground: From Bend, head southwest on Cascade Lakes Highway, which is variously labeled Century Drive, County Road 46, or Forest Road 46. Go 45 miles and turn left onto FR 40. Go 0.4 mile and then turn right onto gravel FR 970. Continue 2 miles on FR 970 and FR 620. The campground entrance is on the right off FR 620 just after you cross the bridge over the Deschutes River.

About the campground: Along the Deschutes River where it feeds into Crane Prairie Reservoir, you will find this quiet camp in the lodgepole pines. The sites are rustic and open. Boaters are restricted to a speed of 10 miles per hour, and anglers have a choice of dipping their line in the river or the reservoir. Ospreys commonly patrol over the water.

98 Crane Prairie

Location: About 48 miles southwest of Bend, on Crane Prairie Reservoir
Season: Mid-April–mid-October
Sites: 140 basic sites; no hookups
Maximum length: 30 feet
Facilities: Tables, grills, vault toilets, drinking water, 2 boat launches, dock, fish-cleaning station
Fee per night: $$
Management: Deschutes National Forest
Contact: (541) 383–4000; www.fs.fed.us/r6/centraloregon/recreation
Finding the campground: From U.S. Highway 97 at Wickiup Junction, 27 miles south of Bend, head west on County Road 43 and then Forest Road 42, traveling a total of 16.5 miles. Turn right (north) onto FR 4270 and proceed 4.2 miles to this camp on the left.

About the campground: The sites of this campground are distributed across a gentle slope of lodgepole pines above and along Crane Prairie Reservoir, which is noted for its nesting ospreys. Despite the size of this camp, the sites are nicely arranged for comfort, and they are partially or fully shaded by the mature trees. Views of the reservoir, its sculpted shore, Mount Bachelor, South Sister, and Broken Top will enhance your stay. Fishing, boating, birding, and relaxing will fill your days.

99 Cultus Corral Horse Camp

Location: About 45 miles southwest of Bend
Season: Late May–mid-October
Sites: 11 basic sites; no hookups
Maximum length: 30 feet
Facilities: Tables, grills, vault toilets, drinking water, community shelter, 4-horse corral at each site
Fee per night: $
Management: Deschutes National Forest
Contact: (541) 383–4000; www.fs.fed.us/r6/centraloregon/recreation
Finding the campground: From Bend, head southwest on Cascade Lakes

Highway, which is variously labeled Century Drive, County Road 46, or Forest Road 46. Go 45 miles and turn right onto gravel Forest Road 4630. Proceed 0.4 mile and turn left to enter the camp.

About the campground: This horse camp rests in a cutover forest of lodgepole pines near the Cultus River. The facility is one of a growing number in the state catering to equestrians. There is a trailhead in the camp and other horse trails a short drive away. Check with the Bend Ranger District about specific rides. This particular camp is sunny and dry, so you might want to bring a shade source.

100 Cultus Lake

Location: About 48 miles southwest of Bend, on Cultus Lake
Season: Late May–September
Sites: 55 basic sites; no hookups
Maximum length: 25 feet
Facilities: Tables, grills, vault toilets, drinking water, boat launch
Fee per night: $$
Management: Deschutes National Forest
Contact: (541) 383–4000; www.fs.fed.us/r6/centraloregon/recreation
Finding the campground: From Bend, head southwest on Cascade Lakes Highway, which is variously labeled Century Drive, County Road 46, or Forest Road 46. Go 46 miles, turn right onto Forest Road 4635, and go 2 miles to enter the camp.

About the campground: This campground offers pleasant, forested sites just above Cultus Lake, a large, natural lake open to boating, fishing, swimming, waterskiing, sailing, and sailboarding. During the day, the area resounds with the roar of boat motors, laughing voices, and general bustle; by night it quiets down. The camp offers direct access to the Winopee Trail, which leads into Three Sisters Wilderness and visits a series of tranquil, high-mountain lakes. Other trails lead from Cultus Lake to Deer and Little Cultus Lakes.

101 Deschutes Bridge

Location: About 41 miles southwest of Bend
Season: Late May–October
Sites: 12 basic sites; no hookups
Maximum length: 30 feet
Facilities: Tables, grills, vault toilets, drinking water
Fee per night: $
Management: Deschutes National Forest
Contact: (541) 383–4000; www.fs.fed.us/r6/centraloregon/recreation
Finding the campground: From Bend, head southwest on Cascade Lakes Highway, which is variously labeled Century Drive, County Road 46, or Forest Road 46. Go 41 miles and turn left (east) onto Forest Road 4270, where you will immediately cross the Deschutes River bridge. Upon crossing, enter the camp on the right.

About the campground: This camp is just off Cascade Lakes Highway in a dense stand of lodgepole pines along a pretty section of the Upper Deschutes River. Here, the river flows narrow, dark, and fast between verdant banks of grass and wildflowers. Giant lupines, false hellebores, bog orchids, and Indian paintbrushes strike a dramatic contrast to the barren ground in the camp. Fishing and birding are popular camp pursuits, and the scenic highway serves as a gateway for sightseers.

102 East Davis

Location: About 65 miles southwest of Bend, on Davis Lake
Season: April–mid-October
Sites: 10 basic sites; no hookups
Maximum length: 40 feet
Facilities: Tables, grills, vault toilets, drinking water
Fee per night: $
Management: Deschutes National Forest
Contact: (541) 433-3200; www.fs.fed.us/r6/centraloregon/recreation
Finding the campground: From Oregon 58, 3.4 miles east of Crescent Lake, turn northeast onto Crescent Cut-off Road, go 3.2 miles to Forest Road 46, and turn left. From U.S. Highway 97 at Crescent, you would go about 9 miles west on County Road 61 (the Crescent Cut-off Road) to FR 46 and turn right. Follow FR 46 north 7.8 miles and turn left onto FR 850. You will come to a T-junction in 0.2 mile. Go left on FR 855 and drive 1.9 miles to the camp entrance on the right.
About the campground: This campground sits alongside Odell Creek on the south shore of Davis Lake; some sites overlook the lakeshore. Views include Maiden Peak, South Sister, Broken Top, and Mount Bachelor. The sites, however, are shadeless. The fire of 2003 swept three-quarters of camp, sparing only the lakeshore, but new grasses have already returned. A lava flow, which dammed the creek, formed this natural lake. Because the lake is a good food source for birds, naturalists will want to keep their binoculars handy. Only fly-fishing is allowed. The lake level fluctuates from year to year, depending on snowfall.

103 Elk Lake

Location: About 31 miles southwest of Bend, on Elk Lake
Season: June–September
Sites: 21 basic sites; no hookups
Maximum length: 25 feet
Facilities: Tables, grills, vault toilets, drinking water, boat launch
Fee per night: $$
Management: Deschutes National Forest
Contact: (541) 383-4000; www.fs.fed.us/r6/centraloregon/recreation
Finding the campground: From Bend, head southwest on Cascade Lakes Highway, which is variously labeled Century Drive, County Road 46, or Forest Road 46. Go 31 miles and turn left into the camp.

About the campground: Lodgepole pines enfold this campground on the north shore of Elk Lake. While the camp has a couple of pull-through sites, many of the sites offer uneven or otherwise difficult parking, so RVers will need to search for the ideal site. Elk Lake is a 390-acre natural lake that hosts boating (10 miles per hour limit), fishing, and sailboarding. A lakeside resort rents boats. Hiking, too, is popular. Across the lake, you can see Mount Bachelor peeking over a ridge.

104 Fall River

Location: About 30 miles southwest of Bend
Season: April–October
Sites: 10 basic sites; no hookups
Maximum length: 25 feet
Facilities: Tables, grills, vault toilet; no drinking water
Fee per night: $
Management: Deschutes National Forest
Contact: (541) 383–4000; www.fs.fed.us/r6/centraloregon/recreation
Finding the campground: From U.S. Highway 97, 17.5 miles south of Bend, 4.9 miles north of the turnoff for La Pine State Recreation Area, turn west onto Forest Road 42 (labeled Vandevert Road and then South Century Drive) and go 12.2 miles to this camp.
About the campground: This camp, which rests in a thinned stand of lodgepole and small ponderosa pines, receives only patchy shade. A sparkling, shallow stretch of spring-fed Fall River flows below the camp. It is open to fly-fishing only. Fall River Fish Hatchery is 3.2 miles northeast of the camp on FR 42.

105 Gull Point

Location: About 46 miles southwest of Bend, on Wickiup Reservoir
Season: Mid-April–mid-October
Sites: 79 basic sites; no hookups
Maximum length: 30 feet
Facilities: Tables, grills, vault and flush toilets, drinking water, dump station, boat launch, fish-cleaning station
Fee per night: $$
Management: Deschutes National Forest
Contact: (541) 383–4000; www.fs.fed.us/r6/centraloregon/recreation
Finding the campground: From U.S. Highway 97 at Wickiup Junction, 27 miles south of Bend, go west on County Road 43 and Forest Road 42 for 15.6 miles. Turn left onto FR 4260 and go 3 miles to the camp entrance on the right.
About the campground: This large camp occupies a peninsula where the Deschutes River Channel meets the main body of Wickiup Reservoir. Davis Mountain and Maiden Peak can be admired from the campground shore. The sites have a nice complement of natural vegetation, and a few big ponderosa pines draw the eyes skyward. Gulls and ospreys fish the reservoir. At the main

reservoir, activities range from fishing and boating to waterskiing, yet the area is wild enough that deer and elk may be seen in the vicinity of the camp. As the water level is drawn down in late summer, marshy areas commingle with the open water.

106 La Pine State Recreation Area

Location: About 27 miles southwest of Bend
Season: Year-round
Sites: 137 full or partial hookup sites, 3 yurts, 5 cabins; water, electric, and sewer hookups
Maximum length: 85 feet
Facilities: Tables, flush toilets, drinking water, showers, dump station, meeting hall
Fee per night: $$
Management: Oregon State Parks and Recreation Department
Contact: (541) 536–2071; (800) 452–5687 for reservations; www.oregonstate parks.org
Finding the campground: From U.S. Highway 97, about 22 miles south of Bend, take the marked turn for the state recreation area and head west. You will reach the campground in just over 5 miles.
About the campground: Site of Oregon's largest ponderosa pine, this state park offers a pleasant camp and day-use area along the Deschutes River and within easy access of the sights and activities of Newberry National Volcanic Monument. Above the river, the camp offers developed, easy-to-access sites in an open stand of lodgepole and small ponderosa pines. The sites with sewers are more closely spaced. Near camp, a trail travels along the rim overlooking the river. A small, gravelly beach at the day-use area is available for unguarded swimming. Because the park terrain does not lend itself to easy river access, anglers may need to do some scouting. A 1,000-foot, paved path descends to Big Tree, the 500-year-old ponderosa pine with a diameter of 8.6 feet.

107 Lava Lake

Location: About 39 miles southwest of Bend, on Lava Lake
Season: April–mid-October
Sites: 43 basic sites; no hookups
Maximum length: 30 feet
Facilities: Tables, grills, vault toilets, drinking water, boat launch
Fee per night: $$
Management: Deschutes National Forest
Contact: (541) 383–4000; www.fs.fed.us/r6/centraloregon/recreation
Finding the campground: From Bend, head southwest on Cascade Lakes Highway, which is variously labeled Century Drive, County Road 46, or Forest Road 46. Go about 38 miles and turn left (east) onto FR 4600.500. Proceed another mile to the camp.
About the campground: Here, on scenic Lava Lake, the campground and

day-use area sit next door to rustic Lava Lake Resort. The campsites occupy a thinned stand of lodgepole pines, while the day-use tables overlook an attractive, multihued wetland. The scalloped shore of Lava Lake is well suited for canoeing. In keeping with the tranquil mood of the lake, the boat speed is limited to 10 miles per hour. Near the boat ramp is Lava Lake Trailhead, a gateway to other area lakes and Edison Ice Cave. Views from the shore include South Sister, Broken Top, and Mount Bachelor.

108 Little Cultus

Location: About 50 miles southwest of Bend, on Little Cultus Lake
Season: Late May–mid-October
Sites: 10 basic sites; no hookups
Maximum length: 30 feet
Facilities: Tables, grills, vault toilets, drinking water, boat launch
Fee per night: $
Management: Deschutes National Forest
Contact: (541) 383-4000; www.fs.fed.us/r6/centraloregon/recreation
Finding the campground: From Bend, head southwest on Cascade Lakes Highway, which is variously labeled Century Drive, County Road 46, or Forest Road 46. Go 46 miles and turn right onto FR 4635. Follow it 0.8 mile and turn left onto gravel FR 4630. Stay on it for 1.7 miles, turn right onto FR 4636, and continue 1 mile to the campground.
About the campground: This appealing campground rests among lodgepole pines on the shore of Little Cultus Lake. Logs frame the camp roads and sites, and in places the lupine is quite lovely. This lake offers a quieter recreational experience than its larger companion, Cultus Lake, where waterskiing is allowed. At Little Cultus, the pace is typically slower and the crowd more sedate. Boats are restricted to a speed of 10 miles per hour. As you troll the waters, you can lean back and enjoy views of Cultus Butte and the distant High Cascades. Area trails lead to Cultus Lake and to mountain lakes in the Three Sisters Wilderness Area.

109 Little Fawn

Location: About 37 miles southwest of Bend, on Elk Lake
Season: June–September
Sites: 20 basic sites; no hookups
Maximum length: 30 feet
Facilities: Tables, grills, vault toilets, drinking water, boat launch
Fee per night: $
Management: Deschutes National Forest
Contact: (541) 383-4000; www.fs.fed.us/r6/centraloregon/recreation
Finding the campground: From Bend, head southwest on Cascade Lakes Highway, which is variously labeled Century Drive, County Road 46, or Forest Road 46. Go 35.5 miles and turn left (east) onto FR 4625, a paved and gravel route, to reach the camp entrance in 1.7 miles.

About the campground: This camp claims a slope on the southeast shore of Elk Lake. A few firs help fill out the lodgepole pine forest. Although some sites are right along shore, all are within easy access of this large, natural lake. Among the recreational opportunities are boating (10 miles per hour limit), fishing, sailboarding, and hiking the Elk Lake Trail, which links the lake recreation sites and delivers new perspectives on the area.

110 Little Lava Lake

Location: About 40 miles southwest of Bend, on Little Lava Lake
Season: April–October
Sites: 12 basic sites; no hookups
Maximum length: 26 feet
Facilities: Tables, grills, vault toilets, drinking water, boat launch
Fee per night: $
Management: Deschutes National Forest
Contact: (541) 383–4000; www.fs.fed.us/r6/centraloregon/recreation
Finding the campground: From Bend, head southwest on Cascade Lakes Highway, which is variously labeled Century Drive, County Road 46, or Forest Road 46. After about 38 miles, turn left (east) onto FR 4600.500. Go 0.7 mile, turn right onto FR 4600.520, and drive another 0.4 mile to the camp.
About the campground: Despite its name, Little Lava Lake is good-sized but smaller than neighboring Lava Lake. It appeals to canoeists because of its beautiful wetland shore and views of Broken Top and Mount Bachelor. The campsites are well spaced in a lodgepole pine forest above the shore. If you enjoy birding, you may spot swallows, ospreys, gulls, ducks, and cormorants at the lake; nuthatches and other woodland varieties in the forest.

111 Mallard Marsh

Location: About 37 miles southwest of Bend, on Hosmer Lake
Season: Late May–October
Sites: 15 basic sites; no hookups
Maximum length: 25 feet
Facilities: Tables, grills, vault toilets, canoe launch (electric motors allowed); no drinking water
Fee per night: $
Management: Deschutes National Forest
Contact: (541) 383–4000; www.fs.fed.us/r6/centraloregon/recreation
Finding the campground: From Bend, head southwest on Cascade Lakes Highway, which is variously labeled Century Drive, County Road 46, or Forest Road 46. Go 35.5 miles and turn left (east) onto FR 4625. Follow it for 1.2 miles and turn right into the camp.
About the campground: A combination of wetland and open water, Hosmer Lake is a picturesque place to canoe. It is stocked with trout and Atlantic salmon for catch-and-release fly-fishing only. Birders and naturalists are drawn here. The upper segment of the lake is three to four times bigger than

Canoeing on Hosmer Lake.

the lower lake; Mount Bachelor and Red Crater are reflected in the open water. The camp is in a tranquil forest of lodgepole pines and firs, and Elk Lake is close by (only about 5 miles to the north) for swimming, sailboarding, or watching the sun set from its Sunset View Picnic Area.

112 McKay Crossing

Location: About 29 miles south of Bend
Season: April–September
Sites: 10 basic sites; no hookups
Maximum length: 26 feet
Facilities: Tables, grills, vault toilets; no drinking water
Fee per night: $
Management: Deschutes National Forest
Contact: (541) 383–4000; www.fs.fed.us/r6/centraloregon/recreation
Finding the campground: From U.S. Highway 97, 23.5 miles south of Bend, turn east onto Forest Road 21, continue 3.2 miles, and turn left onto FR 2120. Go another 2.2 miles to reach the camp.

About the campground: This Paulina Creek campground offers quiet, fairly private sites in a setting of lodgepole and small ponderosa pines. From camp, you can access the Peter Skene Ogden National Recreation Trail, which travels upstream 6 miles to Paulina Lake and caters to multiple use: It is open to foot, horse, and mountain bike travel. Lower Paulina Falls, a picturesque, 25-foot falls on the main creek, is only 500 feet from camp. The many attractions of Newberry National Volcanic Monument (see below) are within easy reach by vehicle.

113 Newberry National Volcanic Monument: Chief Paulina Horse Camp

Location: About 37 miles south of Bend
Season: Late May–October
Sites: 14 basic sites; no hookups
Maximum length: 26 feet
Facilities: Tables, grills, vault toilets, corrals, water for horses; no drinking water
Fee per night: $$
Management: Deschutes National Forest
Contact: (541) 383–4000; www.fs.fed.us/r6/centraloregon/recreation
Finding the campground: From U.S. Highway 97, 23.5 miles south of Bend, head east on Forest Road 21 for 13.9 miles to enter this camp on the right.
About the campground: Situated across FR 21 from Paulina Lake, this equestrian camp puts you right in the heart of Newberry Volcano and gives you easy access to the scenic and recreational opportunities of the area. The camp is in a pleasant, dry forest setting. Area trail rides include tours of the Newberry Crater, Paulina Peak, and Peter Skene Ogden Trails; find the Newberry Crater Trail where it passes through the camp. You can expect dusty trail conditions. Besides riding, you can also fish and boat at Paulina Lake or its twin, East Lake.

114 Newberry National Volcanic Monument: Cinder Hill

Location: About 42 miles south of Bend, on East Lake
Season: Late May–October
Sites: 110 basic sites; no hookups
Maximum length: 30 feet
Facilities: Tables, grills, vault and flush toilets, drinking water, boat launch
Fee per night: $$
Management: Deschutes National Forest
Contact: (541) 383–4000; www.fs.fed.us/r6/centraloregon/recreation
Finding the campground: From U.S. Highway 97, 23.5 miles south of Bend, head east on Forest Road 21 for 17.6 miles. Turn left (north) onto FR 2100.700 and go 0.5 mile to the camp.
About the campground: This camp stretches for 0.7 mile through lodgepole pine forest on the east shore of East Lake. The twin caldera lakes of Newberry

Volcano—East and Paulina—were formed in much the same manner as Crater Lake, and they are equally blue and clear. At camp, grassy spits extend into the lake, shaping quiet coves that attract ducks. East Lake (see below) is a favorite with boaters and anglers, and a rustic resort nearby rents boats. Newberry National Volcanic Monument boasts a superb trail system for hiking, mountain biking, and horseback riding; birding and sightseeing also engage guests. Pumice and ash domes, obsidian slopes, stone pillars, and waterfalls are among the area sights.

115 Newberry National Volcanic Monument: East Lake

Location: About 40 miles southeast of Bend, on East Lake
Season: Late May–October
Sites: 29 basic sites; no hookups
Maximum length: 26 feet
Facilities: Tables, grills, vault and flush toilets, drinking water, boat launch
Fee per night: $$
Management: Deschutes National Forest

Paulina Peak from East Lake.

Contact: (541) 383–4000; www.fs.fed.us/r6/centraloregon/recreation
Finding the campground: From U.S. Highway 97, 23.5 miles south of Bend, turn east onto Forest Road 21 and continue 16.6 miles to the camp entrance on the left.
About the campground: On the south shore of 1,000-acre East Lake, these campsites sit close together in a stand of lodgepole pines. East Lake is one of a pair of deep-water lakes contained in the collapsed bowl of Newberry Volcano. The lake is popular with boaters and with anglers, who vie for rainbow and German brown trout, kokanee, and salmon. A sandy beach is found at the boat launch, and fine trails explore the geologic wonderland of Newberry National Volcanic Monument.

116 Newberry National Volcanic Monument: Hot Springs

Location: About 41 miles southeast of Bend
Season: July–September (only open during high-use periods)
Sites: 50 basic sites; no hookups
Maximum length: 26 feet
Facilities: Tables, grills, vault toilets, drinking water
Fee per night: $$
Management: Deschutes National Forest
Contact: (541) 383–4000; www.fs.fed.us/r6/centraloregon/recreation
Finding the campground: From U.S. Highway 97, 23.5 miles south of Bend, turn east onto Forest Road 21, continue 17.2 miles, and turn right into the camp.
About the campground: This campground is nestled among the lodgepole pines at the foot of a lava flow across the road from East Lake. There is lake access as well as a boat ramp at a day-use area across FR 21 from the camp. A slight odor of sulfur hints at the hot springs at the bottom of the lake. Newberry Crater Trail is accessible from the camp; other easy-to-access trails explore lake, creek, falls, and volcanic attractions. Carry plenty of water as the trails are dusty.

117 Newberry National Volcanic Monument: Little Crater

Location: About 39 miles south of Bend, on Paulina Lake
Season: Late May–October
Sites: 50 basic sites; no hookups
Maximum length: 30 feet
Facilities: Tables, grills, vault toilets, drinking water, boat launch (near entry to camp)
Fee per night: $$
Management: Deschutes National Forest
Contact: (541) 383–4000; www.fs.fed.us/r6/centraloregon/recreation
Finding the campground: From U.S. Highway 97, 23.5 miles south of Bend, turn east onto Forest Road 21. Go 14.5 miles, turn left (north) onto FR 2100.570, and proceed 0.5 mile to the camp.

About the campground: This camp stretches for a half mile through lodgepole pines along the east shore of Paulina Lake, one of two big, clear, azure-blue lakes cradled in Newberry Crater; East Lake is the other. A shoreline trail rings Paulina Lake, traversing forest, obsidian flow, and slopes dotted with junipers and manzanitas. Besides lake views, the trail serves up fine looks at craggy Paulina Peak on the southern skyline. The Peter Skene Ogden and Paulina Falls Trails explore the banks of the outlet. Boating (10 miles per hour speed limit), fishing, birding, mountain biking, horseback riding, and sightseeing are other potential pastimes. The winding, sometimes rough, drive to the top of Paulina Peak delivers a jaw-dropping vista of the Cascade volcanoes, the caldera lakes, Paulina Pinnacles, and Fort Rock.

118 Newberry National Volcanic Monument: Paulina Lake

Location: About 36 miles south of Bend, on Paulina Lake
Season: Late May–October
Sites: 69 basic sites; no hookups
Maximum length: 30 feet
Facilities: Tables, grills, vault toilets, drinking water, boat launch
Fee per night: $$
Management: Deschutes National Forest
Contact: (541) 383–4000; www.fs.fed.us/r6/centraloregon/recreation
Finding the campground: From U.S. Highway 97, 23.5 miles south of Bend, turn east onto Forest Road 21, go 12.9 miles, and turn left into the camp.
About the campground: Below Paulina Peak, on the south shore of picture-pretty Paulina Lake, you will find these closely spaced campsites among the lodgepole pines. This is one of two azure-blue lakes cradled in Newberry Crater; East Lake is the other. From camp, you will find easy access to the Paulina Lake, Peter Skene Ogden, and Paulina Falls Trails, as well as to fishing, sailing, and boating (10 miles per hour limit) on Paulina Lake. Sightseeing stops and short hikes unravel the volcanic story of Newberry Volcano.

119 North Davis Creek

Location: 56 miles southwest of Bend, on Wickiup Reservoir
Season: April–September
Sites: 17 basic sites; no hookups
Maximum length: 25 feet
Facilities: Tables, grills, vault toilets, drinking water, boat launch
Fee per night: $
Management: Deschutes National Forest
Contact: (541) 383–4000; www.fs.fed.us/r6/centraloregon/recreation
Finding the campground: From Bend, head southwest on Cascade Lakes Highway, which is variously labeled Century Drive, County Road 46, or Forest Road 46. Go 56 miles and turn left to enter the camp.
About the campground: This campground occupies a stand of young lodgepole pines on a long inlet arm of Wickiup Reservoir. In the late 1980s, the site

Paulina Pillars at Newberry National Volcanic Monument.

was logged due to a pine beetle infestation. Sparkling North Davis Creek merges with the reservoir here. The inlet bay is clear and quickly grows deep, but the sandy shore broadens as the water level drops later in the year. Although a poor shade source, the tight array of trees contributes a bit of privacy to sites. Besides fishing and boating, you can lace on the hiking boots and head for Moore Creek Trailhead. Hike destinations include Davis, Bobby, and Charlton Lakes and Gerdine Butte and The Twins. You can reach the trailhead by taking the signed road across the highway from the camp.

120 North Lava Flow

Location: 65 miles southwest of Bend, on Davis Lake
Season: May–October
Sites: 25 basic sites; no hookups
Maximum length: 25 feet
Facilities: Tables, fire rings, vault toilets, boat ramp; no drinking water

Fee per night: $
Management: Deschutes National Forest
Contact: (541) 433–3200; www.fs.fed.us/r6/centraloregon/recreation
Finding the campground: From Oregon 58, 3.4 miles east of Crescent Lake, turn northeast onto Crescent Cut-off Road, go 3.2 miles to Forest Road 46, and turn left. From U.S. Highway 97 at Crescent, you would go about 9 miles west on County Road 61 (the Crescent Cut-off Road) to FR 46 and turn right. Follow FR 46 north for 7.8 miles and turn left onto FR 850. You will come to a T-junction in 0.2 mile. Head right to reach the camp in 1.6 miles.
About the campground: This family campground rests in a mixed forest alongside a lava flow at Davis Lake, a large natural lake. Fire, though, has altered the vegetation of the lake basin. The camp's southern counterpart, consisting of 3 dispersed sites, expands the camping opportunity after September. Until then, nesting bald eagles have the sole occupancy of South Lava Flow Campground. Davis Lake is open to fly-fishing only. Because the shallow lake provides essential habitat for wildlife, small, quiet boats are in order.

121 North Twin

Location: About 43 miles southwest of Bend, on North Twin Lake
Season: April–October
Sites: 19 basic sites; no hookups
Maximum length: 30 feet
Facilities: Tables, grills, vault toilets, drinking water, boat launch
Fee per night: $
Management: Deschutes National Forest
Contact: (541) 383–4000; www.fs.fed.us/r6/centraloregon/recreation
Finding the campground: From the Wickiup Junction on U.S. Highway 97, 27 miles south of Bend, turn west onto County Road 43, go 11 miles, and continue west on Forest Road 42 for another 4.6 miles. Turn left onto FR 4260, go 0.2 mile, and turn left into the camp.
About the campground: This campground in the pines sits on the shore of perfectly round North Twin Lake. The sites have gravel parking and not much privacy, given the open spacing of the trees and the lack of ground vegetation. The postcard-pretty lake edged with grasses and snags invites quiet boating (no motors allowed), swimming, and fishing. A trail leads 1 mile from the camp to the lake's mirror image, South Twin Lake, where there is a rustic resort.

122 Pine Mountain

Location: About 33 miles southeast of Bend
Season: April–November
Sites: 12 basic sites; no hookups
Maximum length: 30 feet
Facilities: Tables, vault toilets; no drinking water
Fee per night: None

Management: Deschutes National Forest
Contact: (541) 383-4000; www.fs.fed.us/r6/centraloregon/recreation
Finding the campground: From Bend, go east on U.S. Highway 20 for 25 miles to Millican and turn south onto Pine Mountain Road/FR 2017, leaving the pavement. Go 7.7 miles toward Pine Mountain Observatory to reach the camp. Much of the winding route is on washboard.
About the campground: Near the University of Oregon Pine Mountain Observatory, you will find this campground among the pines at an elevation of 6,250 feet. Lupine and bunchgrasses pierce the needle mat. The observatory operates three telescopes and is typically open to the public on Friday and Saturday evenings, from Memorial Day weekend through the last weekend in September; a donation is suggested, and "dark moons" are the best times to visit. Amateur astronomers bring their own telescopes to the lofty locale. Although stargazing is the chief activity, birders enjoy the spot, too. The open sage summit also supplies panoramic views of the encompassing forest, the Cascade volcanoes, and the High Desert. There are no open fires during summer and fall because of fire danger, but it also preserves the viewing darkness. Keep the noise down during the day so as not to disturb the astronomers' sleep.

123 Point

Location: 34 miles southwest of Bend, on Elk Lake
Season: June–October
Sites: 9 basic sites; no hookups
Maximum length: 25 feet
Facilities: Tables, grills, vault toilets, boat launch; no drinking water
Fee per night: $
Management: Deschutes National Forest
Contact: (541) 383-4000; www.fs.fed.us/r6/centraloregon/recreation
Finding the campground: From Bend, head southwest on Cascade Lakes Highway, which is variously labeled Century Drive, County Road 46, or Forest Road 46. Go 34 miles and turn left into the camp.
About the campground: This campground claims the forested southwest corner of Elk Lake, a large natural lake. Across the water, you can see Mount Bachelor, Broken Top, and South Sister. The lake welcomes fishing, swimming, and boating (10 miles per hour maximum). Next door to the camp is Beach Picnic Area, which offers a broad sandy beach and a nice sandy lake bottom for wading, but no lifeguard. At the picnic area, you can access the Elk Lake Trail.

124 Prairie

Location: About 27 miles south of Bend
Season: Late April–October
Sites: 16 basic sites; no hookups
Maximum length: 30 feet

Facilities: Tables, grills, vault toilets, drinking water
Fee per night: $$
Management: Deschutes National Forest
Contact: (541) 383–4000; www.fs.fed.us/r6/centraloregon/recreation
Finding the campground: From U.S. Highway 97, 23.5 miles south of Bend, turn east onto Forest Road 21, go 3.1 miles, and turn right into the camp.
About the campground: Situated in a mixed pine forest, this camp offers nice, big sites overlooking Paulina Prairie and Creek. It is a picturesque place to kick back and relax, but it also offers a base from which to explore Newberry National Volcanic Monument (see campgrounds 113–118), the Deschutes River, Wickiup Reservoir, and the Bend area.

125 Pringle Falls

Location: About 35 miles southwest of Bend
Season: April–October
Sites: 7 basic sites; no hookups
Maximum length: 25 feet
Facilities: Tables, grills, vault toilet; no drinking water
Fee per night: $
Management: Deschutes National Forest
Contact: (541) 383–4000; www.fs.fed.us/r6/centraloregon/recreation
Finding the campground: From U.S. Highway 97 at Wickiup Junction, 27 miles south of Bend, go west on County Road 43 for 7.4 miles and turn right (north) onto gravel Forest Road 4330.500. Go 0.2 mile, turn left at the camp turnoff, and continue about 0.5 mile to the camp.
About the campground: You will find this pine-shaded campground on the Deschutes River, near the parklike stands of ponderosa pines in Pringle Falls Experimental Forest. The river next to camp is deep, swift, and channel-like. Fishing, rafting, and canoeing are popular; you can put in right at camp. According to a sign at the turn onto FR 4330.500, Tetherow Boat Launch is 3 miles downstream.

126 Quinn Meadow Horse Camp

Location: About 32 miles southwest of Bend
Season: June–September
Sites: 24 basic sites; no hookups
Maximum length: 30 feet
Facilities: Tables, grills, vault toilets, drinking water, tie stalls and corrals, community shelter, manure dump
Fee per night: $$
Management: Deschutes National Forest
Contact: (541) 383–4000; (877) 444–6777 for reservations (which are required); www.fs.fed.us/r6/centraloregon/recreation
Finding the campground: From Bend, head southwest on Cascade Lakes Highway, which is variously labeled Century Drive, County Road 46, or For-

est Road 46. Go 31 miles and turn left (east) onto the camp entrance road. Follow it 0.5 mile into the camp.

About the campground: This beautiful campground caters to equestrians. Sites are dispersed among the lodgepole pines, mountain hemlocks, and firs at the edge of Quinn Meadow, a long, broad sweep of grass threaded by Quinn Creek. The sites are ample and private and encourage reclining at camp. Trails from the camp follow Quinn Creek or lead into the Three Sisters Wilderness and the Horse Lakes Area, giving riders numerous choices.

127 Quinn River

Location: About 48 miles southwest of Bend, on Crane Prairie Reservoir
Season: Mid-April–mid-September
Sites: 41 basic sites; no hookups
Maximum length: 30 feet
Facilities: Tables, grills, vault toilets, drinking water, boat launch
Fee per night: $$
Management: Deschutes National Forest
Contact: (541) 383–4000; www.fs.fed.us/r6/centraloregon/recreation
Finding the campground: From Bend, head southwest on Cascade Lakes Highway, which is variously labeled Century Drive, County Road 46, or Forest Road 46. After about 48 miles, turn left into the camp.
About the campground: This camp occupies a lodgepole pine flat along Quinn River at Crane Prairie Reservoir. The forest is semi-open as a result of a pine beetle infestation and a winter blow-down. The large boat ramp accesses a snag-riddled section of the reservoir where Quinn River empties into it. Boaters are restricted to a speed of 10 miles per hour, and there is no anchoring within 100 feet of any trees that hold osprey nests. Billy Quinn Historical Trail starts at the camp and visits Quinn River Spring (the source of this short river), the Cy Bingham lodgepole pine, and the grave of Billy Quinn, a pioneer sheepman. The trail ends at Osprey Observation Point (which can also be reached by car, less than 1 mile south on Cascade Lakes Highway). More than half of the ospreys in Oregon nest at Crane Prairie Reservoir.

128 Reservoir

Location: About 60 miles southwest of Bend, on Wickiup Reservoir
Season: April–September
Sites: 28 basic sites; no hookups
Maximum length: 30 feet
Facilities: Tables, grills, vault toilets, boat launch; no drinking water
Fee per night: $
Management: Deschutes National Forest
Contact: (541) 383–4000; www.fs.fed.us/r6/centraloregon/recreation
Finding the campground: From Bend, head southwest on Cascade Lakes Highway, which is variously labeled Century Drive, County Road 46, or Forest Road 46. Go 58 miles, turn left onto FR 44, and proceed 1.7 miles to the camp.

About the campground: This campground sprawls along a lodgepole pine flat on the southwest shore of Wickiup Reservoir. Although the pines are small, they grow densely enough to lend privacy to the campsites. You will need to bring a shade source, however. If you get a lakeside site, you can moor your boat on the sandy shore right next to your camp. At this large reservoir, boating and fishing are the primary draws; kokanee is among the catch.

129 Rock Creek

Location: About 50 miles southwest of Bend, on Crane Prairie Reservoir
Season: Mid-April–October
Sites: 31 basic sites; no hookups
Maximum length: 30 feet
Facilities: Tables, grills, vault toilets, drinking water, boat launch, fish-cleaning station
Fee per night: $
Management: Deschutes National Forest
Contact: (541) 383–4000; www.fs.fed.us/r6/centraloregon/recreation
Finding the campground: From Bend, head southwest on Cascade Lakes Highway, which is variously labeled Century Drive, County Road 46, or Forest Road 46. Go about 50 miles and turn left into the camp.
About the campground: On the west shore of Crane Prairie Reservoir, you will find this camp in a semi-open stand of lodgepole pines and bitterbrush. Cross-reservoir views are of Mount Bachelor and South Sister; Cultus Butte rises to the north. Songbirds animate the trees in the camp, while an osprey's screech may draw your eyes skyward. The camp is just 2.5 miles south of Osprey Observation Point, an interpretive and viewing site. The snags of the reservoir provide nesting sites for the lake's osprey population. Trout fishing and boating (10 miles per hour maximum) are the primary activities.

130 Rosland

Location: About 28 miles south of Bend
Season: Mid-April–mid-October
Sites: 5 hookup sites, 6 basic sites; water, electric, and sewer hookups
Maximum length: 40 feet
Facilities: Tables, grills, flush toilets, drinking water, showers, laundry
Fee per night: $$
Management: La Pine Parks and Recreation District
Contact: (541) 536–2223
Finding the campground: From U.S. Highway 97, 2 miles north of La Pine and 27 miles south of Bend, turn west onto Burgess Road toward Wickiup Reservoir and go 1.5 miles to find the campground on the left.
About the campground: Along the winding, willow-lined Little Deschutes River, this campground occupies a habitat of lodgepole pines, bitterbrush, and native grasses. Sites have limited shade. Back in the 1820s, this location was used as a base by trappers. It is lightly trafficked and peaceful, but becoming better known. Fishing is the most popular pastime.

131 Sand Spring

Location: About 41 miles southeast of Bend
Season: April–November
Sites: 5 basic sites; no hookups
Maximum length: 25 feet
Facilities: Some tables, pit toilets; no drinking water
Fee per night: None
Management: Deschutes National Forest
Contact: (541) 383–4000; www.fs.fed.us/r6/centraloregon/recreation
Finding the campground: From U.S. Highway 20, 22 miles east of Bend, turn south onto County Road 23, go 6 miles, and bear left, proceeding on Forest Road 23, a wide gravel road. Continue 12.8 miles, turn right onto FR 22, and immediately make a second right turn into the camp.
About the campground: Across the road from Sand Spring, which is ringed by a pole fence, this primitive camp is a place for the do-it-yourselfer. The camp occupies an open flat of lodgepole pines and bunchgrass surrounded by sagebrush. Your stay here can be one of uncommon solitude or one paired with engine roars: En route to camp, you may have noticed the signs indicating that you are in the East Fort Rock Off-Highway-Vehicle Area. This camp is an excellent place from which to stargaze, and it is also in the general vicinity of Lavacicle Cave. Access to this cave is restricted; it is only shown by guided tour. To make reservations, contact the Bend/Fort Rock Ranger District at the above phone number.

132 Sheep Bridge

Location: About 43 miles southwest of Bend, on Wickiup Reservoir
Season: April–October
Sites: 18 basic sites; no hookups
Maximum length: 30 feet
Facilities: Tables, grills, vault toilets, drinking water, boat launch
Fee per night: $
Management: Deschutes National Forest
Contact: (541) 383–4000; www.fs.fed.us/r6/centraloregon/recreation
Finding the campground: From U.S. Highway 97 at Wickiup Junction, 27 miles south of Bend, go west on County Road 43 and Forest Road 42 for 15.6 miles. Turn left onto FR 4260, go 0.8 mile, and turn right to reach the camp.
About the campground: You will find this small campground in a mixed age forest of lodgepole pines along the meandering Deschutes River Channel of Wickiup Reservoir. Younger trees shape the outskirts of camp; a few bigger pines within the camp afford at least some shade. The heart of the campground is open due to random parking and heavy foot traffic. Boats are limited to 10 miles per hour on the channel. Fishing is popular.

South Sister from Sparks Lake, near Soda Creek campground.

133 Soda Creek

Location: About 26 miles southwest of Bend, on Sparks Lake
Season: June–October
Sites: 10 basic sites; no hookups
Maximum length: 25 feet
Facilities: Tables, grills, vault toilets; no drinking water
Fee per night: None
Management: Deschutes National Forest
Contact: (541) 383–4000; www.fs.fed.us/r6/centraloregon/recreation
Finding the campground: From Bend, head southwest on Cascade Lakes Highway, which is variously labeled Century Drive, County Road 46, or Forest Road 46. Go 26 miles and turn left (east) onto FR 400 at the sign for Sparks Lake. Drive 0.1 mile to the camp area.
About the campground: This camp sits at the northern end of Sparks Lake and Meadow, where Soda Creek feeds into the lake. The sites are situated among the pines and firs at the edge of the meadow, which stretches for more than a mile and is almost as wide. The High Cascades contribute to views. The

area is noted for its abundance of wildlife; watch for elk, deer, and birds. Canoeing, fly-fishing, and hiking into the Three Sisters Wilderness are ways to enjoy your stay. Interpretive boards tell the history of Soda Creek, and a short drive following the signs to the trailheads on FR 400 leads to the Ray Atkeson Nature Trail. The trail honors the Oregon photographer laureate by showcasing one of his favorite images—a stunning view of Sparks Lake with South Sister and Broken Top.

134 South

Location: About 37 miles southwest of Bend, on Hosmer Lake
Season: Late May–October
Sites: 23 basic sites; no hookups
Maximum length: 26 feet
Facilities: Tables, grills, vault toilets, boat launch (at Mallard Marsh Campground); no drinking water
Fee per night: $
Management: Deschutes National Forest
Contact: (541) 383–4000; www.fs.fed.us/r6/centraloregon/recreation
Finding the campground: From Bend, head southwest on Cascade Lakes Highway, which is variously labeled Century Drive, County Road 46, or Forest Road 46. Go 35.5 miles and turn left (east) onto FR 4625. Follow it for 1.2 miles and turn right into the camp.
About the campground: Together with Mallard Marsh campground (see campground 111), this camp provides access to Hosmer Lake, a scenic wetland and open water that is stocked with trout and Atlantic salmon for catch-and-release fly-fishing only. The large lake is ideal for canoeing. You can paddle through reeds, grasses, and water lilies; watch for wildlife; and enjoy the watery reflections of Mount Bachelor and Red Crater. Like Mallard Marsh, this camp is situated among the lodgepole pines and firs.

135 South Twin

Location: About 45 miles southwest of Bend, on South Twin Lake at Wickiup Reservoir
Season: Mid-April–mid-October
Sites: 24 basic sites; no hookups
Maximum length: 26 feet
Facilities: Tables, grills, vault and flush toilets, drinking water, boat launches
Fee per night: $$
Management: Deschutes National Forest
Contact: (541) 383–4000; www.fs.fed.us/r6/centraloregon/recreation
Finding the campground: From U.S. Highway 97 at Wickiup Junction, 27 miles south of Bend, go west on County Road 43 and Forest Road 42 for 15.6 miles. Turn left onto FR 4260, go 2 miles, and turn left into the camp.
About the campground: This camp is housed in a mature forest of lodgepole and ponderosa pines along South Twin Lake, a picturesque, circular body of

water cupped by forest. Its fortress-like ring of trees differentiates it from North Twin Lake, where a grassy shore holds back the trees. A mile-long trail links the two lakes. Activities at South Twin include fishing, nonmotorized boating, and swimming. For additional fishing and boating, across FR 4260 from the camp is a boat launch on the Deschutes River Channel (10 miles per hour maximum). A neighboring resort puts a cup of espresso just strides from the camp.

136 Swamp Wells Horse Camp

Location: About 18 miles southeast of Bend
Season: April–November
Sites: 6 basic sites; no hookups
Maximum length: 25 feet
Facilities: Tables, grills, vault toilets, watering troughs; no drinking water
Fee per night: None
Management: Deschutes National Forest
Contact: (541) 383–4000; www.fs.fed.us/r6/centraloregon/recreation
Finding the campground: From U.S. Highway 97, 4 miles south of Bend, turn east onto Forest Road 18, go 5.4 miles, and turn right (south) onto FR 1810. Continue 5.8 miles, turn left (east) onto FR 1816, and drive another 3 miles to reach this camp.
About the campground: This camp occupies a cutover stand of pines and offers access to area trails and jeep tracks for horseback riding, hiking, and all-terrain-vehicle travel. Buttes in the area supply impressive vistas and make for fairly easy cross-country hikes. Although the terrain appears relatively flat, the camp occupies the skirt of Newberry Volcano, which shows a steady, gradual incline to the caldera rim. Swamp Wells Trail travels 9 miles south to the crater; the trail's northern destination is Horse Butte. If you continue east on FR 18 past its junction with FR 1810, you will come to a series of lava caves that are fun to explore but can be rugged. Carry a flashlight and two backup light sources. If you venture into Wind Cave, you will have to scramble over jumbled rock. Wear long pants, boots, gloves, and something to protect your head from the low arches and pointed lavacicles.

137 Todd Creek Horse Camp

Location: About 25 miles southwest of Bend
Season: July–October
Sites: 8 basic sites; no hookups
Maximum length: 30 feet
Facilities: Tables, grills, vault toilet, corrals; no drinking water
Fee per night: Northwest Forest Pass
Management: Deschutes National Forest
Contact: (541) 383–4000; www.fs.fed.us/r6/centraloregon/recreation
Finding the campground: From Bend, head southwest on Cascade Lakes Highway, which is variously labeled Century Drive, County Road 46, or For-

est Road 46. Go 24 miles and turn left on FR 4600.390. Proceed 0.6 mile to the horse camp.

About the campground: Below Mount Bachelor, this equestrian campground is located in the lodgepole pines at Todd Creek, but bring your own shade source. Riders find access to the long-distance Metolius–Windigo Trail, which is being set up with a series of horse camps a day's ride apart. When not on the trail, you can check out the sights and activities afforded along the scenic highway.

138 Tumalo State Park

Location: About 5 miles northwest of Bend
Season: March–November
Sites: 23 hookup sites, 58 basic sites, 7 yurts, 2 tepees, some hike/bike sites; water, electric, and sewer hookups
Maximum length: 44 feet
Facilities: Tables, grills, flush toilets, drinking water, showers, telephone, playground
Fee per night: $$–$$$
Management: Oregon State Parks and Recreation Department
Contact: (541) 382-3586; (800) 452-5687 for reservations; www.oregonstate parks.org
Finding the campground: From the junction of U.S. Highway 20 and US 97 at the north end of Bend, go west on US 20 for 3.7 miles. Turn south at the sign for the park onto the Old McKenzie–Bend Highway and proceed 1.1 miles to the campground entrance on the left. A day-use area is on the right.
About the campground: This campground rests along the Deschutes River, where the water has been drawn down for irrigation. Picturesque rocks and yellow irises may complement the water. The sites have paved parking, but some of the basic sites will require more RV leveling than others. The camp is set in a juniper forest, with a few aspen trees and grassy plots tucked between the sites. Most sites have partial shade. A designated swimming area in the day-use area is popular in summer. The attractions of Bend may call you away from the camp.

139 West South Twin

Location: About 45 miles southwest of Bend, on Wickiup Reservoir
Season: Mid-April–mid-October
Sites: 24 basic sites; no hookups
Maximum length: 30 feet
Facilities: Tables, grills, vault and flush toilets, drinking water, boat launches
Fee per night: $$
Management: Deschutes National Forest
Contact: (541) 383-4000; www.fs.fed.us/r6/centraloregon/recreation
Finding the campground: From U.S. Highway 97 at Wickiup Junction, 27 miles south of Bend, go west on County Road 43 and Forest Road 42 for 15.6

miles. Turn left onto FR 4260, go 2 miles, and turn right into the camp.

About the campground: Located along the Deschutes River Channel of Wickiup Reservoir, this structured campground retains its native ground vegetation, which contributes to the privacy of the sites and the attractiveness of the camp. Lodgepole and ponderosa pines make up the surrounding forest. From camp, you have direct access to the river channel for boating (10 miles per hour maximum) and fishing. Just across FR 4260 is South Twin Lake, where you can engage in nonmotorized boating or hike the 1-mile trail to North Twin Lake.

140 Wickiup Butte

Location: About 44 miles southwest of Bend, on Wickiup Reservoir
Season: April–October
Sites: 10 basic sites; no hookups
Maximum length: 25 feet
Facilities: Tables, grills, vault toilets, boat launch; no drinking water
Fee per night: $
Management: Deschutes National Forest
Contact: (541) 383–4000; www.fs.fed.us/r6/centraloregon/recreation
Finding the campground: From U.S. Highway 97 at Wickiup Junction, 27 miles south of Bend, go west on County Road 43 for 10.5 miles and turn left onto gravel Forest Road 4380. Go 3.6 miles, turn left onto FR 4260, and continue 2.7 to the boat area (and primitive camping) or 3 miles to the campground.

About the campground: This campground is on the east shore of Wickiup Reservoir at the foot of Wickiup Butte. It has defined sites, earthen parking, and a setting of mixed pines. Views from camp are of Davis Mountain, Maiden Peak, The Twins, and the broad, open reservoir. The small size of the camp and the gravel access roads help to keep away the crowds. Fishing, boating, birding, and waterskiing top the list of recreational pursuits. The launch is at the boating area that you pass en route to camp. There, next to the dam, you will find a 6-site no-frills camp.

141 Wyeth

Location: 8 miles west of La Pine
Season: April–October
Sites: 4 basic sites; no hookups
Maximum length: 25 feet
Facilities: Tables, grills, vault toilets, boat take-out; no drinking water
Fee per night: $
Management: Deschutes National Forest
Contact: (541) 383–4000; www.fs.fed.us/r6/centraloregon/recreation
Finding the campground: From U.S. Highway 97, 2 miles north of La Pine and 27 miles south of Bend, head west Burgess Road (County Road 43) toward

Wickiup Reservoir. Go 7.9 miles and turn left onto gravel FR 4370 at the sign for the campground. Go 0.2 and turn left into the camp.

About the campground: This rustic campground with its partly shaded sites sits beside the Deschutes River in a ponderosa pine forest punctuated by a few big yellow bellies (old-growth pines). Anglers find easy fishing access to the smooth, fast stretch of river. Birdsongs and fish splashes add to the peace found at camp.

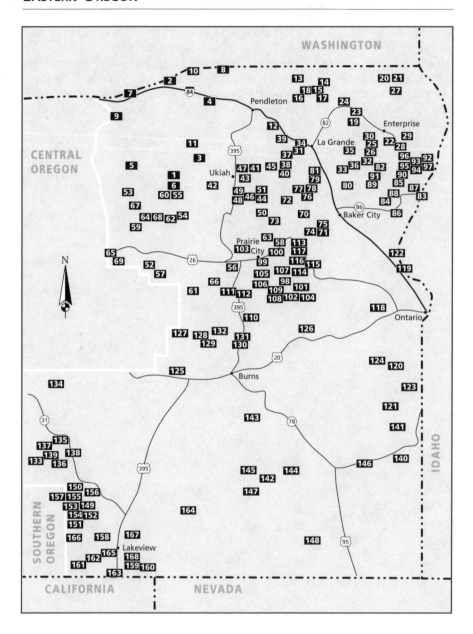

Eastern Oregon

Eastern Oregon rolls out an exciting canvas for discovery. It unites John Day Fossil Beds; Steens Mountain; the history, beauty, and wildlife of the Blue Mountains; and the chiseled, icy grandeur of the Elkhorn and Wallowa Mountains. It also cradles the harsh beauty of Hells Canyon, unbroken desert expanses, enormous desert lakes, hot springs, and the weathered orange canyonlands at the southeast corner of the state. Yes, Eastern Oregon rolls out wide-open spaces and extends a lifetime ticket to adventure. It is a land that supports black bears, coyotes, deer, antelope, elk, bighorn sheep, mountain goats, golden and bald eagles, sturgeon, and wild horses. The land wears the tracks of the Oregon Trail and the telltale signs of dashed mining hopes. Topping it all is the glittery vault of the midnight sky.

Settlement in the eastern part of the state is light and generally far-scattered. Interstate 84 strings together the larger communities at the northeast corner of the state, with Pendleton, La Grande, Baker City, and Ontario. Lakeview and Burns are the "big cities" of the southern extreme. Because of this light development, travelers need to be more self-sufficient and better prepared for the unexpected. Filling gas tanks; having a reliable spare tire, some tools, electrical tape, and other items for emergency repairs; carrying extra water and blankets; and checking on road and weather conditions are all cornerstones to safety.

This region typically experiences four seasons (although some are rushed), with extremes of heat and cold often registered. The extent of snow depends largely on elevation and your location, with regard to the storm track. Chilly dry realms or snowy wonderlands can be found in winter. Summer bakes the desert reaches, making the mountain cool all the more desirable.

Hiking, fishing, birding, horseback riding, hunting, whitewater rafting, rock collecting, boating, skiing, snowmobiling, and snowshoeing are among the active pursuits. Museums, rodeos, county fairs, and historic sites expand the region's appeal.

Columbia Plateau Area

1 Anson Wright Memorial Park

Location: 25 miles south of Heppner
Season: May–mid-November
Sites: 23 hookup sites, 20 basic/tent sites; water, electric, and sewer hookups
Maximum length: 35 feet
Facilities: Tables, fire rings, flush toilets, drinking water, showers, dump station, playground, fishing pond and creek
Fee per night: $–$$
Management: Morrow County
Contact: (541) 989–9500, reservations accepted; www.heppner.net/parks
Finding the campground: It is west off Oregon 207, 25 miles south of Heppner.
About the campground: At the foot of the western slope of Rock Creek Canyon, ponderosa pines and Douglas firs shade this quiet camp. The cool nights sometimes catch campers off guard, so keep the blankets handy. Campers will find routes to walk, and anglers can try their luck in the pond or Rock Creek. Swimming, rock hunting, and simply relaxing complete a stay.

Columbia Plateau Area

		Hookup sites	Total sites	Maximum RV length	Hookups	Toilets	Showers	Drinking water	Dump station	Recreation	Fee	Can reserve
1	Anson Wright Memorial Park	23	43	35	WES	F	•	•	•	HF	$–$$	•
2	Boardman Marina Park	63	63	80	WES	F	•	•	•	SFBL	$$$	•
3	Cutsforth County Park	20	36	35	WES	F	•	•		HF	$–$$	•
4	The Fort Henrietta RV Park	9	9	40	WES	F	•	•	•		$$	•
5	J. B. Burns Park	23	23	40	WES	F	•	•	•		$$	•
6	Morrow County OHV Park		25	none		NF		•		O	$	
7	Port of Arlington Marina and RV Park	11	31	40	WES	F		•		FBL	$–$$	
8	Sand Station Recreation Area		15	40		NF				SFB		
9	Sherman County RV Park	33	33	40	WESC	F	•	•	•		$–$$	•
10	Umatilla Marina and RV Park	26	36	60	WES	F	•	•	•	SFBL	$$–$$$	•
11	Willow Creek		23	23	40	WES	F	•	•	•	FBL	$$	•

2 Boardman Marina Park

Location: In Boardman, on Lake Umatilla
Season: Year-round, but only a handful of sites are open in winter
Sites: 63 hookup sites, tent camping area (open Friday and Saturday nights only); water, electric, and sewer hookups
Maximum length: 80 feet
Facilities: Tables, flush toilets, drinking water, showers, dump station, telephone, playground, recreation hall, sports field, horseshoe pits, marina, launch, docks
Fee per night: $$$
Management: Boardman Parks
Contact: (541) 481-7217; (888) 481-7217 for reservations: www.eoni.com /~parkdu
Finding the campground: From Interstate 84 at Boardman, take exit 164 and head north to reach the park in less than 1 mile.
About the campground: This camp rests on a grassy Columbia River flat, with leafy shade trees and wind fences at the more open sites. There are both back-in and pull-through spaces; all are paved. Lake Umatilla (the harnessed Columbia River) invites recreation, with a designated swimming area and fishing and boating. Stiff winds common to the gorge may fill the sails of sailboats and sailboards. At the day-use area, look for petroglyphs rescued from when the dam was built. Binoculars come in handy as McNary and Irrigon Wildlife Areas and Umatilla National Wildlife Refuge are all in the vicinity.

3 Cutsforth County Park

Location: 20 miles southeast of Heppner
Season: May–mid-November
Sites: 20 hookup sites, 16 basic sites; water, electric, and sewer hookups
Maximum length: 35 feet
Facilities: Tables, grills, flush toilets, drinking water, showers, playground, fishing pond, sale of ice and ice cream
Fee per night: $-$$
Management: Morrow County
Contact: (541) 989-9500, reservations accepted; www.heppner.net/parks
Finding the campground: From Oregon 207 at the south end of Heppner, turn east onto Willow Creek Road, Blue Mountain Scenic Byway, and go 20 miles to this park on the right.
About the campground: The primary campground occupies the eastern half of this park. The sites are dispersed through a mixed forest of pine, spruce, fir, and larch. The pond and a day-use area, as well as the dry camp, claim the park's more open western half. The pond is stocked with pan-sized trout and is fun for the whole family. In this natural setting, deer, bear, coyote, muskrat, and raccoons have been spied. Campers should cover and safely store food at night to prevent raccoon raids.

4   The Fort Henrietta RV Park

Location: In Echo, about 10 miles southeast of Hermiston
Season: Year-round
Sites: 9 hookup sites, open lawn for tent camping, overflow camping in gravel parking lot; water, electric, and sewer hookups
Maximum length: 40 feet
Facilities: Some tables, flush toilets, drinking water, showers, dump station, Oregon Trail interpretive panel
Fee per night: $$
Management: City of Echo
Contact: (541) 376–8411 for information and reservations; www.echo-oregon.com/fort
Finding the campground: From Interstate 84, take exit 188 and go south on Old Pendleton River Road for Echo. In 1.1 mile bear right per the trailer emblem, and in another 0.3 mile turn right on West Main in Echo. Go 0.2 mile to reach the park on the left before the Umatilla River bridge.
About the campground: Along the Umatilla River at the western edge of Echo, you will find this small, attractive city park and overnight wayside. The park recalls Oregon's past: Pioneers on the Oregon Trail camped and crossed the river here, and this was the site of the frontier post Fort Henrietta. The park's replica blockhouse recalls the old fort, as do Henrietta Days, held the second weekend in September. Then, tepees dot the park grounds, and people in buckskins mill about.

5   J. B. Burns Park

Location: In Condon
Season: Closes in winter
Sites: 23 hookup sites, tent camping area; water, electric, and sewer hookups
Maximum length: 40 feet
Facilities: Flush toilets, drinking water, showers, dump station, picnic pavilion
Fee per night: $$
Management: Gilliam County
Contact: (541) 384–5395, reservations accepted
Finding the campground: It is at Gilliam County Fairgrounds, off Oregon 19 at the north end of Condon.
About the campground: This camp serves participants and attendees of Gilliam County Fairground events as well as through travelers, when events are not ongoing. Hookup sites have gravel parking and are typically shadeless, but a few sites edge a grassy area where fir trees grow. Tent camping is allowed on a designated lawn. The park is near the Gilliam County Historical Society Museum, which features a restored 1884 log cabin and complex of early 1900s buildings.

6 Morrow County Off-Highway-Vehicle Park

Location: About 30 miles south of Heppner
Season: Year-round, except during fire danger or heavy snow
Sites: 25 basic sites; no hookups
Maximum length: None
Facilities: Tables, fire rings, portable toilets, drinking water, concession
Fee per night: $
Management: Morrow County
Contact: (541) 989–9500; www.morrowcountyparks.org
Finding the campground: From Heppner go south on Oregon 207 about 30 miles and turn left (east) onto Forest Road 21 at the marked turnoff for the park. The entrance is on the right in about 500 yards.
About the campground: Adjacent to OR 207, this campground is the product of ATV fees and the cooperative efforts of Morrow County and the Oregon Department of Parks and Recreation. At a 4,300-foot elevation, the park consists of rolling pine-clad hills, covering 6,200 acres. The park's track system allows you to match your skill level with the selected route. Quads, dirt bikes, and 4x4s are welcome, with snowmobiles picking up the slack in winter. The sites are all pull-throughs, and the camp setting intermingles pines and open grass. Ask the camp host about purchasing a map. ATV stickers are required on all off-highway vehicles.

7 Port of Arlington Marina and RV Park

Location: In Arlington
Season: Year-round
Sites: 11 RV hookup sites, 20 RV dry sites, no tent sites; water (except in winter), electric, and sewer hookups
Maximum length: 40 feet
Facilities: Some aluminum tables, flush toilets, drinking water, boat launch
Fee per night: $–$$
Management: Port of Arlington
Contact: (541) 454–2868
Finding the campground: From Interstate 84, take exit 137 and go north to the waterfront in Arlington.
About the campground: This overnight facility is located on a strip of land between the port channel and the main Columbia River. In addition to the assigned hookup sites, dry camping is allowed at the paved parking lot that overlooks the port channel. The area serves as a convenient, although sometimes noisy, overnight stop and puts boaters and anglers smack in the middle of the Columbia River action.

8   Sand Station Recreation Area

Location: About 12 miles east of Umatilla
Season: Year-round
Sites: 5 basic sites, 10 walk-in tent sites; no hookups
Maximum length: 40 feet
Facilities: Covered tables at basic sites, tables and barbecues at tent sites, vault toilets, telephone; no drinking water
Fee per night: None
Management: U.S. Army Corps of Engineers
Contact: (541) 922–2268; www.nww.usace.army.mil/corpsoutdoors/camping.htm
Finding the campground: From the intersection of Interstate 82 and U.S. Highway 730 in Umatilla, go east on US 730 for 11.5 miles to enter this camp on the left.
About the campground: On the shore of Lake Wallula sits this small, dry camp. A few black locust trees provide modest but treasured shade on this otherwise sun-drenched flat. Cross-lake views are of the steppes and tablelands of Washington State. A designated swimming area and fishing keep camp guests entertained. At night, truck travel on US 730 can break the calm.

9   Sherman County RV Park

Location: In Moro
Season: Year-round
Sites: 33 hookup sites, tent camping area; water, electric, sewer, and cable hookups
Maximum length: 40 feet
Facilities: Tables, barbeques, flush toilets, drinking water, showers, laundry, dump station, playground, horse stalls, telephone
Fee per night: $–$$
Management: Sherman County
Contact: (541) 565–3127 for information and reservations; www.shermcty.biz /rvpark
Finding the campground: From U.S. Highway 97 in Moro, turn east on First Street and go 0.8 mile to this RV park at the Sherman County Fairgrounds.
About the campground: This campground occupies an open plateau next to the Sherman County Fairgrounds and serves fairground participants and through travelers. Wheatfields spread in all directions; views feature Mounts Hood and Adams. Sites have grassy divides with young planted trees but no shade yet. Wind, a signature of the Columbia Plateau, is common here, so hold onto your paper plates. The county historical museum in town may invite a look, May through October.

10 Umatilla Marina and RV Park

Location: In Umatilla, on Lake Umatilla
Season: Year-round
Sites: 26 hookup sites, 6 basic sites, 4 tent sites; water, electric, and sewer hookups
Maximum length: 60 feet
Facilities: Tables, flush toilets, drinking water, showers, dump station, covered shelters, telephone, boat launch
Fee per night: $$–$$$
Management: Umatilla Marina
Contact: (541) 922-3939; www.nww.usace.army.mil/corpsoutdoors/camping.htm
Finding the campground: From the intersection of Interstate 82 and U.S. Highway 730, go west on US 730 for less than 0.1 mile, turn right on Brownell Boulevard, and continue 0.3 mile. Turn left on Third Street for another 0.3 mile before turning right on Quincy to enter the park.
About the campground: This is a split-level facility, with the marina and day-use area fronting the river and the campground on the upper plateau. The campground is landscaped, with lawn and planted shade trees that are starting to fill out. Sites have gravel parking and a nice spacing. Superb fishing and boating on the Columbia River (here, Lake Umatilla) attract park guests. In the day-use area, you will find a designated swimming area; elsewhere, trails lead to McNary Nature Trail and McNary National Wildlife Refuge.

11 Willow Creek

Location: About 1 mile southeast of Heppner
Season: March–October
Sites: 23 hookup sites, manager will try to accommodate tent campers; water, electric, and sewer hookups
Maximum length: 40 feet
Facilities: Some tables, flush toilets, drinking water, showers, dump station, telephone, boat launch, pool
Fee per night: $$
Management: City of Heppner
Contact: (541) 676-9618, reservations accepted; www.heppner.net/wcpd
Finding the campground: From Oregon 207 at the south end of Heppner, turn east on Willow Creek Road, Blue Mountain Scenic Byway, and go 0.6 mile to this park on the left.
About the campground: Near the dam, this campground terraces an open, grassy slope above Willow Creek Lake. The facility has paved roads and site parking and small planted trees. Awnings make for more comfortable stays. The openness allows for views of the lake and its rimming grassland hills and folded terrain. The lake supports trout, crappie, and bass. Besides anglers in fishing boats, you may see water-skiers on the reservoir.

Northern Blue Mountains

12 Emigrant Springs State Park

Location: About 26 miles southeast of Pendleton
Season: Mid-April–late October
Sites: 20 hookup sites, 32 basic sites, 3 horse campsites, 8 cabins; water, electric, and sewer hookups
Maximum length: 60 feet
Facilities: Tables, grills, flush toilets, drinking water, showers, community building, corrals at horse sites, Oregon Trail exhibit
Fee per night: $$
Management: Oregon State Parks and Recreation Department
Contact: (541) 983–2277; www.oregonstateparks.org
Finding the campground: From Interstate 84, 25 miles southeast of Pendleton, take exit 234 for the state park and follow the signs to the park on the west side of the freeway in less than 1 mile.
About the campground: This camp rests in a deep woods setting of fir and spruce just off the interstate and along the historic Oregon Trail. On a wooded rise at the north end of the park, the horse camp is isolated from both the family campground and the day-use area. Horse trails and nature trails invite exploration. Historically, the emigrants of the Oregon Trail camped here, filling their barrels at a spring. South of the park, at the Spring Creek exit, you will find another Oregon Trail site, the Forest Service's Blue Mountain Crossing interpretive site and trail, where, you can see actual ruts left by the pioneer wagons.

Northern Blue Mountains

	Hookup sites	Total sites	Maximum RV length	Hookups	Toilets	Showers	Drinking water	Dump station	Recreation	Fee	Can reserve
12 Emigrant Springs State Park	20	63	60	WES	F	•	•		HR	$$	
13 Harris Memorial Park: Gene Palmer	26	31	40	WE	F		•		HFO	$$	•
14 Jubilee Lake		50	40		F,NF		•		HFBL	$$	
15 Target Meadows		20	20		NF		•		H	$$	
16 Umatilla Forks		16	30		NF		•		HF	$	
17 Woodland		7	30		NF					$	
18 Woodward		18	20		NF		•			$$	

13 Harris Memorial Park: Gene Palmer

Location: About 13 miles southeast of Milton-Freewater
Season: Year-round; self-contained RVs only in winter
Sites: 26 hookup sites, 5 tent sites; water and electric hookups
Maximum length: 40 feet
Facilities: Tables, grills, flush toilets, drinking water; picnic shelter, playground, and horseshoe pits at day-use area
Fee per night: $$
Management: Umatilla County
Contact: (541) 938-5330, reservations accepted; www.co.umatilla.or.us /harris_park.htm
Finding the campground: At the south end of Milton-Freewater, turn east off Oregon 11 (South Main) onto Fourteenth Street, signed for Harris County Park and Upper Walla Walla River. Signs will then point you through a couple of quick turns before the road becomes Walla Walla River Road, leaving town. After 5 miles, bear right on South Fork Walla Walla River Road and proceed 7.3 miles more to the park (the final 2 miles are on gravel).
About the campground: Along the South Fork Walla Walla River, below a basalt-tiered, arid grassland hill is this comfortable county campground, with two camping areas. You may choose between the side-by-side hookup sites along a neatly trimmed lawn, or the individual hookup sites (with paved spurs) in the pine-scrub outskirts. Driving 0.4 mile past the camp, you will reach a trailhead for the South Fork Walla Walla River Trail, which dishes up a splendid river canyon tour; this trail is open to both nonmotorized and motorcycle travel.

14 Jubilee Lake

Location: About 11 miles north of Tollgate
Season: Maintained mid-June–September
Sites: 46 basic sites, 4 tent sites; no hookups
Maximum length: 40 feet
Facilities: Tables, grills, flush and vault toilets, drinking water, boat launch
Fee per night: $$
Management: Umatilla National Forest
Contact: (509) 522-6290; www.fs.fed.us/r6/uma
Finding the campground: In Tollgate (20.2 miles east of Weston, 21.8 miles west of Elgin), turn north off Oregon 204 onto gravel Forest Road 64, indicated for Target Meadows Campground and Jubilee Lake. Go 11 miles and turn right on FR 250 to enter the camp.
About the campground: Jubilee Lake is manmade, in a beautiful mountain setting. It welcomes boating (self-propelled or electric motor) and is stocked with trout. Sites claim the high-elevation forest above the lake; some are better suited for RVs than others. Most enjoy good privacy. A 2.5-mile trail, partially paved, encircles the lake, allowing for new perspectives and access for shore fishing. For more avid hikers, the Wenaha–Tucannon Wilderness lies to the lake's northeast.

15 Target Meadows

Location: About 3 miles north of Tollgate
Season: Maintained mid-June–mid-September
Sites: 20 basic sites; no hookups
Maximum length: 20 feet
Facilities: Tables, grills, vault toilets, drinking water
Fee per night: $$
Management: Umatilla National Forest
Contact: (509) 522–6290; www.fs.fed.us/r6/uma
Finding the campground: In Tollgate (20.2 miles east of Weston, 21.8 miles west of Elgin), turn north off Oregon 204 onto gravel Forest Road 64, indicated for Target Meadows Campground and Jubilee Lake. Go 0.3 mile and turn left on FR 6401. Go another 1.5 miles, and turn right on FR 050 to enter camp in 0.5 mile.
About the campground: This quiet camp occupies the spruce and true fir perimeter of Target Meadows, a moist, textured meadow expanse, which is especially pretty when the stalks of false hellebore sport creamy floral crowns. Burnt Cabin Trailhead is found at the end of FR 050; the trail from there leads to the South Fork Walla Walla River. From the 1800s to 1906, Target Meadows was used as a U.S. Army firing range; mounds in the area still hold cavalry bullets.

Camping in Umatilla National Forest.

16 Umatilla Forks

Location: About 35 miles east of Pendleton
Season: Mid-May–mid-October
Sites: 7 basic sites, 9 tent sites; no hookups
Maximum length: 30 feet
Facilities: Tables, grills, pit toilets, drinking water
Fee per night: $
Management: Umatilla National Forest
Contact: (509) 522–6290; www.fs.fed.us/r6/uma
Finding the campground: From Mission Junction, 2 miles north of Interstate 84 at exit 216, east of Pendleton, head east on Mission Road. At the intersections, follow the route indicated for Gibbon, continuing northeast along the Umatilla River for 27 miles to reach the Umatilla Forks Campground on Forest Road 32.
About the campground: Along the South Fork Umatilla River above the North Fork confluence, this linear campground, with a separate tent area, stretches below bald hills and long grassy ridges. A few pines and firs shade the sites, while cottonwoods and alders favor the riverbank. The camp offers quiet and access to trails for hiking and horseback riding; several enter the North Fork Umatilla Wilderness. Wildflowers abound, and wildlife sightings are common. Hunting, fishing, and trail bike riding (on trails outside the wilderness) are other area pursuits.

17 Woodland

Location: About 5 miles southeast of Tollgate, 17 miles northwest of Elgin
Season: Maintained mid-June–mid-September
Sites: 7 basic sites; no hookups
Maximum length: 30 feet
Facilities: Tables, grills, vault toilets; no drinking water
Fee per night: $
Management: Umatilla National Forest
Contact: (509) 522–6290; www.fs.fed.us/r6/uma
Finding the campground: It is east off Oregon 204, 16.5 miles northwest of Elgin, 5.2 miles southeast of Tollgate.
About the campground: With a single pull-through site for larger RVs, this small campground occupies a ridge forest of spruce, lodgepole pine, and western larch. Campers may choose between deep shade and partially sunny sites. The camp is convenient for travelers, relatively quiet, and serves as a base for hunters. Umatilla Breaks Viewpoint is not far from the camp.

18   Woodward

Location: West end of Tollgate
Season: Maintained mid-June–mid-September
Sites: 18 basic sites; no hookups
Maximum length: 20 feet
Facilities: Tables, grills, vault toilets, drinking water, picnic shelter
Fee per night: $$
Management: Umatilla National Forest
Contact: (509) 522–6290; www.fs.fed.us/r6/uma

Finding the campground: On the west side of Tollgate, this campground is south off Oregon 204 on Forest Road 020. Find the turn 20 miles east of Weston, 22 miles west of Elgin.

About the campground: This forested campground sits on the west shore of marshy ringed Langdon Lake, which is private. Although the lake can be admired from camp, there is no access. Camasses favor the moist shore, and grasses grade to the open water. Lichens drape the true firs and spruce. Short paths explore out from sites 1 and 13.

Enterprise Area

19 Boundary

Location: About 8 miles south of Wallowa
Season: May–October
Sites: 8 tent sites; no hookups
Maximum length: Suitable for tents only
Facilities: Tables, grills, vault toilets; no drinking water
Fee per night: None
Management: Wallowa–Whitman National Forest
Contact: (541) 426–4978; www.fs.fed.us/r6/w-w/recreation
Finding the campground: From Oregon 82 in Wallowa, head southwest for 0.3 mile on West First Street and turn left at Bear Creek Road/Forest Road 8250, which begins paved and changes to gravel, following it for 7.1 miles. Bear right on FR 8250.040 to pass through the campground in 0.7 mile.
About the campground: Straddling the end of FR 8250.040, just before the Bear Creek Trailhead, is this rustic camp. Many of the sites line the shore of Bear Creek; most are fully shaded by the mature fir-spruce forest. While there are gravel parking pads, the narrowness of the road and the restricted mobility in the canyon make these sites better suited for tents. Bear Creek courses beautiful and clear; its parallel trail offers a fine introduction to Wallowa–Whitman National Forest and the Eagle Cap Wilderness.

Enterprise Area

	Hookup sites	Total sites	Maximum RV length	Hookups	Toilets	Showers	Drinking water	Dump station	Recreation	Fee	Can reserve
19 Boundary		8	T		NF				HF		
20 Coyote		24	20		NF						
21 Dougherty		12	small		NF						
22 Hurricane Creek		8	T		NF				HF	$	
23 The Lions Park		open	40		NF		•	•		donation	
24 Minam State Park		12	70		NF		•		FBL	$	
25 Shady		12	16		NF				HF	$	
26 Two Pan		8	T		NF				HF	$	
27 Vigne		7	18		NF		•			$	
28 Wallowa Lake State Recreation Area	121	213	90	WES	F	•	•	•	HSFBLR	$$–$$$	•
29 Wallowa Park	10	11	40	WE	NF		•		HFR	$	•
30 Williamson		9	15		NF				HF	$	

20   Coyote

Location: About 41 miles northeast of Enterprise
Season: May–October
Sites: 24 basic sites; no hookups
Maximum length: 20 feet
Facilities: Most sites with tables and grills, pit toilets; no drinking water
Fee per night: None.
Management: Wallowa–Whitman National Forest
Contact: (541) 426–4978; www.fs.fed.us/r6/w-w/recreation
Finding the campground: From Enterprise, take Oregon 3 north from town at the sign for Flora and Lewiston; it is Northwest First Street in town. Go 14.7 miles and turn right onto Forest Road 46 (Wellamotkin Drive), which begins paved and becomes gravel. A sign at the turn indicates Starvation and Davis Creeks. Continue 26.3 miles and turn left on FR 4650 at a sign for the camp. Sites are on the right, 0.1 mile ahead. Be alert for free-ranging cattle on FR 46.
About the campground: This campground in the "boonies" has a blended habitat of open grassland and conifer groves; the sites are well scattered for privacy. Generally, though, your camp companions tend to be wildlife, not humans. When it tests safe, intermittent Coyote Spring can serve as a camp water source, but plan on bringing a drinking supply, because it is a long way back to town. Red Hill Lookout, passed en route to camp, offers vistas out the Pevine and Joseph creek drainages. In fall, hunting brings more faces to camp.

21   Dougherty

Location: About 47 miles northeast of Enterprise
Season: May–October
Sites: 12 sites; no hookups
Maximum length: Small units, best suited for tents
Facilities: Some tables or fire rings, vault toilets; no drinking water
Fee per night: None
Management: Wallowa–Whitman National Forest
Contact: (541) 426–4978; www.fs.fed.us/r6/w-w/recreation
Finding the campground: From Enterprise, take Oregon 3 north from town at the sign for Flora and Lewiston; it is Northwest First Street in town. Go 14.7 miles and turn right on Forest Road 46 (Wellamotkin Drive), which begins paved and becomes gravel. A sign at the turn indicates Starvation and Davis Creeks. Continue 32.3 miles to enter this campground on the left. Be alert for free-ranging cattle along FR 46.
About the campground: Near Dougherty Spring, this primitive outpost is a great place for solitude, reflection, and nature study. In the fall, it attracts hunting parties. The undeveloped sites dot a broad plateau of open meadow and clustered conifers. Wildflowers sprinkle color through the meadow.

Bear Creek in Wallowa–Whitman National Forest.

22   Hurricane Creek

Location: About 6 miles south of Enterprise, 4 miles southwest of Joseph
Season: May–October
Sites: 8 tent sites; no hookups
Maximum length: Suitable for tents only
Facilities: Some tables, grills or fire rings, vault toilets; no drinking water
Fee per night: $
Management: Wallowa–Whitman National Forest
Contact: (541) 426–4978; www.fs.fed.us/r6/w-w/recreation
Finding the campground: From Joseph, turn west off Oregon 82 onto West Wallowa Avenue at the sign for the airport and Hurricane Creek; this road later becomes Airport Lane. Follow it for 2.1 miles. Here, the paved road curves, meeting Hurricane Creek Road. Turn left on gravel Hurricane Creek Road and go 1.8 miles to reach the campground (bearing right on paved Hurricane Creek Road takes you into Enterprise).
About the campground: This primitive camp overlooks the impressive waters of Hurricane Creek, a racing Wallowa Mountain waterway. The sites are fully forested, snuggled among the Douglas and true firs, maples, and shrubs. A rough, narrow gravel and rock–studded road stitches together the crude but well-spaced sites. The condition of the camp road, together with the short, uneven parking spaces, makes this primarily a tent camp. Upstream on Hurricane Creek Road (Forest Road 8250), you will find a trailhead for the superb Hurricane Creek Trail and its side trails that explore the Eagle Cap Wilderness.

23   The Lions Park

Location: In the city of Wallowa
Season: April–October
Sites: Open camping area; no hookups
Maximum length: 40 feet
Facilities: Few tables and grills, chemical toilets, drinking water, dump station
Fee per night: Donation
Management: The Lions Club
Contact: (541) 886–3027
Finding the campground: From Oregon 82 at the west end of Wallowa, turn north on the Truck Route and go 0.1 mile to this park on the left.
About the campground: An open lawn and a few dotting pines shape the scene at this convenient travelers' wayside. Willows and cottonwoods edge the camp. The Wallowa County Museum may suggest an outing; among its collection are Nez Perce artifacts. The Wallowa Mountains region is noted for its outdoor recreation.

24 Minam State Park

Location: At Minam, about 13 miles west of Wallowa
Season: March–October
Sites: 12 basic sites; no hookups
Maximum length: 70 feet
Facilities: Tables, grills, vault toilets, drinking water, raft put-in (below the bridge)
Fee per night: $
Management: Oregon State Parks and Recreation Department
Contact: (541) 432–4185; www.oregonstateparks.org
Finding the campground: From Oregon 82, 15 miles east of Elgin, 13.4 miles west of Wallowa, turn north at the sign for the state park and follow the gravel road downstream 1.6 miles to the campground.
About the campground: This canyon campground occupies a flat above the Wallowa River, downstream from the Minam–Wallowa confluence. It offers groomed lawns, with paved roads and parking. Big ponderosa pines and smaller firs spot shade across the park grounds. A fuller wooded slope rises at the back of the camp, while cross-river views feature a steep canyon wall topped by a basalt crest. A foot trail and abandoned jeep trail downstream from the camp provide fishing access. Rafting and spring and fall steelhead fishing are popular.

25 Shady

Location: About 17 miles south of Lostine
Season: May–October
Sites: 8 basic sites, 4 tent sites; no hookups
Maximum length: 16 feet
Facilities: Tables, grills, vault toilets; no drinking water
Fee per night: $
Management: Wallowa–Whitman National Forest
Contact: (541) 426–4978; www.fs.fed.us/r6/w-w/recreation
Finding the campground: From Oregon 82 at Lostine, go south on Lostine River Road/Forest Road 8210 for the Lostine River Campgrounds. The road begins paved and becomes gravel, with areas of heavy washboard. The campground is on the right in 16.6 miles.
About the campground: This camp pairs up with the sparkling beauty of the Lostine Wild and Scenic River and trails leading into the Eagle Cap Wilderness. Outfitters operate along FR 8210 for anyone wanting to get well into the Wallowa Mountains backcountry. Lakes, meadows, pristine streams, alpine forests, and wildlife await. If relaxing at camp is more to your liking, this campground merits a look, with the song of the river and conifer shade.

26 Two Pan

Location: About 17 miles south of Lostine
Season: May–October
Sites: 2 basic sites, 6 tent sites; no hookups
Maximum length: Small units, best suited for tents
Facilities: Tables, grills, vault toilets; no drinking water
Fee per night: $
Management: Wallowa–Whitman National Forest
Contact: (541) 426–4978; www.fs.fed.us/r6/w-w/recreation
Finding the campground: From Oregon 82 at Lostine, go south on Lostine River Road/Forest Road 8210 for the Lostine River Campgrounds. The road begins paved and becomes gravel, with sometimes heavy washboard. Reach the campground at the road's end in 17.3 miles.
About the campground: This small, rustic campground is often hectic, because it doubles as a popular gateway to the Eagle Cap Wilderness. A fir-spruce forest houses the camp, but the ground is well trampled. Trails from camp follow the east and west forks of the Lostine River upstream into the high-mountain splendor, with Minam Lake, the Wallowa Lakes Basin, and the Minam River as possible destinations. Besides hiking, fishing is popular.

27 Vigne

Location: About 40 miles northeast of Enterprise
Season: May–October
Sites: 7 basic sites; no hookups
Maximum length: 18 feet
Facilities: Tables, grills, pit toilets, drinking water
Fee per night: $
Management: Wallowa–Whitman National Forest
Contact: (541) 426–4978; www.fs.fed.us/r6/w-w/recreation
Finding the campground: From Enterprise, take Oregon 3 north from town at the sign for Flora and Lewiston; it is Northwest First Street in town. Go 14.7 miles and turn right on Forest Road 46 (Wellamotkin Drive), which begins paved and becomes gravel. Now, go 13.7 miles, turn right on narrow, paved, sometimes rough FR 4625 and proceed 11.3 miles to enter the campground on the right. The final 1.5 miles is on gravel; entry to the camp requires a difficult right-hook turn.
About the campground: This lightly used rustic campground occupies a corridor of pine, fir, and shrubs along Chesnimnus Creek, a small, shallow creek threading through a pretty canyon. Sites have dirt parking, and the road through camp is dirt. A turnaround loop helps ease access to and from the sites.

A Wallowa Mountain peak.

28 | Wallowa Lake State Recreation Area

Location: About 6 miles south of Joseph, on Wallowa Lake
Season: Mid-April–late October
Sites: 121 hookup sites, 89 basic sites, 2 yurts, 1 cabin; water, electric, and sewer hookups
Maximum length: 90 feet
Facilities: Tables, flush toilets, drinking water, showers, dump station, telephone, marina, launch, moorage, picnic shelters
Fee per night: $$–$$$
Management: Oregon State Parks and Recreation Department
Contact: (541) 432-4185; (800) 452-5687 for reservations; www.oregonstate parks.org
Finding the campground: From Joseph, drive 6 miles south on Oregon 82 and bear right at the fork to reach the state park campground.
About the campground: This popular campground sits on the south shore of Wallowa Lake, a large glacial moraine lake that is watched over by snowy peaks. In a lawn and forest setting, the camp offers comfortable, developed sites within footsteps of the oval lake, its recreation, and prized trails into the Eagle Cap Wilderness. Nearby attractions include Chief Joseph's grave, the steepest vertical-lift gondola in North America (Wallowa Lake Tramway), horse concessions for trail rides, and Wallowa Loop Scenic Drive.

29 | Wallowa Park

Location: About 7 miles south of Joseph
Season: Memorial Day weekend–Labor Day weekend
Sites: 10 hookup sites, 1 basic site; water and electric hookups
Maximum length: 40 feet
Facilities: Tables, fire pits, vault toilets, drinking water
Fee per night: $
Management: Pacific Power Company
Contact: (503) 813-6666 for general information, (541) 432-4902 for information and reservations, which are required; www.pacificpower.net
Finding the campground: From Joseph, drive 6 miles south on Oregon 82 and bear left at the fork to reach this campground at road's end. It's located next to the power plant and the Wallowa Lake State Park day-use area.
About the campground: This quiet campground sits in the forest at the foot of one of the steeply rising Wallowa mountains. It is conveniently located for hiking the trails along the Wallowa River forks or heading up to Aneroid Lake, taking in the recreation at Wallowa Lake, or exploring Joseph and its street of bronze sculptures.

30 Williamson

Location: About 11 miles south of Lostine
Season: May–October
Sites: 9 basic sites; no hookups
Maximum length: 15 feet
Facilities: Tables, grills, vault toilets; no drinking water
Fee per night: $
Management: Wallowa–Whitman National Forest
Contact: (541) 426–4978; www.fs.fed.us/r6/w-w/recreation
Finding the campground: From Oregon 82 at Lostine, go south on Lostine River Road/Forest Road 8210 for the Lostine River Campgrounds. The road begins paved and becomes gravel, with areas of heavy washboard. The campground is on the right in 10.8 miles.
About the campground: This primitive campground occupies a wooded slope above the Lostine Wild and Scenic River, one of the prized waterways of the region and the state. Lodgepole pine, fir, and larch create partial shade, and the parking spaces tend to be small and uneven. Fishing and hiking amuse visitors, with area packers offering an easier way into the wilderness. Dispersed sites can be found along FR 8210 for additional camping options.

Aneroid Lake in the Wallowa Mountains.

La Grande Area

31 Birdtrack Springs

Location: About 15 miles west of La Grande
Season: Early May–late November
Sites: 22 basic sites; no hookups
Maximum length: 40 feet
Facilities: Tables, grills, vault toilets; no drinking water
Fee per night: $
Management: Wallowa–Whitman National Forest
Contact: (541) 963–7186; www.fs.fed.us/r6/w-w/recreation
Finding the campground: From Interstate 84 north of La Grande, take exit 252 and go 5.4 miles west on Oregon 244 to this campground on the left. (The camp turnoff is 42 miles east of Ukiah.)
About the campground: This campground enjoys a peaceful setting of tall ponderosa pines, firs, and larches. Wild rose, grass, and currant contribute to the forest carpet. The sites are well spaced, with gravel parking. Songbirds complement a stay. At the camp's western edge, a rail fence surrounds the namesake natural spring. Although it can supply water when it tests pure, play it safe and bring what you will need. Across OR 244, visitors can access the Grande Ronde River for fishing.

La Grande Area

	Hookup sites	Total sites	Maximum RV length	Hookups	Toilets	Showers	Drinking water	Dump station	Recreation	Fee	Can reserve
31 Birdtrack Springs		22	40		NF				F	$	
32 Buck Creek Trailhead		4	small		NF				HR	$	
33 Catherine Creek State Park		20	30		F		•		F	$	
34 Hilgard Junction State Park		18	30		F		•		FBL	$	
35 Moss Springs		11	25		NF				HR	$	
36 North Fork Catherine Creek		7	small		NF				HFR	$	
37 Red Bridge State Park		20	30		F		•		F	$	
38 Spool Cart		9	40		NF				F	$	
39 Spring Creek		4	35		NF						
40 Umapine		7	none		NF				O		

32   Buck Creek Trailhead

Location: About 18 miles southeast of Union, 33 miles southeast of La Grande
Season: June–October
Sites: 4 basic sites; no hookups
Maximum length: Best suited for tents and small units
Facilities: Tables, grills, vault toilets, corrals; no drinking water
Fee per night: $
Management: Wallowa–Whitman National Forest
Contact: (541) 963-7186; www.fs.fed.us/r6/w-w/recreation
Finding the campground: From Union, go 11 miles southeast on Oregon 203 and turn left onto gravel Forest Road 7785. Go about 3 miles and turn right on FR 7787, which leads to Buck Creek Trailhead and Camp in about another 4 miles.
About the campground: This ridgetop camp sits in an open lodgepole pine forest, which provides patchy shade. The primary attraction is the gateway to Buck Creek Trail, which leads into Eagle Cap Wilderness.

33   Catherine Creek State Park

Location: 8 miles southeast of Union
Season: Mid-April–October
Sites: 20 basic sites; no hookups
Maximum length: 30 feet
Facilities: Tables, grills, flush toilets, drinking water
Fee per night: $
Management: Oregon Department of Parks and Recreation
Contact: (800) 551-6949; www.oregonstateparks.org
Finding the campground: From Union, go 8 miles southeast on Oregon 203 to this state park on the right.
About the campground: This state park picnic area and campground sits along a half-mile stretch of the broad, smooth-flowing Catherine Creek. Planted deciduous and native ponderosa pine trees shade the lawns, while cottonwoods tower above the creek. Despite its proximity to OR 203, the location exudes tranquility. Visitors can fish, cool their ankles, or seek out area trails into Wallowa–Whitman National Forest and the Eagle Cap Wilderness.

34   Hilgard Junction State Park

Location: About 10 miles west of La Grande
Season: March–November
Sites: 18 basic sites; no hookups
Maximum length: 30 feet
Facilities: Tables, grills, flush toilets, drinking water, horseshoe pits, rafting access
Fee per night: $

Management: Oregon State Parks and Recreation Department
Contact: (800) 551-6949; www.oregonstateparks.org
Finding the campground: From Interstate 84 north of La Grande, take exit 252 and follow the signs to the park. It is on the west side of the freeway off Oregon 244.
About the campground: This campground occupies a narrow strip between I-84 and the Grande Ronde River. It is a pretty spot but can be noisy when large trucks tackle the interstate grade. Usually, though, the river wins out. Cottonwoods shade the dandelion-sprinkled lawn, and a forested slope rises across from camp. This is an Oregon Trail site, and to its northwest off I-84 is Blue Mountain Crossing, a Forest Service interpretive site and trail, where the original wagon ruts can be seen. Fishing and rafting are popular river activities.

35 Moss Springs

Location: About 8 miles east of Cove
Season: June-October
Sites: 11 basic sites; no hookups
Maximum length: 25 feet
Facilities: Tables, grills, vault toilets, corrals, horse-loading ramp; no drinking water
Fee per night: $
Management: Wallowa-Whitman National Forest
Contact: (541) 963-7186; www.fs.fed.us/r6/w-w/recreation
Finding the campground: From OR 237 in Cove, turn east on French Street (opposite the high school) for Moss Springs Campground. French Street then bends into Mill Creek Lane, which later becomes Forest Road 6220. Follow these paved and gravel routes for 8.4 miles to the campground.
About the campground: This camp occupies a forested rim at a popular hiker and equestrian gateway to the Eagle Cap Wilderness. The sites are well spaced, comfortable, and well used, especially during hunting season. Horse Ranch Trail descends from this Wallowa Mountain plateau, passing through a historic horse ranch at the bottom of the canyon, to meet the pristine Minam River and its trail to discovery. If you visit the ranch area, travel lightly, and pitch backpack and horse camps well away from this fragile historical resource. The terrain resembles Hells Canyon as much as the Wallowa high country: View basalt-tiered grassland rims and rocky summits.

36 North Fork Catherine Creek

Location: About 17 miles southeast of Union
Season: June-October
Sites: 7 basic sites; no hookups
Maximum length: Best suited for tents or pickup campers
Facilities: Tables, fire rings, vault toilets, horse-loading ramp; no drinking water

North Fork Catherine Creek.

Fee per night: $
Management: Wallowa–Whitman National Forest
Contact: (541) 963–7186; www.fs.fed.us/r6/w-w/recreation
Finding the campground: From Union, go 11 miles southeast on Oregon 203 and turn left (east) on Catherine Creek Lane/Forest Road 7785, a single-lane road. The trailhead and its parking is at the road's end in 5.7 miles. The campsites, being redesigned, will dot the sides of FR 7785 leading up to the trailhead.
About the campground: This rustic camp offers a quiet, no-frills getaway and access to the Eagle Cap Wilderness. Mature conifers offer shade, while wildflowers decorate the grasses. North Fork Catherine Creek is a racing, black satin stream spilling between shrub-lined banks. From the trailhead, the North Fork Catherine Creek Trail heads across a creek bridge and swings up-canyon to visit engaging high meadows and enter the wilderness.

37 Red Bridge State Park

Location: About 16 miles west of La Grande
Season: March–November
Sites: 20 basic sites; no hookups
Maximum length: 30 feet
Facilities: Tables, grills, flush toilets, drinking water, horseshoe pits
Fee per night: $
Management: Oregon State Parks and Recreation Department
Contact: (800) 551–6949; www.oregonstateparks.org
Finding the campground: From Interstate 84 north of La Grande, take exit 252 and go 7.3 miles west on Oregon 244 to reach this park on the left. A fee station is at the parking area.
About the campground: At this Grande Ronde River park, RVers can dry camp in the parking lot, and tent campers are welcome to walk in and pitch their tents along the grassy, pine-clad river bench at the park's east end. Ponderosa pines create a scenic, shady rest, while red rosier dogwoods grow toward shore. Fishing is the pastime.

38 Spool Cart

Location: About 25 miles southwest of La Grande
Season: Early May–late November
Sites: 9 basic sites; no hookups
Maximum length: 40 feet
Facilities: Tables, grills, vault toilets; no drinking water
Fee per night: $
Management: Wallowa–Whitman National Forest
Contact: (541) 963–7186; www.fs.fed.us/r6/w-w/recreation
Finding the campground: From Interstate 84 north of La Grande, take exit 252 and go 11.7 miles west on Oregon 244. (If following OR 244 from Ukiah, it is 35 miles east.) Turn south on Grande Ronde Road/Forest Road 51, cross-

ing the bridge over the river. Go 4.5 miles to find this camp on the right.

About the campground: At this Grande Ronde River campground, large, extra-wide paved parking spaces help get you settled. The camp claims a relaxing spot on the river for reverie or fishing. The sites are fully or partially shaded by a forest of ponderosa pine, fir, larch, and spruce.

39 Spring Creek

Location: About 14 miles northwest of La Grande
Season: Early May–late November
Sites: 4 basic sites; no hookups
Maximum length: 35 feet

The Oregon Trail enters Oregon south of Vale and journeys north and west to The Dalles.

Facilities: Tables, grills, vault toilets; no drinking water
Fee per night: None
Management: Wallowa–Whitman National Forest
Contact: (541) 963–7186; www.fs.fed.us/r6/w-w/recreation
Finding the campground: From Interstate 84, 13 miles north of La Grande, take exit 248 for Spring Creek Road/Forest Road 21 and go west 1.4 miles to this campground on the right.
About the campground: Conveniently located off I–84, near an Oregon Trail interpretive site, this camp occupies an attractive meadow-and-forest setting. Sites are relatively level and radiate off the campground loop road. The surrounding area is a winter range for elk (December–April), as well as a woodpecker nesting area; keep an eye on the ponderosa pines for clues. Bats, too, can be seen. The Oregon Trail site is reached heading 3 miles north from the exit, following signs. A lovely carved entrance sign welcomes you.

40 Umapine

Location: About 39 southwest of La Grande
Season: June–October
Sites: 7 basic sites; no hookups
Maximum length: None
Facilities: Tables, grills, vault toilets; no drinking water
Fee per night: None
Management: Wallowa–Whitman National Forest
Contact: (541) 963–7186; www.fs.fed.us/r6/w-w/recreation
Finding the campground: From Interstate 84 at Hilgard Junction, 9 miles west of La Grande, head west on Oregon 244 for about 22 miles. Turn south onto gravel Forest Road 5160, following it 8 miles to the marked campground turnoff.
About the campground: This camp caters to the needs of off-highway-vehicle and dirt bike enthusiasts, with trails knitted through the surrounding area. The camp is mostly open with a few small western larch. A shade source will make your time in camp more comfortable.

Ukiah Area

41 Bear Wallow

Location: 11 miles east of Ukiah
Season: June–October
Sites: 7 basic sites; no hookups
Maximum length: 35 feet
Facilities: Tables, grills, vault toilets; no drinking water
Fee per night: $
Management: Umatilla National Forest
Contact: (541) 427–3231; www.fs.fed.us/r6/uma/recreation
Finding the campground: From Ukiah, go east on Oregon 244 for 11 miles and turn north to enter this campground.
About the campground: This camp rests at the foot of a slope of ponderosa pines where Bear Wallow Creek supplies a pleasant backdrop murmur. The slope holds many of the big, red-trunked pines, with a few right in camp. The barrier-free Bear Wallow Creek Interpretive Trail leads you through the streamside habitat, where interpretive panels describe how the creek is managed for steelhead. Big larches, false hellebore bogs, and wildflowers add to the discovery.

Ukiah Area

	Hookup sites	Total sites	Maximum RV length	Hookups	Toilets	Showers	Drinking water	Dump station	Recreation	Fee	Can reserve
41 Bear Wallow		7	35		NF				H	$	
42 Divide Well		8	40		NF						
43 Drift Fence		5	40		NF						
44 Driftwood		5	small		NF				FB		
45 Frazier		16	40		NF				O	$	
46 Gold Dredge		6	20		NF				F		
47 Lane Creek		6	40		NF				F	$	
48 Tollbridge		7	25		NF				F	$	
49 Ukiah–Dale Forest State Scenic Corridor		27	40		F		•		F	$	
50 Welch Creek		5	30		NF				F	$	
51 Winom Creek Off-Highway-Vehicle Campground		7	40		NF				HO		

42   Divide Well

Location: About 24 miles west of Ukiah
Season: June–October
Sites: 8 basic sites; no hookups
Maximum length: 40 feet
Facilities: Tables, crude fire rings, vault toilets; no drinking water
Fee per night: None
Management: Umatilla National Forest
Contact: (541) 427–3231; www.fs.fed.us/r6/uma/recreation
Finding the campground: From U.S. Highway 395 near Ukiah, go west on Forest Road 53 for about 14 miles to Four Corners, turn left onto FR 5327, and continue southeast for about 9 miles to enter the camp. Expect some heavy washboard.
About the campground: This rustic camp offers a peaceful retreat among the pines and firs, while the large flat gives horse trailers maneuvering room. Generally, the camp is lightly trafficked, serving hunters in the fall and a wagon train retracing history in the summer. Mule deer and Rocky Mountain elk dwell in the area of the camp, and 11 miles south via FR 5316 (not suitable for RVs) is Potamus Point, which delivers an overlook of the John Day River drainage and interesting rock formations.

43   Drift Fence

Location: About 8 miles southeast of Ukiah, 45 miles northwest of Granite
Season: June–October
Sites: 5 basic sites; no hookups
Maximum length: 40 feet
Facilities: Tables, vault toilet; no drinking water
Fee per night: None
Management: Umatilla National Forest
Contact: (541) 427–3231; www.fs.fed.us/r6/uma/recreation
Finding the campground: From Forest Road 52 (Blue Mountain Scenic Byway), 7.5 miles southeast of Ukiah, 44.5 miles northwest of Granite, turn south to enter this camp.
About the campground: At this traditional hunter's camp on Blue Mountain Scenic Byway, the sites occupy a full, mature forest of ponderosa pine and western larch at the edge of a wildflower meadow. Bridge Creek Interpretive Trail, located 2.4 miles northwest of the camp (toward Ukiah), offers a 0.5-mile walk on a gravel-surfaced trail to an overlook of the Bridge Creek drainage, where elk and other wildlife can be spied.

44 Driftwood

Location: About 20 miles southeast of Ukiah
Season: June–October
Sites: 5 basic sites; no hookups
Maximum length: Small units
Facilities: Tables, fire rings, vault toilets, raft put-in; no drinking water
Fee per night: None
Management: Umatilla National Forest
Contact: (541) 427-3231; www.fs.fed.us/r6/uma/recreation
Finding the campground: From U.S. Highway 395, 1 mile north of Dale and 14 miles south of the junction of US 395 and Oregon 244 near Ukiah, turn east onto gravel Texas Bar Road for Olive Lake. In 0.6 mile, go left on Forest Road 55, and after another 4.2 miles, turn right to enter the camp.
About the campground: This forest camp on the North Fork John Day Wild and Scenic River affords beautiful views of the river and the basalt rims of the downstream canyon. A small gravel beach allows for easy river access. This waterway hosts the only natural run of chinook salmon in the John Day watershed; special fishing regulations apply. The river also invites rafting and tube floating. Ponderosa pines shade the camp.

45 Frazier

Location: About 18 miles east of Ukiah
Season: June–October
Sites: 16 basic sites; no hookups
Maximum length: 40 feet
Facilities: Tables, grills, vault toilets, all-terrain-vehicle loading ramp, covered picnic area; no drinking water
Fee per night: $
Management: Umatilla National Forest
Contact: (541) 427-3231; www.fs.fed.us/r6/uma/recreation
Finding the campground: From Ukiah, go east on Oregon 244 for 17 miles and turn south on gravel Forest Road 5226 to enter this camp on the left in 0.5 mile.
About the campground: Pine and larch trees partially shade these well-spaced sites along Frazier Creek. The primary camp user is the all-terrain-vehicle enthusiast; the Butcher Knife ATV Trail leaves from camp. A legend at the entry kiosk shows an entire network of possible ATV tours. Oddly enough, the camp is also rich in wildflowers; even the untrained amateur can detect scores of species. A wildflower checklist is available at the North Fork John Day Ranger District Office in Ukiah.

46   Gold Dredge

Location: About 22 miles southeast of Ukiah
Season: June–October
Sites: 6 basic sites; no hookups
Maximum length: 20 feet
Facilities: Tables, grills, pit toilets; no drinking water
Fee per night: None
Management: Umatilla National Forest
Contact: (541) 427–3231; www.fs.fed.us/r6/uma/recreation
Finding the campground: From U.S. Highway 395, 1 mile north of Dale and 14 miles south of the junction of US 395 and Oregon 244 near Ukiah, turn east onto gravel Texas Bar Road for Olive Lake. At 0.6 mile, go left on Forest Road 55 and continue 4.8 miles. Now proceed straight on FR 5506 for 1.9 miles to reach the campground off FR 030.
About the campground: With a difficult turn into and out of the camp, individuals driving larger units may choose to bypass this facility. The camp, however, extends a shady retreat along the North Fork John Day River, with parking on the grassy river bench. False hellebore adorns the moist meadow reaches, and in spring the camp hawthorn bushes wear white blossoms. Special fishing regulations apply to protect the anadromous fishery of this watershed. The camp's name reflects the gold mining that took place along the river in the early 1900s.

47   Lane Creek

Location: 10 miles east of Ukiah
Season: June–October
Sites: 6 basic sites; no hookups
Maximum length: 40 feet
Facilities: Tables, grills, vault toilets; no drinking water
Fee per night: $
Management: Umatilla National Forest
Contact: (541) 427–3231; www.fs.fed.us/r6/uma/recreation
Finding the campground: From Ukiah, go east on Oregon 244 for 10 miles and turn north to enter this camp.
About the campground: Tiny Lane Creek flows at the eastern edge of this rustic camp, where towering ponderosa pines and western larches thread through the forest. Sites are bathed in a mix of sun and shadow. Fishing on Camas Creek (along OR 244) may divert campers from their leisure; otherwise, this is an eat, sleep, yawn-and-stretch destination.

48   Tollbridge

Location: About 16 miles south of Ukiah
Season: June–October
Sites: 7 basic sites; no hookups
Maximum length: 25 feet
Facilities: Tables, fire rings, pit toilets; no drinking water
Fee per night: $
Management: Umatilla National Forest
Contact: (541) 427–3231; www.fs.fed.us/r6/uma/recreation
Finding the campground: From U.S. Highway 395, 1 mile north of Dale and 14 miles south of the junction of US 395 and Oregon 244 near Ukiah, turn east onto gravel Texas Bar Road for Olive Lake and Forest Road 10. In 0.6 mile, bear right on FR 10, and in another 0.1 mile, turn right to enter the camp.
About the campground: Below FR 10, this camp claims the narrow meadow shore of Desolation Creek just upstream from its confluence with the North Fork John Day River. Hawthorn, box elder, a conifer or two, and a lilac bush dot the camp flat. High canyon rims overlook the setting. The camp is a favorite of hunters and fishermen; be sure to check the sportfishing regulations for special rules.

49   Ukiah–Dale Forest State Scenic Corridor

Location: About 2 miles south of Ukiah
Season: Mid-April–late October
Sites: 27 basic sites; no hookups
Maximum length: 40 feet
Facilities: Tables, grills, flush toilets, drinking water
Fee per night: $
Management: Oregon State Parks and Recreation Department
Contact: (541) 523–2499; www.oregonstateparks.org
Finding the campground: It is east off U.S. Highway 395, 1.4 miles south of the junction of US 395 and Oregon 244 near Ukiah, 14 miles north of Dale.
About the campground: This attractive wayside is located along a scenic corridor embracing a 14-mile stretch of Camas Creek, a beautiful, alternately glassy and riffling waterway contained by meadow and shrub shores. The creek appeals to anglers, kayakers, and rafters. Ponderosa pines shade this comfortable camp. Cross-creek views are of a rock-and-forest slope. All sites have paved parking; some directly overlook the creek. The camp water source is an artesian well.

50 Welch Creek

Location: About 30 miles southeast of Ukiah
Season: June–October
Sites: 5 basic sites; no hookups
Maximum length: 30 feet
Facilities: Tables, fire rings, vault toilets; no drinking water
Fee per night: $
Management: Umatilla National Forest
Contact: (541) 427-3231; www.fs.fed.us/r6/uma/recreation
Finding the campground: From U.S. Highway 395, 1 mile north of Dale and 14 miles south of the junction of US 395 and Oregon 244 near Ukiah, turn east onto gravel Texas Bar Road for Olive Lake and Forest Road 10. After 0.6 mile, bear right onto FR 10, continue 14 miles, and turn right to enter the camp.
About the campground: This primitive camp occupies an open meadow flat along Desolation Creek, which is large and swift-flowing. Pine and larch trees rim the camp, while the slope across the creek reveals a congestion of lodgepole pines and a maze of interlocking logs. The camp is well used by hunters in the fall, and an off-highway-vehicle trail starts to the camp's east, off FR 10. Bird watching and fishing (special regulations apply) are other diversions.

51 Winom Creek Off-Highway-Vehicle Campground

Location: About 25 miles southeast of Ukiah, 29 miles northwest of Granite
Season: June–October
Sites: 7 basic sites; no hookups
Maximum length: 40 feet
Facilities: Tables, grills, vault toilets, group picnic shelters, OHV loading ramp; no drinking water
Fee per night: None
Management: Umatilla National Forest
Contact: (541) 427-3231; www.fs.fed.us/r6/uma/recreation
Finding the campground: From Forest Road 52, 24 miles southeast of Ukiah and 28 miles northwest of Granite, turn south and follow the winding, coarse-grade gravel road 0.7 mile to the OHV camp.
About the campground: At the outskirts of the Tower Fire Zone, this basic forest camp is tucked away in the Winom Creek Valley, in a setting of tall, thin lodgepole pines punctuated by big larch trees. The Tower Fire had a hit-or-miss pattern, sparing the camp but altering its views. This camp is a gateway to the North Fork John Day Wilderness, which is open only to foot and horse travel, and it is an OHV staging area for the Winom–Frazier OHV Trail System.

John Day Country

52 Barnhouse

Location: About 18 miles southeast of Mitchell
Season: May–October
Sites: 6 basic sites; no hookups
Maximum length: 20 feet
Facilities: Tables, a few fire rings, pit toilets; no drinking water
Fee per night: None
Management: Ochoco National Forest
Contact: (541) 477–6900; www.fs.fed.us/r6/centraloregon/recreation

John Day Country

	Hookup sites	Total sites	Maximum RV length	Hookups	Toilets	Showers	Drinking water	Dump station	Recreation	Fee	Can reserve
52 Barnhouse		6	20		NF						
53 Bear Hollow County Park		13	25		NF		•			$	
54 Big Bend Recreation Site		4	40		NF				FS	$	
55 Bull Prairie Recreation Area		28	40		NF		•	•	HFBL	$$	
56 Clyde Holliday State Recreation Site	31	33	60	WE	F	•	•	•	FB	$$	
57 Cottonwood		6	20		NF						
58 Deerhorn Camp		5	25		NF				F	$	
59 Donnelly–Service Creek River Access		6	40		NF				SFBL	$	
60 Fairview		5	20		NF						
61 Frazier		10	20		NF						
62 Lone Pine Recreation Site		4	40		NF				F	$	
63 Middle Fork		10	30		NF				F	$	
64 Muleshoe Recreation Site		9	35		NF				SFBL	$	
65 Ochoco Divide		28	32		NF		•			$$	
66 Oregon Mine		3	22		NF						
67 Shelton Wayside State Park		36	35		NF		•		H	$	
68 Spray Riverfront Park		5	40		NF		•		FBL	$$	
69 Wildwood		5	T		NF						

Finding the campground: From U.S. Highway 26, 13 miles east of Mitchell, turn south on Forest Road 12. Go 5 miles, ascending to the camp turnoff on the right.

About the campground: In a full forest of fir, pine, and larch, you will find these primitive campsites; most have tables, and a few have a grill or fire ring. Parking is what you make of it. The buzzing of insects or the knocking of a woodpecker only magnifies the quiet. Hiking and hunting can be done near-by.

53 Bear Hollow County Park

Location: About 7 miles southeast of Fossil
Season: May–November
Sites: 13 basic sites; no hookups
Maximum length: 25 feet
Facilities: Tables, grills, vault toilets, drinking water
Fee per night: $
Management: Wheeler County
Contact: (541) 763-2911
Finding the campground: It is west off Oregon 19, 6.5 miles south of Fossil and 12.5 miles north of the junction of OR 19 and OR 207 South (near Service Creek).

About the campground: This camp has a restful appeal, set in a forest of grand and Douglas firs. Although most of the parking spaces are graveled, they still require some leveling. This park is popular in the fall with hunters and serves John Day Country travelers.

54 Big Bend Recreation Site

Location: 3 miles northeast of Kimberly
Season: Year-round
Sites: 4 basic sites; no hookups
Maximum length: 40 feet
Facilities: Tables, fire rings (fires and smoking prohibited June–mid-October), vault toilets; no drinking water
Fee per night: $
Management: Prineville District Bureau of Land Management
Contact: (541) 416-6700; www.or.blm.gov/prineville
Finding the campground: The recreation site is south off the Kimberly–Long Creek Highway, 3 miles northeast of Kimberly, 11 miles south-west of Monument.

About the campground: These well-spaced sites claim a broad river bench, where the North Fork John Day River swings a lazy bend. Each site is paired with at least one juniper for shade; parking is on the grassy flat. Across from the camp rises a steep, grassy slope with rimrock tiers and showings of mountain mahogany. You can fish, swim, or explore the John Day Country. Deer sometimes frequent the river.

55 Bull Prairie Recreation Area

Location: About 20 miles north of Spray, on Bull Prairie Reservoir
Season: Late May–mid-October
Sites: 28 basic sites; no hookups
Maximum length: 40 feet
Facilities: Tables, grills, vault and pit toilets, drinking water, dump station, boat launch, wheelchair-accessible fishing platform and trail
Fee per night: $$
Management: Umatilla National Forest
Contact: (541) 676–9187; www.fs.fed.us/r6/uma/recreation
Finding the campground: From Oregon 207, 17 miles north of Spray and 38 miles south of Heppner, turn east on Forest Road 2039, go 3 miles, and bear right to enter the recreation area.
About the campground: At this relaxing family retreat, campsites are tucked throughout the mature, mixed conifer forest surrounding Bull Prairie Reservoir, a scenic, manmade lake ringed by cattails and stocked with trout. In keeping with the quiet of the setting, the lake is open to nonmotorized boating only. The 1.25-mile Lake Shore Trail travels the lake perimeter for a pleasant start or cap to your day.

56 Clyde Holliday State Recreation Site

Location: 8 miles west of John Day
Season: March–November
Sites: 31 hookup sites, 2 tepees; water and electric hookups
Maximum length: 60 feet
Facilities: Tables, grills, flush toilets, drinking water, showers, dump station, telephone, horseshoe pits
Fee per night: $$
Management: Oregon State Parks and Recreation Department
Contact: (541) 932–4453; www.oregonstateparks.org
Finding the campground: It is south off U.S. Highway 26, 8 miles west of John Day.
About the campground: In the shadow of the Blue Mountains and in the heart of John Day Country you will find this attractive, landscaped campground on the John Day River. Fishing and sightseeing are popular activities. In John Day, be sure to look for the Kam Wah Chung State Heritage Site, a Chinese trading post and apothecary from the mid- to late 1800s. It is shown by guided tour daily, May through October; phone (800) 551–6949 for information and hours. Elsewhere, the units of the John Day Fossil Beds National Monument unfold an exciting geologic timeline and spectacular scenery. The John Day River offers rafting opportunities.

John Day Fossil Beds National Monument.

57 Cottonwood

Location: About 27 miles southeast of Mitchell
Season: May–October
Sites: 6 basic sites; no hookups
Maximum length: 20 feet
Facilities: A few tables and crude fire rings, pit toilets; no drinking water
Fee per night: None
Management: Ochoco National Forest
Contact: (541) 477–6900; www.fs.fed.us/r6/centraloregon/recreation
Finding the campground: From U.S. Highway 26, 13 miles east of Mitchell, turn south onto Forest Road 12, which begins paved and becomes gravel, for a hefty ascent. Go 13.5 miles and turn left on FR 200, proceeding 0.3 mile more to the camp.
About the campground: This is a campground for the do-it-yourself camper. Sites are informal, with just a table or a fire ring marking the spot. The location unites a mature pine-fir forest, false hellebore meadow, and a prairie meadow for a pleasant place to kick back and relax. In fall, hunters often base here.

58 Deerhorn Camp

Location: About 22 miles northeast of Prairie City
Season: Late May–mid-October
Sites: 5 basic sites; no hookups
Maximum length: 25 feet
Facilities: Tables, grills, vault toilets; no drinking water
Fee per night: $
Management: Malheur National Forest
Contact: (541) 820–3800; www.fs.fed.us/r6/malheur
Finding the campground: From the junction of Main Street and U.S. Highway 26 in Prairie City, go east on US 26 for 15.3 miles, turn north on Oregon 7 for Sumpter and Baker City, and go another 1.1 miles. There, turn left on County Road 20 toward Susanville and travel 5.1 miles to this camp on the left.
About the campground: This small rustic camp occupies a transition habitat, where a false hellebore meadow and ponderosa pine forest meet. It rests along the picturesque Middle Fork John Day River and engages guests with fishing, wildlife viewing, and hunting.

59 Donnelly–Service Creek River Access

Location: About 13 miles southwest of Spray
Season: Year-round
Sites: 6 walk-in tent sites; no hookups
Maximum length: 40 feet
Facilities: Tables, vault toilets, primitive boat launch; no drinking water
Fee per night: $
Management: Prineville District Bureau of Land Management
Contact: (541) 416–6700; www.or.blm.gov/prineville
Finding the campground: From the junction of Oregon 19 and Oregon 207 South, near Service Creek (12.3 miles southwest of Spray), turn south on OR 207 and proceed 0.3 mile to this recreation site on the left.
About the campground: Primarily a base for rafters, this camp occupies an arid flat on the John Day River. Only a couple of pines and scattered junipers dot the flat; the tables are paired with these trees for a retreat from the sun. The setting is one of basalt-tiered grassland rims, butte-dressed skylines, and river canyon cliffs. Fishing and swimming are other amusements.

60 Fairview

Location: 39 miles south of Heppner
Season: June–October
Sites: 5 basic sites; no hookups
Maximum length: 20 feet
Facilities: Tables, grills, pit toilets; no drinking water
Fee per night: None
Management: Umatilla National Forest

Contact: (541) 676–9187; www.fs.fed.us/r6/uma/recreation
Finding the campground: It is west off Oregon 207, 16 miles north of Spray, 39 miles south of Heppner.
About the campground: On a slope below OR 207, in a ponderosa pine stand, you will find these five well-spaced campsites. Part of the campground looks out at a burn. The camp is convenient for travelers and welcomes lazing about.

61 Frazier

Location: About 28 miles northeast of Paulina
Season: May–October
Sites: 10 basic sites; no hookups
Maximum length: 20 feet
Facilities: Tables, crude fire rings, pit toilets; no drinking water
Fee per night: None
Management: Ochoco National Forest
Contact: (541) 477–6900; www.fs.fed.us/r6/centraloregon/recreation
Finding the campground: From Paulina (56 miles east of Prineville), go east on County Road 112, the Paulina Highway, for 4.2 miles and turn left on gravel CR113/Forest Road 58. Stay on FR 58, following this paved and gravel route for 22.2 miles. Turn left on narrow, sometimes rough FR 5800.500 and proceed 1.6 miles to the camp.
About the campground: This primitive forest camp provides a quiet escape from everyday demands. It has a pine-meadow setting and well-spaced, informal sites for personal privacy. Aspens with dancing leaves shade a headwater spring of Frazier Creek. The camp, a favorite with hunters, is also just a short hop away from the South Fork John Day River via FR 58 eastbound.

62 Lone Pine Recreation Site

Location: About 2 miles northeast of Kimberly
Season: Year-round
Sites: 4 basic sites; no hookups
Maximum length: 40 feet
Facilities: Tables, fire rings, vault toilets; no drinking water
Fee per night: $
Management: Prineville District Bureau of Land Management
Contact: (541) 416–6700; www.or.blm.gov/prineville
Finding the campground: It is off the Kimberly–Long Creek Highway, 1.7 miles northeast of Kimberly.
About the campground: On a flat along the North Fork John Day River rests this small campground, which lacks improved parking. A grove of cottonwoods shades a pair of sites, while the other two are mostly sunny. Nighttime unites the song of the river and the click of crickets and brings on the erratic flight of bats. Days are filled with fishing, swimming, and exploring the John Day Country and the scattered units of John Day Fossil Beds National Monument.

63 Middle Fork

Location: About 23 miles northeast of Prairie City
Season: Mid-May–mid-October
Sites: 10 basic sites; no hookups
Maximum length: 30 feet
Facilities: Tables, grills, pit toilets; no drinking water
Fee per night: $
Management: Malheur National Forest
Contact: (541) 820–3800; www.fs.fed.us/r6/malheur
Finding the campground: From the junction of Main Street and U.S. Highway 26 in Prairie City, go east on US 26 for 15.3 miles and turn north on Oregon 7 toward Sumpter and Baker City. Go 1.1 miles and turn left on County Road 20 for Susanville. Proceed 6.6 miles to the campground on the left.
About the campground: This linear campground stretches alongside the Middle Fork John Day River, with most of its sites overlooking the river; all having gravel parking. The young and middle-aged pines and firs that dress the flat provide at least partial shade for the sites. Alders, a few dogwoods, and meadow vegetation claim the shore. The camp appeals to outdoor interests, with fishing and hunting, and is near Vinegar Hill–Indian Rock Scenic Area.

64 Muleshoe Recreation Site

Location: About 10 miles west of Spray
Season: Year-round
Sites: 6 basic sites, 3 walk-in tent sites; no hookups
Maximum length: 35 feet
Facilities: Tables, vault toilet (wheelchair accessible), primitive boat launch; no drinking water
Fee per night: $
Management: Prineville District Bureau of Land Management
Contact: (541) 416–6700; www.or.blm.gov/prineville
Finding the campground: From Spray, go 10.3 miles west on Oregon 19 North/207 South, to reach this camp on the left.
About the campground: This campground rests on a small plateau above the John Day River. The walk-in sites are tucked into a juniper grove; the basic sites have gravel parking spurs and claim an open sagebrush flat that offers unobstructed river views. The folded tableland ridges, cliffs, and rims that shape the canyon contribute to the beauty. Below camp, hackberry and wild rose grow near the popular raft put-in/take-out site. Fishing, rafting, and swimming attract visitors to this region and camp.

65 Ochoco Divide

Location: 18 miles southwest of Mitchell
Season: Late May–September
Sites: 28 basic sites, bicycle camp; no hookups
Maximum length: 32 feet
Facilities: Tables, grills, vault toilets, drinking water
Fee per night: $$
Management: Ochoco National Forest
Contact: (541) 416–6500; www.fs.fed.us/r6/centraloregon/recreation
Finding the campground: It is east off U.S. Highway 26, 30 miles northeast of Prineville, 18 miles southwest of Mitchell.
About the campground: At Ochoco Pass on US 26, you will find this camp among the old-growth ponderosa pines and firs. The camp primarily caters to the passer-through, so individuals who opt to linger generally enjoy quiet days perfect for birding and relaxing. An old road leads away from the campground for an easy leg stretch. The Painted Hills Unit of John Day Fossil Beds National Monument is a half-hour's drive northeast of the camp.

66 Oregon Mine

Location: About 32 miles southwest of John Day
Season: Late May–mid-October
Sites: 3 basic sites; no hookups
Maximum length: 22 feet
Facilities: Tables, grills, pit toilet, corral; no drinking water
Fee per night: None
Management: Malheur National Forest
Contact: (541) 820–3800; www.fs.fed.us/r6/malheur
Finding the campground: From U.S. Highway 26, 13 miles east of Dayville, 18 miles west of John Day, turn south on paved Fields Creek Road/Forest Road 21. Follow it for 13.4 miles and turn right onto gravel FR 2170 to enter the campground on the left in 0.4 mile.
About the campground: This small, out-of-the-way, primitive campground has great charm, with its shrub and meadow floor, towering ponderosa pine trees, rustic rail fencing, and shrub-lined Murderers Creek flowing at its back. Deer sometimes visit the camp, and the lilting voices of songbirds invite an early rising. Nearby, a national recreation trail explores a rare Alaskan cedar grove for a 2.2-mile round-trip hike: Return to FR 21 and go 3.5 miles north. There, turn left (west) on FR 2150, following it 6 miles to find the trailhead on the right.

67 Shelton Wayside State Park

Location: About 10 miles southeast of Fossil
Season: May–November
Sites: 36 basic sites; no hookups

Maximum length: 35 feet
Facilities: Tables, grills, vault toilets, drinking water
Fee per night: $
Management: Leased to Wheeler County
Contact: (541) 763–2911
Finding the campground: It is west off Oregon 19, 10.3 miles south of Fossil, 8.7 miles north of the junction of OR 19 and OR 207 South.
About the campground: Service Creek flows through this linear campground, which stretches for a mile at the foot of a forested ridge traversed by trail. The camp has a meadow floor, which is partially shaded by the pine-fir complex. Arnica and mock orange lend seasonal color. The wayside offers a base for exploring the scattered units of John Day Fossil Beds National Monument or participating in the John Day River recreation.

68 Spray Riverfront Park

Location: In Spray
Season: Usually March–December, closing during flood stage
Sites: 5 basic sites; no hookups
Maximum length: 40 feet, but large units may have difficulty taking the turn into the camp
Facilities: Tables, grills, vault toilets, fee boat launch/landing, drinking water
Fee per night: $$
Management: City of Spray
Contact: (541) 468–2069
Finding the campground: From U.S. Highway 26/Oregon 19 in Spray, turn south on Main Street, follow it 0.2 mile, and turn left at the river bridge to enter the campground.
About the campground: Located on a grassy flat on a bend in the John Day River, this camp offers anglers, drift boaters, and rafters convenient access. Seasonally, the locust trees and birdhouses are noisy with birds. Desert canyon rims and ridges add to the scenery. The park has gravel parking at the sites and the boat landing. The Spray Pioneer Museum, built in 1912, may suggest a trip into town.

69 Wildwood

Location: About 34 miles northeast of Prineville
Season: May–September
Sites: 5 tent sites; no hookups
Maximum length: Suitable for tents only
Facilities: Tables, grill, pit toilets; no drinking water
Fee per night: None
Management: Ochoco National Forest
Contact: (541) 416–6500; www.fs.fed.us/r6/centraloregon/recreation
Finding the campground: From U.S. Highway 26, 27 miles northeast of Prineville and 21 miles southwest of Mitchell, turn east onto gravel Forest

Road 2630. Go 4 miles, turn left on FR 2210, and proceed another 3 miles to the camp.

About the campground: Along the old Prineville–Mitchell Highway, this camp has long been a traveler's wayside, although now it is farther off the beaten track for greater relaxation. Its remoteness appeals to great horned owls. The primitive camp occupies a pine-fir slope, with a needle-and-cone-strewn floor. It is another place to commune with nature, read a book, or seek out area trails or hunting opportunities.

Granite–Sumpter Area

70 McCully Forks

Location: About 3 miles northwest of Sumpter
Season: Mid-May–September
Sites: 6 basic sites; no hookups
Maximum length: 18 feet
Facilities: Tables, grills, vault toilets; no drinking water
Fee per night: $
Management: Wallowa–Whitman National Forest
Contact: (541) 523–4476; www.fs.fed.us/r6/w-w/recreation
Finding the campground: From Sumpter (about 30 miles west of Baker City, via Oregon 7 and Sumpter Highway), go 2.8 miles north on Sumpter Highway to find this camp on the right.
About the campground: Along Elkhorn Scenic Byway, this small rustic camp straddles McCully Creek. Fir and spruce trees shade the sites. Farther from the creek grow lodgepole pines, and dogwoods are common. Because of the narrowness of the canyon, parking is constrained, but the camp remains popular, filling on summer weekends. Recreational gold panning is allowed on the camp stream, but take care to avoid straying (claim jumping). The historic Sumpter Valley Railroad may suggest a side trip.

71 Millers Lane

Location: About 9 miles southeast of Sumpter, on Phillips Lake
Season: Mid-May–September
Sites: 7 basic sites; no hookups
Maximum length: 20 feet
Facilities: Tables, grills, vault toilets, boat ramp (at Southwest Shore Campground); no drinking water
Fee per night: $

Granite–Sumpter Area

	Hookup sites	Total sites	Maximum RV length	Hookups	Toilets	Showers	Drinking water	Dump station	Recreation	Fee	Can reserve
70 McCully Forks		6	18		NF				F	$	
71 Millers Lane		7	20		NF				HSFB	$	
72 North Fork John Day		15	40		NF				HFR	$	
73 Olive Lake		23	30		NF				HFBL	$	
74 Southwest Shore		18	35		NF				HSFBL	$	
75 Union Creek	24	70	40	WES	F	•	•	•	HSFBL	$$–$$$	

Management: Wallowa–Whitman National Forest
Contact: (541) 523–4476; www.fs.fed.us/r6/w-w/recreation
Finding the campground: From Oregon 7, 22.2 miles west of Baker City and 3.8 miles east of the Sumpter Junction, turn south on paved Hudspeth Lane for Southwest Shore and Millers Lane Campgrounds. Go 1.2 miles and turn left on gravel Forest Road 2220 to reach this campground on the left in another 1.3 miles.
About the campground: Along the south shore of Phillips Lake, a large, manmade platter that fluctuates, you will find this small campground with exceptional cross-lake viewing of the Elkhorns. Sites occupy a ponderosa pine forest, with a rail fence separating the camp from the shore. Adjacent to camp are dry meadows. Fishing, swimming, and boating make this campground popular on summer weekends. A path follows the lakeshore for hiking.

72 North Fork John Day

Location: About 8 miles north of Granite
Season: June–October
Sites: 8 basic sites, 3 walk-in tent sites, 4 horse sites; no hookups
Maximum length: 40 feet
Facilities: Tables, grills, vault toilets, horse feeding station, loading ramp, and corrals; no drinking water
Fee per night: $
Management: Umatilla National Forest
Contact: (541) 427–3231; www.fs.fed.us/r6/uma/recreation
Finding the campground: It is off Forest Road 52 at its intersection with FR 73, 8.3 miles north of Granite, 39 miles southeast of Ukiah.
About the campground: Along the North Fork John Day Wild and Scenic River at the intersection of the Elkhorn and Blue Mountain Scenic Byways is this pleasant, sunny camp in the lodgepole pines. The North Fork John Day National Recreation Trail leaves one end of the camp and follows the river into the North Fork John Day Wilderness. It travels past mounds of tailings, active claims, and decaying cabins, all part of the mining era here. Special fishing regulations protect the anadromous fishery.

73 Olive Lake

Location: 12 miles west of Granite
Season: June–mid-October
Sites: 21 basic sites, 2 tent sites; no hookups
Maximum length: 30 feet
Facilities: Tables, grills, vault toilets, boat dock and launch; no drinking water
Fee per night: $
Management: Umatilla National Forest
Contact: (541) 427–3231; www.fs.fed.us/r6/uma/recreation
Finding the campground: From Granite, travel 12 miles west on Forest Road 10, a good, wide gravel road, to reach this camp on the left off FR 480. From

U.S. Highway 395 north of Dale, follow FR 55 east 0.6 mile to FR 10, then continue east on FR 10 for another 26.2 miles to reach the campground turnoff.
About the campground: This camp is on the east shore of peaceful Olive Lake. Lodgepole pines, firs, spruces, and larches contribute to the forested basin. Enlarged by an earthen dam, the lake invites fishing and boating. Fremont Powerhouse Historic District (8 miles east of camp) makes an interesting side trip. This restored station powered the gold boom of Eastern Oregon. Its wooden pipeline can be seen in several places throughout the area. Near camp, trails venture into North Fork John Day Wilderness and Indian Rock–Vinegar Hill Scenic Area.

74 Southwest Shore

Location: About 9 miles southeast of Sumpter, on Phillips Lake
Season: Mid-May–September
Sites: 18 basic sites; no hookups
Maximum length: 35 feet
Facilities: Tables, grills, vault toilets, boat ramp; no drinking water
Fee per night: $
Management: Wallowa–Whitman National Forest
Contact: (541) 523-4476; www.fs.fed.us/r6/w-w/recreation
Finding the campground: From Oregon 7, 22.2 miles west of Baker City and 3.8 miles east of the Sumpter Junction, turn south on paved Hudspeth Lane for Southwest Shore and Millers Lane Campgrounds. Go 1.2 miles and turn left on gravel Forest Road 2220 to reach this campground on the left in another 0.5 mile.
About the campground: On the south shore of Phillips Lake, a large, recreational reservoir in the shadow of the Elkhorn Mountains, sits this popular campground with prized views. Sites receive a mix of sun and shade and are generally well spaced across the ponderosa pine and sagebrush flat. Fishing, boating, swimming, and hiking the south shore trail for photographs and nature study busy guests. At the marshy ends of the reservoir are nesting boxes for geese.

75 Union Creek

Location: About 10 miles southeast of Sumpter, on Phillips Lake
Season: Mid-May–October
Sites: 24 hookup sites, 34 basic sites, 12 walk-in tent sites; water, electric, and sewer hookups
Maximum length: 40 feet
Facilities: Tables, grills, flush toilets, drinking water, showers, dump station, telephone, docks, paved multilane boat ramp, fish-cleaning station
Fee per night: $$–$$$
Management: Wallowa–Whitman National Forest
Contact: (541) 523-4476; concessionaire: (541) 894-2505; www.fs.fed.us/r6/w-w/recreation

Finding the campground: It is south off Oregon 7, 19 miles west of Baker City, 7 miles east of the Sumpter Junction.

About the campground: On the north shore of 5-mile-long, 2,450-acre Phillips Lake sits this fully developed campground. Sites terrace the pine-forested slope of the lake basin, with paths leading to the lakeshore, launch, and picnic area. Visitors can enjoy a full day of fun in the sun on the lake and then retreat to the shade of the camp. The roped-off swimming area suggests a refreshing dip, or you can walk the shoreline trail exploring this vast im-poundment on the Powder River. Fresh-caught bass or trout may top the dinner menu. Historic Sumpter and Baker City suggest short road trips.

North Powder–Anthony Lakes Area

76 Anthony Lakes

Location: About 40 miles northwest of Baker City
Season: Mid- to late June–September
Sites: 16 basic sites, 21 tent sites; no hookups
Maximum length: 22 feet
Facilities: Tables, grills, vault toilets, drinking water, boat ramp
Fee per night: $$
Management: Wallowa–Whitman National Forest
Contact: (541) 523–4476; concessionaire: (541) 894–2505; www.fs.fed.us/r6 /w-w/recreation
Finding the campground: From Interstate 84, take the North Powder–Anthony Lakes exit (exit 285) and go west on North Powder River Lane and Forest Road 73 for 20 miles, following the signs to Anthony Lakes. The camp is on the left off FR 73.
About the campground: This camp occupies a high-elevation forest of small-diameter firs and lodgepole pines along Anthony Lake (elevation 7,100 feet). Campers are treated to a breathtaking setting that pairs the stunning granite peaks of the Elkhorn Crest with the midnight blue of the mountain lake. Anthony Lake welcomes trout fishing, human-powered boating, or a shoreline stroll. More challenging hikes are boundless, with several high lakes destinations and the Elkhorn Crest. For vehicle sightseeing, this campground is on the 106-mile Elkhorn Scenic Byway, which makes a loop.

North Powder–Anthony Lakes Area

	Hookup sites	Total sites	Maximum RV length	Hookups	Toilets	Showers	Drinking water	Dump station	Recreation	Fee	Can reserve
76 Anthony Lakes		37	22		NF		•		HFBL	$$	
77 Grande Ronde Lake		8	16		NF		•		HFBL	$	
78 Mud Lake		8	16		NF		•		HFB	$	
79 Pilcher Creek Reservoir Recreation Site		12	40		NF				FBL		
80 Thief Valley Recreation Area		12	32		NF		•		FBL		
81 Wolf Creek–Guy Smith Lake and Dam Recreation Area		open	40		NF				FBL		

77 Grande Ronde Lake

Location: About 41 miles northwest of Baker City
Season: Mid- to late June–September
Sites: 8 basic sites; no hookups
Maximum length: 16 feet
Facilities: Tables, grills, vault toilets, drinking water, primitive boat ramp
Fee per night: $
Management: Wallowa–Whitman National Forest
Contact: (541) 523-4476; concessionaire: (541) 894-2505; www.fs.fed.us/r6 /w-w/recreation
Finding the campground: From Interstate 84, take the North Powder–Anthony Lakes exit (exit 285) and go west on North Powder River Lane and Forest Road 73 for 21 miles, following the signs to Anthony Lakes. Turn right on FR 43, go 0.2 mile, and bear left to enter the camp.
About the campground: The campsites sit in a high-elevation conifer forest overlooking the broad, wet wildflower meadow that separates this camp from Grand Ronde Lake. The submerged grasses and dotting cow lilies add to the charm of this small, circular mountain lake, where quiet boating is allowed and the trout fishing can be good. This camp puts visitors within easy access of the Anthony Lake–Elkhorn Crest recreation, a lineup that includes hiking, sightseeing, photography, and scenic driving.

78 Mud Lake

Location: About 40 miles northwest of Baker City
Season: Mid- to late June–September
Sites: 5 basic sites, 3 tent sites; no hookups
Maximum length: 16 feet
Facilities: Tables, grills, vault toilets, drinking water
Fee per night: $
Management: Wallowa–Whitman National Forest
Contact: (541) 523-4476; concessionaire: (541) 894-2505; www.fs.fed.us/r6 /w-w/recreation
Finding the campground: From Interstate 84, take the North Powder–Anthony Lakes exit (exit 285) and go west on North Powder River Lane and Forest Road 73 for about 20 miles, following the signs to Anthony Lakes. The camp is on the right.
About the campground: Across the road from Anthony Lake and the Anthony Lakes Ski Area, this camp is set back from Mud Lake, tucked away in lodgepole pines and spruce. Shallow Mud Lake is ringed by a broad meadow expanse. Although the setting is serene, mosquitoes can be bothersome. Visitors enjoy the high-country splendor of the Elkhorn Mountains: chiseled granite peaks, high lakes, lush meadows, elk herds, and wildflower showcases. You may hike, fish, row your boat, and sightsee.

79 Pilcher Creek Reservoir Recreation Site

Location: About 30 miles northwest of Baker City
Season: May–mid-October
Sites: 12 basic sites; no hookups
Maximum length: 40 feet
Facilities: Tables, barbecues or fire rings, vault toilets, primitive boat launch; no drinking water
Fee per night: None
Management: Union County
Contact: (541) 963–1001
Finding the campground: From Interstate 84, exit 285 (the North Powder exit), go west on North Powder River Lane, proceeding straight at the junction. After 7.6 miles, turn right on gravel Tucker Flat Road, go 2 miles, and turn right to enter the camp.
About the campground: The centerpiece here is the broad platter of Pilcher Creek Reservoir, cupped by low, rounded meadow-and-forest rises and a

Pilcher Creek campsite.

scenic aspen-filled dip. Views include the rugged beauty of the Elkhorn Mountains. The camp offerings are primitive, and the primary activities are boating (5 miles per hour) and fishing. With Elkhorn Wildlife Area bordering the recreation site, deer, elk, and other wildlife can be seen at the camp. In spring, balsamroot colors the meadow.

80 Thief Valley Recreation Area

Location: About 15 miles south of Union
Season: May–mid-October
Sites: 12 basic sites; no hookups
Maximum length: 32 feet
Facilities: Tables, barbecues, vault toilets, drinking water, boat launch
Fee per night: None
Management: Union County
Contact: (541) 963–1001
Finding the campground: From Oregon 237, 7.8 miles south of Union and 7.3 miles north of Interstate 84, exit 285 (the North Powder exit), turn east on Telocaset Lane, a good gravel road. After 1.8 miles, turn left to remain on Telocaset Lane and continue 4.2 miles more before turning right for the reservoir. Go 1.5 miles to the recreation area.
About the campground: This shadeless flat overlooks the broad, open water of Thief Valley Reservoir, built for irrigation and open to recreation. Low sage-grass ridges shape the basin, while a few willows cluster along the lake rim. The reservoir is open for boating, fishing, swimming, and windsurfing. The jetty offers fishing access for individuals with disabilities. Some big trout are pulled from the reservoir, but by June an algae bloom overtakes the lake, ending the catch. In winter, the lake is open for ice fishing.

81 Wolf Creek–Guy Smith Lake and Dam Recreation Area

Location: About 25 miles northwest of Baker City, on Wolf Creek Lake
Season: May–mid-October.
Sites: Open camping near the dam and along the north shore; no hookups
Maximum length: 40 feet
Facilities: Some lattice-roofed picnic tables, vault toilets, boat launch, dock; no drinking water
Fee per night: None
Management: Union County
Contact: (541) 963–1001
Finding the campground: From Interstate 84 north of the community of North Powder, take exit 283 and go west on Wolf Creek Lane for 4 miles. The recreation area is on the left.
About the campground: This moderate-sized reservoir is open to boating, fishing, and waterskiing. Low, rounded sage-grass hills shape the reservoir neighborhood, with the regal Elkhorns or valley farmlands seen in the distance. Ospreys, ducks, geese, goldfinches, and killdeer can hold the attention of birders.

Richland–Halfway Area

82 Boulder Park

Location: About 40 miles northeast of Baker City and 52 miles southeast of La Grande
Season: June–October
Sites: 8 basic sites; no hookups
Maximum length: Best suited for tents and smaller units
Facilities: Tables, grills, vault toilets, stock feeders, holding facilities, trailer parking; no drinking water
Fee per night: $
Management: Wallowa–Whitman National Forest
Contact: (541) 963-7186; www.fs.fed.us/r6/w-w/recreation
Finding the campground: From Oregon 203 at Medical Springs, head southeast on Collins Road/Eagle Creek Drive for Boulder Park. The road soon widens and becomes gravel. Go 1.6 miles and turn left onto Forest Road 67. Continue 13.5 miles, turn left (west) on FR 77, and go another 0.7 mile to FR 7755. There, turn right on FR 7755 and proceed about 3.8 miles to this campground; Main Eagle Trailhead is 0.25 mile past the camp at road's end.
About the campground: Tucked among the mixed conifers, Boulder Park sits at the Main Eagle Trailhead and is primarily intended to serve people traveling with stock animals. The Main Eagle Trail is a popular southern approach to Eagle Cap Wilderness, and the nearby Fake Creek Trail offers a chance to vary your travels. Beautiful views of the Wallowa Mountains and Eagle Creek, a Wild and Scenic Waterway, are just strides away, with some views obtained right from camp. Campers without stock will likely prefer the family sites at nearby Two Color Campground (see campground 91).

Richland– Halfway Area

	Hookup sites	Total sites	Maximum RV length	Hookups	Toilets	Showers	Drinking water	Dump station	Recreation	Fee	Can reserve
82 Boulder Park		8	small		NF				HR	$	
83 Copperfield Park	62	72	40	WE	F	•	•	•	SFBL	$–$$	
84 Eagle Forks		7	20		NF		•		HF		
85 Fish Lake		15	15		NF		•		HFBL	$	
86 Hewitt/Holcomb County Parks	27	62	30	WE	F	•	•		FBL	$$	•
87 Lake Fork		10	22		NF		•		HF	$	
88 McBride		11	16		NF		•				
89 Tamarack		24	22		NF		•		F	$	
90 Twin Lakes		6	15		NF				HF		
91 Two Color		14	22		NF		•		F	$	

83 Copperfield Park

Location: About 17 miles east of Halfway, on the Snake River
Season: Year-round
Sites: 62 hookup sites, 10 tent sites; water and electric hookups
Maximum length: 40 feet
Facilities: Tables, barbecues or grills, flush toilets, drinking water, showers, dump station, telephone (along Oregon 86 near camp), boat launch (0.6 mile downstream from park)
Fee per night: $–$$
Management: Idaho Power
Contact: (800) 422–3143, no reservations accepted; www.idahopower.com /riversrec/parksrec
Finding the campground: From Halfway, go east on OR 86 for 16.6 miles to enter this park at the river.
About the campground: On the one-time site of the rough-and-tumble mining city of Copperfield, Oregon, sits this pleasant, groomed, developed park,

Copperfield Park on Hell's Canyon Reservoir.

with lots of open lawn and a few big pines. The park offering includes a swimming area on the broad, harnessed Snake River, with boating access nearby. The river here, Hells Canyon Reservoir, is popular with fishermen; warmwater fish species are the primary catch. North (downstream) from the camp, Hells Canyon Reservoir Trail offers a wonderful hike, with views of the steepwalled canyon and broad, cloudy river. Its trailhead parking, though, is limited, with no developed turnaround.

84 Eagle Forks

Location: About 10 miles north of Richland
Season: June–October
Sites: 7 basic sites; no hookups
Maximum length: 20 feet
Facilities: Tables, grills, vault toilets, drinking water
Fee per night: None
Management: Wallowa–Whitman National Forest
Contact: (541) 742-7511; www.fs.fed.us/r6/w-w/recreation
Finding the campground: At the western edge of Richland, turn north off Oregon 86 at a sign for Sparta, following Sparta Road 2.3 miles to Newbridge. There, continue north on Eagle Creek Road/Forest Road 7735, which changes to dirt. Go another 7.3 miles and turn left for the campground.
About the campground: On a wooded rise, this camp threaded by Little Eagle Creek overlooks Eagle Creek, a wild and scenic waterway. Pines and firs shade the camp, while alders and willows fan Eagle Creek. At the upstream end of the camp, you will find the 7-mile Martin Bridge Trail, which pursues the creek upstream for an engaging canyon tour. The trail ends at Martin Bridge, a former stage stop on the Union–Cornucopia Wagon Road that linked the historic gold-mining districts of this area to Union and Baker City. The creek is open to fishing and to gold panning for a touchstone to the past.

85 Fish Lake

Location: About 20 miles north of Halfway, on Fish Lake
Season: July–September
Sites: 15 basic sites; no hookups
Maximum length: 15 feet; best suited for tents
Facilities: Tables, grills, vault toilets, drinking water, boat launch (small boats)
Fee per night: $
Management: Wallowa–Whitman National Forest
Contact: (541) 742-7511; www.fs.fed.us/r6/w-w/recreation
Finding the campground: From Halfway–Cornucopia Highway (County Road 413) in Halfway, turn north onto East Pine Creek Road at the sign for Fish Lake. Go 3.2 miles and turn left onto gravel Fish Lake Road/Forest Road 66, which is indicated for a snow park. Stay on it for 16.5 miles to enter the campground on the left.
About the campground: At an elevation of 6,600 feet, you will find this

inviting mountain lake in a basin of spired trees, meadow, and scree. A small earthen dam has enlarged the lake, a couple of islands contribute to its charm, and avalanche lilies decorate its shore as the snow recedes. The rustic campsites line the shore just below the road shoulder parking. Come prepared for mosquitoes and cold nights. For hiking options, you have Fish Creek Trail (2 miles south of camp), Lake Fork Trail (0.3 mile south), and Clear Creek and Deadman Trails (leaving near camp). Fishing, though, remains the biggest draw.

86 Hewitt/Holcomb County Parks

Location: About 2 miles east of Richland
Season: Year-round
Sites: 27 hookup sites, 20 basic sites, 15 tent sites; water and electric hookups
Maximum length: 30 feet
Facilities: Tables, barbecues, flush toilets, drinking water, showers, telephone, covered gazebos, playground, boating and angling docks, boat launches, fish-cleaning station
Fee per night: $$
Management: Baker County
Contact: (541) 523-8342; (541) 893-6147 for reservations; www.bakercounty.org/parks
Finding the campground: From Richland, go east on Oregon 86 for 0.8 mile and bear right on the road indicated to Hewitt Park, proceeding 1.5 miles to the park campground at road's end.
About the campground: This campground stretches along the Powder River Arm of Brownlee Reservoir. The park's sloping acre of green lawn stands in contrast to the dusky dry grass canyon. Most visitors come for the boating and fishing, for which the lake is noted. The RV camping area is an extensive paved lot, with numbered sites and accompanying tables and barbecues and planted shade trees at its perimeter. A separate tent camping area on a constructed terrace close to the water provides tenters with a flat spot to camp beneath the trees. All sites, though, are just steps from the water, and trophy catfish can entice anglers out at night.

87 Lake Fork

Location: About 18 miles northeast of Halfway
Season: June–November
Sites: 10 basic sites; no hookups
Maximum length: 22 feet
Facilities: Tables, grills, vault toilets, drinking water
Fee per night: $
Management: Wallowa–Whitman National Forest
Contact: (541) 426-4978; www.fs.fed.us/r6/w-w/recreation
Finding the campground: From Oregon 86, 10 miles east of Halfway, turn north on Forest Road 39, the Wallowa Mountain Loop Road, and go 8 miles to reach this camp on the left.

About the campground: This quiet camp along Lake Fork Creek consists of shady, well-spaced sites in a multistory mixed forest of fir, pine, and larch. Just north of the camp, the Lake Fork Trail offers hikes to Big Elk Creek (2 miles) or Fish Lake (11 miles). The camp is conveniently located along Wallowa Mountain Loop Road, which accesses the sights, trails, and attractions of Wallowa–Whitman National Forest and Hells Canyon National Recreation Area.

88 McBride

Location: About 16 miles northwest of Halfway
Season: Mid-May–October
Sites: 8 basic sites, 3 tent sites; no hookups
Maximum length: 16 feet
Facilities: Tables, grills, vault toilets, drinking water
Fee per night: None
Management: Wallowa–Whitman National Forest
Contact: (541) 742-7511; www.fs.fed.us/r6/w-w/recreation
Finding the campground: From Oregon 86 just west of the summit, 6 miles west of Halfway and 47 miles east of Baker City, turn north on gravel, washboard Forest Road 77. Follow it for 10.4 miles to enter the camp on the left.
About the campground: Along Brooks Ditch, this camp extends a quiet forest retreat. In fall, hunters swell the camp population. Opposite the campground turnoff is FR 7715, which travels 4.5 miles to the road's end and Summit Point Trailhead and a vista. Views pan south-southwest. Hiking the Cliff River Trail from here leads past Summit Point Lookout Tower, which is reached via the spur at 0.6 mile. Destinations include Little Eagle Meadows, Nip and Tuck Passes, and some prized high-mountain lakes, if you are a power hiker or backpacker. Bears frequent the Summit Point area.

89 Tamarack

Location: About 36 miles northeast of Baker City
Season: June–October
Sites: 12 basic sites, 12 tent sites; no hookups
Maximum length: 22 feet
Facilities: Tables, grills, vault toilets, drinking water
Fee per night: $
Management: Wallowa–Whitman National Forest
Contact: (541) 742-7511; www.fs.fed.us/r6/w-w/recreation
Finding the campground: From Oregon 203 at Medical Springs (20 miles northeast of Baker City), turn southeast on Collins Road/Eagle Creek Drive for Boulder Park. The road quickly widens and changes to gravel. Go 1.6 miles and turn left on Forest Road 67. Continue 13.5 miles, turn right (east) on FR 77, and go 0.6 mile to the camp.
About the campground: This campground occupies a sunny location above Eagle Creek, with log-defined parking, grassy sites, and an open forest of larch, spruce, and fir. The creek adds a scenic ribbon and a restful voice. By

taking FR 7750 north off FR 77, 0.3 mile west of camp, you can access the Two Color Trail, which travels to Two Color Lake. But you need not hike far to enjoy the walk and attain a peek at the Wallowa Mountains' signature grandeur.

90 Twin Lakes

Location: About 25 miles northeast of Halfway
Season: July–September
Sites: 6 basic sites; no hookups
Maximum length: 15 feet; best suited for tents
Facilities: Tables, grills, vault toilets; no drinking water
Fee per night: None
Management: Wallowa–Whitman National Forest
Contact: (541) 426–4978; www.fs.fed.us/r6/w-w/recreation
Finding the campground: From Halfway–Cornucopia Highway (County Road 413) in Halfway, turn north onto East Pine Creek Road for Fish Lake. Go 3.2 miles and turn left on gravel Fish Lake Road/Forest Road 66, which is indicated for a snow park. Stay on it for 21.6 miles to enter the campground on the left.
About the campground: Despite the camp's name, a trio of meadowy ponds shape a cloverleaf alongside this split-level campground. Lodgepole pines, firs, and larches dress the area, and Russel Mountain presides over the Twin Lakes area. The sites are rustic, and parking is constricted. Twin Lakes and Sugarloaf Trails begin near camp, with the latter leading to Russel Mountain Lookout. A fire several years ago left a wake of silver snags and logs that continue to be a part of the Twin Lakes mosaic. At the camp, a ramp spans the meadowy shore to provide fishing access on the open water.

91 Two Color

Location: About 36 miles northeast of Baker City
Season: June–October
Sites: 14 basic sites; no hookups
Maximum length: 22 feet
Facilities: Tables, grills, vault toilets, drinking water
Fee per night: $
Management: Wallowa–Whitman National Forest
Contact: (541) 963–7186; www.fs.fed.us/r6/w-w/recreation
Finding the campground: From Oregon 203 at Medical Springs (20 miles northeast of Baker City), turn southeast on Collins Road/Eagle Creek Drive for Boulder Park. The road soon widens and becomes gravel. Go 1.6 miles and turn left onto Forest Road 67. Continue 13.5 miles, turn left (west) on FR 77, and go another 0.7 mile to FR 7755. There, turn right to reach the campground in 0.5 mile. Turnouts are fairly frequent and wide to accommodate RVs.
About the campground: In a mixed conifer stand, boulders mark off the

grassy campsites; some are more level than others. Flowing past camp is Eagle Creek, wide and clear-rushing, with richly vegetated banks and overhanging logs. Meadows fan out from the camp. By following FR 7755 north to its end, in about 3 miles, you will find Fake Creek and Main Eagle Trails. They roll out long-distance hikes but also have satisfying scenery and stops for day hikers.

Upper Imnaha River Area

92 Blackhorse

Location: About 36 miles southeast of Joseph
Season: May–October
Sites: 16 basic sites; no hookups
Maximum length: 25 feet
Facilities: Tables, grills, vault toilets, drinking water
Fee per night: $
Management: Wallowa–Whitman National Forest
Contact: (541) 426-4978; www.fs.fed.us/r6/w-w/recreation
Finding the campground: From Oregon 82 in Joseph, turn east on East Wallowa Avenue at the sign for Imnaha and Halfway; it later becomes the Imnaha Highway. Go 7.8 miles and turn right (south) on Wallowa Mountain Loop Road. Continue 28.6 miles to the camp on the left.
About the campground: Along the Imnaha Wild and Scenic River and Wallowa Mountain Loop Road, you will find this camp with well-spaced sites. Meadow openings intersperse the forest of fir, ponderosa pine, and larch, creating a mix of sun and shade. The Imnaha River is captivating: its color, clarity, and overall persona. Besides fishing, camp guests may take a short drive to Hells Canyon Overlook or check out the trails at Indian Crossing (look for the signed turns, south on Wallowa Mountain Loop Road).

93 Coverdale

Location: About 41 miles southeast of Joseph
Season: May–October
Sites: 11 basic sites; no hookups
Maximum length: 15 feet; primarily a tent area
Facilities: Tables, grills, vault toilets; no drinking water
Fee per night: $

Upper Imnaha River Area	Hookup sites	Total sites	Maximum RV length	Hookups	Toilets	Showers	Drinking water	Dump station	Recreation	Fee	Can reserve
92 Blackhorse		16	25		NF		•		F	$	
93 Coverdale		11	15		NF				F	$	
94 Hidden		13	25		NF		•		F	$	
95 Indian Crossing		15	20		NF		•		HFR	$	
96 Lick Creek		12	25		NF					$	
97 Ollokot		12	30		NF		•		F	$	

Management: Wallowa–Whitman National Forest
Contact: (541) 426–4978; www.fs.fed.us/r6/w-w/recreation
Finding the campground: From Oregon 82 in Joseph, turn east on East Wallowa Avenue at the sign for Imnaha and Halfway; it later becomes the Imnaha Highway. Go 7.8 miles and turn right (south) on Wallowa Mountain Loop Road. Continue 29 miles and turn right on Forest Road 3960. Near milepost 4 on FR 3960, turn left onto FR 100 to enter this campground.
About the campground: At the edge of a riparian wildflower meadow in an open flat of mixed age ponderosa pine sits this primitive Imnaha River campground. Sites spread across the untamed, natural setting, which can be overgrown in places. Shrubs edge the clear-rushing river. The rustic camp holds great tranquility, but the mosquitoes can annoy. Fishing, hiking, and horseback riding are area pursuits.

94 Hidden

Location: About 44 miles southeast of Joseph
Season: May–October
Sites: 13 basic sites; no hookups
Maximum length: 25 feet
Facilities: Tables, grills, vault toilets, drinking water
Fee per night: $
Management: Wallowa–Whitman National Forest
Contact: (541) 426–4978; www.fs.fed.us/r6/w-w/recreation
Finding the campground: From Oregon 82 in Joseph, turn east on East Wallowa Avenue at the sign for Imnaha and Halfway; it later becomes the Imnaha Highway. Go 7.8 miles and turn right (south) on Wallowa Mountain Loop Road. Continue 29 miles and turn right on Forest Road 3960. Go 6.9 miles more to enter this campground on the left.
About the campground: This nicely forested campground has bookend outcrops. Footpaths from each site lead to the Imnaha Wild and Scenic River. Sites enjoy partial to full shade beneath a canopy of fir, pine, and larch. Upstream, the river is braided by meadow islands; downstream, it is rushing. Campers pass their days fishing, watching wildlife, and exploring area trails.

95 Indian Crossing

Location: About 46 miles southeast of Joseph
Season: May–October
Sites: 9 basic sites, 6 horse sites; no hookups
Maximum length: 20 feet
Facilities: Tables, grills, vault and pit toilets, drinking water, and horse hitching rails, troughs, and ramp
Fee per night: $
Management: Wallowa–Whitman National Forest
Contact: (541) 426–4978; www.fs.fed.us/r6/w-w/recreation
Finding the campground: From Oregon 82 in Joseph, turn east on East Wal-

lowa Avenue at the sign for Imnaha and Halfway; it later becomes the Imnaha Highway. Go 7.8 miles and turn right (south) on Wallowa Mountain Loop Road. Continue 29 miles and turn right on Forest Road 3960. Go 8.7 miles to this campground and trailhead at road's end.

About the campground: As a main gateway to the Eagle Cap Wilderness, this open-forest campground is popular with hikers, equestrians, anglers, and hunters. The camp straddles the Imnaha Wild and Scenic River, with the horse camp claiming the north shore, the family sites the south shore. Nearby trails pursue the river upstream into the wilderness and climb the ridge to Duck Lake. The camp road can be rough.

96 Lick Creek

Location: About 23 miles southeast of Joseph
Season: May–October
Sites: 12 basic sites; no hookups
Maximum length: 25 feet
Facilities: Tables, grills, vault toilets; no drinking water
Fee per night: $
Management: Wallowa–Whitman National Forest
Contact: (541) 426-4978; www.fs.fed.us/r6/w-w/recreation
Finding the campground: From Oregon 82 in Joseph, turn east on East Wallowa Avenue at the sign for Imnaha and Halfway; it later becomes the Imnaha Highway. Go 7.8 miles and turn right (south) on Wallowa Mountain Loop Road. Continue 15.1 miles to the campground.

About the campground: In a meadow setting along Lick Creek, among the scattered firs and lodgepole pines, sits this fine campground for the family. The campground has paved roads, with gravel parking, including a couple of small pull-through sites. Deer commonly browse in the wildflower meadow. False hellebore with its showy crown of flowers gives the meadow dimension and texture. Wallowa Mountain Loop Road is the yellow brick road to many trails and sights in Hells Canyon National Recreation Area and the Eagle Cap Wilderness.

97 Ollokot

Location: About 37 miles southeast of Joseph
Season: May–October
Sites: 12 basic sites; no hookups
Maximum length: 30 feet
Facilities: Tables, grills, vault toilets, drinking water
Fee per night: $
Management: Wallowa–Whitman National Forest
Contact: (541) 426-4978; www.fs.fed.us/r6/w-w/recreation
Finding the campground: From Oregon 82 in Joseph, turn east on East Wallowa Avenue at the sign for Imnaha and Halfway; it later becomes the Imna-

ha Highway. Go 7.8 miles and turn right (south) on Wallowa Mountain Loop Road. Continue 29.1 miles to enter the campground on the left.

About the campground: On a low plateau above the Imnaha Wild and Scenic River, this east shore campground occupies a ponderosa pine stand, with a parklike open spacing and meadow floor. The campsites have gravel parking and are generally sunny. Campers can access the river fairly easily for fishing and admiring. Wallowa Mountain Loop Road is the avenue to outward exploration, hiking, and sightseeing.

Prairie City Area

98 Crescent

Location: About 17 miles south of Prairie City
Season: Late May–mid-October
Sites: 5 basic sites; no hookups
Maximum length: 18 feet
Facilities: Tables, grills, pit toilets; no drinking water
Fee per night: None
Management: Malheur National Forest
Contact: (541) 820–3800; www.fs.fed.us/r6/malheur
Finding the campground: From U.S. Highway 26 in Prairie City, turn south on Main Street, go 0.3 mile, and turn left on Bridge Street, which later becomes County Road 62. Proceed south for 16.6 miles and turn right to enter the campground.
About the campground: Along the John Day River, in a forest of fir, spruce, and lodgepole pine, sits this tiny campground. Sites are partially shaded and have gravel parking. Here, the river spans 5 to 7 feet wide and flows clear and fast. The river fishery is acclaimed, but no taking of Dolly Varden (bull trout).

99 Depot Park

Location: In Prairie City
Season: May–October
Sites: 20 RV hookup sites, open lawn for tent camping; water, electric, and sewer hookups

Prairie City Area

	Hookup sites	Total sites	Maximum RV length	Hookups	Toilets	Showers	Drinking water	Dump station	Recreation	Fee	Can reserve
98 Crescent		5	18		NF				F		
99 Depot Park	20	20	40	WES	F	•	•	•		$$	
100 Dixie		11	25		NF		•			$	
101 Elk Creek		5	T		NF						
102 Little Crane Creek		5	30		NF						
103 Magone Lake		23	16		NF		•		HSFBL	$$	
104 North Fork Malheur		5	T		NF				HF		
105 Slide Creek Horse Camp and Campground		6	30		NF				HR		
106 Strawberry		12	16		NF		•		H	$	
107 Trout Farm		6	30		NF		•		F	$	

Maximum length: 40 feet
Facilities: Tables, flush toilets, drinking water, showers, dump station, telephone, picnic shelter
Fee per night: $$
Management: Prairie City
Contact: (541) 820-3605
Finding the campground: From U.S. Highway 26 in Prairie City, turn south on Main Street and go 0.3 mile to find this city park on the left at the intersection with Bridge Street.
About the campground: This charming city park welcomes weary travelers with its neatly trimmed lawns, shade trees, and babbling Strawberry Creek. Sites are available on a first come, first served basis. The park offering includes a 1910 historic depot (museum), railroad boxcar, wagon, rustic statue, gazebo, and picnic shelter. Each RV space has paved parking and a lawn meridian with a table. Tent campers can make use of the picnic shelter when preparing and eating meals. Seasonally open for tours, the museum has 10 rooms of pioneer memorabilia.

100 Dixie

Location: About 10 miles east of Prairie City
Season: Late May–mid-October
Sites: 11 basic sites; no hookups
Maximum length: 25 feet
Facilities: Tables, grills, vault toilets, drinking water
Fee per night: $
Management: Malheur National Forest
Contact: (541) 820-3800; www.fs.fed.us/r6/malheur
Finding the campground: From the intersection of Main Street and U.S. Highway 26 in Prairie City, go east on US 26 for 9.5 miles and turn left (north) on Forest Road 2600.848 to enter the camp.
About the campground: At Dixie Summit (elevation 5,000 feet), this terraced campground occupies a lodgepole pine–dominated forest, with larch and fir in the mix. Dwarf and true huckleberry grow beneath the trees. Sites are partially shaded, with gravel parking. Set back from US 26, the campground offers a quiet night's sleep. Hunting and berry picking are among the activities. In winter a snow park attracts visitors to the area.

101 Elk Creek

Location: About 25 miles southeast of Prairie City
Season: Late May–mid-October
Sites: 5 basic sites; no hookups
Maximum length: Best-suited for tents or pickup campers
Facilities: Tables, grills, pit toilets; no drinking water
Fee per night: None
Management: Malheur National Forest

Contact: (541) 820–3800; www.fs.fed.us/r6/malheur
Finding the campground: From U.S. Highway 26 in Prairie City, turn south on Main Street, go 0.3 mile, and turn left on Bridge Street, which later becomes County Road 62. Proceed south for 7.8 miles and turn left on Forest Road 13 (an improved surface and paved route). Continue 15.7 miles to FR 16 and head right (south) on FR 16 to reach the camp in another 1.5 miles. From US 395 at Seneca, go east on FR 16 for 40 miles to reach the camp.
About the campground: This small, lightly developed campground is sandwiched by FR 16 and Elk Creek. Ponderosa and lodgepole pines dominate the camp, with a few grand firs and Douglas firs interwoven. Despite its proximity to FR 16, the camp conveys a feeling of isolation, and it is not far from the hiking at North Fork Malheur River (southwest of camp, taking FR 1675 off FR 16) and Little Malheur River (northeast of camp off FR 1672).

102 Little Crane Creek

Location: About 31 miles southeast of Prairie City
Season: Late May–mid-October
Sites: 5 basic sites; no hookups
Maximum length: 30 feet
Facilities: Tables, grills, vault toilets; no drinking water
Fee per night: None
Management: Malheur National Forest
Contact: (541) 820–3800; www.fs.fed.us/r6/malheur
Finding the campground: From U.S. Highway 26 in Prairie City, turn south on Main Street, go 0.3 mile, and turn left on Bridge Street, which later becomes County Road 62. Proceed south for 7.8 miles and turn left on Forest Road 13 (an improved surface and paved route). Continue 15.7 miles to FR 16 and head right (south) on FR 16 to reach this camp in another 7 miles. From US 395 at Seneca, go east on FR 16 for 34.5 miles to reach the camp.
About the campground: This quiet retreat claims a scenic mixed conifer setting alongside Little Crane Creek. The camp has gravel roads and site parking and serves anglers and hunters. The camp is close to the hiking at North Fork Malheur River (east on FR 16 and then south on FR 1675).

103 Magone Lake

Location: About 19 miles northwest of Prairie City
Season: Late May–mid-October
Sites: 23 basic sites; no hookups
Maximum length: 16 feet
Facilities: Tables, grills, vault toilets, drinking water, dock, boat launch for human-powered craft
Fee per night: $$
Management: Malheur National Forest
Contact: (541) 820–3800; www.fs.fed.us/r6/malheur
Finding the campground: From Prairie City, drive west on U.S. Highway 26

for 3.4 miles and turn north on Bear Creek Road (County Road 18). Go 13 miles and turn left on Forest Road 3620, following it for 1.5 miles. Turn right on FR 3618 to reach the campground in 1.5 miles more. Signs point the way along the paved and gravel route. An alternative entry is east off U.S. 395, 9 miles north of Mount Vernon: Follow County Road 32/FR 36 and FR 3618 10 miles to the camp.

About the campground: This popular campground occupies the forested shore of Magone Lake. In the 1800s a natural landslide captured the waters of Lake Creek to form this 50-acre lake, which now offers swimming, fishing, and quiet boating. Muskrats and duck families inhabit the lake. A 1.5-mile trail encircles the lake, and the 0.5-mile Magone Slide Trail leaves FR 3618 near the day-use area.

104 North Fork Malheur

Location: About 26 miles southeast of Prairie City
Season: Late May–mid-October
Sites: 5 basic sites; no hookups
Maximum length: Best-suited for tents or smaller units
Facilities: Tables, grills, vault toilets; no drinking water
Fee per night: None
Management: Malheur National Forest
Contact: (541) 820–3800; www.fs.fed.us/r6/malheur
Finding the campground: From U.S. Highway 26 in Prairie City, turn south on Main Street, go 0.3 mile, and turn left on Bridge Street, which later becomes County Road 62. Proceed south for 7.8 miles and turn left on Forest Road 13 (an improved surface and paved route). Continue 15.7 miles to FR 16 and head right (south) on FR 16 to reach this camp in another 2.2 miles. From US 395 at Seneca, go east on FR 16 for 39.3 miles to reach this campground.
About the campground: Rimmed by fence, this picturesque camp unites a lovely forest of ponderosa pine and larch, a meadowy shore and islands, and the braided, glimmering water of the North Fork Malheur Wild and Scenic River. At either end of the camp, gates provide access to the river, where angler paths travel along shore. Following FR 1675 past the camp for less than 1 mile leads to the North Fork Malheur Trailhead. Because of its minimal turnaround space, you should leave RVs at the camp and hike FR 1675 to the trailhead. The trail extends for a dozen miles, offers a wonderful river-forest sojourn, and accesses the Crane Creek Trail 2.5 miles downstream.

105 Slide Creek Horse Camp and Campground

Location: About 9 miles south of Prairie City
Season: Mid-May–mid-November
Sites: 3 basic sites, 3 horse sites; no hookups
Maximum length: 30 feet
Facilities: Tables, grills, vault toilets, corrals at horse camp; no drinking water
Fee per night: None

Management: Malheur National Forest
Contact: (541) 820–3800; www.fs.fed.us/r6/malheur
Finding the campgrounds: From U.S. Highway 26 in Prairie City, turn south on Main Street, go 0.3 mile, and turn right on Bridge Street. The route begins paved and becomes gravel, and the name changes to Forest Road 6001 upon entering the national forest. Reach these two camp areas in about 9 miles.
About the campgrounds: These small rustic camps near the confluence of Slide and Strawberry Creeks have grassy floors and an open-forest look. As an entryway to the Strawberry Mountain Wilderness, the camps are popular with hunters and hikers. Near these camps, the Slide Creek Connector Trail heads east off FR 6001 and links up with the wilderness trail network near Slide Lake.

106 Strawberry

Location: About 11 miles south of Prairie City
Season: Maintained mid-June–mid-October
Sites: 12 basic sites; no hookups
Maximum length: 16 feet
Facilities: Tables, grills, vault toilets, drinking water
Fee per night: $
Management: Malheur National Forest
Contact: (541) 820–3800; www.fs.fed.us/r6/malheur
Finding the campground: From U.S. Highway 26 in Prairie City, turn south on Main Street, go 0.3 mile, and turn right on Bridge Street. It begins paved and becomes gravel, and the name changes to Forest Road 6001 upon entering the national forest. Reach the camp in 10.8 miles.
About the campground: At more than a mile high, this popular camp is the primary base and access to Strawberry Mountain Wilderness, a prized area of high lakes, snow-patched peaks, tinsel-like streams, waterfalls, and wildflower-spangled meadows and crests. A mixed high-elevation forest enfolds the camp. Adjacent to the camp is trailhead parking, and the Strawberry Basin Trail is your pass to the grandeur.

107 Trout Farm

Location: About 15 miles south of Prairie City
Season: Late May–mid-October
Sites: 6 basic sites; no hookups
Maximum length: 30 feet
Facilities: Tables, grills, vault toilets, drinking water, picnic shelter
Fee per night: $
Management: Malheur National Forest
Contact: (541) 820–3800; www.fs.fed.us/r6/malheur
Finding the campground: From U.S. Highway 26 in Prairie City, turn south on Main Street, go 0.3 mile, and turn left on Bridge Street, which later be-

comes County Road 62. Proceed south for 14.9 miles and turn right for the campground.

About the campground: Along the upper John Day River and a small fishing pond sits this tranquil campground in a full fir forest. Often the pond shows a thick vegetation, but small trout and families of ducks still animate the water. A barrier-free trail partially rims the pond, providing fishing access for all.

Seneca–Logan Valley Area

108 Big Creek

Location: About 19 miles northeast of Seneca
Season: Late May–mid-October
Sites: 14 basic sites; no hookups
Maximum length: 25 feet
Facilities: Tables, grills, vault toilets, drinking water
Fee per night: $
Management: Malheur National Forest
Contact: (541) 820–3800; www.fs.fed.us/r6/malheur
Finding the campground: From U.S. Highway 395 at Seneca, turn east onto paved Forest Road 16 and go 18.7 miles. Turn left onto gravel FR 815 for the camp.
About the campground: This camp with closely spaced sites occupies a flat of ponderosa and lodgepole pines between Big Creek and Logan Valley, an expansive meadow with a kaleidoscope of wildflowers and abundant wildlife. Sightings of deer, antelope, sandhill crane, and coyote are common. An egress in the camp's rail fence leads to Big Creek, with its alder-lined banks and deep pools. Consult the camp information board for details about the Big Creek Area mountain bike trails, which make use of nearby seldom-used and closed forest roads.

109 Murray

Location: About 20 miles northeast of Seneca
Season: Late May–mid-October
Sites: 5 basic sites; no hookups
Maximum length: 25 feet
Facilities: Tables, grills, pit toilets; no drinking water
Fee per night: None
Management: Malheur National Forest

Seneca–Logan Valley Area

	Hookup sites	Total sites	Maximum RV length	Hookups	Toilets	Showers	Drinking water	Dump station	Recreation	Fee	Can reserve
108 Big Creek		14	25		NF		•		FC	$	
109 Murray		5	25		NF				F		
110 Parish Cabin		20	35		NF		•		F	$	
111 Starr		8	30		NF					$	
112 Wickiup		9	22		NF				F		

Contact: (541) 820–3800; www.fs.fed.us/r6/malheur

Finding the campground: From U.S. Highway 395 at Seneca, turn east onto paved Forest Road 16 and go 17.2 miles. Turn left on gravel FR 1600.924 and proceed 2.6 miles to the camp. It is on the left before the junction with FR 1648.

About the campground: This informal, primitive camp occupies a semi-open mixed forest along Lake Creek. Within camp, look for a regal, old-growth ponderosa pine that reigns over the area. Lake Creek is a fast-rushing water, with forested shores. A half mile south of camp, near the Lake Creek Organizational Camp, you will find Trail 307, a closed jeep trail to explore.

110 Parish Cabin

Location: 11 miles northeast of Seneca
Season: Late May–mid-October
Sites: 20 basic sites; no hookups
Maximum length: 35 feet
Facilities: Tables, grills, vault toilets, drinking water
Fee per night: $
Management: Malheur National Forest
Contact: (541) 820–3800; www.fs.fed.us/r6/malheur
Finding the campground: From U.S. Highway 395 at Seneca, turn east onto paved Forest Road 16 and go 11 miles to enter this camp on the left. From US 26 at John Day, go south on US 395 for 10.1 miles, and turn left (east) onto County Road 65/Forest Road 15 at the sign for Canyon Meadows and Wickiup Campground. Proceed 13.7 miles and turn right on FR 16 to find the campground on the right in 0.1 mile.

About the campground: This campground occupies a flat of lodgepole pines along picturesque Bear Creek. Lush meadow banks decorated in wildflowers and shrubs contain the meandering stream. The sites have partial shade and gravel parking spaces; a few sites have pull-through parking. Look for indications of beaver along the creek.

111 Starr

Location: About 16 miles south of John Day
Season: Late May–mid-October
Sites: 8 basic sites; no hookups
Maximum length: 30 feet
Facilities: Tables, grills, pit toilets; no drinking water
Fee per night: $
Management: Malheur National Forest
Contact: (541) 820–3800; www.fs.fed.us/r6/malheur
Finding the campground: From John Day, go south on U.S. Highway 395 for 15.5 miles to enter the campground on the right at the summit (elevation 5,125 feet).

About the campground: This campground occupies a ponderosa pine forest and shrub-meadow flat. Across the road from the camp is a winter sports area, with warming hut and sledding hill. The closed roads that serve cross-country skiers and snowshoers in winter double as hiking trails in summer. The camp is near Fall Mountain Lookout, a 20-foot fire tower built in 1933. Although the public can no longer enter it, they may still choose to visit the historic fire tower. North of the campground, take Forest Road 4920 northwest off US 395 to FR 4920.607 and the lookout. Altogether, it is about a 4-mile side trip; the final mile on FR 607 requires either a high-clearance vehicle or hiking to the top. Wildflowers and mountain mahoganies dress the summit; views are to the east and south.

112 Wickiup

Location: About 23 miles northeast of Seneca
Season: Late May–mid-October
Sites: 9 basic sites; no hookups
Maximum length: 22 feet
Facilities: Tables, grills, vault toilets; no drinking water
Fee per night: None
Management: Malheur National Forest
Contact: (541) 820–3800; www.fs.fed.us/r6/malheur
Finding the campground: From U.S. Highway 26 at John Day, go south on US 395 for 10.1 miles, and turn left (east) on paved County Road 65/Forest Road 15 at the sign for Canyon Meadows and Wickiup Campground. Proceed 7.7 miles to reach this camp on the right off FR 1516, which heads to Dry Soda Lookout.
About the campground: At the foot of a forested slope, this campground occupies a pine-fir flat along Canyon Creek at the Wickiup confluence. The sparkling water courses over a pebble-and-rock bed, creating a restful backdrop rush. Wild roses and dogwoods accent the flat. West of the camp off FR 15 is the trailhead for Table Mountain Loop, and few hikers can resist the call of the nearby Strawberry Mountain Wilderness.

Unity Area

113 Oregon

Location: About 13 miles northwest of Unity
Season: Mid-May–mid-October
Sites: 8 basic sites; no hookups
Maximum length: 30 feet
Facilities: Tables, grills, vault toilets, drinking water
Fee per night: $
Management: Wallowa–Whitman National Forest
Contact: (541) 446-3351; www.fs.fed.us/r6/w-w/recreation
Finding the campground: Find it north off U.S. Highway 26, 12.7 miles west of Unity, 23.6 miles east of Prairie City.
About the campground: Ideal for US 26 travelers, this camp provides fully to partially shaded sites in a forest of ponderosa pine and fir. Shrubs and wildflowers decorate the understory. The sites have gravel parking. From the camp, an off-highway-vehicle trail heads north to the bridge outage on North Fork Burnt River. Unity Reservoir, Monument Rock Wilderness, and the historic Sumpter Valley Railroad also suggest outings.

114 South Fork

Location: About 7 miles southwest of Unity
Season: Mid-May–mid-October
Sites: 12 basic sites; no hookups
Maximum length: 28 feet
Facilities: Tables, grills, pit toilets, drinking water
Fee per night: None
Management: Wallowa–Whitman National Forest
Contact: (541) 446-3351; www.fs.fed.us/r6/w-w/recreation
Finding the campground: From U.S. Highway 26 at Unity, go 7.3 miles southwest on South Fork Road (County Road 600/Forest Road 6005) to reach this campground on the left; the final 3.2 miles is on gravel.

Unity Area

	Hookup sites	Total sites	Maximum RV length	Hookups	Toilets	Showers	Drinking water	Dump station	Recreation	Fee	Can reserve
113 Oregon		8	30		NF		•		O	$	
114 South Fork		12	28		NF		•		F		
115 Unity Lake State Park	35	37	40	WE	F	•	•	•	SFBL	$$	
116 Wetmore		12	18		NF		•		H	$	
117 Yellow Pine		21	25		NF		•		H	$	

About the campground: This quiet camp hugs the pretty South Fork Burnt River. A meadow floor spills beneath the towering pines, firs, and larches. Several of the sites overlook the sparkling river and its alder banks. If you steal up to the water, fishing is possible, and hikers may choose to investigate nearby Monument Rock Wilderness.

115 Unity Lake State Park

Location: About 4 miles north of Unity
Season: Mid-April–late October
Sites: 35 hookup sites, 2 tepees; water and electric hookups
Maximum length: 40 feet
Facilities: Tables, fire rings, flush toilets, drinking water, showers, dump station, telephone, boat launch, dock
Fee per night: $$
Management: Oregon State Parks and Recreation Department
Contact: (541) 932–4453; www.oregonstateparks.org
Finding the campground: From Unity, go west on U.S. Highway 26 for 1.7 miles and turn north on Oregon 245 toward Hereford and Baker City. Go another 2.5 miles, turn left at the sign for Unity Lake State Park, and proceed into the park.
About the campground: At this landscaped campground, the planted shade trees have yet to reach a size to be considered dependable shade, but the adjoining day use is well shaded. Unity Lake harnesses the Burnt River and rests in an arid basin in the Blue Mountains. Views are of the surrounding sage grass hills and their volcanic crests. The blue water is a strong enticement to fish, boat, swim, or windsurf. Best fishing is during the spring and fall; the catch is trout, bass, and crappie.

116 Wetmore

Location: About 10 miles northwest of Unity
Season: Mid-May–mid-October
Sites: 12 basic sites; no hookups
Maximum length: 18 feet
Facilities: Tables, grills, vault and pit toilets, drinking water
Fee per night: $
Management: Wallowa–Whitman National Forest
Contact: (541) 446–3351; www.fs.fed.us/r6/w-w/recreation
Finding the campground: This campground is north off U.S. Highway 26, 10.2 miles west of Unity, 27.1 miles east of Prairie City.
About the campground: This family campground occupies a rolling terrain of fir, ponderosa pine, and larch. An understory of mixed shrubs and wild roses attracts browsing deer. At the west end of the camp, a 0.5-mile, paved barrier-free trail journeys along a gurgling tributary and past old-growth pines and volcanic outcrops to switchback uphill to neighboring Yellow Pine Campground. Possible car outings include Unity Reservoir or the Sumpter Valley Railroad.

117 Yellow Pine

Location: About 11 miles northwest of Unity
Season: Mid-May–mid-October
Sites: 21 basic sites; no hookups
Maximum length: 25 feet
Facilities: Tables, grills, pit toilets, drinking water
Fee per night: $
Management: Wallowa–Whitman National Forest
Contact: (541) 446-3351; www.fs.fed.us/r6/w-w/recreation
Finding the campground: The campground is north off U.S. Highway 26, 10.8 miles west of Unity, 26.5 miles east of Prairie City.
About the campground: Tucked off US 26, in a gently rolling terrain punctuated with mature yellow-bellied ponderosa pines is this pleasant campground. Younger pines and firs fill out the forest. From the east end of the camp, a barrier-free nature trail travels 0.5 mile to Wetmore Campground. Deer sometimes visit the camp.

Ontario Area

118 Bully Creek Reservoir County Park

Location: About 11 miles northwest of Vale, on Bully Creek Reservoir
Season: April–mid-November
Sites: 40 hookup sites; electric hookups
Maximum length: 40 feet
Facilities: Tables, grills, flush toilets, drinking water, showers, dump station, telephone, boat launch, dock
Fee per night: $$
Management: Malheur County
Contact: (541) 473-2969
Finding the campground: From U.S. Highway 20 at the west end of Vale, go northwest on Graham Boulevard for 7 miles and continue northwest on Bully Creek Reservoir Road for another 4 miles to enter the campground on the left.
About the campground: This landscaped campground rests in the basin of grassy hills that contains Bully Creek Reservoir, the centerpiece to recreation. The reservoir offers catches of panfish, boating, and swimming. Along the shore, shade is rare. Campsites have gravel parking, and a few sites are shaded by fuller trees.

119 Farewell Bend State Recreation Area

Location: About 26 miles northwest of Ontario, on Brownlee Reservoir
Season: Year-round
Sites: 101 hookup sites, 35 basic sites, 3 walk-in tent sites, 2 covered camper wagons, 3 tepees, 2 cabins; water and electric hookups
Maximum length: 56 feet

Ontario Area

	Hookup sites	Total sites	Maximum RV length	Hookups	Toilets	Showers	Drinking water	Dump station	Recreation	Fee	Can reserve
118 Bully Creek Reservoir County Park	40	40	40	E	F	•	•	•	SFBL	$$	
119 Farewell Bend State Recreation Area	101	146	56	WE	F	•	•	•	SFBL	$$	•
120 Lake Owyhee State Park	31	58	55	WE	F	•	•	•	SFBL	$$	
121 Leslie Gulch–Slocum Creek		12	20		NF				HSFBL		
122 Spring Recreation Site		35	30		NF	•			SFBL	$	
123 Succor Creek State Park		19	small		NF				H		
124 Twin Springs Recreation Site		5	20		NF				O		

Facilities: Tables, grills, flush toilets, drinking water, showers, dump station, telephone, playground, sand volleyball, horseshoe pits, fishing docks, boat launch, Oregon Trail exhibit

Fee per night: $$

Management: Oregon State Parks and Recreation Department

Contact: (541) 869–2365; (800) 452–5687 for reservations; www.oregonstate parks.org

Finding the campground: From Interstate 84, take exit 353 (25 miles northwest of Ontario), and go north on U.S. Highway 30 Business toward Huntington to enter the park on the right in 1 mile.

About the campground: Here, along the Snake River, you can camp where the Oregon pioneers did more than 150 years ago. But there are a couple of notable differences: The accommodations are now first-class, and the river is contained as Brownlee Reservoir. Arid canyon hills overlook this oasis of lawn and trees. The hookup sites occupy two distinct areas: one with privacy hedges, mature shade trees, and a central lawn; the other in the arid Snake River Canyon, with open lawn and young trees. Boating, swimming, fishing for bass and catfish, hunting (outside the park), and rockhounding in the outlying area entertain guests.

120 Lake Owyhee State Park

Location: 33 miles southwest of Nyssa

Season: Mid-April–October

Sites: 31 hookup sites, 25 basic sites, 2 tepees; water and electric hookups

Maximum length: 55 feet

Facilities: Tables, grills, flush toilets, drinking water, showers, dump station, boat launch, dock, fish-cleaning station

Fee per night: $$

Management: Oregon State Parks and Recreation Department

Contact: (800) 551–6949; www.oregonstateparks.org

Finding the campground: The park is off Owyhee Reservoir Road, 33 miles south of Nyssa: From Nyssa, go south on Oregon 201 about 12 miles and turn right for Lake Owyhee, following Owyhee Avenue and Owhyee Reservoir Road the remaining way to the park. Road signs help point the way.

About the campground: In a stunning desert canyon in the remote southeast corner of the state, the park's V. W. McCormack Campground offers landscaped sites above Lake Owyhee. Lake Owyhee is an attractive, 52-mile-long, 14,000-acre reservoir open to boating, swimming, and waterskiing and known for its bass fishing. Attractive reddish cliffs, terraced walls, and unusual geological formations frame the reservoir. A nearby resort rents boats.

121 Leslie Gulch–Slocum Creek

Location: About 47 miles southwest of Adrian, on Owyhee Reservoir
Season: In dry weather, April–October
Sites: 12 basic sites; no hookups
Maximum length: 20 feet
Facilities: Tables, vault toilet, boat launch; no drinking water
Fee per night: None
Management: Vale District Bureau of Land Management
Contact: (541) 473-3144; www.or.blm.gov/vale
Finding the campground: From Oregon 201, 8 miles south of Adrian, go southwest on Succor Creek Road and then west on Leslie Gulch Road (both are improved surface roads), for a combined distance of about 39 miles. The camp is on the left before the Owyhee Reservoir boat launch at the road's end.
About the campground: This sun-drenched camp has limited amenities, but it enjoys a front row seat to the reservoir and an exciting canyon location. Stargazing is unmatched. The reservoir is noted for its scenery, fishing, and boating. Washes in the Leslie Gulch Area shape natural dry-weather hiking trails through the colorful volcanic ash formations: shields, beehives, hollows, and monoliths that tickle the imagination. Visitors have the opportunity to spy bighorn sheep, coyotes, bats, and golden eagles, but be alert for snakes. The camp sits at the mouth of Slocum Gulch for morning or evening strolls. Bring plenty of water, hats, sunscreen, and a free-standing shade source. A reservoir dunking is almost always in order, but water levels can fluctuate drastically, especially in drought and by late summer.

122 Spring Recreation Site

Location: About 33 miles northwest of Ontario, on Brownlee Reservoir
Season: March–November
Sites: 20 basic sites, 15 tent sites; no hookups
Maximum length: 30 feet
Facilities: Tables, grills, vault toilets, drinking water, boat launch, docks, fish-cleaning station
Fee per night: $
Management: Vale District Bureau of Land Management
Contact: (541) 473-3144; www.or.blm.gov/vale
Finding the campground: From Interstate 84, take exit 353 (25 miles northwest of Ontario), and go 5 miles north on U.S. Highway 30 Business to Huntington. There, turn right on paved Snake River Road for a 3.4-mile winding canyon drive to the camp.
About the campground: Along Brownlee Reservoir on the Snake River, both the tent and RV camping areas rim a gravel parking lot. The tent sites are just a short walk away in an area of established shade trees. The RV spaces are typically paired with smaller trees. In this narrow, steep-sided canyon, the walls help shadow the camp. Fishing, boating, and swimming attract people to this spot.

123 Succor Creek State Park

Location: About 23 miles southwest of Adrian
Season: In dry weather, March–October
Sites: 19 basic sites; no hookups
Maximum length: Small units only
Facilities: Tables, vault toilet; no drinking water
Fee per night: None
Management: Oregon State Parks and Recreation Department
Contact: (800) 551–6949; www.oregonstateparks.org
Finding the campground: From Oregon 201, 8 miles south of Adrian, go southwest on improved surface Succor Creek Road for 15 miles to reach this park.
About the campground: This isolated state park serves up a fine dose of solitude in a grand desert canyon setting. Succor Creek halves the camp, and the bigger trees within the camp offer prized shade. There are no established trails, but the jeep trails and landmarks of the canyon terrain suggest short

Succor Creek State Park.

cross-country outings. Photography, wildlife viewing, stargazing, and relaxing at camp entertain individuals who venture here. When scrambling among the rocks, be alert for snakes. Temporarily, until the creek bridge is repaired, expect fewer available sites.

124 Twin Springs Recreation Site

Location: About 33 miles southwest of Vale
Season: In dry weather, April–November
Sites: 5 basic sites; no hookups
Maximum length: 20 feet
Facilities: Tables, grills, vault toilets; no drinking water
Fee per night: None
Management: Vale District Bureau of Land Management
Contact: (541) 473–3144; www.or.blm.gov/vale
Finding the campground: From the junction of U.S. Highway 20 and US 26 in Vale, go 4.6 miles west on US 20, and turn south on paved Russell Road, which is signed for Rock Canyon and Dry Creek. Follow it for 2.2 miles and turn left off the pavement onto a dirt-and-gravel road signed for Twin Springs and Dry Creek. Go 0.5 mile, and turn left, passing through a pair of gates. The road here traverses private property; resecure the gates after you. In 9 miles, bear left to avoid a jeep road to the right, and 3.5 miles farther, bear right per the sign for Twin Springs. Proceed 12.7 miles more to find this campground straddling the road. High clearance is recommended.
About the campground: After a complicated drive on bumpy dirt roads, campers can settle back among the shade trees at this out-of-the-way, spring-fed oasis. A few free-ranging cows and screeching hawks are your neighbors. The immediate area allows for some motorcycle use, hunting, rockhounding, and cross-country exploration (for the knowledgeable), but most users seem content just to bask in the solitude and tranquility of camp.

Burns Area

125 Chickahominy Recreation Site

Location: 31 miles west of Burns, on Chickahominy Reservoir
Season: Year-round, maintained April–September
Sites: 28 basic sites; no hookups
Maximum length: 35 feet
Facilities: Tables, fire rings, vault toilets, drinking water, shade shelters, fish-cleaning station, boat launch
Fee per night: $
Management: Burns District Bureau of Land Management
Contact: (541) 573–4400; www.or.blm.gov/burns
Finding the campground: It is north off U.S. Highway 20, 31 miles west of Burns and 99 miles east of Bend.
About the campground: This camp rests along the open flat of Chickahominy Reservoir, which holds back the water of Chickahominy Creek. It is a sparkling, big, elongated water body in an arid basin of mixed grasses and sagebrush. Juniper-studded buttes and ridges rise in the backdrop. Bird watching, fishing, and boating are the pastimes. The sites have gravel pull-through parking, and shelters protect some of the tables from wind and sun. Bringing a sturdy shade source and plenty of sunscreen lotion remains a good idea.

126 Chukar Park

Location: 6 miles north of Juntura
Season: Mid-April–October
Sites: 18 basic sites; no hookups
Maximum length: 28 feet
Facilities: Tables, grills, vault toilets, drinking water

Burns Area

	Hookup sites	Total sites	Maximum RV length	Hookups	Toilets	Showers	Drinking water	Dump station	Recreation	Fee	Can reserve
125 Chickahominy Recreation Site		28	35		NF		•		FBL	$	
126 Chukar Park		18	28		NF		•		F	$	
127 Delintment Lake		26	30		NF		•		HFBL	$	
128 Emigrant Creek		6	25		NF		•		F	$	
129 Falls		6	22		NF		•		F	$	
130 Idlewild		23	30		NF		•		H	$	
131 Joaquin Miller Horse Camp		15	35		NF		•		R		
132 Yellowjacket		20	30		NF		•		FBL	$	

Fee per night: $
Management: Vale District Bureau of Land Management
Contact: (541) 473–3144; www.or.blm.gov/vale
Finding the campground: From U.S. Highway 20 at Juntura, go 6 miles north on Beulah Reservoir Road.
About the campground: This campground is a pleasing oasis along the North Fork Malheur. It sits in a rugged countryside, where the chukar, an introduced gameland partridge, is hunted in the fall. The camp unites lawn and native juniper-grassland vegetation. The 20- to 25-foot-wide North Fork Malheur races past the camp. Scenic cliffs across the river add to views. The camp is 9 miles south of Beulah Reservoir for fishing and boating.

127 Delintment Lake

Location: About 42 miles northwest of Burns/Hines, on Delintment Lake
Season: June–mid-October
Sites: 26 basic sites; no hookups
Maximum length: 30 feet
Facilities: Tables, grills, vault toilets, drinking water, boat launch
Fee per night: $
Management: Malheur National Forest
Contact: (541) 573–4300; www.fs.fed.us/r6/malheur
Finding the campground: From U.S. Highway 20 at the west end of Hines, turn north on Burns-Izee Road (County Road 127) for Yellowjacket and Delintment Lakes. Go 11.7 miles and turn left on Forest Road 41. Proceed 26.2 miles and keep left to remain on FR 41. Reach the lake in another 4 miles, with the camp entrance ahead.
About the campground: This comfortable family campground occupies the treed shore of Delintment Lake, a onetime beaver pond enlarged by an earthen dam to its present 57-acre size. The fishing is good, with the rainbow trout measuring on average between 12 and 18 inches. Across the road from the camp, the 5-mile Delintment Creek Trail explores forest and meadow edge along gurgling Delintment Creek.

128 Emigrant Creek

Location: About 34 miles northwest of Burns/Hines
Season: June–mid-October
Sites: 6 basic sites; no hookups
Maximum length: 25 feet
Facilities: Tables, grills, vault toilets, drinking water
Fee per night: $
Management: Malheur National Forest
Contact: (541) 573–4300; www.fs.fed.us/r6/malheur
Finding the campground: From U.S. Highway 20 at the west end of Hines, turn north on Burns-Izee Road (County Road 127) for Yellowjacket and Delint-

ment Lakes. Go 23.2 miles and bear left on Forest Road 43. Proceed 9.9 miles, turn left on gravel FR 4340, and follow it 0.3 mile into the campground.

About the campground: This campground is situated among the big ponderosa pines along meadow-banked Emigrant Creek. The picturesque, meandering waterway invites you to explore along its banks or go fishing. The forest has a lovely meadow and shrub understory, and sites offer gravel parking. At the edges of day, deer can be spied as they drift to and from the creek.

129 Falls

Location: About 32 miles northwest of Burns/Hines
Season: June–mid-October
Sites: 6 basic sites; no hookups
Facilities: Tables, grills, vault toilets, drinking water
Maximum length: 22 feet
Fee per night: $
Management: Malheur National Forest
Contact: (541) 573–4300; www.fs.fed.us/r6/malheur
Finding the campground: From U.S. Highway 20 at the west end of Hines, turn north on Burns-Izee Road (County Road 127) for Yellowjacket and Delintment Lakes. Go 23.2 miles and bear left on Forest Road 43. Proceed 8.2 miles and turn left onto gravel FR 4300.050 to reach the campsites in 0.2 mile.

About the campground: This campground occupies a ponderosa pine flat at a bend on Emigrant Creek. The beautiful, towering red-trunked pines complement the green banks and dark, meandering flow of the creek. Above the camp, a few volcanic boulders stud the forest slope. The camp promises a quiet retreat, and a short, rugged trail travels the west shore downstream.

130 Idlewild

Location: 17 miles north of Burns
Season: Maintained end of May–mid-October
Sites: 23 basic sites; no hookups
Maximum length: 30 feet
Facilities: Tables, grills, vault toilets, drinking water, picnic shelter
Fee per night: $
Management: Malheur National Forest
Contact: (541) 573–4300; www.fs.fed.us/r6/malheur
Finding the campground: The campground is east off U.S. Highway 395, 17 miles north of Burns, 53 miles south of John Day.

About the campground: At meadow's edge, in a scenic ponderosa pine forest sits this pleasant campground, a convenient stopover for the US 395 traveler. Planted aspen and natural mountain mahogany vary the look of the forest. The campground roads and parking spaces are paved, with a few pull-through sites to accommodate longer vehicles. Short hiking trails explore out from the camp: the 1-mile Idlewild Loop and the 2-mile Devine Summit Loop.

131 Joaquin Miller Horse Camp

Location: 19 miles north of Burns
Season: Maintained end of May–mid-October
Sites: 15 basic sites; no hookups
Maximum length: 35 feet
Facilities: Tables, grills, pit toilets, drinking water, corrals
Fee per night: None
Management: Malheur National Forest
Contact: (541) 573-4300; www.fs.fed.us/r6/malheur
Finding the campground: The camp is west off U.S. Highway 395, 19 miles north of Burns, 51 miles south of John Day.
About the campground: At this camp, you will find paved roads and parking spaces and several long pull-through sites to accommodate the horse camping public. The corrals rest at the far west edge of the camp. The sites are partially shaded by ponderosa pines. Although there are commonly used horse routes next to the camp, there are no formal horse trails.

132 Yellowjacket

Location: About 34 miles northwest of Burns/Hines, on Yellowjacket Lake
Season: Maintained end of May–mid-October
Sites: 20 basic sites; no hookups
Maximum length: 30 feet
Facilities: Tables, grills, pit toilets, drinking water, primitive boat launch
Fee per night: $
Management: Malheur National Forest
Contact: (541) 573-4300; www.fs.fed.us/r6/malheur
Finding the campground: From U.S. Highway 20 at the west end of Hines, turn north on Burns-Izee Road (County Road 127/Forest Road 47) for Yellowjacket and Delintment Lakes. Go 30.1 miles and turn right (east) onto FR 37. Go 2.5 miles and turn right on gravel FR 3745. Go 0.8 mile to the campground on the right.
About the campground: This family campground occupies a gentle, pine-clad slope above the west shore of Yellowjacket Lake. A small earthen dam creates this elongated lake at the foot of a low ridge. At the lake's north and south ends, willows and marsh claim the shallows, and coots and ducks rear their young. The deeper water toward the lake's center is suitable for fishing tubes and small boats. On summer weekends and holidays, the camp can fill up.

Silver Lake Area

133 Antler

Location: About 20 miles southwest of the city of Silver Lake
Season: May–mid-November
Sites: 5 basic sites, 4 walk-in tent sites; no hookups
Maximum length: 30 feet
Facilities: Tables, grills, vault toilets, drinking water, corral, hitching posts
Fee per night: None
Management: Fremont National Forest
Contact: (541) 576-2107; www.fs.fed.us/r6/frewin
Finding the campground: From Oregon 31, 0.8 mile northwest of Silver Lake, turn south on paved County Road 4-11/Forest Road 27 for Silver Creek Marsh and Thompson Reservoir. Go 9 miles, turn right on gravel FR 2804, and go 2.5 miles. Head left on FR 7645 for 5.6 miles, turn left on FR 036, and continue 1.5 miles. Turn right on FR 038 and go 0.6 mile to the camp on the right. Some intersection signs will help point the way.
About the campground: On Fremont National Recreation Trail, this campground is a gateway to Yamsay Mountain Roadless Area. The sites receive partial shade in a select-cut forest of lodgepole pine and fir. The camp serves hiker and equestrian. Yamsay Mountain—an all-day ride or backpack—is an intriguing, volcanic dome, with exceptional views and herds of wild elk ranging its flank. The Scenic Rock Loop Trail offers a shorter excursion, touring forest, meadow, and scenic rock near the camp.

134 Cabin Lake

Location: About 32 miles southeast of La Pine
Season: April–November
Sites: 14 basic sites; no hookups

Silver Lake Area

	Hookup sites	Total sites	Maximum RV length	Hookups	Toilets	Showers	Drinking water	Dump station	Recreation	Fee	Can reserve
133 Antler		9	30		NF		•		HR		
134 Cabin Lake		14	30		NF		•				
135 Duncan Reservoir		4	22		NF				FBL		
136 Eastbay		17	40		NF		•		FBL	$	
137 Silver Creek Marsh		17	40		NF		•		HFR		
138 Summer Lake Wildlife Area		20	40		NF				HF		
139 Thompson Reservoir		19	35		NF		•		FBL		

Maximum length: 30 feet
Facilities: Tables, grills, vault toilets, drinking water
Fee per night: None
Management: Deschutes National Forest
Contact: (541) 383–4000; www.fs.fed.us/r6/centraloregon/recreation
Finding the campground: From U.S. Highway 97, at La Pine, turn east on Forest Road 22, go 26.4 miles, and turn right (south) on FR 18. Continue 6 miles to the camp on the right. From Fort Rock, it is 11 miles north via County Road 511/FR 18.
About the campground: This camp claims an attractive stand of mature ponderosa pines at the transition zone between forest and southeastern desert. This little-used camp offers solitude, bird watching, and an opportunity to explore. It takes its name from tiny Cabin Lake, which was located across from the guard station and is now dry. Suggesting an outing from the camp is Fort Rock State Park, where a natural rock fortress rises from the desert floor. The feature has an interesting geological and archaeological tale, related by the interpretive boards at the park; find the turnoff 9 miles south of the camp off FR 18/CR 511.

135 Duncan Reservoir

Location: About 10 miles southeast of the city of Silver Lake, on Duncan Reservoir
Season: Year-round, depending on weather
Sites: 4 basic sites; no hookups
Maximum length: 22 feet
Facilities: Tables, fire rings, vault toilets, boat launch; no drinking water
Fee per night: None
Management: Lakeview District Bureau of Land Management
Contact: (541) 947–2177; www.or.blm.gov/lakeview
Finding the campground: From Silver Lake, go east on Oregon 31 South for 5.4 miles and turn right on gravel County Road 4-14 at the sign for Duncan Reservoir. Proceed 0.9 mile and turn right on BLM 6197, a narrow washboard road, and continue 4.1 miles to the camp.
About the campground: This small, primitive camp occupies a juniper-sage shore of Duncan Reservoir, a moderate-sized body of water cradled in an arid basin. Anglers troll the lake in hopes of catching evening supper. Stargazing is a pleasant way to cap the day.

136 Eastbay

Location: About 15 miles southwest of the city of Silver Lake, on Thompson Reservoir
Season: Early May–mid-November
Sites: 17 basic sites; no hookups
Maximum length: 40 feet
Facilities: Tables, barbecues, vault toilets, drinking water, boat launch, dock

Fee per night: $
Management: Fremont National Forest
Contact: (541) 576–2107; www.fs.fed.us/r6/frewin
Finding the campground: From Oregon 31, 0.3 mile northwest of Silver Lake, turn south onto paved County Road 4-12/Forest Road 28 for Eastbay Campground. Go 13.2 miles and turn right on FR 014. Go another 1.5 miles to enter this campground.
About the campground: On the east shore of 1,532-acre Thompson Reservoir, this comfortable campground borders a quiet cove, offers paved parking, and receives partial shade from its mixed age pine forest. Thompson Reservoir harnesses Silver Creek for irrigation and is open to fishing and boating. Boat speeds are limited to 10 miles per hour. The lake has an attractive shoreline when full and serves up western views of Yamsay Mountain. The south end of the lake boasts nesting bald eagles, while the lake island is a waterfowl nesting area.

137 Silver Creek Marsh

Location: About 11 miles southwest of the city of Silver Lake
Season: Early May–mid-November
Sites: 17 basic sites; no hookups
Maximum length: 40 feet
Facilities: Tables, grills, vault toilets, drinking water, corrals, hitching posts
Fee per night: None
Management: Fremont National Forest
Contact: (541) 576–2107; www.fs.fed.us/r6/frewin
Finding the campground: From Oregon 31, 0.8 mile northwest of Silver Lake, turn south on paved County Road 4-11/Forest Road 27 for Silver Creek Marsh and Thompson Reservoir. Go 10 miles to this campground on the left.
About the campground: This campground hugs the West Fork Silver Creek, a tiny creek with a few deep pools for fish. A semi-open pine flat, with big ponderosa pines, houses the camp. The sites have gravel parking, receive a mix of sun and shade, and can serve either as a stop or a base for exploring the Fremont National Recreation Trail, which traverses a corner of the camp. Thompson Reservoir, 5 miles southeast, offers more dependable fishing and also boating (10 miles per hour).

138 Summer Lake Wildlife Area

Location: About 1 mile southeast of the community of Summer Lake
Season: Year-round
Sites: 4 camping areas for a total of 20 basic sites; no hookups
Maximum length: 40 feet
Facilities: A few tables, nonflush toilets; no drinking water
Fee per night: None
Management: Oregon Department of Fish and Wildlife
Contact: (541) 943–3152; www.dfw.state.or.us/wildlifearea/summerlake.htm

Finding the campground: At the south end of the community of Summer Lake, turn east off Oregon 31 at the sign for the wildlife area. Pick up a refuge map at the office, and follow the road tour into the wildlife area to the designated camping areas at Windbreak, River, Bullgate, and River Ranch.

About the campground: The refuge offers minimalist camping on broad, gravel flats; comfort is what you bring. Views are of the richly textured refuge lands: open water, channels, marsh, mudflat, and arid brush. To the west rises imposing Winter Ridge. Bird watching and hunting are the chief draws, with the refuge road to drive and the dikes to hike. A cacophony of sound delights, as do the evening stars. Mosquitoes can be menacing, but remember they are part of the food chain sustaining the birds. Insect repellent, hats, binoculars, scopes, and telephoto lenses are among the preferred gear.

139 Thompson Reservoir

Location: About 16 miles southwest of the city of Silver Lake, on Thompson Reservoir
Season: Early May–mid-November
Sites: 19 basic sites; no hookups
Maximum length: 35 feet
Facilities: Tables, grills, pit toilets, drinking water, primitive boat launch
Fee per night: None
Management: Fremont National Forest
Contact: (541) 576-2107; www.fs.fed.us/r6/frewin
Finding the campground: From Oregon 31, 0.8 mile northwest of Silver Lake, turn south on paved County Road 4-11/Forest Road 27 for Silver Creek Marsh and Thompson Reservoir. Go 14 miles and turn left on gravel FR 287 to reach this campground in another 1.1 miles.

About the campground: This rustic campground is on the pine-forested north basin slope of Thompson Reservoir. The large, roundish irrigation reservoir has a piney rim, treed points, and a riddling of snags. Fishing boats (10 miles per hour) ply the clear, blue water. When the reservoir is full, so, too, is this freebie campground. Look for mergansers, bald eagles, ospreys, and migratory shorebirds and waterfowl.

Southeast Desert

140 Antelope Reservoir Recreation Site

Location: About 13 miles southwest of Jordan Valley, on Antelope Reservoir
Season: Year-round
Sites: 4 basic sites, plus dispersed camping; no hookups
Maximum length: 25 feet
Facilities: Tables, grills, vault toilets, primitive boat launch; no drinking water
Fee per night: None
Management: Vale District Bureau of Land Management
Contact: (541) 473-3144; www.or.blm.gov/vale
Finding the campground: From U.S. Highway 95, 12 miles west of Jordan Valley and 21 miles east of Rome, head south on gravel Antelope Reservoir Road. At 1.2 miles, reach the campground on the left.
About the campground: On Antelope Reservoir's west shore, this campground occupies points of land on either side of the rocky dam; sites dot the barren, shadeless shore. The reservoir claims a gentle basin, with skyline views of arid rims. Beyond camp stretches open sage-grassland. Fishing and boating engage visitors. Killdeers can animate the shore.

141 Cow Lakes Recreation Site

Location: About 19 miles northwest of Jordan Valley
Season: Year-round, except after heavy rains
Sites: 10 basic sites; no hookups
Maximum length: 30 feet
Facilities: Tables, fire rings, vault toilet, boat ramp (small boats for trolling or rowing); no drinking water

Southeast Desert

	Hookup sites	Total sites	Maximum RV length	Hookups	Toilets	Showers	Drinking water	Dump station	Recreation	Fee	Can reserve
140 Antelope Reservoir Recreation Site		4	25		NF				FBL		
141 Cow Lakes Recreation Site		10	30		NF				FBL		
142 Fish Lake Recreation Site		23	24		NF			•	FBLR	$	
143 Jackman Park Recreation Site		6	24		NF			•		$	
144 Mann Lake Recreation Site		open	35		NF				FBL		
145 Page Springs Recreation Site		31	24		NF			•	HF	$	
146 Rome Launch Site		5	40		NF			•	FBL		
147 South Steens Recreation Site		36	35		NF			•	HFR	$	
148 Willow Creek Hot Springs Recreation Site		4	small		NF						

Fee per night: None
Management: Vale District Bureau of Land Management
Contact: (541) 473–3144; www.or.blm.gov/Vale
Finding the campground: From Jordan Valley, head west on U.S. Highway 95 South for 5 miles and turn right onto gravel Danner Loop Road; a sign indicates this route to Cow Lakes. Continue following the signs to Cow Lakes, heading northwest via Danner Loop and Lower Cow Creek Roads, reaching the campground in 14 miles.
About the campground: This sun-drenched camp sits between Upper and Lower Cow Lakes. The area is surrounded by sage tablelands and the Jordan Craters Lava Flow. Upper Cow Lake is a fluctuating, 1,000-acre reservoir that attracts anglers with catches of white crappie, largemouth bass, and brown bullhead. Besides fishing, guests can swim, bird watch, or go hunting. For people interested in exploring the lava beds, contact the BLM for information. North of Danner, history trackers may seek out the grave of Jean Baptiste Charbonneau; he was the son of Sacajawea and Toussaint Charbonneau of the Lewis and Clark party.

142 Fish Lake Recreation Site

Location: About 78 miles southeast of Burns
Season: June–October
Sites: 23 basic sites; no hookups
Maximum length: 24 feet
Facilities: Tables, grills, vault toilets, drinking water, boat ramp
Fee per night: $
Management: Burns District Bureau of Land Management
Contact: (541) 573–4400; www.or.blm.gov/burns
Finding the campground: From Frenchglen (61 miles south of Burns on Oregon 205), head east on gravel Steens Mountain Loop Road to enter this camp on the right at about 17 miles.
About the campground: This family campground occupies the shore of a mountain lake, which is large enough to support fishing and motorless boating. Willows claim the shore and aspens dress the slope near camp, but the sites sit mostly in the open. Nearby are corrals for public use. Discovery of both Steens Mountain and Malheur National Wildlife Refuge awaits. High-clearance vehicles are necessary at Steens Mountain, and four-wheel drive is recommended to complete Steens Mountain Loop.

143 Jackman Park Recreation Site

Location: About 80 miles southeast of Burns
Season: July–October
Sites: 6 basic sites; no hookups
Maximum length: 24 feet
Facilities: Tables, grills, vault toilets, drinking water
Fee per night: $

Management: Burns District Bureau of Land Management

Contact: (541) 573–4400; www.or.blm.gov/burns

Finding the campground: From Frenchglen (61 miles south of Burns on Oregon 205), head east on gravel Steens Mountain Loop Road for almost 20 miles to enter this camp on the right.

About the campground: This small camp has a split character, with the northern half of the loop showing dry meadows and sagelands dotted with juniper and mountain mahogany and the southern half showing wet meadows and aspen groves. The camp offers a base for exploring Steens Mountain, a rugged, high-clearance-vehicle area. West of the camp are Honeymoon and Pate Lakes.

144 Mann Lake Recreation Site

Location: About 89 miles southeast of Burns, on Mann Lake

Season: Year-round, depending on winter weather

Sites: Random camping; no hookups

Maximum length: 35 feet

Facilities: Vault toilets, 2 primitive boat launches; no drinking water

Fee per night: None

Management: Burns District Bureau of Land Management

Contact: (541) 573–4400; www.or.blm.gov/burns

Finding the campground: From U.S. Highway 20/395 in Burns, go east on Oregon 78 for 65 miles. Turn right onto the gravel road indicated for Andrews, Fields, and Denio (Fields-Denio Road) and go 23.6 miles. Turn right for Mann Lake.

About the campground: Named for an early-day rancher, Mann Lake, the centerpiece for this Oregon outback stay, is a glassy, broad natural platter at the eastern foot of Steens Mountain. This is a do-it-yourself camping area on the open plain. A shade source is desirable, along with plenty of water and sunscreen. Rainbow and the Mann Lake cutthroat trout survive in this low-oxygen water. Fishing is best early in the year before the algae builds. A wildlife viewing area encompasses the lake. Alvord Hot Springs can be found some 18 miles farther south; look for rising steam and the tin changing cell on the east side of the road.

145 Page Springs Recreation Site

Location: About 64 miles southeast of Burns

Season: Mid-April–mid-November

Sites: 31 basic sites; no hookups

Maximum length: 24 feet

Facilities: Tables, grills, vault toilets, drinking water

Fee per night: $

Management: Burns District Bureau of Land Management

Contact: (541) 573–4400; www.or.blm.gov/burns

Finding the campground: From Frenchglen (61 miles south of Burns on Oregon 205), head east on gravel Steens Mountain Loop Road to enter the camp on the right in about 3 miles.

About the campground: Beneath a basalt rim along the Donner und Blitzen River sits this arid grassland camp. Both sunny and tree-shaded sites are available. The camp makes a fine base for visiting its next-door neighbor, Malheur National Wildlife Refuge, where you will find exceptional birding and natural and cultural discoveries. It is equally convenient for exploring Steens Mountain, a fascinating alpine fault-block mountain rising from the desert plain; high-clearance vehicles are needed. Steens, chiseled canyons reveal superb scenery and seclude the Kiger wild horses. Page Springs, though, is no ugly stepsister, with the sparkling Donner und Blitzen River, its own birdlife, and the long-distance Desert Trail, which passes through camp.

146 Rome Launch Site

Location: 33 miles west of Jordan Valley, near Rome
Season: Early March–mid-November
Sites: 5 basic sites; no hookups
Maximum length: 40 feet
Facilities: Tables, vault toilets, drinking water, raft take-out/put-in
Fee per night: None
Management: Vale District Bureau of Land Management
Contact: (541) 473–3144; www.or.blm.gov/vale
Finding the campground: It is south off U.S. Highway 95 at the eastern outskirts of Rome, 105 miles southeast of Burns, 33 miles west of Jordan Valley.
About the campground: The sites edge an open, gravel plateau above the Owyhee River. A sage-grass hillside and rocky crest overlook the camp, and planted cottonwoods provide a bit of shade. The Owyhee—one of the originally designated wild and scenic rivers—flows glassy and welcoming. A rafting permit system is in effect. A nearby attraction is the Pillars of Rome. These 100-foot-tall white rock towers suggested the ruins of Rome to early travelers.

147 South Steens Recreation Site

Location: About 90 miles southeast of Burns
Season: June–October
Sites: 21 basic sites, 15 horse sites; no hookups
Maximum length: 35 feet
Facilities: Tables, grills, vault toilets, drinking water, hitching posts in horse camp
Fee per night: $
Management: Burns District Bureau of Land Management
Contact: (541) 573–4400; www.or.blm.gov/burns

Fishing on the Donner und Blitzen River.

Finding the campground: From U.S. Highway 20/395 in Burns, go east on Oregon 78 for 1.7 miles and turn right (south) on OR 205. Proceed another 69 miles and turn left on South Steens Loop Road at the sign for Upper Blitzen. Drive 18.8 miles to the horse camp or 18.9 miles to the family campground.

About the campground: These side-by-side campgrounds sit at the mouth of Big Indian Gorge and offer similar convenience and amenities. Sites are dispersed through a juniper sage-grassland and are either sunny or partially shaded. A trail explores Big Indian Gorge, following Big Indian Creek upstream from the camp. With high-clearance vehicles, visitors can drive the Steens Mountain Loop Back Country Byway for stunning vistas and scenery. Wildflowers and wildlife further recommend a visit.

148 Willow Creek Hot Springs Recreation Site

Location: About 43 miles east of Fields
Season: Dry weather access only
Sites: 4 basic sites; no hookups
Maximum length: Small units only
Facilities: Vault toilet; no drinking water
Fee per night: None
Management: Vale District Bureau of Land Management
Contact: (541) 473–3144; www.or.blm.gov/vale
Finding the campground: From Burns Junction (the intersection of Oregon 78 and U.S. Highway 95), 92 miles southeast of Burns and 46 miles west of Jordan Valley, go south on US 95 for 20 miles and turn southwest (right) on gravel Whitehorse Road. Proceed 21 miles and turn south following a dirt, dry-weather road along a fenceline for 2.3 miles and bear right at the information board to reach the hot springs in 0.25 mile.

About the campground: This remote destination is reserved for the adventurous. The austere camp exists because of two adjoining, modestly developed hot springs pools in a natural outdoor setting of dry grass and sage. Each of the pools can accommodate several people. The hotter one is clear, with a sandy bottom, and 3 feet deep. The milder pool is cloudy, with a muddy bottom, and 4.5 feet deep. Biting flies can annoy, but the stars dazzle.

Paisley–Gearhart Mountain Area

149 Campbell Lake

Location: About 30 miles southwest of Paisley, on Campbell Lake
Season: July–October
Sites: 16 basic sites; no hookups
Maximum length: 25 feet
Facilities: Tables, grills, pit toilets, drinking water, boat launch and dock at day-use area
Fee per night: None
Management: Fremont National Forest
Contact: (541) 943–3114; www.fs.fed.us/r6/frewin
Finding the campground: From Oregon 31 at Paisley, turn west on Mill Street, which becomes Forest Road 33. After 20 miles, you will come to a T-junction; turn right on paved FR 28. Go 8.4 miles and turn left on FR 033 to reach this campground on the left in 1.8 miles.
About the campground: This inviting campground occupies the lodgepole pine perimeter of Campbell Lake, a pretty, circular mountain lake below Deadhorse Rim. The tight pine forest affords nearly complete shade, and the sites are well spaced for privacy. The lake is stocked with rainbow trout and open to small fishing boats. Trails from the camp traverse Deadhorse Rim en route to neighboring Deadhorse Lake. The small pond near the trailhead is sometimes loud with frogs.

Paisley–Gearhart Mountain Area	Hookup sites	Total sites	Maximum RV length	Hookups	Toilets	Showers	Drinking water	Dump station	Recreation	Fee	Can reserve
149 Campbell Lake		16	25		NF		•		HFBL		
150 Chewaucan Crossing Trailhead and Campground		5	small		NF				HF		
151 Corral Creek Forest Camp		6	30		NF				H		
152 Dairy Point		4	25		NF		•		F		
153 Deadhorse Lake		9	16		NF		•		HFBL		
154 Happy Camp		12	25		NF				F		
155 Lee Thomas		7	20		NF		•		F		
156 Marsters Spring		10	30		NF		•		HF		
157 Sandhill Crossing		5	30		NF		•		F		

150 Chewaucan Crossing Trailhead and Campground

Location: About 8 miles southwest of Paisley
Season: Mid-April–October
Sites: 5 basic sites; no hookups
Maximum length: Best suited for smaller units (only 1 pull-through site)
Facilities: Tables, grills, vault toilets; no drinking water
Fee per night: None
Management: Fremont National Forest
Contact: (541) 943–3114; www.fs.fed.us/r6/frewin
Finding the campground: From Oregon 31 at Paisley, turn west on Mill Street, which becomes Forest Road 33 at the Y-junction, and proceed to the campground near milepost 8.
About the campground: This camp on a pine and juniper flat along the Chewaucan River is a gateway to the long-distance Fremont National Recreation Trail, which travels in both directions from the camp. On this growing forest trail, 82 miles currently stretch north to Yamsay Mountain, 33 miles lead south to Cox Pass. A pedestrian bridge spans the river at the camp, linking the trail segments. Fishing the river, anglers can match wits with the rainbow and brook trout. The canyon also engages guests with its varieties of birds and wildflowers.

151 Corral Creek Forest Camp

Location: About 30 miles northeast of Bly
Season: Mid-May–October
Sites: 6 basic sites; no hookups
Maximum length: 30 feet
Facilities: Tables, grills, vault toilets; no drinking water
Fee per night: None
Management: Fremont National Forest
Contact: (541) 353–2427; www.fs.fed.us/r6/frewin
Finding the campground: From Oregon 140 at Quartz Mountain (13 miles east of Bly, 30 miles west of Lakeview), turn north on Forest Road 3660. Go 16 miles to FR 34 and turn right. Continue 0.2 mile more and turn left on FR 012, going 0.3 mile on dirt road to reach the camp on the left.
About the campground: At this relaxing getaway, the sites are nicely spaced for privacy in a setting of meadow and lodgepole pines. A rail fence isolates the camp from the picturesque meadow stream of Corral Creek. An egress in the fence allows access for fishing or admiring. At the trailhead at the end of FR 012, you will find wilderness entry and the Gearhart Mountain Trail System.

152 Dairy Point

Location: About 22 miles southwest of Paisley
Season: Mid-May–October
Sites: 4 basic sites; no hookups
Maximum length: 25 feet
Facilities: Tables, grills, pit toilets, drinking water
Fee per night: None
Management: Fremont National Forest
Contact: (541) 943-3114; www.fs.fed.us/r6/frewin
Finding the campground: From Oregon 31 at Paisley, turn west on Mill Street, which becomes Forest Road 33, following the signs to Marsters Spring and Dairy Creek. After 20 miles, you will come to a T-junction; turn left on paved FR 28. Go 2.1 miles and again turn left to enter the camp.
About the campground: A rail fence encloses this small, pleasant flat that edges a meadow and is just removed from Dairy Creek. The camp enjoys a combined setting of meadow and mature ponderosa pines. This is a place to commune with nature or attempt fishing along Dairy Creek. The lilting notes of birds and wails of coyotes are among the melodies heard at the camp.

153 Deadhorse Lake

Location: 32 miles southwest of Paisley
Season: July–October
Sites: 9 basic sites; no hookups
Maximum length: 16 feet
Facilities: Tables, grills, pit toilets, drinking water, boat launch, dock
Fee per night: None
Management: Fremont National Forest
Contact: (541) 943-3114; www.fs.fed.us/r6/frewin
Finding the campground: From Oregon 31 at Paisley, turn west on Mill Street, which becomes Forest Road 33. After 20 miles, you will come to a T-junction. Turn right on paved FR 28, go 8.4 miles, and turn left on FR 033. Go 3.2 miles to the campground.
About the campground: This campground in the lodgepole pines sits on the shore of Deadhorse Lake. This elongated lake is one of two attractive mountain lakes below Deadhorse Rim; the other is Campbell Lake. This tranquil mountain retreat welcomes fishing, boating (5 miles per hour), and hiking. The lake is stocked with rainbow trout. Trails travel Deadhorse Rim to Campbell Lake and follow Deadcow Drainage.

154 Happy Camp

Location: About 24 miles southwest of Paisley
Season: Mid-May–October
Sites: 9 basic sites, 3 rustic Adirondack-style shelters; no hookups
Maximum length: 25 feet
Facilities: Tables, grills, pit toilets; no drinking water

Fishing for rainbow trout on Deadhorse Lake.

Fee per night: None
Management: Fremont National Forest
Contact: (541) 943–3114; www.fs.fed.us/r6/frewin
Finding the campground: From Oregon 31 at Paisley, turn west on Mill Street, which becomes Forest Road 33, following the signs to Marsters Spring and Dairy Creek. After 20 miles, you will come to a T-junction. Turn left on paved FR 28, go 2 miles, then turn right on dirt FR 047. Proceed 2.4 miles to enter the camp on the left. FR 047 has some rough, rock-studded segments and washboard.
About the campground: This campground is loaded with rustic charm. It rests on the north shore of pretty Dairy Creek. The meadow flat of the camp is dotted by aspens and ponderosa and lodgepole pines. It is place where you can awaken to bird songs. Fishing, reading a book, or napping are popular activities (or inactivities).

155 Lee Thomas

Location: 36 miles southwest of Paisley
Season: June–October
Sites: 7 basic sites; no hookups
Maximum length: 20 feet
Facilities: Tables, grills, pit toilets, drinking water
Fee per night: None
Management: Fremont National Forest
Contact: (541) 943-3114; www.fs.fed.us/r6/frewin
Finding the campground: From Oregon 31 at Paisley, turn west on Mill Street, which becomes Forest Road 33. After 20 miles, you will come to a T-junction. Turn right on paved FR 28, go about 11 miles, and turn left on FR 3411, heading toward Lee Thomas and Sandhill Crossing Campgrounds. Go 5 miles to this campground on the left.
About the campground: This campground unites a lodgepole pine stand, a marmot-inhabited rock outcrop, wildflower meadows punctuated by willow clumps, and the lovely Sprague Wild and Scenic River. A pole fence encircles camp, with an egress to the river for fishing or gazing at its sparkle. The Lee Thomas Trailhead is 1 mile east of the camp; from it, the Deadhorse Rim Trail travels 6 miles to Deadhorse Lake, with Campbell Lake, a possible destination beyond that.

156 Marsters Spring

Location: 7 miles southwest of Paisley
Season: Mid-May–October
Sites: 10 basic sites; no hookups
Maximum length: 30 feet
Facilities: Tables, grills, vault toilets, drinking water
Fee per night: None
Management: Fremont National Forest
Contact: (541) 943-3114; www.fs.fed.us/r6/frewin
Finding the campground: From Oregon 31 at Paisley, turn west on Mill Street, which becomes Forest Road 33, following the signs to Marsters Spring and Dairy Creek. After 7 miles, turn left to enter the camp.
About the campground: This campground fronts the picturesque Chewaucan River, presently being studied for wild and scenic river classification. The relaxing camp is sheltered by a mixed woods of pine, juniper, cottonwood, willow, and alder. Some sites directly overlook the swift river. Chewaucan Crossing Trailhead, 1 mile upstream on FR 33, offers access to the Fremont National Recreation Trail, a long-distance trail that is still growing. Fishing is also popular.

157 Sandhill Crossing

Location: About 38 miles southwest of Paisley
Season: June–October
Sites: 5 basic sites; no hookups
Maximum length: 30 feet
Facilities: Tables, grills, pit toilets, drinking water
Fee per night: None
Management: Fremont National Forest
Contact: (541) 943–3114; www.fs.fed.us/r6/frewin

Finding the campground: From Oregon 31 at Paisley, turn west on Mill Street, which becomes Forest Road 33. After 20 miles, you will come to a T-junction. Turn right on paved FR 28, go about 11 miles, and turn left on FR 3411, heading toward Lee Thomas and Sandhill Crossing Campgrounds. Go 7.3 miles to this campground on the left.

About the campground: This campground in the lodgepole pines overlooks the postcard-pretty Sprague Wild and Scenic River. Wildflower-dotted meadow banks contain the river; among nature's palette are Indian paintbrush, shooting star, and buttercup. Small gravel bars and deep pools are part of the meandering river's character, and fishing provides a challenge. Mosquitoes are the lone detractor; come prepared.

Lakeview Area

158 Cottonwood Meadow

Location: About 30 miles northwest of Lakeview
Season: June–mid-October
Sites: 21 basic sites; no hookups
Maximum length: 22 feet
Facilities: Tables, grills, vault toilets, drinking water, boat launch (boating: human-powered or electric motors only), horse facilities
Fee per night: None
Management: Fremont National Forest
Contact: (541) 947–3334; www.fs.fed.us/r6/frewin
Finding the campground: From Oregon 140, 20 miles east of Bly and 23 miles west of Lakeview, turn north on Forest Road 3870 at the sign for Cottonwood Meadow Lake. Go 5.7 miles and turn left on FR 024 to enter the camp in about 1 mile.
About the campground: At this pleasant campground, the sites either line Cougar Creek or rim Cottonwood Meadow Lake. The lake generally has good fishing and is open to rafts, canoes, and small boats. The lake basin features wildflower meadows, scenic stands of ponderosa pine, groves of aspen, and views of Cougar and Grizzly Peaks. Trails explore the greater lake area and climb to the top of Cougar Peak.

Lakeview Area

	Hookup sites	Total sites	Maximum RV length	Hookups	Toilets	Showers	Drinking water	Dump station	Recreation	Fee	Can reserve
158 Cottonwood Meadow		21	22		NF		•		HFBL		
159 Deep Creek Forest Camp		4	16		NF				F		
160 Dismal Creek Forest Camp		3	16		NF				F		
161 Dog Lake		6	20		NF		•		FBL		
162 Drews Creek		5	25		NF		•		F		
163 Goose Lake State Recreation Area	47	47	50	WE	F	•	•	•	HFB	$$	
164 Hart Mountain National Antelope Refuge		21	T		NF				H		
165 Lake County Fairgrounds and Rodeo Facility	14	14	40	WE	F	•	•	•		$$	
166 Lofton Reservoir		26	30		NF		•		FBL		
167 Mud Creek Forest Camp		7	30		NF						
168 Willow Creek Forest Camp		8	30		NF				F		

159 Deep Creek Forest Camp

Location: About 28 miles southeast of Lakeview
Season: June–mid-October
Sites: 4 basic sites; no hookups
Maximum length: 16 feet
Facilities: Tables, grills, pit toilets; no drinking water
Fee per night: None
Management: Fremont National Forest
Contact: (541) 947–3334; www.fs.fed.us/r6/frewin
Finding the campground: From Lakeview, head north on U.S. Highway 395/Oregon 140 East for 4.7 miles and turn right to remain on OR 140E. Continue 7.2 miles and turn right on South Warren Road/Forest Road 3915 (which begins paved and becomes gravel). Go 10.2 miles to a Y-junction and bear left to remain on FR 3915 for another 5 miles. Bear right on FR 4015, proceed 0.7 mile, and turn right onto FR 011 for the camp.
About the campground: This intimate little campground faces out at Deep Creek and occupies a pine-meadow habitat, with some stout ponderosa pines. Deep Creek is broad, deep, and braided, with cottonwoods and aspens shading its shore. Because site parking is along the road shoulder, this camp is better suited for tents. Campers can try their hands at fishing, but mostly the camp offers quiet leisure.

160 Dismal Creek Forest Camp

Location: About 28 miles southeast of Lakeview
Season: June–mid-October
Sites: 3 basic sites; no hookups
Maximum length: 16 feet
Facilities: Tables, grills, pit toilets; no drinking water
Fee per night: None
Management: Fremont National Forest
Contact: (541) 947–3334; www.fs.fed.us/r6/frewin
Finding the campground: From Lakeview, go north on U.S. Highway 395/Oregon 140 East for 4.7 miles and turn right to remain on OR 140E. Continue 7.2 miles and turn right on South Warren Road/Forest Road 3915 (which begins paved and becomes gravel). Go 10.2 miles to a Y-junction and bear left, remaining on FR 3915 for another 5 miles. Again head left, still on FR 3915, to reach this camp on the left in 1.1 miles.
About the campground: This camp in an open stand of ponderosa pines sits above Deep Creek, along the stair-stepped waters of Dismal Creek. With few neighbors in camp, the spot promises quiet, chances for wildlife sightings, and an occasion to fish. Balsamroot adorns the sage-grass floor.

161 Dog Lake

Location: About 27 miles southwest of Lakeview
Season: June–mid-October
Sites: 6 basic sites; no hookups
Maximum length: 20 feet
Facilities: Tables, grills, pit toilets, drinking water, boat launch (boating: 5 miles per hour)
Fee per night: None
Management: Fremont National Forest
Contact: (541) 947–3334; www.fs.fed.us/r6/frewin
Finding the campground: From U.S. Highway 395 in Lakeview, go west on Oregon 140 for 7.3 miles and turn left (south) onto County Road 1-13 for Dog Lake. Go about 4 miles and turn right on CR 1-11D, which becomes Forest Road 4017. Stay on it for about 16 miles to reach the main campground on the right. The day-use area, Dog Lake, and a gravel road to additional sites are all on the left.
About the campground: Dog Lake, the central draw to the area, is an attractive artificial lake. It claims a pretty forested basin and displays area of rush, cattail, and pond lily along its shallows. White pelicans, ducks, geese, killdeer, and yellow-headed and red-winged blackbirds find favor with this lake, as do campers, boaters, and anglers. The main part of the campground sits on a pine-forested knoll above and across FR 4017 from the lake. It is a typical forest camp, with dirt parking; a path links it to the boat launch area. Water is available on the knoll and at the day-use area, but not at the second camping area, which is 0.2 mile from the day-use area via a gravel road. The second camp also rests above shore. Bass and trout are the lake catches.

162 Drews Creek

Location: About 17 miles southwest of Lakeview
Season: June–mid-October
Sites: 5 basic sites; no hookups
Maximum length: 25 feet
Facilities: Tables, grills, vault toilets, drinking water, horseshoe pits
Fee per night: None
Management: Fremont National Forest
Contact: (541) 947–3334; www.fs.fed.us/r6/frewin
Finding the campground: From U.S. Highway 395 in Lakeview, go west on Oregon 140 for 7.3 miles and turn left (south) onto County Road 1-13 for Dog Lake. Go about 4 miles and turn right on CR 1-11D, which becomes Forest Road 4017. Stay on it for 6 miles to reach this campground on the left, crossing over a bridge.
About the campground: Along Drews Creek, this camp sits at the foot of a low hill, in a ponderosa pine setting. It is a popular group camp facility, with a central area of long tables and community parking. A pair of individual site turnouts provide greater privacy. Pole fencing isolates the camp from Drews

Creek, which can flow slow and murky here. For fishing, the camp is 2 miles from Drews Reservoir.

163 Goose Lake State Recreation Area

Location: About 16 miles south of Lakeview
Season: Mid-April–late October
Sites: 47 hookup sites; water and electric hookups
Maximum length: 50 feet
Facilities: Tables, grills, flush toilets, drinking water, showers, dump station, telephone, horseshoe pits (at day-use area), nearby boat launch
Fee per night: $$
Management: Oregon State Parks and Recreation Department
Contact: (541) 947-3111; www.oregonstateparks.org
Finding the campground: From the junction of U.S. Highway 395 and Oregon 140 West in Lakeview, go south on US 395 for 14.7 miles. Turn right at the sign for Goose Lake State Recreation Area, just as California welcomes you, and go 1.1 miles. Turn right for the campground; straight leads to the day-use area.
About the campground: On the Oregon–California border, Goose Lake is an enormous Great Basin lake spanning between distant low ridges. Water levels fluctuate from year to year. The campground is slightly removed from the lake, occupying a flat of lawn and shade trees. The site parking is paved. At the outskirts of camp stretch fields and willows, with mowed passageways through them. Giant lupine and wild rose color these corridors where songbirds flourish. This camp is a favorite with birders. Quail roam through the camp, western tanagers decorate tree branches, and migrant and resident waterfowl visit the lake. Goose Lake welcomes fishing and boating, but the access is away from the camp.

164 Hart Mountain National Antelope Refuge

Location: About 68 miles northeast of Lakeview
Season: Maintained mid-May–October
Sites: 21 tent sites; no hookups
Facilities: Vault and pit toilets, hot springs "bathhouse;" no drinking water
Fee per night: None
Management: Hart Mountain National Antelope Refuge
Contact: (541) 947-3315
Finding the campground: From the town of Plush (40 miles northeast of Lakeview), drive 0.9 mile north and turn east at the sign for Hart Mountain and Frenchglen. Go 23 miles to the headquarters or 27 miles to the camp and hot springs, bearing right at the junction past the headquarters. The route is paved and gravel to the refuge. The rough road into the camp is not recommended for trailers or RVs.
About the campground: The route to the refuge is part of the Lakeview to Steens National Back Country Byway. The refuge road system then continues

the discovery, serving up wildlife sightings and stunning dry landscapes. Antelope are the primary attraction. The isolated camp consists of a casual cluster of primitive sites radiating out from the refuge hot springs, a pleasant, 5-foot-deep steamy pool. The camp claims an aspen-shaded grassy flat between Rock and Bond Creeks. Scenic hillsides of sage, juniper, and mountain mahogany frame the setting. Near the headquarters, you will find a small museum and nature garden.

165 Lake County Fairgrounds and Rodeo Facility

Location: In Lakeview
Season: Year-round, but no water October–March
Sites: 14 hookup sites, with dry camping and tent camping available; water and electric hookups
Maximum length: 40 feet
Facilities: Flush toilets, drinking water, showers, dump station, telephone, food concessions when open
Fee per night: $$
Management: Lake County
Contact: (541) 947–2925
Finding the campground: The fairgrounds is north off Oregon 140 (North Fourth Street) at the east end of Lakeview. You will find the RV camp to the left off the West Gate Entrance.
About the campground: This austere but practical RV camp primarily caters to fair-goers and participants, but it is also available to area travelers. It occupies a shadeless, gravel parking area, with hookup posts. For individuals looking to dry camp or tent camp, ask at the office about suitable areas.

166 Lofton Reservoir

Location: About 38 miles northwest of Lakeview
Season: May–October
Sites: 26 basic sites; no hookups
Maximum length: 30 feet
Facilities: Tables, grills, pit toilets, drinking water, boat launch, accessible fishing pier for individuals with disabilities
Fee per night: None
Management: Fremont National Forest
Contact: (541) 353–2427; www.fs.fed.us/r6/frewin
Finding the campground: From Oregon 140, 13 miles east of Bly and 30 miles west of Lakeview, turn south onto paved Forest Road 3715 for the reservoir. Go 7.2 miles and turn left on FR 013 to reach the camp in 1.2 miles.
About the campground: In a location that has been largely cut over, a full forest of ponderosa pine and white fir shelters this family campground along the shore of Lofton Reservoir. The lake was built to hold water for irrigation, but it is open to recreation. Lofton is at its prettiest when full, and the fishing is generally good. Electric motors are allowed on the lake; boating speed is limited to 5 miles per hour.

167 Mud Creek Forest Camp

Location: About 20 miles northeast of Lakeview
Season: June–mid-October
Sites: 7 basic sites; no hookups
Maximum length: 30 feet
Facilities: Tables, grills, pit toilets; no drinking water
Fee per night: None
Management: Fremont National Forest
Contact: (541) 947-3334; www.fs.fed.us/r6/frewin
Finding the campground: From Lakeview, go north on U.S. Highway 395/ Oregon 140 East for 4.7 miles and turn right to remain on OR 140E. Continue 8.5 miles and turn left on North Warren Road/Forest Road 3615. Proceed 7 miles to enter this camp on the right.
About the campground: At the edge of a sage prairie and along the wet meadow threaded by tiny Mud Creek sits this quiet camp in a forest of lodgepole pine and white fir. Mud Creek is a meandering black ribbon. Across FR 3615 from the camp is Bull Prairie, a private property where the springtime camas bloom creates seas of purple. Area trails can be reached 2.2 miles south of the camp, and Drake Peak Lookout might suggest a drive. Fishing and hunting are other pursuits. Come ready for mosquitoes in early summer.

168 Willow Creek Forest Camp

Location: About 23 miles southeast of Lakeview
Season: June–mid-October
Sites: 8 basic sites; no hookups
Maximum length: 30 feet
Facilities: Tables, grills, pit toilets; no drinking water
Fee per night: None
Management: Fremont National Forest
Contact: (541) 947-3334; www.fs.fed.us/r6/frewin
Finding the campground: From Lakeview, go north on U.S. Highway 395/ Oregon 140 East for 4.7 miles and turn right to remain on OR 140E. Continue 7.2 miles and turn right onto South Warren Road/Forest Road 3915 (which begins paved and becomes gravel). Go 10.2 miles to a Y-junction and bear right on FR 4011. Go 0.7 mile and turn right on FR 011, followed by a right on FR 012 to enter the camp in 0.3 mile.
About the campground: A rail fence separates this campground from the meadow of Willow Creek. A mixed woods of ponderosa pine and aspen enfolds the camp, and arnica sometimes lends a cheery yellow glow to the forest floor. Signs of beaver are evident throughout the meadow. Fishing is the lone activity at this camp.

Campground Index

About the Authors

For decades, Rhonda and George Ostertag have traveled throughout their home state of Oregon, seeking its secrets and treasures. They have documented their journey in more than a half dozen Oregon guidebooks, hundreds of articles, and calendar and postcard images. The duo speaks from firsthand knowledge of the campgrounds, backroads, waters, and trails. They have weathered the raindrop, braved the wind, and rejoiced in the splendor.

Among their other Oregon titles are *Best Short Hikes in Northwest Oregon, 100 Hikes in Oregon, 75 Hikes in Oregon's Coast Range and Siskiyous*, and *50 Hikes in Hells Canyon and Oregon's Wallowas*, all with The Mountaineers Books of Seattle, and *Backroads of Oregon*, from Voyageur Press (Stillwater, Minnesota).

Although Oregon is their primary playground, the Ostertags have found time to travel, adding California and East Coast titles to their resume: *California State Parks: A Complete Recreation Guide* (The Mountaineers Books) and *Scenic Driving Pennsylvania, Hiking Pennsylvania, Hiking Southern New England,* and *Hiking New York*, all FalconGuides with The Globe Pequot Press.

George and Rhonda Ostertag, Eagle Cap Wilderness.

  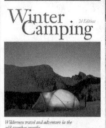
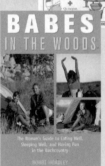 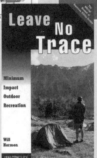